Man is the Cruelest Animal

Essays on the Human-Animal Link

By Lyle Munro

Man is the Cruelest Animal

Essays on the Human-Animal Link

By Lyle Munro

COMMON
GROUND

First published in 2021
as part of the *Interdisciplinary Social Sciences* Book Imprint
doi:10.18848/978-0-949313-46-1/CGP (Full Book)

Common Ground Research Networks
60 Hazelwood Drive
University of Illinois Research Park
Champaign, IL
61820

Library of Congress Cataloging-in-Publication Data

Names: Munro, Lyle, author.
Title: Man is the cruelest animal : essays on the human-animal link / by
  Lyle Munro.
Description: Champaign, IL : Common Ground Research Networks, 2021. |
  Includes bibliographical references. | Summary: "Man is the Cruelest
  Animal features four main themes: History, Cruelty, Activism and
  Perspectives with each section comprised of four peer-reviewed essays.
  History describes the centuries-old animal protection societies that
  preceded the modern movement that emerged in the 1970s. Cruelty explains
  what drives activist campaigns against factory farming, vivisection and
  hunting. Activism analyses the educational and intervention strategies
  and the varied tactics of animal activists in the USA, the UK and
  Australia. Perspectives identifies some of the conflicts involving
  counter movements against the theory and practice of animal rights; the
  prospect for achieving common cause in resolving the worst features of
  human-animal interactions is also discussed. The concluding section is
  in two parts: Part 1 focuses on Pandemics and Life Chances, a topic that
  is of obvious relevance in the current era while Part 2 features an
  annotated guide to recommended reading on the four main themes covered
  in the book"-- Provided by publisher.
Identifiers: LCCN 2020050194 (print) | LCCN 2020050195 (ebook) | ISBN
  9780949313447 (hardback) | ISBN 9780949313454 (paperback) | ISBN
  9780949313461 (adobe pdf)
Subjects: LCSH: Animal welfare--United States--History. | Animal
  welfare--Great Britain--History. | Animal welfare--Australia--History. |
  Animal rights activists--United States--History. | Animal rights
  activists--Great Britain--History. | Animal rights
  activists--Australia--History. | Animal rights--United States--History.
  | Animal rights--Great Britain--History. | Animal
  rights--Australia--History.
Classification: LCC HV4764 .M877 2021 (print) | LCC HV4764 (ebook) | DDC
  179/.309--dc23
LC record available at https://lccn.loc.gov/2020050194
LC ebook record available at https://lccn.loc.gov/2020050195

Cover Photo Credit: Animal Rescue League, c.1940. Roger Kingston Collection, New York.

Table of Contents

List of Figures

List of Tables

Introduction

I have sometimes been asked why I took an academic interest in animal protection issues. There are a couple of reasons. As a child, I attended St Francis of Assisi primary school where a picture of the animal-friendly saint adorned one of the walls. It was at that school that I first heard mention of the Royal Society for the Prevention of Cruelty to Animals (RSPCA) and I remember being surprised that there was a phenomenon known as cruelty to animals. For my six-year-old self, it was difficult to imagine how anyone could ill-treat a dog like my cocker spaniel "Silver" let alone other creatures great and small. Years later, I learned that my great grandfather was a jockey who rode the winner of the Melbourne Cup in 1886 on a horse called "Arsenal". As a nineteen year-old apprentice jockey, Billy English saw how some of the horses were being harshly flayed by their riders and decided to allow his mount to cross the finishing line un-whipped, despite a strong challenge by a New Zealand champion, "Trenton", the future sire of two Melbourne Cup winners. These were the early influences that prompted my developing interest in animal welfare and the animal rights movement campaigns to challenge cruelty to animals.

My first book on animal rights *Compassionate Beasts: The Quest for Animal Rights* featured the history, sociology and philosophy of the animal protection movement in Australia, the UK and the USA. The main focus was on grassroots activism in the streets and organizational advocacy in "the suites". The study was based on interviews with about 50 animal protection activists and advocates and comparative surveys on attitudes toward the treatment of nonhuman animals. I concluded that the style of animal protection groups was different in the three case study countries:

UK: Grassroots activism > Organizational advocacy

USA: Organizational advocacy > Grassroots activism

Australia: Grassroots activism + Organizational advocacy

Note > denotes "greater than"; < denotes "less than"; + denotes an "equivalence"

According to Freud, people need love and work to give their lives meaning. Intuitively, the idea is sound, and a moment's reflection should convince most people that love and work are central to most people's well-being. If love and work help to make people's lives meaningful, then we can expect that people will seek every opportunity to maximise both in their everyday lives, even in their extracurricular activities encompassing such things as leisure, social and political pursuits. I was not consciously aware of the possibilities of the love/work couplet when I began the research for this study. Yet, on reflection, the questions I asked of my informants in the interviews could be seen as an exploration of the relationship between commitment and campaigning, which is a more formal description of the notion of love and work in social movement participation.

Soon after the publication of *Compassionate Beasts,* my PhD dissertation[1] used much of the empirical data of that book to produce a more theoretical study of the sociology of the animal protection movement. The initial research proposal I drew up for approval from Monash University's Ethics Committee was called "Animal liberationists and their campaigns". From the outset, the focus was on the individual animal liberationists (their personal background, motives, involvement and commitment to the movement etc.) and what they did in their campaigns (the actual work involved in being an activist or advocate). The research question which frames the thesis is "Why and how do people campaign on behalf of a species that is not their own?" Questions used in the interview schedule focused on the meaning of animal activism and the nature of the key campaigns; the why and how of social movement involvement are therefore central to the thesis and correspond to new social movement theory and resource mobilization theory respectively.

The thesis contends that people support the animal movement because of their abhorrence of cruelty, of what the animal movement labels as speciesism. While speciesism comes in many forms, there are three main practices—vivisection, factory farming and blood sports, which have been identified as among the worst abuses and hence have become seminal campaigns of animal rights activism. Animal movement supporters want people to see animal abuse in these contexts as a social problem not unlike child abuse, spousal abuse or elder abuse; that is, as morally objectionable because the victims are vulnerable populations of human and nonhuman animals.

The most useful sociological theories and concepts were derived from the social movement and social problems literatures. I perceived social problems and social movements to be two sides of the same coin. I argued that animal abuse was a social problem which, like other similar social issues, was a social construction: it had to be objectively identified and labelled as a problem society would be better off without before it could be challenged as such. For example, it took many decades before behaviours involving sexual harassment, elder abuse and the like were recognised and named as deviant or criminal acts that could make offenders subject to legal prosecution.

Social movement theorists had developed what they claimed were the three framing tasks of every social movement: diagnostic framing, prognostic framing and motivational framing. I used this typology to explain that the diagnostic frame of animal activists came down to their claims of widespread institutional cruelty of nonhuman animals. Activists then built affinity groups and social movement organizations small and large to press their claims against "the animal-industrial

---

[1] The PhD was titled *Beasts Abstract Not: A Sociology of Animal Protection*, 2002, Monash University.

complex"[2]; the third task was the mobilizing of a movement to challenge the individuals and institutionalised practices that were against the interests of animals' welfare.

My second book, *Confronting Cruelty: Moral Orthodoxy and the Challenge of the Animal Rights Movement,* was based on my doctoral thesis. It included an extensive literature review on "the animal problem in social context" that consisted of three sections: 1. Animals as a social problem (e.g. feral cats and dogs); 2. Campaigns against cruelty as a social problem (e.g. protesters as violent); and 3. The exploitation of animals as a social problem (e.g. animal cruelty in factory farms). The third (social problem) was the main focus of the book, in which I argued that animal protectionists engage in intellectual, practical and emotional work in prosecuting their campaigns. Based on the empirical evidence I had gathered, the most important campaigns were against the use of animals in food production, in animal experimentation and as targets in hunting and field sports.

My research following these two books focused on four broad topics: 1. The early history of the animal movement; 2. The idea that "man is the cruelest animal" (Nietzsche); 3. Activists and academics involved in the movement; and 4. Various perspectives on the movement, including its increasing relevance to the existential threats of pandemics and the climate crisis. In the remainder of this introduction, I outline the topics I have researched during and since the publication of my two books on the animal movement. For convenience, I have divided the book into four sections and have also added a conclusion that is part of fourth and final section.

1. History: Most people assume the animal rights movement began in recent times with the publication of Peter Singer's *Animal Liberation* in 1975. In fact, early animal protection societies such as the RSPCA in the UK and Australia and the SPCA in the USA go back to the early 19th century. Furthermore, philosophers of animal rights as well as ethical vegetarian advocates were promoting the cause of animal protection decades earlier. In writing my first book, I found most pleasure in the study of these pioneer individuals and organizations; for example, I discovered campaigns for the rights of animals preceded those for the rights of children. This and other interesting facts, especially in Keith Thomas's excellent *Man and the Natural World: Changing Attitudes in England 1500-1800,* are among the most enjoyable books I encountered in the research. I should also mention Coral Lansbury's *The Old Brown Dog: Women, Workers and Vivisection in Edwardian England* as another classic in the literature.[3] The present book also covers the early history of animal protection in Australia, along with the more recent developments inspired by Singer's manifesto published in 1975.

2. Cruelty: This section focuses on what drives the animal movement worldwide, namely its opposition to speciesism or the cruel treatment of nonhuman animals. The

---

[2] Barbara Noske (1989) *Humans and Other Animals*, London: Pluto Press.
[3] Coral Lansbury is the mother of Australia's 29th Prime Minister, Malcolm Turnbull.

discussion begins with some reflections on what constitutes a "decent" society i.e. one that practices compassion as opposed to cruelty to sentient beings. Included in the discussion are some reflections on how social scientists have defined cruelty and the related term "speciesism" as well as compassion, empathy, caring and commitment. The argument in this early part of the book is that animal activists practice social problems *work* in defending the rights of animals; many committed animal protectionists claim their activism is a form of work that is motivated by the love of animals. As philosophers have been described as "midwives" to the movement, the arguments of some of the leading philosophers are explained; also included are the views of some prominent academics opposed to animal rights. The case study of duck hunting in Victoria, Australia is used to demonstrate why animal protectionists see duck shooting as a cruel sport that should be banned. The duck rescuers use dramatic visual images of "spectacles of slaughter" in an effort to persuade the public to demand an end to the killing of Australian water birds. How dramatic and disturbing TV images of animal cruelty are used to mobilize the public against cruel practices is described in another case study involving the "bloody business" of live animal exports from Australia to Indonesian slaughterhouses. Why that campaign was only partially successful and did not succeed in banning "the cruel trade" is explained from the perspective of social movement theory. My interest in this campaign originated in seeing Laurie Levy, the so-called "Duck Protector-General of Victoria", in several television programs. He turned out to be a most helpful interviewee and committed proponent of animal rights.

For the past three decades, animal activists led by Laurie Levy, have been confronting duck hunters in the wetlands of Victoria, the home of duck shooting in Australia. Australia's Coalition Against Duck Shooting (CADS) founded by Levy, frames duck shooting as a social problem and as an injustice with moral, legal and environmental consequences. The small animal rights group has succeeded in dramatically reducing the practice of duck hunting in Victoria and is still trying to ban the practice. The Coalition's framing work with the public via the electronic media involves three parts: a diagnosis (assembling claims), a prognosis (presenting claims) and a motivational frame (contesting claims), all of which construct hunting as a cruel, anti-social blood sport that ought to be banned.[4]

Television coverage of the opening of the duck-shooting season in March each year has become a media ritual in Victoria where duck rescuers confront duck hunters in the wetlands in their attempt to have duck shooting banned. Television simultaneously reflects and distorts the campaign by CADS which uses the media to promote its animal liberation cause. The three frames used to structure television's

---

[4] Laurie Levy once thanked me for understanding the Coalition's strategy. Little did he know that he was enacting social movement framing theory well before academic theorists had utilized the three-staged process. The exception is John Wilson who in 1973 introduced the 3 tasks of SM framing in his *Introduction to Social Movements*. New York: Basic Books Inc.

narrative of "Duck Wars" reveal that while the duck–rescue operation is predominantly represented as a law and order issue and the rescuers as deviant protesters, the strongly emotive images of wildlife slaughter appeal, as only television pictures can, to the viewing public's moral sensibilities and sense of outrage. It is these images that produce moral shocks activists believe will ensure victory in the "Duck Wars". However, television is an unreliable friend to environmentalists and grassroots activists who cannot predict how the media tell their story.

One recent television exposé on live animal exports is an exception. A media campaign by Animals Australia and the RSPCA in association with the Australian Broadcasting Commission (ABC) exposed the cruelties of the live animal export trade in Australia. The television story 'A Bloody Business' aired by the country's leading investigative programme *Four Corners* caused an immediate and unprecedented expression of anger by thousands of viewers who were horrified by the spectacle of Australian cattle being abused in a number of Indonesian abattoirs. I reported on the activists' campaign to ban the trade which both confirmed and challenged a number of social movement theories and concepts. As a classic 'hot cognition' issue, the moral crusade against the trade seemed destined to succeed such was the publicity the program generated. However, an increasingly nervous and vulnerable government lifted its temporary ban on the trade only a month after the controversy began. I wrote to the leaders of the campaign suggesting they might utilise ideas from the social movement literature to their advantage in their future campaigns. I see this kind of activity as activist-academic collaboration. There was no response to my suggestions.

3. Activism: It is important to understand that a social movement is what it does as much as why it does it, an idea that is particularly important in the case of the animal rights movement which is often demonised as extremist and violent. Critics of the movement claim that animal activists use letter bombs, arson attacks and threats to intimidate those they see as animal abusers and that violent direct action of this kind is typical of the movement as a whole. I argue that the mainstream animal movement in the USA, the UK and Australia is overwhelmingly non-violent and that its core strategies and tactics have two broad aims, namely to gain publicity for the cause of animals and to challenge conventional thinking about how we treat nonhuman animals. This is achieved primarily by the deployment of the key tactical mechanisms of persuasion, protest, non-cooperation and intervention. These tactics may be deployed collectively or as DIY (Do- It- Yourself) activism which many grassroots animal activists aptly described as 'caring sleuths'[5] seem to prefer. Demonstrations and pamphleteering are examples of publicity strategies or liberal governance

---

[5] Ken Shapiro (1994) The caring sleuth: Portrait of an animal rights activist, *Society and Animals* 2, 2:145-65.

strategies[6] as well as critical governance strategies or interference strategies such as a hunger strike, ethical vegetarianism and undercover surveillance.

I discovered during my research that there is little empirical work by sociologists on social movement organizations (SMOs) such as People for the Ethical Treatment of Animals (PETA) or Animals Australia, a situation I have attempted to change. One early study I completed was on the four campaigns of one such SMO in the Blue Mountains west of Sydney. The group is known as Mountain Residents for Animal Rights (MRAR), whose activists have focused on liberating animals from exploitation by humans for food, for entertainment or display, and being exploited as objects in scientific and medical experiments. I was also interested in what drove activist leaders such as MRAR's Anne Elliott. A more prominent animal rights activist and advocate was a later interest in the research. Based on a fair amount of secondary material, I wrote a profile of the late American animal activist Henry Spira, whose campaign strategies and tactics suggest a number of links with the nineteenth century pioneers of animal protection as well as with approaches favoured by contemporary animal activists.

Spira's style of animal advocacy differed from conventional approaches in the mainstream animal movement in that he preferred to work with rather than against animal user industries. To this end, he pioneered the use of "reintegrative shaming"[7] in animal protection, an accommodation strategy which relied on moralising with opponents as opposed to the more common approach in protest politics of adversarial vilification, and hence disintegrative shaming.

Henry Spira is a classic example of an issue entrepreneur who used a variety of legal tactics, both conventional and unconventional, to achieve his animal welfare goals. His strategy was unusual for an animal protectionist in that he sought to make instances of animal cruelty public only as a last resort. Ever the pragmatist, his primary goal was to reduce the level of suffering and cruelty to animals, preferably by persuasive communication and only when that failed, by coercion. Sometimes Spira worked alone, and sometimes he formed affinity groups from existing animal rights organizations to achieve his ends. His tactics were always designed to achieve maximum benefits in terms of saving animals' lives and ranged across the spectrum of tactical mechanisms: persuasion, facilitation, bargaining, and coercion. I suggest these mechanisms can best be thought of as a continuum with persuasion as the most moderate tactic at one end and the more direct confrontational tactic of coercion at the other end. Not surprisingly, persuasion, facilitation and bargaining tend to be the preferred tactics of organisational advocates "in the suites", while coercive tactics are usually more commonly observed in grassroots campaigns in the streets.

---

[6] Peter Newell (2000) Environmental NGOs and globalization: The governance of TNCs, in R. Cohen and S. Rai (Eds.) *Global Social Movements*, London and New Brunswick, NJ: Athlone Press.
[7] John Braithwaite (1989) *Crime, Shame and Reintegration*, Cambridge: Cambridge University Press.

Finally in this section on activism, my paper on "Women's Standing in the Animal Protection Movement" analysed the different attitudes of men and women in the movement and found they are contingent upon such things as early socialisation, gendered work and leisure patterns, affinity with companion animals, ambivalence about science and a history of opposition to animal abuse by generations of female activists and animal advocates. It is rare to find a social movement in which the standing of women eclipses those of their male colleagues.[8] I suggest the movement remains a bastion of female activism and advocacy because women care about blood, flesh and pain (according to the female leader of Animal Liberation Victoria) and unlike earlier generations of animal activists, women are no longer seen as a liability to the success of the movement.

4. Perspectives: As indicated in the background to this book, I have found social movement and social problems theories of most use in analysing the much-misunderstood animal rights movement. Both literatures are overflowing with definitions and concepts that serve only to confuse many readers not familiar with social and political movements. I have tried to use plain language and only a limited number of relevant concepts in my work. I do believe theory is essential to any sociological study and ascribe to the dictum: "There is nothing as practical as a good theory". [9] There is not enough space to elaborate on the various perspectives on animal rights, suffice to say, advocates and adversaries seek the moral high ground in pressing their claims. I have explored this idea in several papers reproduced in this book on "moral capital", "human versus nonhuman interests", "vilification of adversaries versus accommodating their different views" and on philosophical debates on "the genetic engineering of nonhuman animals".

Concluding the volume is a section that is not in the style of a conventional conclusion. Instead, I have suggested how readers might learn about one of the last great causes confronting humans as ethical individuals. In my recent book *Life Chances, Education and Social Movements*[10] I argue how our individual life chances are greatly enhanced by a sound education and collectively, by the work of social movements. One of the themes of the book is that a well-informed, educated citizenry is needed to solve some of the most pressing problems humanity faces. It is also argued that social movements are vital actors in mitigating the impact of existential threats such as pandemics and climate change, both of which incidentally, are linked to animal agriculture in the contexts of Concentrated Animal Feeding Operations (CAFOs) and live animal wet markets. However, the movement or movements must be supported by a well-informed, committed citizenry. As a contribution to this project, a list of annotated readings is provided on the book's four main themes: history, cruelty, activism and perspectives.

---

[8] An exception is Mothers Against Drunk Driving (MADD).
[9] Attributed to Kurt Lewin's work in the 1940s.
[10] Published in 2019 by Anthem Press, London and New York.

History

Chapter 1

A Short History of Animal Protection

It was no battle of words in which we were engaged but one of ethical conduct.

—Henry Salt,1921

The Genealogy of Animal Rights

It is often said that the modern animal rights movement began around 1975, the year that Peter Singer's *Animal Liberation: A New Ethics for our Treatment of Animals* was published. While this is undoubtedly the case, the animal protection movement has much deeper roots that go back to Pythagoras's arguments for vegetarianism in the sixth century BC. According to Magel (1989) the first publication in English to use the term "rights" in connection with animals was written in 1683 by Thomas Tyron, a Christian theologian. This chapter outlines some of that history by noting the continuity between the "old" humanitarian/welfare movements and the "new" animal liberation/rights movement associated with Singer's name. For more comprehensive historical accounts of our relationship with other animals, there are no better sources than the excellent studies by Thomas (1983) and Ritvo (1987).

Anglo-American Pioneers of Animal Protection

The history of animal protection in the Anglo-American world reveals the continuity of the early campaigns against cruelty with contemporary protests on behalf of animals as well as similarities in the emergence of the movement in the UK and the USA. The first cruelty law in Anglo-American jurisprudence was inscribed in the statutes of the Puritan founding fathers in 1641. However, as Tannenbaum (1995) points out, the statutes never became law in any of the American colonies, nor even in Massachusetts after it achieved statehood. England was first to secure the protection of animals in the statute books early in the nineteenth century although for the rest of the century, animal protection developed along similar lines on both sides of the Atlantic. It was a different story, however, in the eighteenth century, as told by the cultural historian Ann Fairfax Withington (1991) in her book which covers the American Revolution in the period from 1764 to1776. Cockfighting was a popular pastime in eighteenth century England and before Congress banned the practice, it was part of the colonial life south of New England. But in the political climate in revolutionary America, the vices associated with cockfighting and horse racing posed a threat to the values colonists needed in order to resist English tyranny or defeat them morally at least. "Both activities seemed frivolous and extravagant. They diverted people from work; they produced nothing of benefit to society; and, by encouraging competition and gambling, they weakened community cohesiveness" (Withington 1991:199). Animals were treated better in England than in the American colonies, an observation often made by visitors to both countries. The treatment of animals on both sides of the Atlantic came to symbolise the moral virtues, or lack of them, of the protagonists in pre-revolutionary America.

It was in the year of the Revolution in 1776 that Humphry Primatt published his dissertation on *The Duty of Mercy and the Sin of Cruelty to Brute Animals* which Turner (1980:11) praised for containing virtually all the intellectual arguments that had for more than a century and a half shaped Anglo-American attitudes towards animals. In an introduction to a 1992 edition of the book, Richard Ryder (1989) goes even further by noting that Primatt's ideas were remarkably similar to those of leading Anglo-American scholars during the next two hundred years. Primatt even drew a comparison between our treatment of brutes and other races thus anticipating the link between speciesism and racism that Singer was to make two centuries later.

> Pain is pain, whether it be inflicted on man or on beast; and the creature that suffers it, whether man or beast, being sensible of the misery of it whilst it lasts, suffers *evil*; and the sufferance of evil, unmerited, unprovokedly, where no offence has been given, and no good can possibly be answered by it, but merely to exhibit power or gratify malice, is cruelty and injustice in him that occasions it (Primatt 1992:21).

This 1776 statement against "the sin of cruelty" contains the essential elements of pain, sentience, injustice and cruelty which became the core motifs of the modern animal protection movement. The influence of Primatt's writings, however, was confined to like-minded souls of his own generation, "a small number of enthusiasts for whom concern for animals had a strong emotional force" (Turner 1980:14). Yet Turner notes that by the end of the eighteenth century, most of "the middling and upper classes" at least believed that morality demanded kindness to the brute creation. It would take another century or more for these changing attitudes to trickle down to the bulk of the population in the Anglo-American world. Much of that task would fall to the genteel patrons of the Society for the Prevention of Cruelty to Animals.

Societies for the Prevention of Cruelty to Animals in the 19th Century

Inspired by Primatt's sentiments, the Royal Society for the Prevention of Cruelty to Animals (RSPCA) found a receptive audience in the Victorian era. Primatt's dissertation emphasised the rational over the emotional and focussed explicitly on animal pain and suffering. England produced the first enduring anti-cruelty law in 1822 when the Martin Act was passed to prevent cruelty to cattle; in 1835 it was extended to include all domestic animals. By that time, the Society for the Prevention of Cruelty to Animals (SPCA) had been founded in 1824 in London as the first national animal protection society in the world, although the Liverpool Society for Preventing Wanton Cruelty to Brute Animals, which was set up in 1809, has the distinction of being the world's oldest animal welfare group. In 1840, the national group received royal patronage and became the Royal Society for the Prevention of Cruelty to Animals.

According to Harrison (1973), the history of the RSPCA has been neglected by scholars even though it was one of the most influential "cause groups" in the nineteenth century. Harrison attributes its success to its respectability and to the strategy of never running too far ahead of public opinion, especially among the more respectable members of the public. The RSPCA derived its philosophy, rhetoric and its moral force from evangelicalism; the objects of its campaigns against cruelty were almost exclusively the cruel sports of the lower orders. In Thompson's view, the organisation was swimming with the tide, not creating it, as it was "just one weapon in a whole armoury which included Sunday schools, temperance, popular education, and personal hygiene, that was intended to persuade or compel the working classes to adopt approved standards of behaviour rooted in religious belief" (Thompson 1988:280).

Another historian dates the humanitarian tide as having begun in the previous century: "Throughout the eighteenth century, humanitarian reform had played a major causal role in (the) cultural reconstruction of pain, identifying a range of formerly unquestioned practices as unacceptable cruelties and demanding that virtuous people, men and women of sensibility, endeavour to put a stop to such practices" (Haltunen 1995:318). These included blood sports, public executions, harsh treatment of the insane, flogging in the armed services, corporal punishment of children, and sport which caused serious injury. Still another historian noted that eighteenth-century women empathised more with animals than they did with peasants or slaves. Barker-Benfield sees the eighteenth century as an age of sensibility in which women campaigned against male barbarity. "From Margaret Cavendish through Francis Power Cobbe, women made the connection between men's treatment of animals and their treatment of women" (Barker- Benfield 1992:232). Cobbe had written an article in 1878 called "Wife-Torture in England" in which she put the abuse of women by men on a par with vivisection which she condemned for experimenting on the nerves of living dogs and torturing dozens of cats in a single experiment.

Animal protectors in the RSPCA had to work hard to change the way animals were treated by "the lower orders". In the early 1800s, legislation against bull-baiting did not invoke the cruelty argument, because the concept would not resonate in a predominantly rural England, which depended on the daily slaughter of animals (Harrison 1973:786). For example, some thought the House of Commons had reached a low ebb when in 1880 it had a bill before it on the abolition of bull baiting (Ritvo 1987:125). By the end of the century, argues Harrison, kindness to animals was the widespread expectation of an urban society that had become used to the RSPCA's strong appeals for compassion towards "the brute creation". One humanitarian crusader noted approvingly how far animal protection had come over the past one hundred years; in Anglo-Saxon countries, especially, tenderness towards sentient creatures, he observed, was now commonplace (cited in Ritvo 1987:126). And as described by Ryder (1989), the RSPCA in the second half of the 19th century succeeded in promoting a number of important legal protections for animals such as dogs used to draw carts, wild birds, laboratory animals, animals in transit and even wild animals.

Notwithstanding these achievements, and similar ones in the USA, the organisation on both sides of the Atlantic was, as a creature of the Victorian age, characterised by a belief in "kindness, mildness and self-restraint", virtues unlikely to upset the status quo (Turner 1980). It became glaringly obvious that on some issues, most notably the vexed question of hunting with hounds, the RSPCA would not challenge the proclivities of the upper classes. Working class habits were a different matter as the records of the Society's inaugural meeting in 1824 revealed. Ritvo notes that the chairman made it clear to members that the Society's purpose was not only "to prevent the exercise of cruelty towards animals, but to spread amongst the lower orders of the people a degree of moral feeling which would compel them to think and act like those of a superior class (1987:135).

According to Turner, for most of the nineteenth century the SPCAs in North America followed in the footsteps of the English RSPCA by cultivating a conservative, middle-class constituency and by keeping women from ascending to leadership positions in the organisation. "The RSPCA largely expelled the unconventional; its American counterparts simply ignored them" (Turner 1980:53). The American Society for the Prevention of Cruelty to Animals (ASPCA) was established in 1866 and in the next three years SPCAs spread to Boston, Philadelphia, and San Francisco. The founder of the ASPCA, Henry Bergh persuaded the State Legislature in New York to include all animals in the 1867 animal protection statute. The first section of the statute has been incorporated in many American state anti-cruelty laws and Tannenbaum (1995:567) notes that even the wording closely resembles the language of present-day statutes:

> If any person shall over-drive, over-load, torture, torment, deprive of necessary sustenance, or unnecessarily or cruelly beat, or needlessly mutilate or kill, or cause or procure to be over-driven, over-loaded, tortured any living creature, every such offender shall, for every such offense, be guilty of a misdemeanour (quoted in Tannenbaum 1995:567).

Although legislation to protect animals was first enacted in England, animal protection could be described as an Anglo-American tradition. According to Turner (1980), the Anglo-American world in the nineteenth century was a separate cultural entity within the larger European civilization. Thus, it is not surprising that animal protection in both countries followed a similar pattern. Worster also writes of a distinctive Anglo-American tradition in the ecology movement in the late twentieth century, which while "never wholly a consensus, but withal a single dialogue carried on in a single tongue" (1977: ix).

Australia's early efforts in animal protection were also part of this dialogue. An Australian RSPCA was established in 1891 and by the end of the 19th century each of the colonies had its own society modelled after the English parent organization. Like its Anglo-American counterparts, the Australian RSPCA consisted of predominantly middle-class urbanites, although in the Australian case, the RSPCA attracted affluent people from rural areas as well. Yet aside from these similarities the animal protection movement in Australia developed along different lines and in ways which were unique.

Cruelty in the Australian Bush

The most comprehensive study of the early history of the animal protection movement in Australia is Jennifer MacCulloch's (1993) analysis of the period 1880-1930 in which she documents the activities of the Animal Protection Society of NSW (APS) founded in 1873 and the Women's Society for the Prevention of Cruelty to Animals established in 1886. The APS's moral purpose was not unlike the RSPCA's in that it derived its motivation from "the prevalence of cruelty to animals amongst a certain class of persons in this community (which) has excited the indignation and disgust of the educated and humane" (MacCulloch 1993:43). Opposition to cruelty was to be the driving force of the early animal protectionists in their campaigns to save both domestic and wild animals in Australia. While the brutality of working- class men particularly towards street horses had been the target of the early campaigners, most of whom were women, the anti-plumage campaign targeted women for their indirect cruelty to birds. The anti-plumage campaign became a synonym for anti-cruelty and united both animal protectionists and preservationists. One of MacCulloch's most important findings was that these two movements were irrevocably intertwined, and in the popular imagination, were synonymous.

It is perhaps not surprising in a country with a relatively small population that animal protectionists and preservationists would find it necessary to join forces in their respective causes. But according to MacCulloch, the preservationists were keenly conscious of the disadvantages of being associated with "the emotionalism, hysteria and religiosity of the animal protection movement" (1993: 202). More importantly, then as now, both movements had different purposes and ideologies; the preservationists focussed their campaigns on saving species and habitats and thought little of the animal protectionists' concern for preventing cruelty to individual animals. MacCulloch argues, however, that the animal protection movement's lasting legacy was to shape the means by which communication about nature with the public was possible. According to MacCulloch, the preservationists realized that however much they were out of kilter with the animal protectionists, the concept of cruelty was needed to mobilise a sympathetic, sensitive public into action. The early alliance of the two movements in Australia was therefore a marriage of convenience since the preservationists needed the moral appeal of their partner's anti-cruelty focus. In her conclusion MacCulloch describes what still rings true a century later: "For no matter how affecting, or even tragic, it was to witness the destruction of a single, beautiful tree or scenic area, it lacked the pathos of cruelty to animals. A tree was a living thing, but it did not bleed, it did not suffer, it did not have babies" (1993:369).

Animal protectionists have always known the power of cruelty as a moral weapon, yet it was rarely widely invoked on behalf of native Australian fauna. It featured prominently in the anti-plumage campaign and most effectively in what was to become the preservation movement's symbol of success, the campaign to protect the koala. Of all Australian fauna the koala provided the highest quality fur and hunting them for profit led to the destruction of vast numbers of the animals. Although numbers are imprecise, MacCulloch reports that one leading fur company held over one million koala skins for export to Russia in 1896.

Animal protectionists and preservationists had little difficulty promoting the virtues of the "bushland baby and toy" to city people as "a morally blameless infant which lived on gum leaves and harmed no-one and nothing"(MacCulloch 1993:299). To many rural people, however, the koalas were vermin to be exterminated. To counter this hostility, the campaigners were obliged to transform the koala's status from commercial success to national pet. The modern meaning of "koala", writes MacCulloch, is as "an emotional rather than commercial resource" much the same as the social value of children changed from an economic to an emotional resource after the Industrial Revolution (Zelizer 1985). But in the early part of the century koalas were hunted as pests. If people were to see them as anything other than vermin, an effective campaign would need to be waged. Cruelty was the answer, for how could anyone "murder" this quintessentially cute and cuddly creature?

The koala was therefore constructed as a lovable pet, an Australian teddy bear which one reporter described as a "charming little creature, a more perfect natural pet is not to be found anywhere in the world" (MacCulloch 1993:300). MacCulloch points out that this construction was only possible once the koala had ceased to be of commercial value after overhunting had decimated their numbers. For this reason, she argues, the koala was a good choice as a symbol for the preservation movement. The koala was "an amalgam of the values and messages of the animal protection and preservation movements the conduit which connected the two in the popular mind" (1993:301). According to MacCulloch, animal protectionists needed the preservationists since the animal lobby had virtually run out of steam by 1914. MacCulloch concludes that this was due to the movement's transformation from a social reform lobby to a group of pet enthusiasts who emphasised the genteel promotion of kindness to domestic animals, especially cats and dogs. "This loss of purpose both mirrored and was reinforced by the growing feminisation of the cause. Increasingly, the cause of animal protection was given over to women, and subsequently, children" (MacCulloch 1993:45-6).

Elsewhere within the animal protection movement itself unity of purpose has not always been easily achieved. At least in the nineteenth century the RSPCA provided a solid foundation for a united voice to be raised in defence of animals. What there was of a single voice in the movement however was to dissipate in the first half of the twentieth century. Part of the reason was a growing tension within the animal protection movement between moderate welfarists in the RSPCA and SPCAs and the abolitionists in the anti -vivisection movement. According to French, by 1875-76, the RSPCA had distanced itself from "the hysteria and sensationalism" in the anti-vivisection movement and even took to discrediting it publicly (1975: 82). As the tension between the two movements remains unresolved at the end of the 20th century, it is worth outlining the history of anti -vivisectionism.

Early Opposition to Animal Experimentation

Time will disperse with certain hand and sure

This swarm of buzzing idlers, whose obscure

Humanitarians foul humanity

–Zoophilist, 1835 cited in Elston 1990:259

These inflammatory words were among the many directed against those who campaigned against the use of live animals in scientific experiments in America and in England in the 19th century. The term vivisection originally meant the dissection of, or the surgical intervention upon, living animals for research purposes (Maehle and Troehler, 1990:14). Vivisection has always been a controversial scientific procedure, but it was not until the second half of the 17th century that it became a moral issue.

In the first half of the 17th century Descartes maintained that animals were automata devoid of rationality, a soul and feeling. Unlike many of his disciples, Descartes did not believe that animals were entirely devoid of sentience and towards the end of his life he conceded the possibility of some inferior feelings in brutes. But the early vivisectionists who followed the Cartesian concept of the "beast-machine" believed they could not harm animals; the cries of animals subjected to vivisection were interpreted as no different to the sounds emitted by an object struck by a hammer. Here was a rock-solid rationalization for exempting humans from any qualms they might have about their treatment of other animals. But by the end of the 17th century the rock became increasingly shaky as educated individuals, vivisectors among them, insisted that animal experimentation was cruel.

Robert Hooke (1635-1703) for example, had experimented on a dog in which he cut away the thorax and diaphragm of the living creature in order to observe the motions of the animal's heart and lungs. He managed to keep the dog alive for more than an hour by pumping air into its windpipe by means of a pair of bellows. His observation of the animal during the process moved Hooke to vow never to repeat the experiment "because of the torture of the creature" (Maehle and Troehler 1990:23).

While there were scientists who found vivisection abhorrent, the majority of vivisectors rarely mentioned the torture they inflicted on their living tools.

The Vivisection Debate

Samuel Johnson (1709-1784) rejected Cartesianism and believed, no doubt by observing his own pets, that animals felt pain and had feelings. His attack in 1758 on physicians who experimented on animals rates as the fiercest denunciation up to that time: "Among the inferior Professors of medical knowledge, is a race of wretches, whose lives are only varied by varieties of cruelty" (quoted in Maehle and Troehler 1990:32). His arguments against vivisection, while not original, were effective because they were anthropocentric: first, cruelty towards animals may lead to cruelty towards men and second, he denied any therapeutic consequences of animal experimentation, suggesting that "these horrid operations make the physician more dreadful than the gout or stone" (Maehle and Troehler 1990:33).

William Hogarth's depiction of the fate of Tom Nero in *The Four Stages of Cruelty* (1750) graphically captured these sentiments in pictorial form. Nero progresses from torturing animals in the streets of London to beating a horse and then to killing his mistress for which he hanged. In the fourth stage of the tale, the still breathing body of Nero is the subject of an anatomy lecture during which his entrails are consumed by the surgeon's mastiff. Immanuel Kant, who argued that the considerate treatment of animals was a duty to man himself, apparently used Hogarth's prints to illustrate in his own lectures the widely held idea that cruelty to animals may lead to cruelty against one's fellows.

But it was left to Jeremy Bentham to produce what was probably the first serious counterargument to Kant's doctrine that "our duties towards animals are merely indirect duties towards humanity" (Kant 1930:230). Kant evidently believed that painful experiments on animals were to be avoided if the results could be otherwise obtained; but it was what the experiments did to the experimenter rather than the animal that chiefly concerned Kant. In stark contrast to Kant's human-centred, contractual doctrine, Bentham's (1789) oft-quoted dictum "the question is not, Can they *reason*? nor, Can they *talk*? But, Can they *suffer*?" called for an entirely different relationship between humans and animals. This right of animals to be treated humanely as sentient beings was to be the basis for Singer's (1975) *Animal Liberation* almost two centuries later.

Victorian Values and Vivisection

It was not until the 1870s that the vivisection controversy reached its peak in Victorian England. "What elevated anti-vivisectionism from a mostly latent sense of outrage into a ferocious public agitation was the large-scale importation of experimental physiology into Britain and the United States after 1870" (Turner 1980:89).

Articles, letters, advertisements, books, prize essay contests, placards, flyers, pamphlets, periodicals as well as antivivisectionist novels and paintings were among the many ways the moral atrocities of animal experimentation as described openly in Sanderson's *Handbook for the Physiological Laboratory* of 1873 were widely publicised. As French (1975:254) points out, the printed word was the single most important medium for mobilizing anti -vivisection support.

Opposition to vivisection was such that the biomedical establishment was compelled to organize its members against the twin charges that animal experimentation was both cruel and useless. Rupke points out that the antivivisectionists suffered a setback in 1881 when the scientists rallied in London for the International Medical Congress and unanimously endorsed animal experimentation as indispensable to medicine and therefore "in the interests of man and of animals" (quoted in Rupke 1990:191-2). Insult was added to injury when the journal *Nature* criticized leading antivivisectionists for their apparent hypocrisy: Francis Power Cobbe, for example, was ridiculed for wearing ostrich feathers ("plucked from the *living bird*") and for being seen in public carrying an ivory-handled umbrella ("*cut out* of the dying elephant's jaw"). The people in glass houses taunt would be used whenever animal protectionists could be faulted for not living up to the high moral standards of their most militant colleagues.

Rupke suggests that the defence of vivisection by reference to the cruelties of blood sports was no more than an attack on the middle class and aristocratic membership of the antivivisectionist societies (1990:203). However, the single most important motive for defending animal experiments, he argues, was that the antivivisectionists threatened not just the progress of biomedical science, but the status of the scientists whose position and privilege had steadily improved during the Victorian period (1990:198).

Nor was opposition to vivisection confined to animal protectionists. The biomedical fraternity also had to contend with the less strident, but sometimes more effective arguments of the Humanitarian League (1891-1919) founded by Henry Salt. It argued against the use of animals in experiments because they were too much like humans and opposed the use of a vaccine made from calf lymph as an example of "the animalization of humans" (Weinbren 1994:99). According to Weinbren, the League introduced a fresh perspective to the antivivisection debate by inserting new issues such as its critique of state intervention, the importance of education and the promotion of a wholesome lifestyle (1994:98). The League's approach, while relying more on education than vilification, was nonetheless designed to shame those who they thought were cruel to animals.

Vilification was used by the experimentalists as well. In America, "the nightmare humanitarians of antivivisection" (Fleming 1987:145) were subjected to extreme abuse by the experimentalists whose rhetoric of vilification has continued well into the twentieth century. One of the most colourful examples was penned by the historian David Fleming in the 1950s in his study of the rise of modern medicine in the United States. To this modern-day defender of animal experimentation, the anti-vivisection movement of the nineteenth century was:

> a world alliance of overlapping animal lovers, vegetarians, anti-Listerians, anti-bacteriologists, and anti-inoculationists; soft muddle-headed women, cold-blooded Amazons and publicity seekers of both sexes, bluff advocates of the old-fashioned godliness and soap-and-water but not carbolic-acid cleanliness, maudlin religionists not averse to blasphemy, medical sectaries (ie. sects), and academic and professional cast-offs all engaged in a travesty of the intellectual life, snooping about laboratories and ransacking the pages of scientific journals for ammunition (Fleming 1954/1987: 147).

Turner (1980:93) points out that American antivivisectionists relied almost exclusively on the literature of their English colleagues, who as in animal welfare generally, took the lead in campaigning against cruelty. On one matter, however, the Americans proved to be the more innovative. America's vivisectors saw themselves as rational men of science whose work on behalf of humanity was being retarded by middle-class, city-based female "cranks" in humane societies. In 1906, a prominent American neurologist, Charles Loomis Dana foresaw "catastrophe" for science if the antivivisectionists succeeded in their plans to regulate laboratories.

His solution was to pronounce the opponents of animal experimentation victims of zoophil-psychosis, an illness he diagnosed as among the "obsessive insanities" (Buettinger 1993:5). Women, some of whom it was alleged coddled their pets and loved them more than their babies, were held to be more susceptible than men to the disease. Buettinger refers to one physician who maintained that zoophil-psychosis affected people without children and without a serious occupation in life. Not surprisingly, women who joined animal protection societies, or worse, who campaigned against vivisection, were easily portrayed as afflicted by the malady. The *New York Times* of March 1909 explained: "This is because animals make a small and strictly limited demand for affection and care, and therefore are favorite objects of those with little to bestow" (Buettinger 1993:8). The newspaper's verdict has become a popular refrain among critics of the present-day animal movement.

By 1914, notes Buettinger, the charge of zoophil-psychosis had become commonplace, despite the lack of any scientific evidence for the malady. And although anti-vivisectionists refused to be intimidated by the label or the labellers, the movement began to run out of steam by 1925 (Buettinger1993:10). Yet it was not Dana's invention of zoophil-psychosis which retarded the progress of the antivivisectionists.

Lederer (1990:253) argues that the causes were more varied, including the antivivisectionists' own excesses, their continued support for obsolete medical therapies, the making of unhelpful alliances, and their strident attacks on medical progress in understanding disease. Articles in the quality press such as the *New York Times* like the example quoted above, important as they were, would not have had the same impact as an essay which appeared in the Encyclopedia Britannica of 1910-11. The piece carried the imprimatur of the Britannica which presented a six-page, 9000-word argument supporting vivisection by Stephen Paget, honorary secretary of the Research Defence Society. Paget invited readers to compare the fate of the 86 277 research animals in Great Britain in 1909 to the much worse predicament of "an equal number of the same kinds of animals, either in a state of nature, or kept for sport, or used for the service of human profit or amusement"(quoted in Cockburn 1996:28). Cockburn suggests that the article's inclusion in the 11th edition was in response to the strength of the anti-vivisection movement at that time. It is more likely that the editors were confident of the article being in tune with a public that had already been for the most part won over by the case for vivisection.

In any event, according to Lederer, by 1914, moderate animal protectionists sympathised with medical researchers about the excesses of their more militant colleagues. Anti-vivisectionism had lost much of the moral capital it had enjoyed in the 1870s but by no means did the movement disappear altogether.

Animal Protection in the 20th Century

According to Ryder (1989), royal support of the RSPCA continued until the end of the nineteenth century but declined after World War 1 and with it, the fortunes of the RSPCA. Elsewhere, Ryder (1979:11) suggests that from 1918 to the 1960s, serious intellectual debate on animals' rights ebbed. And when one looks at the literature on the animal protection movement in the first half of the twentieth century there is an apparent falling off in interest by scholars. On the other hand, social movements professing to be against *all* cruelty were much in evidence at the turn of the century. Henry Salt's Humanitarian League is the best example of a multi-purpose anti-cruelty campaign. Its mission included Poor Law, Criminal and Prison Law reform as well as cruelty to animals in vivisection, in slaughterhouses, the trade in feathers, blood sports and the "evil trade" that involved the shipping of live cattle abroad (Weinbren 1994:88). Unlike the RSPCA, which was reluctant to harass the hunting fraternity, the Humanitarian League campaigned vigorously against blood sports. In 1924 it established the League for the Prohibition of Cruel Sports, the most recent campaigns of which are organised by the League Against Cruel Sports (LACS). Salt saw his organisation as "a fighting, not a talking Society" (Hendrick and Hendrick 1989:46). He had little patience for hair-splitting over the meaning of "rights" and the like which today still preoccupy philosophers.

Salt believed, and many modern animal welfare/liberation organisations agree, that animal welfare reform can best be achieved via education and legislation. His firm faith in education was matched by his lack of it in established religion. His only religion was his self-styled *Creed of Kinship* which he hoped would have an educative, civilizing effect on those who considered its principles—"a belief that in years to come there will be a recognition of the brotherhood between man and man, nation with nation, human and sub-human, which will transform a state of savagery as we have it, into one of civilization." (From the cremation address in 1939 composed by Salt himself and cited in Winsten 1951:203).

Legislation, the second weapon in Salt's reformist armoury, was by no means the lesser strategy, for Salt argued that it was more important than preventive cruelty. Legislation such as the reforms which abolished slavery and the Factory Acts provided "the record, the register, of the moral sense of the community" (Salt, 1980:124). Time and again, animal protection staff in organisations which advocated moderate piecemeal reforms in animal welfare echoed Salt's sentiments. Not surprisingly, the most striking example of an organisation choosing the "legislative" track as a strategy against cruelty, is the League Against Cruel Sports, the group Salt's Humanitarian League had established in 1924.

Thus, it would be mistaken to conclude that the animal protection movement had run entirely out of steam in the first three-quarters of the 20th century. Organisations like the RSPCA did not disappear, nor was it the case that no new groups emerged during this comparatively quiet period. For example, in one list of major British animal protection organisations that were formed in the nineteenth and twentieth centuries, half were founded between 1900 and 1969 (Garner 1993: 43). Lederer (1992) has described the durability of the anti-vivisection movement during this period and its capacity to exert pressure on the medical research fraternity. Moreover, as long as there were individuals like Henry Salt who devoted their lives to the humanitarian cause, the animal movement would continue to move, however slowly. Small numbers of supporters would join the true believers as in any social movement whose grievances had not been resolved. Eminent individuals such as Gandhi who attributed his conversion to vegetarianism to Henry Salt would add lustre to the movement and more importantly, moral capital. Gandhi's belief in *Ahisma* non-violence, of causing no harm to humans or other animals is the cornerstone of Hindu ethics and continues to guide animal liberation philosophers such as Tom Regan and Peter Singer, a vegan and vegetarian respectively. This brings us to a period in the first half of 20th century animal protection that demands an explanation. Critics of 'animal people', vegans and vegetarians sometimes invoke the proposition in hopes of undermining the movement's promotion of compassion that many Nazis were fervent animal protectors, and that Hitler was a committed vegetarian.

Nazi Animal Protection Policies

Nothing contrasts more starkly with the Gandhian approach to animal rights than the politics of animal protection in Nazi Germany. It is surely one of the ironies of history and an episode of acute discomfort to animal protectionists that some of the most progressive animal protection legislation this century was enacted in Germany during the reign of the Nazis. Just as animal protectionists are pleased to invoke Gandhi's vegetarianism but not Hitler's, there exists little more than an explanatory footnote to the seemingly incongruous attitude by one of history's most genocidal regimes to the world of nature. However, the recent debate sparked by Arluke and Sax (1992) provides a deeper insight into this apparent contradiction. Arluke and Sax suggest three reasons for the paradox: first, the leading Nazi's love of animals may have been a psychological response or a coping device to counter their inhumanity towards "inferior" humans; second, their professed love of animals may have been a convenient guise to attack inconvenient people like Jews, homosexuals and gypsies; and third, the Nazis may have blurred the boundaries between humans and other animals so as to be able to designate certain undesirable humans as lower in moral worth than nonhuman animals.

Elsewhere, Arluke and Sanders (1996) claim the Nazis' blurring of the animal/human boundary and their alteration of the conventional distinctions of what in the West constitutes the animal and the human was achieved in three ways: the moral elevation of nonhuman animals, their identification with them as noble beasts, and the animalization of certain humans.

While critics of modern-day animal protectionists are quick to connect their activities with the Nazis' attitudes toward animals, no mainstream animal liberationist would accept the boundary work practised by the Nazis. First, the moral "elevation" of animals does not usually feature in animal liberation campaigns. There is nothing in the contemporary animal movement approaching the Nazi's cult worship of animals or the distinction made in the Third Reich between good (Aryans) and bad animals (Jews and other "inferior races"). Nor do animal liberationists claim, as the Nazis did, that animals like the "sacred" pig were moral beings. Second, Nazi identification with animals at a personal level is not unusual; most of the leading Nazis from Hitler down, kept pets and professed their mutual devotion in the same way that all pet owners typically do. Hitler and Goebbels were different in that they preferred animals to humans, a preference which is rarely expressed by animal liberationists. (Of the 50 or so individuals interviewed for this book, only two confessed to feeling this way).

According to Arluke and Sanders (1996:165) the Nazis identified with animals that symbolized "ideal" qualities such as fearlessness, loyalty, obedience and strength. Politically, however, identifying with animals was important as Nazi propaganda because it directed people's compassion away from suffering Jews to innocent animals who the Nazis claimed were victims of Jewish butchers and vivisectors. And Goering, the avid hunter, promised "to commit to concentration camps those who still think they can continue to treat animals as inanimate property" (quoted in Arluke and Sax 1992:7). While Goering's own love of hunting did not constrain his contempt for such people, it symbolized the fundamental contradictions inherent in Nazi attitudes towards animals and humans. Further, the animalization of humans as "vermin", "beasts", "wild animals" is a technique of demonization not confined to the Nazis. Animal liberationists constantly challenge the unthinking labelling of criminals and deviants as "animals" by pointing out the injustice of attributing to animals what humans alone are guilty of.

According to Luc Ferry the animal protection law (*Tierschutzgesetz*) of 24 November, 1933 and the law for the protection of nature (*Reichsnaturschutzgesetz*) two years later represented for the first time in history an attempt to reconcile political and ecological interests (1995:92). Compared to other animal protection laws in Europe, the Nazis' *Tierschutzgesetz* stood out as a rejection of anthropocentrism and as a principle that animals were to be protected in their own right and not as a means to shield humans from the ill effects of cruelty. Arluke and Sax (1992:9) dispute this, however. They argue that the Nazi laws did not go much beyond those in Britain, the country which had pioneered animal protection. Phillips and Sechzer (1989:12) support this view when they point to the similarities between the Nazi law of 1934 and the British law of 1876 which they explain as a consequence of Hitler's selective admiration for British values. What made the German law different was the severity of the punishment meted out to those found guilty of mistreating animals (Arluke and Sax 1992; Brunner 1995). Arluke and Sax give the example of one such penalty a fine plus two years imprisonment for the "rough mistreatment" of a dog.

What continues to intrigue scholars however is that the purpose of Nazi animal protection was, in the words of the *Tierschutzgesetz*, "to awaken and strengthen compassion as one of the highest moral values of the German people" (quoted in Arluke and Sax 1992:8). Among the first reforms the Nazis implemented when they came to power in 1933 was the law in relation to Jewish ritual slaughter. Laws on animal experimentation, the protection of wildlife and a law forbidding the boiling of crabs, lobsters and other crustaceans soon followed. The Arluke and Sax paper stimulated several responses to these contradictions: the idea of protecting animals while murdering people; the avoidance of meat but not blood sports; the receptivity of the Nazi regime's evil intentions in a highly cultivated society and so on. Some commentators have warned of the danger of making too much of the Nazi paradox. Herzog, for example, makes the compelling point that "moral inconsistency is the hallmark of our relations with other species" (1993:82). Nevertheless, while much more needs to be done to improve animal welfare, there has been progress in several countries such as in Australia.

Animal Liberation in Australia

Since the 1990s, there have been several significant improvements to animal welfare in Australia; the most important perhaps and this applies to the movement's achievements worldwide as well is the growth in vegetarianism and to a much lesser extent, veganism. While meat eating continues to be popular in affluent countries like Australia, vegetarianism is no longer seen as an irrational taboo. Popular animal movement slogans "Meat is Murder" and "Go Veg" have been promoted because activists insist that "meat eating is the most oppressive and extensive institutionalized violence against animals" (Adams 1990: 70).

'Go Veg': The Dietary Future of Humankind?

The easier and more palatable alternative to a vegan diet would be a mass conversion to vegetarianism, which as Elias (1978) predicted, is likely to be the dietary future of humankind. There is an increasing number of vegetarian advocates and practitioners who call for an ethical diet that does not include meat with vegans recommending a diet and lifestyle that is completely free of dairy and animal products such as leather and fur.

According to Newton's (2019) research the number of people worldwide choosing a meat-free diet has increased significantly over one or two generations; there were five main reasons respondents gave for 'going veg': 1. health (64%); 2.animal protection (41%); 3. environmental issues (37 %); 4.disgust (36 %) and 5. taste (21%). The reason for the increase in the 'disgust' factor may have to do with the many visual images and stories of animal cruelty in the social and mainstream media in the last few decades. While this single survey cannot be a firm guide for the future eating habits of the population, it does demonstrate vegetarianism's appeal in that it is widely perceived as a better dietary choice for the health of humans, animals and the environment than the meat-eating alternative. Australians stating they are on a vegetarian or mostly vegetarian diet in the period from 2011/2 (9.7%) to 2015/6 (11.2%) means vegetarianism has seen only a modest increase of 1.5% in these six years. (Statistical Research Department, accessed online on 16 May 2020).

Ethical vegetarianism involves people's conversion to a meat-free diet because it reduces animal cruelty while pragmatic vegetarianism is based on consumer awareness of the risk of eating contaminated meat; both these motivations are radical in so far as they represent a boycott on meat products which ultimately makes a huge dent in the ideology of speciesism. This is the subversive potential of vegetarianism when defects in food regulations are revealed that shock consumers into converting to a vegetarian (or vegan) diet (Frank 2004).

It is also evident, according to Hughes (2020) that animal-free dairy products and plant-based meats are increasingly on the menu, for example in Hungry Jack's in Australia. She notes how the food animal industry is fighting back with what it ridicules as a 'vegan fantasyland' of animal-free foods. Hughes, on the other hand, explains why the Australian dairy industry 'is already in deep cow manure' with New Zealand's dairy products it's most valuable export likely to be in much less demand in 20-25 years with the consumption of synthetic milk sold worldwide. Healthy food is an issue upon which animal protectionists could unite in common cause with public health, consumer, food security, environmental and other like-minded groups to promote a vegetarian or vegan lifestyle.

For such a mass movement to be mobilised, the public first needs to be convinced about the many negative consequences of the intensive confinement and abuse of animals that have been identified by animal activists. Additionally, as Akhtar (2013) argues, there is the need to include animal protectionism in public health policies as well as the importance of educating the public that emerging infectious diseases (EIDs) are linked to the cruel treatment of animals.

At the time of writing, the Chinese Communist Party's (CCP) failure to alert the world immediately to a virus outbreak in Wuhan is seen as the most likely culprit responsible for the catastrophic global impact of the Covid-19 pandemic. In the months to come, the pandemic will be debated as to who or what was responsible for the worldwide havoc; it is too soon to be certain of anything except that our treatment of food animals has severe consequences for the health of the human race.

Conclusion

Like many other aspects of our lives, it has taken Covid-19 to compel us to consider our relations with and our treatment of animals. Abattoirs and meat works in many countries including developed economies such as Germany and Australia have been revealed as hot spots for spreading the coronavirus. While there has been much publicity on slaughterhouses and their infected workers, very little media attention has been given to the thousands of wet and live animal markets or the trade in exotic wildlife particularly in countries in Asia and Africa. The well-known animal rights slogan 'Meat is Murder' now carries a new and grim message in the era of a global pandemic.

Vegetarianism has long been advocated as the alternative to meat, which if adopted on an increasing scale globally, will reduce greenhouse emissions, improve human health and reduce the numbers of animals raised for food. While vegetarianism has a long history and only a minority of followers worldwide, the current crisis will surely induce many more people to reduce or eschew animal products all together. The animal protection movement (APM) has historically used animal exploitation as its *modus operandi*; the time is now opportune to add the health risks of meat consumption to its campaigns on behalf of humans, animals and the environment. The risk of further pandemics to our wellbeing is taken up in the book's conclusion.

REFERENCES

Adams, C. (1990) *The sexual politics of meat: A feminist-vegetarian critical theory,* Polity Press: Cambridge.

Akthar, A. (2012) *Animals and public health: Why treating animals better is critical to human welfare,* Houndmills, UK/New York: Palgrave Macmillan.

Arluke, A. and Sanders, C R (1996) *Regarding animals,* Temple University Press: Philadelphia.

Arluke, A.and Sax, B. (1992) "Understanding Nazi animal protection and the Holocaust", *Anthrozoos,* 5: 6-31.

Barker-Benfield, G J (1992) *The culture of sensibility: Sex and society in eighteenth-century Britain,* The University of Chicago Press: Chicago.

Brunner, P. (1995) "Tierschutz in Deutschland und im Vereinigten Koenigsreich" (Animal protection in Germany and the United Kingdom), PhD diss., Munich: University of Munich.

Buettinger, C. (1993) "Anti-vivisection and the charge of zoophilia- psychosis in the early twentieth century", *The Historian,* 55 (2): 277-288.

Cockburn, A. (1996) "A short, meat-oriented history of the world: From Eden to the Mattole", *New Left Review,* No. 215, January/February, pp 16-42.

Elias, N (1978) *The civilising process, Vol 1, The history of manners,* Oxford: Basil Blackwell.

Elston, M. (1990) "Women and anti-vivisection in Victorian England 1870 to 1900" in Nicholaas Rupke (ed.) *Vivisection in historical perspective,* London and New York: Routledge.

Ferry, L. (1995) *The new ecological order,* Chicago: The University of Chicago Press.

Fleming, D. (1987) *William H. Welch and the rise of modern medicine,* Baltimore: Johns Hopkins University.

Frank, J. (2004) "The role of radical animal activists as information providers to consumers", *Animal Liberation Philosophy and Policy Journal,* 2 (1): 1-13.

French, R.D. (1975) *Antivivisection and medical science in Victorian Society,* Princeton: Princeton University Press.

Garner, R. (1993) *Animals, politics and morality,* Manchester: Manchester University Press.

Harrison, B. (1973)"Animals and the state in nineteenth century England" in J.M. Wallace-Hadrill and J.M.Roberts (Eds) , The English Historical Review, 88:.(349): pp. 786-820.

Haltunen, K (1995) 'Humanitarianism and the philosophy of pain in Anglo-American culture', *The American Historical Review,* 100(2) 303-334.

Hendrick, George and Hendrick, Willene (1989) (eds.) *The savour of Salt: A Henry Salt anthology,* The Centaur Press, Fontwell, Sussex.

Herzog, Harold (1993) "The movement is my life: The psychology of animal rights activism", *Journal of Social Issues,* 49, pp 103-119.

Hughes, L. (2020) "The milk of human genius: On the end of the cow and the future of food", *The Monthly,* March, 44-50.

Kant, I. (1930) Lectures on Ethics, London: Methuen.

Kean, H. (1998) *Animal rights: Political and social change in Britain since 1800,* Reakion Books Ltd, London.

Lederer, S (1992) "'Political animals.' The shaping of biomedical research literature in twentieth-century America", *ISIS,* 83, pp.61-79.

MacCulloch, Jennifer (1993) C*reatures of culture: The animal protection and preservation movements in Sydney, 1880-1930,* Unpublished PhD thesis, University of Sydney.

Maehle, A.H. and Troehler, U. (1990) "Animal Experimentation from Antiquity to the end of the eighteenth century: Attitudes and Arguments" in A.R. Nicholass (Ed) *Vivisection in Victorian perspective,* London: Routledge.

Magel, C. (1989) *Keyguide to information sources in animal rights,* Mansell Publishing, London.

Magel, C. (1992) (editor) J. Howard Moore's *the universal kinship,* The Centaur Press, Fontwell, Sussex.

Newton, D. (2019) *Vegetarianism and veganism: A reference handbook,* Contemporary World Issues (Society), Santa Barbara CA: ABC-CLIO.

Phillips, M;T. and Sechzer, J.A. (1989) *Animal research and ethical conflict: An analysis of the scientific literature, 1966-1986,* New York: Springer Verlag.

Primatt, H. (1776/1992) *The duty of mercy and the sin of cruelty to brute animals*, A Kinship Classic, Sussex: Centaur Press, Fontwell.

Ritvo, H. (1987) *The animal estate: The English and other creatures in the Victorian age*, Harvard University Press: Cambridge, Massachusetts.

Rupke, N. (ed.) (1990) Vivisection in Victorian Perspective, London: Routledge.

Ryder, R. (1979) "The struggle against speciesism" in D. Paterson and R.Ryder (eds.) Animal rights: A symposium, Sussex, Fontwell: Centaur Press Ltd.

Ryder, R. (1989) *Animal revolution: Changing attitudes towards speciesism*, Basil Blackwell: Oxford.

Salt, H. (1980/1892) *Animals' rights considered in relation to social progress: With a bibliographical appendix*, New York: Macmillan.

Singer, P. (1975) *Animal liberation: A new ethics for our treatment of animals*, New York: New York Review and Random House.

Tanenbaum, E (1995) *Animal transport through Brightlingsea: Report of an opinion survey*, Department of Government: University of Essex.

Thomas, K. (1983) *Man and the natural world: Changing attitudes in England 1500-1800*, Penguin Books: Middlesex, England.

Thompson, F.M.L (1988) *The rise of respectable society: A social history of Victorian Britain 1830-1900*, Cambridge, M.A: Harvard University Press.

Turner, J (1980) *Reckoning with the beast: Animals, pain and humanity in the Victorian mind*, The Johns Hopkins University Press: Baltimore.

Weinbren, D. (1994) "Against all cruelty: The Humanitarian League, 1891-1919", *History Workshop Journal*, 38, 86-105.

Winsten, S. (1951) Salt and his circle, London: Hutchinson & Co.

Withington, A F (1991) *Toward a more perfect union: Virtue and the formation of American republics*, Oxford University Press: New York.

Worster, D. (1977) *Nature's economy: The roots of ecology*, Sierra Club Books: San Francisco.

Zelizer, V. (1985) *Pricing the priceless child: The changing social value of children*, New York: Basic Books.

Chapter 2

A Decade of Animal Liberation

The animal protection lobby has achieved much in the ten years since Peter Singer introduced the concept of animal liberation to *Current Affairs Bulletin* readers in 1983. The following article surveys the changing attitudes and practices in our treatment of non-human animals over the decade and reviews the achievements of animal rights activists—in all their guises—who are engaged in a moral crusade on behalf of non-human animals.

The concept of rights as it applies to both human and non-human animals opens up a complex field of philosophical, legal, moral and social questions which have been the subject of debate for centuries. Proponents of animal rights, as with other categories of rights such as children's rights, can be distinguished as having a protectionist or a liberationist orientation. The former is represented by the relatively long-established humanitarian movement, which seeks to protect animals from human cruelty, and the latter by the modern animal liberation movement, which seeks to include animals along with humans as members of a moral community deserving of moral status and consideration.

The extension of rights to animals is an ethical position which can be seen as a step forward along the humanitarian path towards moral and political progress in an environmental ethics that includes the rights of nature.

This progressive extension of rights from humans to non-humans has been illustrated by Roderick Nash in relation to the United States: American colonists (1776) → slaves (1863) →women (1920) → Native Americans (1924) → labourers (1938) → Blacks (1957) → and finally, with the passage of the Endangered Species Act in 1973, to nature.

Nash notes that the inclusion of nature is arguably the most dramatic expansion of morality in intellectual history. [1]

From Protection to Liberation

The early history of animal liberation has been painstakingly documented by Keith Thomas in his book *Man and the Natural World: Changing Attitudes in England 1500-1800.* According to Thomas, the predominant attitude until the end of the eighteenth century was anthropocentric that is, that mankind was the centre of existence and that nature was subordinate to human needs and wants. By the end of

---

[1] Roderick Nash, *The Rights of Nature: A History of Environmental Ethics,* Primavera Press, Wilderness Society, Leichhardt NSW, 1990, p.7.

the eighteenth century, however, 'a growing number of people had come to find man's ascendancy over nature increasingly abhorrent to their moral and aesthetic sensibilities [2]. Thomas sees the role of pets as of fundamental importance in changing people's attitudes towards animals. By encouraging people to form emotional attachments with animals, pet keeping 'created the psychological foundation for the view that some animals at least were entitled to moral consideration' [3]. In a country where fox-hunting and pet-keeping co-existed as national icons, the English middle and upper classes developed a reputation as animal lovers eager to denounce cruelty by other 'less civilised' peoples. It was in this spirit that the Royal Society for the Prevention of Cruelty to Animals (RSPCA) was formed in 1840. The main target of the new organisation was the brutish treatment of animals by the lower orders. [4]

By the middle of the nineteenth century, cruel sports such as bull-baiting and cock-fighting had virtually disappeared in England while the aristocratic blood sport of fox-hunting continued enthusiastically.

At about the same time, the Australian colonies were inventing their own version of animal sport: 'kangarooing'. It was described as 'an exciting institution, as thoroughly antipodean in every sense of the word as fox-hunting is English'[5]. Killing kangaroos for sport continued into the twentieth century; as late as 1972, the *Bulletin* reported that the popularity of kangaroo hunting, fist fighting, and sodomy rose following the success of the film *Wake in Fright*.

The Australian RSPCA was founded in 1891. Like its English parent, the organisation prohibits cruelty to animals by protecting them against sadistic practices, but not against the myriad of other uses and abuses to which animals are subjected.

Thus the modern RSPCA is essentially an animal welfare organisation, which from its inception has promoted the idea of treating animals with kindness and humanity; provided no cruelty is involved, it does not prohibit the use of animals to satisfy human needs or wants such as in animal experimentation or food production. Human interests are thus given greater weight than animal interests in the ideology of the RSPCA. Anthropocentrism continues to be the moral orthodoxy in most animal welfare groups.

Singer's name is often associated with 'animal rights', an association he is happy to accept since the term is a convenient political slogan. However, Singer does not argue a case for animal rights in the way the noted American philosopher Tom Regan

---

[2] Keith Thomas, *Man and the Natural World: Changing altitudes in England 1500-1800*, P [1] Penguin Books, Middlesex, 1983, p.300.
[3] *Ibid.* p.119.
[4] F.M.L. Thompson, *The Rise of Respectable Society: A Social History of Victorian Britain 1830-1900*, Harvard University Press, Cambridge MA, 1988, p.280.
[5] The Colony of Queensland 1866: 20 as a full field for emigration, *Australian National Dictionary*, Oxford University Press, Melbourne, 1988, D345.

does. [6] Singer's position is that the interests of all sentient beings should be given equal consideration. Pain is pain no matter who feels it, human animals or non-human animals and the latter have an equal interest in avoiding pain. Singer's use of sentience as a reason for treating animals as morally equal to humans is, for many people, more acceptable and understandable than Regan's abstract defence of animals as subjects-of-a-life deserving of the same rights as humans. Furthermore, Regan's fundamentalist position on animal-human issues is more extreme than both the welfarist and pragmatist positions since he wants to abolish most practices involving the use of animals by humans.

Moral Crusaders in a New Social Movement

When animal liberationists challenge the assumptions of speciesism and anthropocentrism they are accused of being misanthropic. They would reject this criticism by pointing out that it is not human beings *per se* that they object to, but rather their prejudices and discriminatory actions against non-human animals.

The charge of hating humans is usually argued in the context of acts of violence perpetrated by extremists on the fringes of the movement The Animal Liberation Front (ALF) and its deviant ally the Animal Rights Militia have raided British laboratories and attacked businesses engaged in 'animal abuse' from butchers to fur retailers. They claim to have initiated about 10,000 'actions' in their ten years of operation, although these have recently been curtailed by stricter police surveillance which has put several activists behind bars.

The most damage ever inflicted by a radical environmental group was estimated at $4.6 million when the American equivalent of the ALF burnt down an animal experimentation facility at the University of California at Davis in 1987. Radical animal liberation groups operate in several countries, including Australia where they have been particularly active in the Melbourne area, damaging property to the value of $1 million between 1986 and 1988. [7]

Mainstream animal activists reject violence as morally reprehensible and politically counterproductive and dissociate their campaigns from the actions of extremists. Nonetheless, if the American experience is anything to go by, opponents of the animal liberation movement paint all activists with the same violent brush, despite the fact that not one person has been killed as a result of direct action by animal liberationists. [8]

---

[6] Tom Regan, *The Struggle for Animal Rights*, International Society for Animal Rights Inc., Clarks Summit PA, 1987.
[7] Rik Scarce, *Eco-Warriors: Understanding the Radical Environmental Movement*, Noble Press Inc., Chicago, 1990, p.125.
[8] Robert Garner, *Animals, Politics and Morality*, Manchester University Press, Manchester, 1993, p.220.

The animal liberation movement, however, has a kind of moral purity that makes involvement extremely rewarding. As a middle-class moral crusade, the animal liberation platform is attractive to people eager to articulate a moral vision of the world around the symbol of the besieged animal. Indeed, Peter Singer argues in the second edition of *Animal Liberation* (1990) that this is the strength of the movement. [9]

Challenging Anthropocentrism

It is speciesism which distinguishes the animal liberation movement from the other major streams of the environmental movement, including resource conservation, human welfare ecology, preservation and ecocentrism. [10] All represent a challenge to anthropocentrism, but the animal liberation movement alone uses humanity's treatment of non-human animals as the symbol of all that is wrong with anthropocentric thinking. To the animal liberation movement, 'the animal as victim has become a symbol of both humanity and nature besieged [in the] vivisection of our planet' [11] Modern animal liberators, like their anti-vivisectionist predecessors in the late nineteenth century, perceive the abuse of animals as the central moral dilemma confronting society. However, Singer's claim to the high moral ground is shared by other strands of the environmental movement. The appeal of new social movements is largely due to the strength of their vision and the fact that they are 'freer than many other movements to take risks, to behave outrageously, to construct a broad-ranging utopian vision [12]. Is it utopian to believe that animals can be liberated from human exploitation in laboratories, in factory farms, in sport and entertainment?

We need to know how ordinary people think about animals and how attitudes change in response to campaigns on their behalf.

How do people relate to animals? In an article in *Current Affairs Bulletin,* Stone and Stone suggest four distinct relationships between ourselves and other animals. [13] These can be illustrated with reference to crocodiles. First, humans are used by animals as prey. Fear of crocodiles is largely responsible for the public's indifference to crocodile hunting in Australia: if they can eat us, as they sometimes do, we can kill them. The toothy croc of *Crocodile Dundee* engenders the opposite emotion to the kindness and affection aroused by the 'dolphin's smile'. Second, humans use animals

---

[9] Peter Singer, *Animal Liberation* (2nd edition 1990), xiii.

[10] Robyn Eckersley, *Environmentalism and Political Theory: Towards an Ecocentric Approach,* University College London Press, London, 1992, pp.42-45.

[11] Susan Sperling, *Animal Liberators: Research and Morality,* University of California Press, Berkeley CS, 1988, chapter 5.

[12] Barbara Epstein, *Political Protest and Cultural Revolution: Nonviolent Direct Action in the 1970s and 1980s,* University of California Press, Berkeley, 1991, p.242.

[13] Margaret Stone and Jonathan Stone, 'Principles and Animals', *Current Affairs Bulletin,* Vol.63, No 3, August1986, pp.4-13.

as resources; crocodiles are used for their hides as well as for their meat, both of which may be of secondary importance to the hunt itself. Third, we displace animals by just being here or whenever we build roads, dams and civilisations which disturb their habitat. Finally, and paradoxically, humans seek to protect animals either from individual cruelty or as a species endangered by excesses in any of the above.

In their article, the Stones identify four principles governing the human-animal relationship: responsibility, love, conservation and animal rights. They claim that none of these succeeds in offering a solution to the problem of reconciling human versus animal interests.

Their solution is to look for consensus and compromise rather than assert natural rights which they claim is a distraction from the *realpolitik* of animal welfare issues. Yet it is difficult to see how 'consensus' would work in practice except in the case of animals like crocodiles, sharks and snakes which fail 'the soft and cuddly' test set by the community for measuring its preferences. Different animals are valued for a variety of reasons by different people, scientists, hunters, Kooris, tourists, naturalists and so on. How are we to measure these values in order to achieve community consensus and compromise?

One Australian study examined the different attitudes towards animals of a sample of hunters and animal liberationists, in an attempt to resolve misconceptions and to help policy-makers and wildlife managers who are responsible for mediating between the competing interests of hunters and animal welfare groups.[14] If we are to heed the results of the study, consensus is most likely only for animals at either extreme: for those perceived as most resembling us (e.g. chimpanzees) and for those considered pests (e.g. rodents).

In recognition of the increasing sensitivity of audiences to animal cruelty, the makers of the film *A River Runs Through It* included this disclaimer in the credits: 'No fish were injured during the making of this film'. Closer to home, local filmmakers were compelled to respond to public reactions following the screening of *Kangaroos: Faces in the Mob* on ABC TV in early 1993. The producers from Film Australia wrote a six-page open letter in response to the many viewers who questioned the ethics of the film crew in failing to assist one of the injured animals during the filming. One of the producers, Dr Jan Aldenhoven, appeared on television to explain what a harrowing and difficult experience watching the young kangaroo suffer had been for her.

The Australian public's sensitivity about the treatment of the national icon has changed markedly since *Wake in Fright* twenty years ago, yet while the large scale slaughter of kangaroos and other animals continues; it is difficult to see these manifestations of ethical concern as anything other than idiosyncratic.

---

[14] Mark Fenton and Adelma Hills, 'The Perception of Animals Amongst Animal Liberationists and Hunters', *Australian Psychologist*, Vol.23, 2, July 1988, pp.243-257.

While studies and observations of changing attitudes towards animals are useful up to a point, there is often a wide gap between what people think about animals and what they are prepared to do for them. One of the things people do is join animal welfare organisations. In the last decade these have dramatically increased in size and membership. As one writer noted: 'It is astonishing how many creatures, from whales to hedgehogs, now have their own pressure groups'.[15]

Some Recent Achievements of the Animal Liberation Movement

In order to put the achievements of the animal liberation movement in Australia into a comparative context, a brief inventory of international trends will be useful.

Tom Regan believes that the movement is universally committed to a number of goals including:

- the total abolition of the use of animals in science.

- the total dissolution of commercial animal agriculture.

- the total elimination of commercial and sport hunting and trapping.[16]

Not all animal liberators are abolitionists like Regan, and many would add the elimination of the use of animals in zoos and circuses to his list.

A special issue of the *New Internationalist* on 'Animal rights and wrongs' surveyed worldwide trends in the following four areas.[17]

Animals in Research

Approximately 200 million animals are subjected to painful experiments of which 200,000 are used to test cosmetic and household products.

International cosmetics firms Revlon, Avon, Estée and Max Factor have banned animal testing as a result of protests from animal rights groups.

---

[15] E.S. Turner, *All Heaven in a Rage*, Centaur Press, Fontwell, Sussex, 1992, p.318.

[16] Tom Regan, 'The Case for Animal Rights', in Peter Singer (ed.), *In Defence of Animals*, Harper & Row Publishers, New York, 1985, p.13.

[17] *New Internationalist* Special Feature, 'Targets of Tyranny: Animal Rights and Wrongs', January 1991, pp.16-17.

Animals in Food Production

Human beings consume about 140 million tonnes of meat yearly, i.e. about 30 kilograms per person. Australians consume 103 kilos, second only to the Americans (111 kilos).

The British are in the middle (68 kilos) and Indians at the bottom (1 kilo).

In the UK vegetarianism has doubled among students and school children to one in six, while in the US nearly nine million people claim to be vegetarians. Women far outnumber men.

Hunting and Trapping

One hundred million animals are killed every year for their fur. In the UK blood sports claim the lives of 63,000 foxes yearly and about 12 million pheasants and one million wildfowl are shot.

Zoos and Circuses

More than one million animals are kept in an estimated 5,000 zoos and menageries worldwide.

The *New Internationalist* provides only 'downers' in these last two areas. The list of achievements both abroad and in Australia can be expected to expand. L'Oreal, the world's largest manufacturer of cosmetics, has agreed to discontinue using animals for testing their products after four years of campaigning by animal rights groups in Europe and in the USA.

The successes of the animal liberation movement in Australia are quite impressive when compared to the modest gains internationally. Some achievements, selected from various newsletters and fliers, principally from Animal Liberation (Victoria) and ANZFAS, are listed below.

Science

- LD50 and Draize tests were abolished in Victoria in 1987.

- The use of animals for testing cosmetics was banned in Victoria in 1990.

Agriculture/Food

- Sales of free-range eggs have been increasing in Victoria since 1978; the rate was 278% between 1986 and 1989.

Sport/Hunting/Trapping

- The Coalition Against Fur was formed in 1990; both David Jones and Myer closed their fur salons in Melbourne in 1991. David Jones have since closed their fur salons in Adelaide and Sydney.

- The WA government banned duck shooting in 1990; Victoria has a duck identification program and test for duck shooters; SA, the NT and Victoria have started to phase out the use of lead shot and banned it in some wetland areas.

- The ACT was the first government to ban the use of steel jawed traps and the first to ban rodeos.

Zoos/Circuses

- About 15 local councils in Australia have refused to host circuses in their municipalities.

Animal Rights Issues and Campaigns

What do animal rights advocates want? As part of her doctoral thesis in sociology, Rebecca Richards surveyed more than 1,000 subscribers to *The Animals' Agenda,* an animal rights magazine in the United States. [18] In one set of questions, the researcher sought to uncover the degree of 'ideological consensus' among the subscribers. This consisted of two measures: an index of speciesism and the degree with which respondents identified with the animal rights as opposed to the animal welfare movement. In the latter, 80 percent of the 844 people who responded identified with both movements; that is, most made no distinction between animal rights and animal welfare. The speciesism index was more complicated. Respondents were asked to rank 15 items dealing with the human treatment of animals on a scale from 1 (extremely wrong) to 7 (not at all wrong). Thus, people genuinely concerned about animal welfare were asked to judge the morality of common practices involving non-human animals.

As could be expected the 'least unacceptable' practices on which there was a strong consensus concerned neutering a pet (6.62) and keeping a pet (6.24).

---

[18] Rebecca Richards, *Consensus Mobilisation through Ideology, Networks, and Grievances: A Study of the Contemporary Animal Rights Movement,* PhD dissertation (1990) printed by University Microfilms International, Ann Arbor, 1992, pp.34-35.

There was also strong consensus about the most morally reprehensible practices which respondents ranked in order as follows:

- Using leg-hold traps to capture wild animals (1.06)

- Using animals in cosmetic and other beauty product experiments (1.13)

- Killing an animal to make a fur coat (1.17)

- Selling unclaimed dogs from animal shelters for use in medical experiments (1.29)

- Hunting wild animals with guns (1.49)

- Exposing an animal to a disease as part of a medical experiment (1.62)

- Raising cattle for food in feedlots (1.75).

The survey results also tell us that raising cattle for food in open pastures (ranked 11th) is less objectionable than using horses for racing (8th), eating meat (9th), or keeping animals in zoos (10th).

Animal welfare groups in Australia pointed out similar concerns to the Senate Select Committee on Animal Welfare which was appointed late in 1983. The committee decided to examine the welfare of kangaroos before other issues (e.g. use of animals in experiments and in sport) because of growing public concern, both in Australia and overseas, over their slaughter. It took five years before the committee handed down its findings in 1988 and another five years before any of the twenty-six recommendations were heeded by the Australian government.

The full report runs to over 200 pages and concludes with a simple sketch of a kangaroo showing the point (X) at which to aim to kill the animal humanely. This sanitised drawing of a kangaroo marked for death is emblematic of the report.

Senator Saunders, in a minority report to the committee, chided his colleagues for taking the politically safe line of defending the status quo. In fact, only two of the twenty-six recommendations could be regarded as a challenge to anthropocentrism.

For example, the committee recommended as a firm principle that the kangaroo remain a protected animal but added that it could be killed to protect property. On this point it claimed, 'almost unanimity of opinion that the latter was acceptable when those kangaroos cause unjustifiable levels of damage and no feasible alternative method is available to contain that damage'. Thus, the Senate Select Committee, in paying only lip-service to the principle of protecting the kangaroo, confirmed the anthropocentric bias throughout its lengthy report. The level of protection can be gauged by the quota on the number of kangaroos which can be legally killed; for 1993, the quota was 4,804,100.[19]

Civilising the Appetite: From Meat Eating to Vegetarianism

The sociologist Norbert Elias described 'the civilising process' over several centuries of European history as a gradual process of change involving increasing levels of shame and embarrassment about social habits like eating and drinking.[20] He noted how meat in the modern era is rarely served in a form which too closely reminds diners of what they are eating. Elias suggests that vegetarianism may be the logical long-term dietary future of humanity as the trend towards lowered thresholds of repugnance (such as towards meat eating, and displays of dead animals in butchers' shops) which began in the late eighteenth century continues.

While Elias's prediction is for the twenty- first century at the earliest, others have discerned how meat eating is already on a par with smoking or drug addiction, 'as a relatively vulgar, unhealthy and anti-social indulgence'.[21]

There has in fact been a trend away from red meat consumption in Australia although it cannot be claimed that this is due to increasing thresholds of shame associated with eating animals. The decline over the past two decades has been most evident in mutton and lamb consumption, with an overall drop of about 7 kilograms (1972-82) and 11.5 kilograms (1982-92) in the total consumption of red meat per capita.

The long-term trend in the decline of meat consumption since World War II is evident as is a reverse trend for the consumption of vegetables Again there is no evidence that the trend represents a growing sensitivity towards the treatment of animals or a civilising of the appetite; there are a number of reasons for following a vegetarian diet: moral, health-related, gustatory and ecological.[22] Survey results in England, however, do show that animal welfare issues are about as important as health concerns in people's avoidance of meat. A Gallup survey for Realeat in 1990 found that 28,000 people per week that year were turning to a vegetarian diet with adults citing health (76 per cent) and animal welfare (75 percent) as the main reasons for their conversion; young people put animal welfare as their main motivation with

---

[19]Report by The Senate Select Committee on Animal Welfare: Kangaroos, Commonwealth of Australia, AGPS, Canberra, 1988, P.176.

[20] Norbert Elias, The Civilising Process, Vol 1. *The History of Manners, Basil Blackwell*, Oxford, 1978.

[21] NickFiddes, *Meat: A Natural Symbol*, Routledge, London, 1991.

[22]Alan Beardsworth And Teresa Keil, 'The Vegetarian Option: Varieties,Conversions, Motives and Careers', Sociological Review, 1992, Pp.253-293.

concern about slaughter techniques (76 per cent) and the treatment of livestock (75 per cent) at the top of the list.[23]

Of all the campaigns on behalf of animals, the avoidance of meat may well be the most important, for as one campaigner argues, 'meat eating is the most oppressive and extensive institutionalised violence against animals'.[24] The arguments used to defend vegetarianism today were already in currency when the Vegetarian Society of Great Britain was founded in 1847. At that time, the founding members were confident that future generations would be converted away from meat eating, not least because of the increasing resistance to anthropocentrism and a growing sensibility towards nature.

This article began with reference to Peter Singer's piece in *Current Affairs Bulletin* in 1983. In the *New York Review* in 1985 Singer reviewed ten books about animal welfare (mainly written by philosophers) published in the early 1980s. Since then, dozens of books and several journals on animal rights have been published, including the quarterlies *Anthrozoös* (since 1988) and *Society and Animals* (since January 1993).[25]

Until quite recently, philosophers have been the most prolific writers on the subject; increasingly, social scientists, in particular psychologists and sociologists, are beginning to make their own distinctive contributions to the topic. In 1993, for example, the first edition of the *Journal of Social Issues* took as its theme 'The Role of Animals in Human Society'; the editor noted that just a few years ago the idea of an open discussion on animal rights would have been met with derision. The publication of this issue and specialist journals on the human-animal relationship are further illustrations that animals are being taken more seriously as subjects in their own right. And as one philosopher has suggested, it is this recognition, not philosophical doctrine as such, which is what animal liberation is all about.[26]

---

[23] *The Survey Data cited in Colin Spencer*, Fourth Estate, London, 1993, Pp.336-338.

[24] Carol Adams, *The Sexual Politics of Meat: A Feminist-Vegetarian Critical Theory*, Polity Press, UK, 1990, p.70.

[25] Since this article was published in the early 1990s, the number of books, anthologies and papers on animals and animal rights has increased massively as indicated in the Recommended reading in the Conclusion of the present book.

[26] Anthony Weston, *Toward Better Problems: New Perspectives on Abortion, Animal Rights, the Environment, and Justice*, Temple University Press, Philadelphia, 1992

Cruelty

Chapter 3

Cruelty and Compassion in a Decent Society

The only political commitments worth making are those that seek to reduce the amount of human suffering in the world.

—John Berger, 1990

This chapter focuses on the themes of cruelty and its opposite compassion. No study of the animal protection movement would be complete without an understanding of what moves people to campaign against cruelty to animals. The chapter therefore begins with an outline of some of the main reasons animal protectors give for joining the movement. These are described as fateful moments or turning points in their lives when they "converted" to the cause. This is followed by a broad discussion of cruelty which leads to an explanation of how the animal movement constructs speciesism as a social problem. It has to be understood that such a construction is only possible in a society where it is at least potentially possible, for violence against animals to be taken as seriously as other forms of violence. This has only been possible in the West during the last two centuries. Over this period, the animal movement has amassed the prerequisite moral capital upon which it can mount its campaigns. By the late twentieth century, animal cruelty is now defined by movement analysts sympathetic to the cause as "any act that contributes to the pain or death of an animal or that otherwise threatens the welfare of an animal" (Agnew, 1998: 179). This definition includes not just wanton cruelty involving the torture or maiming of individual animals, but also the death and suffering of large numbers of animals in intensive farming, experimentation and recreational hunting.

For the past two centuries much of the work of animal protection organisations has been concerned with promoting compassion for animals in these contexts. The chapter will therefore examine this side of the cruelty/compassion couplet by focussing on the nature of caring and commitment in the animal movement from the perspective of individuals and an animal welfare organisation in the UK. I begin with an overview in Figure 3.1 of the reasons interviewees gave for joining the animal movement. About half the sample of 53 interviewees identified a specific event or "fateful moment" which caused them to join the animal movement. Many of the remaining informants said they did not experience an epiphany or a turning point and that they came to the movement more gradually and for more general reasons, typically because of their abhorrence of cruelty. One prominent animal protector, John Bryant of the League Against Cruel Sports, claimed that no one will ever know why people join the animal movement. Yet more than two dozen of the interviewees could identify a turning point in their lives when they decided to do something for animals by joining the movement, or in some cases, starting up an organisation of their own. Giddens (1991: 202-203) refers to "fateful moments" as episodes when "an individual is forced to rethink fundamental aspects of her existence and future prospects". A few of the interviewees claimed their conversion to the cause came as an epiphany which Denzin describes as "moments of problematic experience that illuminates personal character" after which "the person is never again quite the same" (1989: 15-18). Whether these turning points are called fateful moments or epiphanies, about half the animal protectors in the sample could identify a specific moment or event in their lives when things were never the same again.

The responses in Figure 3.1 can be divided into intellectual, emotional and practical reasons although there is sometimes some obvious overlap between the categories. For example, while rescuing an animal in distress is often a profoundly emotional experience; the act of rescue itself is a practical one. These particular responses are listed as emotional reasons since the informants narrated the experience as an intensely emotional one. Similarly, Tina's accidental encounter with a healthy vegetarian was an experience that led to her to read up on vegetarian and animal rights issues so that a practical reason for becoming a vegetarian, the positive impression made by her vegetarian acquaintance, developed into an intellectual pursuit. It is interesting to note that these intellectual, emotional and practical reasons for joining the movement correspond to the three dimensions of social problems work elsewhere in the book. It is perhaps not surprising that the motives for joining the movement are closely linked to actual animal protection praxis as in most cases, the interviewees were already engaging in social problems work when they made the decision to change their lives by converting to vegetarianism, starting an animal group, or joining an existing one. The evidence of social problems work is more obvious in some activities—hearing, reading, seeing, rescuing and participating—than in others. Conversion experiences typically mean that people "are called on to take decisions that are particularly consequential for their ambitions, or more generally for their future lives" (Giddens, 1991: 114). This is the first stage of social problems work, when people's intellectual, emotional or practical experiences mean they will never be quite the same again.

Figure 3.1: Reasons informants give for joining the animal movement

Name	Responses
	Intellectual reasons
Elisabeth Ahlston	Hearing a talk on vivisection
Glenys Oogjes	Reading Singer's *Animal Liberation*
Joyce d'Silva	Reading Gandhi's autobiography
Stephanie Ruddick	Hearing a university class on animal experimentation
Scott Williams	Recognising hot dogs as linked to cruelty
	Emotional reasons
"Milly"	Seeing TV images of cattle lorries
"Lisa"	Seeing her cat suffering
"Alan"	Seeing *Faces of Death* video
Collette Kase	Love of pet rabbit, Mr. Charlie
Ann Sparks	Seeing classic pictures of a veal calf
Patty Mark	Seeing goat's head soup in Greece
Mark Berriman	Finding meat "atrocious" in India
Tamara Hamilton	Seeing a pamphlet on vivisection
Wayne Pacelle	Lifelong antipathy towards people who harm animals
Jenny Talbot	Seeing destruction of animals during tree felling
Jim Roberts	Seeing abattoir trucks loaded with animals
Tim O'Brien	Recognising sheep as individuals who should not be eaten
	Practical reasons
"Sid"	Early childhood experience of the RSPCA
"Casey"	Incongruity of loving animals and eating them
"Tina"	Accidental meeting of a healthy vegetarian
"Sherry"	Participating in a duck rescue operation
"Owen"	Discovering vegetarianism
"Roger"	Participating in a duck rescue operation
Andrew Tyler	Writing about the "animal problem" for a newspaper
Cathy Liss	Connecting McDonald's with cruelty
Pat Reilly	Rescuing a river otter from a leg hold trap

Source: Munro (2001)Compassionate beasts: The quest for animal rights.

SOYONS CRUELS!

— Graffiti on the walls of the Sorbonne, May 1968

James Miller has pondered the meaning of *BE CRUEL!* in the work of Foucault and Nietzsche and suggests that to them, cruelty externalised is better than cruelty internalised. One interpretation of being cruel which Miller believes Foucault would endorse is the idea of giving institutions license "to foster brutality and public displays of suffering" so that execution, torture, terror, unleashing lust for revenge and even the spectacular deaths of animals could be celebrated (Miller, 1990: 485). Miller implies that no society would ever accept or even contemplate this kind of regime; nor is he convinced that externalizing cruelty is healthier than suppressing such phantasies within the self. Miller points out that Foucault's views on power and cruelty raise complex theoretical and practical questions, for example, what would it be like to be free of cruel impulses? This is not the place to address philosophical questions of this kind, but suffice it to say that animal protectionists would find nothing of merit in Foucault's response given his celebration of cruelty.

For animal protectionists, the work of Sue Coe strikes a more responsive chord. In her artwork and graphic descriptions of animal suffering in slaughterhouses, Coe startles and shocks the reader in ways reminiscent of Foucault in the opening passages of *Discipline and Punish*: "The feeding lots for cows look like the stocks, an old English device which secured a criminal, whilst the townspeople pelted him with garbage" (Coe, 1995: 47).Coe is however much more interested in depicting the mass cruelty of the slaughterhouse, which she describes, hesitantly, as an animal holocaust:

> *This is the longest train I have ever seen. It takes a full thirty minutes to pass by. There are hundreds of cars, packed with thousands and thousands of cattle on their way to slaughter. Six billion animals are killed each year in the United States for human consumption. The suffering of these animals is mute. For the defenseless, the gentle, the wounded, the ones who cannot speak, life consists of indescribable suffering* (Coe, 1995: 63).

The animal protection movement is united in its opposition to cruelty perpetrated either against individual animals or en masse as in Coe's example. Surprisingly, however, only three out of the more than two dozen groups sampled in this study— the Massachusetts Society for the Prevention of Cruelty to Animals, the League Against Cruel Sports and the Animal Cruelty Investigation Group in the UK—refer to cruelty in their logos and letterheads although most refer explicitly to "animals" and implicitly to their exploitation and suffering. In the interview transcripts however, there were 57 references to cruelty, more than any other code word in *The Ethnograph*, although tactics (55) and strategy (40) were not far behind. Furthermore, cruelty has several cognates of which domination, abuse, oppression, exploitation, pain and suffering among others, are the most common in the animal protectionist's lexicon. To the Australian activist, Roger, opposition to cruelty is the movement's *raison d'etre*:

> There's no excuse for cruelty. I can't think of one. Our society and just about all religions don't accept cruelty. That's a good basis for an organisation. (Interview, 1994).

From the beginning of the humanitarian movement in the nineteenth century, opposition to cruelty has been the movement's driving force in both America and England. The forerunners of the modern animal rights movement were first and foremost anti-cruelty movements. And in Australia too, it was the moral potency of cruelty that united the early conservationists and animal protectors (MacCulloch, 1993). According to MacCulloch, the animal protection movement's lasting legacy was to shape the means by which communication about nature with the public was possible. This communication was founded on the moral potency of cruelty. MacCulloch describes the public's response to this message in the nineteenth century which still rings true a century later:

> For no matter how affecting, or even tragic, it was to witness the destruction of a single, beautiful tree or scenic area, it lacked the pathos of cruelty to animals. A tree was a living thing, but it did not bleed, it did not suffer, it did not have babies (1993: 369).

Cruelty to individual animals evokes strong emotions in most people, especially when the animal is as affecting as the koala. Increasingly, other, less "appealing" animals are being described sympathetically in the public domain. For example, a cover story in *The Economist* featured a battery hen on the cover under the heading "What we owe to animals". The editorial opened with a description of the bird:

> She is confined to a tiny cage with four or five others for her entire adult life squeezed into a space about the size of the picture on our cover, barely enough to move. She may exercise her pecking instinct by pecking out her neighbour's feathers, unless her beak has been cut off with a red-hot blade, probably causing pain for life (*The Economist*, 19 August 1995).

In this editorial, the issue of animal rights is discussed as a noble but futile project, since "without agreement on the rights of people, arguing about the rights of animals is fruitless". Animal liberationists would counter by appealing to people's compassion—does a hen have a right to her beak? This question brings the issue of animal rights down to earth. Phrased in this way, it is no longer a philosophical question, but rather an issue of social justice and humanity. People can identify with the issue when it is put in terms of an animal's bodily integrity. This is how many animal protectors conceive of cruelty, as an assault on an animal's telos.

Informants defined cruelty in both general and very specific terms. For three of the sample, cruelty was everywhere: *It's not possible to walk on this earth without being cruel to animals* (Joan, ARC); *the amount of cruelty is overwhelming* (Patty Mark, ALV); *you don't have to look far to find it* (Cathy Liss, AWI). More informants however claimed cruelty was hidden behind closed doors, with one activist noting *the incredible juxtaposition that there's all this space* (in the countryside*) and they're all shoved inside a shed for the rest of their lives* (Owen, Australian activist). Cruelty for some was defined very specifically and graphically: *it's not legitimate to abuse, mutilate, slaughter, electrocute, burn people, but of course it is legitimate and there are rewards for doing so in respect to animals* (Andrew Tyler, Animal Aid).

The philosopher Tom Regan believes that confronting people with the suffering of animals in different cultures is an effective mobilising strategy:

> *I think the thing that I would do over and over again (as a strategy) is to show people how in Korea, in China and so on, "pets" (so called) are chosen, thrown in boiling water, skinned alive, thrown in vats, drowned, then cooked. And then I would show them what happens to hogs at slaughter. I think the connection just stares you in the face. The only thing that's different is that in Korea and China they're more honest about what they do. It's more public. In the USA and other so called "advanced" nations, it's hidden behind closed doors.* / Interview with author 1997

Strongly expressed sentiments of this kind are intended to shock, as Tyler freely acknowledges and as Regan endorses. Speciesism, on the other hand, does not have the same power as explicit forms of cruelty such as those described by Tyler and Regan.

Speciesism , defined by Singer (1975:7) as "a prejudice or attitude of bias toward the interests of members of one's own species and against those of members of other species", is a term rarely used in the movement. It is primarily employed by movement analysts and philosophers who wish to convey a sense of the interconnectedness between the animal movement and other liberation movements. Thus, Singer's argument that speciesism is a morally reprehensible practice on a par with racism and sexism, explicitly makes the link between animal liberation and movements to liberate women and oppressed ethnic and racial minorities.

For most people the idea that the consumption, exploitation and mistreatment of nonhuman animals deserves the same moral condemnation as attacks against racial groups or women is quite alien. Animal rights activists, by contrast, want to change the way people perceive other animals by linking the exploitation of animals with the oppression of women and racial minorities. La Follette and Shanks put the position as follows: "Animal liberationists compare speciesism with racism to focus our attention on the human tendency to unreflectively accept contemporary moral standards" (1996: 227). They do so by constructing speciesism as a social problem, in much the same way that the Civil Rights and women's movements campaign against racism and sexism as social injustices. The following critique by a prominent animal liberation philosopher clearly identifies speciesism as a moral problem, if not a social problem:

> Morality is a goal-directed activity which aims at making the world a better place in terms of reduced suffering and frustration, increased happiness and fulfilment, a wider reign of fairness and respect for others, and enhanced presence and effectiveness of such virtues as kindness and impartiality. Through our exploitation of nonhuman animals we detract from all of these moral goals. Factory farming, fur trapping and other exploitations of nonhuman animals increase the suffering and frustration in the world and reduce happiness and fulfilment the exact opposite of all these moral goals. Consequently, our goal of making the world a morally better place will be more effectively pursued by liberating from human exploitation all those capable of suffering and happiness and of being treated fairly and virtuously (Sapontzis,1993: 270).

Sapontzis emphasises the goal of "making the world a better place", or "a decent society" in the words of Avishai Margalit (1996). Margalit argues that a decent society is one free of humiliation; people are subjected neither to humiliation by other people nor by institutions such as welfare agencies or prisons. Margalit believes, however, that humiliation runs a close second to the greatest evil physical cruelty, especially the suffering inflicted by other human beings. "Torturing the body causes more acute pain than torturing the soul" (1996:264). A decent society presupposes that physical cruelty has been eliminated. Although he suggests that cruelty toward man or beast is wrong, it is the suffering of human animals not nonhuman animals which concerns Margalit. This is clearly implied in his explanation of humiliation as the treatment of humans as if they were animals, objects or machines. Here the author of *The Decent Society* relegates nonhuman animals to an inferior species, just as people do when they talk about deviant individuals "behaving like animals". This expression of moral outrage is usually directed at people whose actions offend our collective sensibilities. In such cases, the derogatory label "animal" is used to question the offenders' humanity by drawing attention to their animality.

From a non-speciesist, non-anthropocentric perspective, Margalit's argument is also deficient as a prescription for an alternative reality, or as a vision of what a decent society might look like. Nonhuman animals get short shrift. There is only one reference to animals in the book's index and most of the textual references are used to underline the author's explanation of the central concept, humiliation, as a denial of an individual's humanity by the process of animalisation or objectification. Human animals, we are told, are the only animals that suffer mental cruelty or humiliation.

For Margalit, then, humiliation can only be directed at human beings and only humans can suffer humiliation. Thus, in the case of the close confinement of humans in conditions approximating a battery cage, the incarcerated humans suffer physically and mentally while a hen might be expected to be spared the latter. But this is by no means clear. If the result of humiliation in this case, the humiliation of intensive confinement is unnatural behaviour such as cannibalism, then it must be possible for battery hens or tethered sows to suffer anguish and mental cruelty, if not the shameful, demeaning humiliation that confined humans experience.

Margalit is skeptical of societies which preach the extension of respect to all living creatures since he claims that these societies do not always respect human beings. Nazi Germany is the most grotesque example of this phenomenon for it produced progressive animal protection laws in the same breath as its genocidal policies towards the Jews and other "outcasts". But only the most unreasonable of critics of the animal movement would want the moral standing of animals to be compromised by the barbarity of the Nazis. **(See Note 1)**

In noting the contrasting views of Sapontzis and Margalit towards making the world a morally better place, it is clear that only Sapontzis is prepared to include nonhumans in the moral community. Philosophers generally have not been willing to extend the circle of compassion to animals and some like Leahy (1991) have strenuously argued the case against animal liberation. For these and other reasons to be discussed below, animal liberationists have labelled their opponents "speciesists" and have identified speciesism as the basis for what they see as the unjust oppression of one species by another.

Speciesism and Structures of Dominance

Inequality, injustice and oppression are terms commonly used to describe domination of blacks by whites, women by men or of powerful groups over the powerless. According to Iris Young (1990), oppression and domination are social conditions which together constitute and define injustice. Such terms are less common in the context of our relations with other animals which are nonetheless predicated on the dominance of one species over another. Ironically, Young's exclusion of nonhuman animals in her analysis highlights the applicability to animals of some of the "five faces of oppression" she identifies in relation to the treatment of humans. A moment's reflection would convince most animal protectors that exploitation, marginalisation, powerlessness, violence, and even cultural imperialism in the case of Wolfe's (1993) defence of human culture at the expense of nature are some of their most common animal liberation grievances concerning our treatment of other animals.

Weber (1925/1967:322-3) saw domination as an ubiquitous social reality: "Without exception every sphere of social action is profoundly influenced by structures of dominance. Domination constitutes a special case of power". Edward A. Ross also wrote that "no phenomenon is more frequent, persistent and recurrent than domination" (1933:94).

Both Weber and Ross are cited by Moland (1996) in his analysis of what he calls "the structure of dominance" in race-caste and patriarchal systems of oppression. Moland argues that notions of racial superiority and white male dominance have largely been undermined by a number of social and political movements as well as technological change following World War II. According to Moland, pre-War forms of racial and gender etiquette in relation to dominance are either diminishing or losing recognition, but intergroup tensions in race and gender relations have intensified. People whose socialization experience has been associated with the structure of dominance, he claims, believe they have lost control as a result of these social transformations and are anxious to regain whatever lost ground they can.

This backlash by conservative, right wing countermovements has a parallel in our changing relationships with the natural world. Just as notions of white supremacy and patriarchy have been challenged by social movement activists, anthropocentrism is now under threat by what Wolfe (1993:16) calls "the fastest-growing political movements in Western societies", movements concerned with the defence of nature. For the moment, I want to suggest that the word "speciesism" is a modern term for a very old problem. Few animal liberationists use the awkward-sounding term when they talk about our treatment of animals, preferring instead more euphonious and everyday language such as cruelty, oppression, exploitation and abuse. However, as Eckersley (1992) has pointed out, speciesism is what distinguishes the animal liberation movement from the other main streams of environmentalism. It is the animal movement alone which uses humanity's mistreatment of nonhuman animals as the symbol for all that is wrong with anthropocentric thinking. The notion of speciesism is useful also in that it broadens the movement's protest against cruelty to individual animals, a position which puts them at odds with environmentalists with reference to interspecies discrimination. Speciesism is useful in allowing animal protectionists of different persuasions to see their cause in the context of a broader social movement agenda in which animals are listed along with exploited women, blacks, ethnic minorities, children, the disabled, and gays and lesbians, in short, a social problem which generates palpable consequences in the form of societal conflict and confrontation. But outside the animal movement, how sustainable is the analogical argument that links speciesism with sexism and racism?

In their discussion of the rights and wrongs of animal experimentation, LaFollette and Shanks (1996) acknowledge that speciesism and racism are sufficiently similar that their equivalence cannot be dismissed as category mistakes. Speciesists, they suggest, would need to prove that animals and humans are not just biologically different, but different in *morally relevant respects.* LaFollette and Shanks distinguish between bare and indirect speciesism. The bare speciesist claims that the *bare* difference in species between humans and other animals is morally relevant. Thus Wolfe's (1993) claim that humans need to exploit animals in order to be fully human is based on bare speciesism, that is, that humans are entitled to use animals to serve our purposes simply because we are human. LaFollette and Shanks conclude that like racism and sexism, bare speciesism is indefensible. Indirect speciesism is based on the idea that although bare species differences are not morally relevant, there are nonetheless morally relevant differences between species. For example, these might include the idea that animals, unlike humans, cannot claim or assign rights, an argument used by Rose (1991) in his defence of speciesism. **(See Note 2)**

Speciesism, whether bare or indirect, is built on the assumption that cruelty to animals, and more specifically animal pain, does not really matter when human interests are threatened. For bare speciesists, even trivial human interests must be preserved at the expense of animal cruelty. What would the speciesist Alan Wolfe make of Lobster Liberation? This group believes that lobsters do not deserve to be boiled alive just to satisfy human appetites and maintains that lobsters have similar traits to humans in that they have a very long childhood and an awkward adolescence, pregnancies which last nine months, and live to be over one hundred years of age (from *PETA News,* 1989). Wolfe's response is that if we were never to be cruel to other animal species, we would live in a world without fantasy, excitement, and creativity:

> Although it may seem relatively easy to suggest that it is not worth killing animals so that humans can go on with what, to some, are archaic and barbaric practices, the loss to the human capacity for living meaningful lives is great, when, in the name of protecting other species, humans are asked to do without the symbolic richness that follows from ritual and tradition (1993:87-8).

Animal liberationists reject this as others might reject slavery, female genital mutilation, torture and other cruel practices carried out in the name of tradition or national interest.

While speciesism is the term that most broadly identifies the animal movement's diagnostic frame, cruelty has greater resonance which different social movement organisations within the movement recognise and exploit. In the public mind, cruelty to individual animals has an emotional force which speciesism lacks. Some groups like the Farm Animal Reform Movement (FARM) use terms like "eco-friendly eating" or "cruelty-free living" to promote a more positive message; others like the Guardians who campaign against vivisection have replaced their predominantly animal welfare frame with a human welfare focus. Other groups however recognise the dangers inherent in frame transformations; the Coalition Against Duck Shooting (CADS) has rigorously stuck to its anti-cruelty frame and has refused to broaden it to include for example a pro-vegetarian or an anti-gun dimension. Thus, while some groups have used different means to promote their issues, no animal protection organisation or campaign can afford to abandon the opposition to cruelty and speciesism as its primary purpose without devaluing the movement's unifying ideology. Animal protection organisations therefore typically diagnose speciesism by identifying and naming particular abuses such as factory farming and animal experimentation—the two primary examples of speciesism criticised in Singer's *Animal Liberation*—as well as hunting and trapping and a host of other practices which are the focus of particular campaigns by movement organisations.

The Origins of Contemporary Speciesism

The term "speciesism" was coined in 1970 by Richard Ryder, an English animal welfare advocate and clinical psychologist. Ryder used the word to describe "the widespread discrimination that is practised by man against other species" adding that speciesism, racism and sexism disregard the suffering of others (1983:5). Peter Singer (1975) gave the term prominence in his *Animal Liberation: A New Ethics for Our Treatment of Animals* in which he acknowledged Ryder as the originator of the term. Singer identified speciesism as the injustice from which animals had to be liberated, since one's species, like one's race or sex, is seen by animal liberationists as a morally irrelevant criterion upon which to judge a being's worth. During a symposium at Trinity College, Cambridge in August 1977, some 150 individuals signed "A Declaration Against Speciesism", which in part read:

> We do not accept that a difference in species alone (any more than a difference in race) can justify wanton exploitation or oppression in the name of science or sport, or for food, commercial profit or other human gain. We believe in the evolutionary and moral kinship of all animals and we declare our belief that all sentient creatures have rights to life, liberty and the quest for happiness. We call for the protection of these rights.

Singer has reflected that in a hundred years historians may well identify the Trinity College meeting as the starting point for the modern animal rights movement (Singer, 1978: xii). And yet the origin of speciesism as a perceived social problem can be traced back two centuries earlier.

In the introduction to a new edition of a book by Humphrey Primatt, Ryder (1992) explains how in 1976 while browsing through some old texts in an Oxford library, a card fell on to the desk which read " *The Duty of Mercy and the Sin of Cruelty to Brute Animals* by Humphrey Primatt". When Ryder procured the book, he was astonished by how modern the ideas were for a dissertation which was written two hundred years earlier in 1776. In the Preface for example, Primatt argues that "*justice* is a rule of universal extent and invariable obligation. We acknowledge this important truth in all matters in which man is concerned, but then we limit it *to our own species only* "(emphasis added). Misled with this prejudice in our own favour, we overlook *some* of the brutes, as if they were mere excrescences of nature"

Almost certainly, this was the first recorded argument for compassion towards nonhuman animals which was based on a critique of speciesism. In addition to the references to the prejudice and implied injustice of our treatment of other species, Primatt's Preface condemns "wanton cruelty and oppression" as well as extolling "mercy to brutes" as "a doctrine of divine revelation, as it is itself reasonable, amiable, useful, and just" (Primatt, 1992:17). Apart from the religious overtones, the language in this dissertation is immediately familiar to the present-day student of animal liberation. Primatt's thesis, summed up in the following paragraph, would be taken up by Ryder himself two centuries later:

> Pain is pain, whether it be inflicted on man or on beast; and the creature that suffers it whilst it lasts, suffers *evil*; and the sufferance of evil, unmeritedly, unprovokedly, where on offence has been given, and no good end can possibly be answered by it , but merely to exhibit power or gratify malice, is cruelty and injustice in him that occasions it (Primatt, 1992:21).

Ryder's words echoed those of Primatt's when he argued that pain and pleasure should be the bedrock of our morality: "Pain is pain, regardless of the species suffering it" (1989). According to Ryder, who also coined the word "painism", "pain is the quintessence of evil" and it is therefore our moral duty not to cause suffering to human and non-human sentients alike (1983).

For Primatt, cruelty was a sin because it harmed brutes and men alike. As early as 1776, he anticipated twentieth-century arguments by Singer and others that speciesism was on a par with racism:

> And if the difference of complexion or stature does not convey to one man a right to despise and abuse another man, the difference of shape between a man and a brute, cannot give to a man any right to abuse and torment a brute (Primatt, 1992:23).

Ironically, Primatt's masculinist tone was accurate insofar as the perpetrators of cruelty towards animals were largely working-class men and their more educated betters in the scientific and medical fraternities. Women, on the other hand, then and now, were more likely to be among the growing band of animal protectors, who by the middle of the nineteenth century had become a powerful lobby for people who cared about animals. The next section looks at the role of caring and compassion in the contemporary animal movement and how these concepts constitute social problems work.

Caring: Animal Protection as Social Problems Work

This section describes the nature of animal protection work as caring work and the motives that inspire individuals and organisations to care about animals. It also suggests that animal protection work is real work in the sense of a vocation. It is a calling for some, while for others it is experienced as work that needs to be done for either intrinsic or extrinsic reasons.

According to Erickson, labours of love **(See Note 3)** include the labours of people who derive their main sense of vocation and calling from the way they engage in activities that pay them little or nothing but provide them with their most significant investments of self, their most meaningful forms of work, their principal niches in life (Erickson, 1990: 6-7).

Erickson has in mind not just poets and artists, but hobbyists and amateurs, as well as volunteers "who keep parishes alive and hospitals humane". Also applicable to this kind of work is the social problems work of activists and advocates in various social movements, including the animal protection movement.

One of the most striking features of the animal movement is the massive over representation of women in both the nineteenth and twentieth centuries. Wendy Kaminer's (1984) study of volunteering shows how women deprived of career opportunities worked as volunteers in three main areas: cultural activities, moral reform and social service. Animal protection societies and anti- vivisection groups attracted more women than men, although men often occupied the leadership positions in organisations such as the RSPCA. Conventional wisdom in the nineteenth century decreed that women should not work for money or compete in a man's world. Working women were by definition not "ladies". Virtuous women worked as career volunteers for charitable associations in Christian temperance and anti-vice societies as well as in campaigns against slavery designed for the social betterment of the less fortunate. "Religion-inspired service work also provided a satisfying and even consuming career alternative for gentlewomen who would not or could marry" (1984: 26). Religious work vindicated the militancy of some of their campaigns but when they spoke out in public, this was viewed as contrary to nature and against "The Cult of True Womanhood" (1984: 22).

Voluntary work was condemned in the early 1970s by some critics such as the National Organisation of Women as career volunteering. Kaminer however, argues that volunteering was a form of work experience for married women which "gave them work to do in their communities and a sense of usefulness" (1984: 47). She suggests that women in voluntary organisations often drew the public's attention to "low visibility" issues and gives the example of the battered women's shelter to make the point (1984: 6). Similarly, the idea of animal protection had to be promoted by issue entrepreneurs, many of whom were women. "A century ago, volunteering laid the groundwork for women's suffrage and the emancipation of women by bringing them out of the home and into the world of politics, civics, and social affairs" (1984:11).

According to Thomas (1999), for many nineteenth-century theorists including Marx, work was the defining feature of the human species. Beavers might build dams and birds build nests, but these activities were done instinctively rather than as in the case with humans, on the basis of a conscious plan. Thomas points out that there is no single, objective, universally acknowledged definition of work; the *Oxford English Dictionary,* he notes, gives close to forty different meanings for the use of the term as both a noun and a verb. From the latter part of the seventeenth century onwards, the absence of purposeful work meant a loss in both physical and emotional needs, as well as economic deprivations for those without work. In the nineteenth century, enforced idleness amongst middle-class women prompted Florence Nightingale to remark on their sufferings and frustrations due to "the accumulation of nervous energy, which has nothing to do during the day, makes them feel every night, when they go to bed, as if they were going mad"(Thomas, 1999: xix-xx). For many such women, involvement in causes such as prison reform, temperance movements, child welfare and animal protection provided the only outlet for this "nervous energy". These causes, then and now, provide women and men with the opportunities for doing social problems work. Minus the economic component, social problems work in new social movements represents real work with practical, intellectual and emotional elements.

Real work typically means paid work, which would seem to preclude community and political work in new social movements. Yet a case can be made for designating such activities as work. For example, Wadel (1979) has advocated extending the economist's definition of (paid) work to include the hidden work of everyday life. Her concept of work is broad enough to include the notion of work as a source of cultural and social values. In short, work has social worth, since everyday work and political work, discussion, reading newspapers, listening to media reports and making up one's mind about political issues generates social value and helps maintain social institutions. Wadel argues that work is not just socially constructed, "but that work is something that characterises social relations. In other words, a sociological theory of work must treat work as a *relational* concept" (1979: 381). She contends that a new non-economistic concept of work would need to include the mutual activities that build personal and private relations and the collective activities that maintain community and other valued institutions. Social problems work is the name I give to the kinds of work Wadel describes as "hidden" work, which includes the work that activists and advocates perform when they promote the causes of new social movements. In the present study, caring about and for animals constitutes animal protection praxis, the social problems work that is characteristic of the animal movement.

Caring work is not to be confused with emotional labor (Hochschild, 1983), although emotions feature prominently in the movement's seminal campaigns. While Hochschild's concept accurately describes the commercialisation of feelings in many service occupations, especially in the "personality market" (Mills, 1951), it does not apply to the kind of work performed in the caring professions of nursing, social work and the like. In these professions, and in the social problems work of new social movements such as animal welfare, compassion cannot easily be faked. Furthermore, emotional labor, as conceived by Hochschild, refers to how an organisation requires its workers typically in the service industry to manage their emotions in ways which will maximise the organisation's productivity. With caring work, the focus is on resolving or ameliorating problems in the human services, including our relations with other animals.

Caring About and for Animals

While caring is a common thread in a number of social movements such as Amnesty, child protection and ecopax movements, it is at its most salient in the animal movement. Yet for a social movement whose most fundamental motivations are identified by some writers as caring and compassion (e.g. Wynne-Tyson, 1990; Finsen and Finsen, 1994; Shapiro, 1994), it is curious that concepts of compassion, empathy and caring appeared only rarely in the transcripts of interviews with the 53 animal protectionists in this study. Primarily this is because such concepts are integral to the work of animal protectors and are generally not made explicit. It is also partly a reflection of the inadequacies of reporting spoken language, which, even with the aid of computer-assisted data processing, may fail to pick up the nuances of meaning and flashes of feeling that the interviewer can recall when listening to the tapes. For example, the printed word does not convey the strength of feeling in the following reply to my question about animal protection work, which I remember as one of the most sincerely felt responses in the entire study:

> *Certainly, emotions are an important part of it, because we have our hearts involved. You need to keep your heart in something I think to be effective and if it's something that you believe in, you'll be more effective.* (Interview by author with Tamara Hamilton, HSUS, 1996)

Hamilton has not specifically mentioned caring, compassion or empathy, but they are implicit in her reply and in the remainder of the interview. In this short excerpt, she expresses the idea of caring about (*keeping your heart in something*) and taking care of (*being effective*) animals, two of the main forms of caring identified by Tronto (1993) who argues that care implies extending concern beyond the self to others which will lead to some kind of action. Tronto (1993) identifies the main kinds of care as caring about, taking care of, care- giving and care- receiving and suggests that powerful people tend to be associated with the first two types of care, while less powerful people are more likely to give and receive care. These four dimensions of caring suggest an ethic of care based on attentiveness, responsibility, competence, and responsiveness (1993: 127). Each of these dimensions can be applied to the work of animal protectionists which also involves the related concepts of empathy /compassion and protection.

Empathy/Compassion: Attentiveness and Responsibility

Being attentive to the plight of others is the first requirement of an ethic of care. Tronto suggests that " it is probably more morally reprehensible to ignore wilfully that which is close to one's own actions than to fail to be aware of a distant consequence of one's actions" (1993: 129). Thus the failure to assist an injured or sick animal that wanders into one's backyard seems more heartless than an unwillingness to care about the plight of a thousand intensively reared farm animals when one buys meat at the supermarket. *Caring about* implies an acknowledgment that care is necessary; because people know their cat needs food or the dog needs a walk, they can be said to care about their companion animals. People know these things through empathy, an awareness which one of my informants described in an experience she had with her cat:

> *I was in a small flat, he was on his own during the day and then when I got home in the evening I noticed how lonely he was; then a few weeks after getting him, he came down with the cat flu and it sort of struck me that these animals suffer just the same as we do and that was the turning point.* (Lisa, Interview by author, 1992.)

Clark's (1997: 28) research on the etymology of the term, "compassion" in Latin-related languages, suggests that we cannot look on cooly as others suffer; or we sympathize with those who suffer; in other European languages, empathy, or the idea of "co-feeling", is used to convey the same meaning. Animal lovers have little difficulty seeing companion animals as part of a primary relationship which entitles them to the rewards that the bonds of friendship demand. On the other hand, being willing to take care of, or have any responsibility for the plight of millions of intensively farmed, hunted, or laboratory animals is usually not seen as part of an individual's moral brief. This is the work of animal rights/liberation organisations. *Taking care of* lost or abandoned animals is a basic service of animal welfare organisations like the National Canine Defence League (NCDL) discussed below. The issues of factory farming, vivisection, recreational hunting and the liberation of captive animals are the province of the more radical animal rights/liberation groups. The act of taking care of—in the form of campaigns against the exploitation of animals—is the equivalent of the animal movement's prognostic frame. Put differently, taking care of animals in the sense of doing something for them in campaigns against vivisection, factory farming and blood sports is achieved collectively through the work of animal activists and advocates in social movement organisations.

Animal protectionists see it as their responsibility to take care of animals by taking action on their behalf wherever animal exploitation and abuse occurs. Haskell has traced the career of the concept of responsibility to as recently as 1788 and explains that "once an evil is perceived as remediable, some people (not all, certainly) will be exposed to feelings of guilt and responsibility for suffering that was previously viewed with indifference or, at most, aroused only passive sympathy" (1999: 21). He argues that modern societies with high rates of social and technological change foster an expansive sense of agency whereby "people cannot feel responsible enough to do anything about ending suffering as long as they cannot imagine any practicable course of action that will reliably lead to that outcome" (1999: 22). Haskell is mainly concerned with slavery as one of many cruel and exploitative practices. He notes "the startling recency of the humanitarian phenomenon" and points out that there was no serious opposition to slavery before the eighteenth century (1999: 22-23). Similarly, cruel practices perpetrated against animals were not seriously challenged until the latter part of the nineteenth century. Only since the mid-twentieth century has there been an expansion of agency expressed through collective action that has demonstrated the possibility of successfully challenging and preventing animal exploitation, such as factory farming.

The remaining two dimensions of caregiving and care receiving involve direct contact with animals which most animal protectionists do not experience beyond their relationship with companion animals. *Caregiving* which "involves physical work, and almost always requires that care-givers come in contact with the objects of care" (1993: 107) can best be described in the context of the professional work of veterinarians, animal technicians and the like. *Care-receiving* implies that the recipient of the care will respond to it, that caring needs have actually been met. In the case of veterinary care, for example, we would expect the animal's ailments to be remedied.

While Tronto's typology of caring doesn't mention nonhuman animals, the ethic of care which she advocates applies equally well to them with some modifications. When she suggests that care-giving and care-receiving typically occur within less powerful social groups, this takes a different form in the case of animal protection. Tronto argues that competence and responsiveness are the essential ethical ingredients of these kinds of caring. I suggest that the ethical equivalent in the animal movement is the concept of protection.

Protection: Competence and Responsiveness

Caring work must be competently performed. The veterinarian unable to restore a sick animal to health as a consequence of faulty treatment, or who is not concerned with the outcome of the treatment, is acting incompetently. The vulnerability of animals to abuse by humans means that "responsiveness requires that we remain alert to the possibilities for abuse that arise with vulnerability" (Tronto, 1993: 135). For many social critics, the idea of protecting vulnerable humans is deeply suspect. Brown for example, asserts that women have good reason for being wary of the politics of protection:

> Historically, the argument that women require protection by and from men has been critical in legitimating women's exclusion from some spheres of human endeavour and confinement within others. Indeed, to be "protected" by the same power whose violation one fears perpetuates the very modality of dependence and powerlessness marking much of women's experience across widely diverse cultures and epochs (Brown,1995: 170).

Although it is sometimes claimed that the idea of institutionalised animal protection is paternalistic, it would be farfetched to suggest that these caveats apply to the protection of nonhuman animals when it is done competently by people who care about their vulnerable charges. Paternalism is seen by animal protectors as a lesser evil than indifference to animal suffering.

Caring about the wellbeing of animals is the mission of every animal protection organisation in this study. In the case study below and elsewhere in the present study, I look at a cross section of animal protection and humane groups and organisations in Australia, the UK and the USA. The first example is from England, the birthplace of animal protection organisations in the West. This particular organisation was chosen because it represents the hands-on caring work of an animal welfare organisation that helps homeless people and their canine companions.

Caring for Canines and Homeless People at the NCDL

No study of the animal protection movement would be complete without reference to the "hands-on" work of animal shelters, refuges and the like. These are the animal rescue activities of organisations such as the RSPCA and the National Canine Defence League (NCDL). It is perhaps the English disposition towards animals and their reputation as an animal-loving nation which explains the existence of the NCDL. The organisation was established as a charity in 1891 and has the Queen as its patron. It exists "to protect and defend all dogs from abuse, cruelty, abandonment and any form of mistreatment, both in the UK and abroad" (NCDL flyer). While the NCDL's first priority is to dogs, it has demonstrated a strong commitment during its history to the welfare of the poor and needy. In the 1930s, for example, it helped fund refugees and their pets who had fled Nazi Germany. And in its *Annual Report* of 1933, it drew attention to the bond between a destitute man and his dog who, it said, "was probably better fed and groomed than his owner. Yet he cannot part with his dog" (Kean, 1998: 184).

The charity launched its Hope Project in 1994 when it was discovered that there were thousands of unvaccinated dogs roaming the streets of England's big cities with their homeless keepers. Apart from offering homeless people the opportunity to have their dogs vaccinated, wormed and neutered, Hope assists the owners in finding "dog-friendly" accommodation or when this is not available, provides advice on rehoming and temporary care for the animal. Hope also assists dog owners who are faced with eviction because of their pets.

The NCDL believes all dogs should be cared for by responsible owners and that no healthy dog should ever be destroyed. In its first year of operation, Hope reported that they had not come across any case of neglect and noted the importance of companion animals to homeless people: "The unconditional love and friendship that a dog can provide is invaluable and for those who sleep rough, there is the added benefit of physical warmth at night" (undated NCDL information sheet). The sheet also referred to people who are squatting, travelling or living in hostels using the services for their dogs. All of this seems eminently appropriate work for a charity of the NCDL's standing, but it is not without its detractors. Squatters, the homeless and New Age Travellers are perceived as folk devils by many people in Britain as a result of media stereotyping and government hostility. Tory Party politicians including the then Prime Minister John Major have attacked New Age Travellers as a threat to law and order in the countryside. For the Tory government, these people are a blot on the landscape; they are out of place in the countryside which "it seems, belongs to the middle class, to landowners, and to people who engage in blood sports" (Sibley, 1995:107). Sibley notes how the laws of trespass have been strengthened to safeguard rural England from the Travellers as well as from ramblers, hunt saboteurs and environmental protesters.

A tour through the NCDL's headquarters in London reveals portraits of dogs on every wall and hundreds of dogs in residence. Hope's coordinator, Colette Kase spoke enthusiastically about the organisation's devotion to dogs:

> *I'm very pro-companion animal (and) we are a pro- dog organisation. Some of the very well- known animal rights organisations would rather see the end of all domestic animals; they take an abolitionist stance. We would **never** want to see (that); we **love** dogs and want to keep dogs going, but we want them to have wonderful lives.* (Interview with author, 1996)

It is not surprising that NCDL, as the largest dog protection society in the UK and possibly in the world, is critical of the extreme animal rights approach to companion animals, namely that pets represent "both slavery and imprisonment of innocents" (Bryant,1982:9). It is a position not held by the majority of the animal movement's supporters, most of whom keep companion animals. Yet Bryant points to the contradiction of a so-called animal-loving nation, with an estimated dog population of six million, deliberately killing 600,000 young dogs every year. According to the NCDL, this is precisely why it has been campaigning over the past century for the rights of dogs to life. It is the recent inclusion of the dogs of the homeless that adds a different dimension to the organisation's caring work. Because the NCDL is serious about wanting dogs *to have wonderful lives,* the organisation is concerned about the fate of dogs whose owners are homeless and who therefore may be more vulnerable to hardship than their domiciled counterparts.

One of the NCDL's most ambitious projects is concerned with pets and housing. In stark contrast to the strict animal rights position, the NCDL believes in the desirability of pets in society. "All responsible pet owners derive some benefit from their pets. The animals can help to develop a social life, for example, because people will very often talk to others who have animals. Loneliness is a scourge of modern society; for many people an animal may be their only friend." Human welfare and human needs clearly take precedence over the animals' welfare in this statement of what the document calls "the human/animal bond" and about which much has been written (see for example the work of the International Society for Anthrozoology). An umbrella group in the NCDL made up of some of the leading animal welfare SMOs in the UK seeks to encourage housing providers to accept pets where facilities for their proper care exist. As the document makes clear, this is an issue concerning the rights of pet owners rather than an animal welfare issue as such. This is even more so in the case of the Hope Project's campaign for homeless people and their dogs. As Kase points out:

> *The Hope Project is a classic example of where we aren't just looking after dogs; we are helping the owners as well. For example, we do a lot more (human welfare work) women escaping domestic violence is one example. If people want to go into detox units and they have a dog obviously what are they going to do with their dog? So we look after their dog so they can go into detox. Things like that.* (Interview with author, 1996)

While the defence of the canine remains its main objective, caring for the dogs' homeless companions has emerged as an important by-product of the NCDL's advocacy work. This is a classic example of frame bridging which Snow and Benford define as "the linkage of two or more ideologically congruent but structurally unconnected frames regarding a particular issue or problem" (1986: 467). Caring work of the kind achieved by the NCDL and other organisations such as the American Humane Association and its work with children is one the movement's most effective arguments against the charge that the animal movement is misanthropic and indifferent to human concerns.

This chapter has focused on the importance to the animal movement of the concepts of cruelty and compassion. Caring work is the animal movement's response to achieving a decent society in which human and non-human animals can live free of exploitation. Caring is social problems work in which activists care about and take care of animals. It is related to but is not the same as emotional labour which is a feature of work in many service industries. This chapter told the story of the National Canine Defence League and its work with animals and homeless people. While this kind of caring work is characteristic of animal welfare agencies, the campaigns against vivisection, blood sports and factory farming are associated with the activities of the animal rights/liberation movement. These movements are discussed in the chapters which follow.

Note 1: To say that the Nazis were animal lovers who hated "inferior humans" is an oversimplification. Hermann Goering, for instance, while posturing as a protector of animals, was an avid hunter. As in most cultures, attitudes and practices towards human and nonhuman animals alike were full of contradictions although they reached new heights of perversity under the Nazis. Apart from Nazi Germany, it is not clear which societies Margalit has in mind when he makes this point. Is it China whose disregard of human rights is notorious? In China's case, animal rights is an utterly alien concept as WSPA and other animal protection agencies have discovered in their campaigns to ban bear farming in that country. Margalit's admonition seems less impressive when set against Gandhi's famous dictum that "the greatness of a nation and its moral progress can be judged by the way its animals are treated" (Wynne-Tyson, 1990:139).

Note 2: Benton (1993) cites the seminal paper by Francis and Norman (1978) in which they reject the idea of animal rights as a "real liberation movement": "Liberation movements have a character and a degree of moral importance which cannot be possessed by a movement to prevent cruelty to animals" (cited in Benton, 1993:10). However, Leahy (1991: 247), although a critic of animal liberation philosophy, maintains that the term "liberation" is more accurate and effective than legalistic "rights talk".

Note 3: Freidson (1990) focuses on work that is the opposite of alienated labor. He calls this kind of work "labors of love" or the voluntary work which he notes Marx and most other writers have overlooked (151). "In English, the word *volunteer* tends to be used to designate people who are unpaid participants in some purposive program that is often organized as a social movement or a campaign" (156-7). Volunteer workers are found in virtually every area of activity where paid work is available and may even do voluntary work in what are seen as leisure activities. Thus, an individual might be a volunteer at a local school or at a tennis club. What is important is that voluntary work is unpaid and as such, is not recognised as real work. Daniels (1987) calls such activities "invisible work" because they are not part of the institutionalized aspects of life represented by salaried careers and jobs. Her sample consisted of women in civic projects who did fundraising, public relations, organisation building and maintenance, and lobbying as advocates of various causes. In the case of animal protection advocacy and activism, both women and men do this kind of work which is more often than not underpaid or not paid at all.

The danger in describing animal activism and advocacy as work is that any form of participation in social movements might then qualify as work. And even more troublesome is the question; is all social activity or social behaviour work? (Pahl, 1984; 126). "Work" then becomes synonymous with "task" or "activity" and loses its distinctive meaning. According to Pahl (1984: 128), work can be understood only within the context of the specific social relations within which it is embedded. Work cannot include all social activity nor can it be limited to the constraining definition of work as employment.

REFERENCES

Agnew, R.(1998) "The causes of animal abuse: A social-psychological analysis", *Theoretical Criminology*, 2,177-209.

Benton, Ted (1993) *Natural relations: Ecology, animal rights and social justice*,Verso, London.

Berger, John (1990) "Photographs of agony" in *About looking*, Vintage International, Vintage Books, New York.

Brown, Wendy (1995) *States of injury: Power and freedom in late modernity*, Princeton University Press, Princeton, N.J.

Bryant, John (1982) *Fettered kingdoms*, Fox Press, Manchester.

Clark, S.R..L (1997) *Animals and their moral standing*, Routledge London.

Coe, Sue (1995) *Dead meat*, Four Walls Eight Windows, New York and London.

Denzin, N K (1989) *Interpretive interactionism*, Sage Publications, Newbury Park, California.

Eckersley, Robyn (1992) *Environmentalism and political theory: Toward an ecocentric approach*, UCL Press, London

Economist, the (1995) "People and animals: Also, part of creation", 19 August, pp 17-19.

Erikson, Kai (1990) "Introduction" in Kai Erikson and Steven Peter Vallas (eds) *The nature of work: Sociological perspectives*, American Sociological Association, Presidential Series and Yale University Press, New Haven and London.

Finsen, Lawrence and Finsen, Susan (1994) *The animal rights movement in America: From compassion to respect*, Twayne Publishers, New York.

Francis, L P and Norman, R (1978) "Some animals are more equal than others" in *Philosophy*, 53, pp 507-27.

Freidson, Eliot (1990) "Labors of love in theory and practice: A prospectus" in Kai Erikson and Steven Peter Vallas (eds) *The nature of work: Sociological perspectives*, American Sociological Association, Presidential Series and Yale University Press, New Haven and London.

Giddens, Anthony (1991) *Modernity and self-identity: Self and society in late modern age*, Polity, Cambridge

Haskell, Thomas (1999) "Responsibility, convention, and the role of ideas in history" in Peter Coclanis and Stuart Bruchey (1999) *Ideas, ideologies, and social movements: The United States experience since 1800*, University of South Carolina Press, Columbia, South Carolina.

Hochschild, Arlie Russell (1983) *The managed heart: the commercialization of human feeling*, University of California Press, Berkeley.

Kaminer, Wendy (1984) *Women volunteering: The pleasure, pain, and politics of unpaid work from 1830 to the present*, Anchor Books, New York.

Kean, Hilda (1998) *Animal rights: Political and social change in Britain since 1800*, Reakion Books Ltd, London.

LaFollette, H and Shanks, N (1996) *Brute science: Dilemmas of animal experimentation*, Routledge, London.

Leahy, M (1991) *Against liberation: Putting animals in perspective*, Routledge London.

MacCulloch, Jennifer (1993) *Creatures of culture: The animal protection and preservation movements in Sydney, 1880-1930*, Unpublished PhD thesis, University of Sydney.

Margalit, Avishai (1996) *The Decent Society*, Cambridge MA: Harvard University Press.

Miller, James (1990) "Carnivals of atrocity: Foucault, Nietzsche, cruelty", *Political Theory*, Vol 18, No 3, August, pp 470-491.

Mills, C Wright (1951) *White collar: The American middle classes*, Oxford University Press, New York.

Moland, John (1996) "Social change,social inequality, and intergroup tensions" in *Social Forces*, December, 765 (2): 403-421.

Pahl, R E (1984) *Divisions of labour*, Blackwell, London.

Primatt, H. (1776/1992) *The duty of mercy and the sin of cruelty to brute animals*, A Kinship Classic, Sussex, Centaur Press, Fontwell.

Rose, Steven (1991) "Proud to be speciesist" in *New Statesman and Society*, 26 April, p21.

Ross, Edward A (1933) *The outlines of sociology*, Century Company.

Ryder, Richard (1983) *Victims of science: The use of animals in research*, National Anti-vivisection
        Society Limited, London.
Ryder, Richard (1992) (editor) Humphrey Primatt's *the duty of mercy and the sin of cruelty to brute
        animals*, A Kinship Classic, Centaur Press, Fontwell, Sussex.
Sapontzis, Steve (1993) "Aping Persons pro and con" in Paola Cavalieri and Peter Singer (editors), *The
        great ape project: Equality before humanity*, Fourth Estate, London.
Shapiro, Ken (1994) "The caring sleuth: Portrait of an animal rights activist", *Society & Animals,* 2(2) 145-
        165.
Singer, Peter (1978) "Preface" in David Patterson and Richard Ryder (eds) *Animal rights: a symposium*,
        Centaur Press Ltd. Fontwell, Sussex.
Singer, Peter (1975) *Animal liberation: A new ethics for our treatment of animals*, New York: New York
        Review and Random House.
Thomas, Keith (ed) (1999) "Introduction", *The Oxford Book of Work*, Oxford University Press, Oxford.
Tronto, Joan (1993) *Moral boundaries: A political argument for an ethic of care*, Routledge, New York.
Wadel, Cato (1979) "The hidden work of everyday life", in Sandra Wallman (ed) *Social anthropology of
        work,* Academic Press Inc. London.
Weber, Max (1925,1967) *Max Weber on law in economy and society*, edited by Max Rheinstein and
        Translated by Edward Shils and Max Rheinstein, Simon & Schuster.
Wolfe, Alan (1993) *The human difference: Animals, computers and the necessity of* social science: ,
        Berkeley: University of California Press.
Wynne-Tyson, Jon (1990) *The extended circle: An anthology of humane thought*, Cardinal, London.
Young, Iris (1990) *Justice and the politics of difference*, Princeton University Press, Princeton.

Chapter 4

The Compassionate Beast:
A Movement of Hearts and Minds

Philosophy can lead the mind to water but only emotion can make it drink

—Tom Regan, animal rights philosopher

Animals are not affected by how we feel but by what we do

—John Webster, professor of animal husbandry

In this chapter the work of some of the most important critics of the animal movement are outlined and evaluated. Like these writers, I have found it difficult to remain detached, perhaps because of the nature of the subject, the complexity of which is so accurately captured in the epigrams at the head of the chapter. The book is essentially about these two ideas expressed by Regan the animal rights philosopher and Webster the practising animal scientist: (1) what motivates animal protectionists in their campaigns on behalf of animals and (2) what are the results of the strategies and tactics they use?

Activists and advocates invariably perceive nonhuman animals as innocent victims of human cruelty while their campaigns are driven by a desire to end what they see as an outrageous injustice perpetrated by human beings against other animals. The animal movement has been described as "a moral crusade" in which campaigners use emotions and moral shocks as well as atrocity stories about "the suffering of innocents" to mobilise public support for their cause (Jasper and Nelkin 1992; Jasper and Poulsen 1995; Groves1995, 1997). For Finsen and Finsen (1994), the animal movement is the quintessential movement for social justice while to Tester (1991) it is not about animal rights at all but rather about how adherents define their humanity. Conflicting interpretations are a constant theme in the sociological literature on the animal movement just as they are in the work of the philosophers who have shaped the movement from the outset. I will therefore outline some key ideas of a selection of prominent philosophers on both sides of the animal liberation debate.

Singer/Regan, Leahy/Frey and Wolfe

The Australian philosopher Peter Singer has been called the most effective philosopher alive (Appleyard 1995) while critics have denounced his work as "a clear illustration of the moral bankruptcy and intellectual impoverishment of the animal liberation philosophy" (Nicoll, Russell and Lau 1992:60). Similarly, Regan's *The Case for Animal Rights* (1984) is cited by some as the most rigorous and philosophically sophisticated argument for the extension of rights to animals (e.g. Benton and Redfearn 1996:50) while others like Steven Rose (1991) have denounced Regan as "muddle-headed and intellectually dishonest". Yet despite these mixed reviews, every serious book on the animal movement devotes a section or two to the ideas of Peter Singer and Tom Regan (pronounced as in "vegan"). Their most important contributions in guiding us as to how we should treat other animals are outlined below. The Singer/Regan pro-animal liberation perspective will be described alongside the critique by Michael Leahy who utilises R G Frey's case against animal liberation, primarily in *Interests and Rights* (1980) to craft his own rebuttal of Singer/Regan and other animal liberationists. The arguments for and against liberation will then be evaluated within the context of the main arenas of movement activism: factory farming, animal experimentation and blood sports and will conclude with Alan Wolfe's (1993) defense of anthropocentrism. That more space in this chapter is given over to the animal movement's critics can be justified on the ground that the bulk of this book focuses on the views of movement supporters, advocates and activists.

The Singer/Regan Case for Animal Interests/Rights

Although commentators often emphasise the differences between their philosophical positions, Singer and Regan are on the same side in that they both want people to respect animals as sentient beings who deserve to be treated compassionately rather than as if they do not matter. Both philosophers have published as a duo and agree that the worst forms of cruelty perpetrated by humans against animals occur on factory farms, in laboratories and in hunting and trapping. But their differences are important for those who are guided by what they have to say about the way we should treat other animals.

Interests

Singer argues that when we mistreat animals by eating them, dissecting them and killing them for sport, we are guilty of speciesism, an act of discrimination that he claims is on a par with racism and sexism. According to Singer, race, sex and species membership are morally irrelevant criteria upon which to discriminate against other beings. Like the social movements that seek to emancipate oppressed racial/ethnic peoples and women, the animal liberation movement wants to liberate animals exploited and abused by humans.

Anti-speciesism requires that we give equal consideration to the interests of all sentient beings. Pain is pain whether suffered by a boy or a dog and it is in the interests of both to avoid it. Most animals and all humans, unlike trees and rocks, have the capacity for experiencing pain and pleasure. It is not animal rights that Singer advocates, but rather the animal's interest in avoiding pain. Thus, a Singerian would argue, the boy's interests and the dog's deserve equal consideration, but not necessarily equal treatment. A dog might need to be put down if for instance it attacked a boy; but not vice versa. But a dog should not be required to suffer so as to satisfy the curiosity of a research scientist or to forfeit its life in order to facilitate some trivial research project. However, replace the dog with a rodent and most people would probably be less enthusiastic about supporting the proposition. As a utilitarian, Singer accepts that animals' lives may need to be sacrificed for a greater good, but he urges us to weigh carefully the animals' lives against the supposed benefits. This is the theory of utilitarianism which maintains that an act is right if, and only if, in the absence of a better alternative, the amount of good caused by the act outweighs the amount of bad. For instance, that millions of animals die to satisfy our taste for meat, for fur, for cosmetics or for fun, is to the utilitarian, morally wrong.

To Singer, it is the capacity for suffering, not species membership which dictates how we should treat other animals. A human equipped with the powers of imagination and diagnosed as terminally ill suffers in a way that no nonhuman animal can. By the same token, battery hens, tethered sows and caged lions cannot comprehend the reason for their confinement and so it may be that they endure greater stress than the confined convict or slave who at least understands the reason for their incarceration. Thus anti-speciesism requires that we consider the interests of all sentient beings equally so that it is not just humans or charismatic megafauna—whales, white rhinos and pandas—who are the recipients of moral consideration, but the millions of laboratory and food animals that are Singer's principal concern. "As long as we remember that we should give the same respect to the lives of animals as we give to the lives of those humans at a similar level", suggests Singer, "we shall not go far wrong" (Singer 1975:24). As a rule of thumb, this means that if we object to say experiments being conducted on a brain-damaged human, we should logically find similar experiments on a healthy animal morally reprehensible.

Singer's utilitarianism allows for the humane killing of sentient beings under certain circumstances where the positive consequences of the act outstrip the negative. Thus, the deaths of a number of animals in an experiment which leads to the discovery of a vaccine that in due course saves both animal and human lives may, according to a utilitarian calculus, be justified. But in *Animal Liberation* (1975) there would seem to be no justification for the killing of millions of animals annually on factory farms and in laboratories. Killing animals for food, when there is a vegetarian alternative, is for Singer indefensible. With animal experimentation, each case would have to be decided on its merits, since there are instances when the aggregate good of human and nonhuman animals may be served by the sacrifice of individual animals. This is the kind of pragmatism that abolitionists in the movement reject since utilitarianism's cost/benefit calculus allows individuals to be harmed for a greater good, a proposition abhorrent to the likes of the American philosopher Tom Regan.

Rights

Regan's uncompromising abolitionist stance is by definition at odds with Singer's pragmatism regarding how we should treat animals. Regan finds Singer's utilitarianism inadequate for defending the rights of animals to be left alone. They are "subjects of a life" which means they have inherent value that humans should respect. Inherent value is something Regan argues all individual human and nonhuman animals have equally. It is inherent value which is the basis for the claim of rights. If animals have rights, the most basic is the right to bodily integrity, which an activist interviewed for this book graphically described in the case of battery hens, as "the right to own a beak". To Regan, animal rights means an animal has a right to respectful treatment. However, this is more than the utilitarian principle of equal consideration of the animal's interests for rights explicitly mean the right not to be harmed. If the rights of animals are to be taken seriously, no practice—experimentation, commercial agriculture, hunting and trapping—which results in the suffering or death of an animal can be justified. Regan and his animal rights followers therefore call for nothing less than the abolition of these "abuses" irrespective of whatever benefit they may be to other animals or humans. Animal exploitation, like slavery or the oppression of powerless people, is morally wrong. According to this view, zoos, circuses and even pet keeping should be banned.

For freedom-loving people the doctrine of individual rights has enormous appeal since it supports the idea that the individual's liberty cannot be sacrificed for the common good. Yet "rights talk" is fraught with moral pitfalls and can be easily exploited by either left-wingers or right-wingers to argue a convincing case, for instance, about the virtues of big or small government. The New Right can put a strong case for keeping government out of people's private lives—the right to be left alone, including the provision of welfare—while the Left can claim that the failure of government to deliver adequate material assistance to the needy is a violation of human rights. The issue of rights is even more complicated, some would say incomprehensible, when it is applied to the lives of animals. "Rights talk" readily becomes a weapon which critics and sceptics of animal liberation use to undermine the defence of animals' rights. It is too easy, even for those who are sympathetic to the animal cause, to claim that just as people do not have a right not to be eaten by a shark, the shark has no right not to be consumed as flake by humans.

The Case for Animal Rights (1984) contains 400 pages of carefully crafted arguments which most animal supporters find daunting in comparison to Singer's more widely read and cited *Animal Liberation* (1975). In the preface to *The Case*, Regan explains that the book was written with three audiences in mind: supporters of the animal movement, his professional peers in philosophy and finally those who work with animals such as veterinarians and scientists. The book contains virtually nothing on the actual conditions of animals in the contexts that Regan seeks to abolish in factory farms, laboratories and in the wild, since its purpose is to provide a philosophical defense of animal rights in general and to explain what it means to ascribe rights to nonhuman animals. In the terminology used in *Compassionate Beasts,* Regan's book is about animal rights advocacy or claims making while Singer's *Animal Liberation* is directed more to the activist and gives detailed descriptions of the conditions under which animals suffer as well as prescriptions for action by those who want to support the cause.

Critics of the movement will exploit philosophical differences in order to discredit the movement as ideologically confused. Yet the differences matter little to the many supporters, advocates and activists interviewed and surveyed for this book. Similarly, for those critical of the movement or for those who find the concepts of animal interests and animal rights questionable, the Singer/Regan position is essentially seen as *for* animal liberation and therefore untenable.

The Leahy/Frey Case Against Liberation

Pain

Michael Leahy's (1991) intention of *putting animals in perspective* derives its inspiration from Wittgenstein's language-games and theories about how language works. According to Wittgenstein language works in the context of human experience and a word's meaning is determined by the context of a series of language-games. Leahy's main idea is that animals are "primitive beings" that lack the power of speech and all that that entails including desires, interests and beliefs as we understand these concepts. Animals therefore cannot have beliefs because they lack language and being speechless, they cannot have desires.

How is an animal protectionist to take seriously Wittgenstein's claim as reported by Leahy that to attribute pain to animals does not make *sense*? Pain in the Wittgensteinian sense applies to human beings and only in diluted form to lesser beings. This defies the experience of anyone who has had any long-term association with animals as companions, on farms or in the wild. An official complaint of cruelty lodged by animal activists against an intensive piggery in Australia described "how two of the prolapses were seething with maggots and how *one pig screamed in pain* as another pig stood on its prolapse" (Barrowclough, Neales and Brew-Bevan 1997:16). Leahy's excessive adherence to the doctrine of language-games would denigrate the activists' description as anthropomorphic while the assertion that it makes no *sense* to describe the pig's scream as evidence of suffering is surely a failure of *common sense*, if not a sign of moral apathy.

The neo-Cartesian John S Kennedy argues that it is dangerous to unthinkingly assume that animals are conscious (1992:157). To do so, is to be guilty of the sin of anthropomorphism, that is, the attribution of human mental experiences to nonhumans. Kennedy claims that it is not possible scientifically to determine from their behaviour whether or not animals have feelings. Animal protectionists, like environmentalists confronted with the proposition that there is no evidence of an impending ecological catastrophe, say from global warming, would prudently invoke the "precautionary principle" to ensure that if there is any element of doubt about whether animals feel pain, then we should desist from treating them as insentient rather than unthinkingly assuming they are unconscious. Kennedy seeks to dilute the severity of pain with reference to reports of people on the sports field and battlefield or of those admitted to hospital with severe injuries who may be completely unaware of the pain. In much the same way that environmental cornucopians serve vested economic interests, Kennedy's attack on the new anthropomorphism serves the interests of animal abusers.

Suffering

Leahy agrees with Singer that human beings *suffer* more than animals in many cases because animals, unlike humans are incapable of pondering the associated torments, the loss of potential happiness, living to a ripe old age, opportunities and regrets about the past and so on. Yet this has little to do with pain or cruelty as the focus of animal liberation campaigns. It is possible to argue, as some philosophers do, that pain is a greater evil than suffering.

Many pet keepers armed with stories of animals pining for their lost companions, human and nonhuman, would contest the assertion that only humans suffer mental torment. And animal watchers, notably Masson and McCarthy (1995), would refute the proposition with their observation of the existence of complex emotions in animals which Leahy would no doubt dismiss as an extreme form of anthropomorphism. Furthermore, it is not fanciful to suggest that animals in distress might suffer more than their human counterparts since unlike us they are unable to engage in the human capacity to exercise mind over matter in order to relieve their torment. Put more succinctly: "They have less capacity for distancing themselves" (Rodd 1992:73).

Leahy's perspective on animals is too abstract to be convincing to anyone other than those who seek to rationalise their exploitation of other animals. Lawrence Johnson (1993:5) charges Leahy with "linguistic Cartesianism" and rightly suggests that the use of Wittgenstein's language-games to counter animal liberation attacks against speciesism is as absurd as Descartes' "animals as machines" analogy of the seventeenth century. It is true that humans alone are able to give meaning to mental cruelty or abuse by labelling such things as instances of "torturing the soul". But this is not an argument that sentient beings incapable of articulating their pain or suffering do not experience it, as I have tried to show in the previous paragraph. Endless debates and language-games about animal consciousness, the nature of animal pain and suffering will never satisfy individuals like the Australian activists mentioned above who have heard the pig's scream.

The American philosopher R.G. Frey (1983;1980) is frequently invoked by opponents of animal liberation to support the moral orthodoxy of keeping animals in perspective. Yet Frey is as much a utilitarian as Singer; their philosophical differences are more of degree than of kind. Singer argues that most human uses of animals are unethical, especially those associated with factory farming, animal experimentation and recreational hunting. According to Singer's calculus, the cost of these practices in terms of animals' lives and suffering greatly outweighs the benefits to humans and therefore the practices are morally reprehensible. Frey's utilitarianism, on the other hand, sees the benefits of meat eating, improvements to human health, happiness and well-being and so on as justifying the use of animals for these purposes. For him, animals can be eaten, dissected and hunted provided there is good reason to do so and the killing is done humanely, that is in the absence of gratuitous cruelty. Regan's insistence that animals are subjects-of-a-life who have rights is however rejected by Frey for all the usual reasons critics of "rights talk" use to question the concept of animal rights. There is therefore more common ground between Frey's "concerned individual" and Singer's more pragmatic position on animal liberation than there is with the militantly abolitionist stance taken by Regan. What then do critics of animal rights have to say about the treatment of animals in commercial agriculture, in research and in zoos and hunting?

Eating Animals

The issue of meat is crucial to the animal protection cause since liberationists argue that if people believe that there is nothing wrong with eating animal flesh, then this is effectively a licence for humans to use animals as they please. Leahy's defence of killing animals for food seems to be that it is acceptable as long as there is no avoidable cruelty involved in their rearing, transport and slaughter. The arguments in favour of vegetarianism—moral, health, environmental and gustatory as canvassed by proselytes like Singer (1975), Robbins (1987), Fiddes (1991), Cox (1992), and Hill (1996) among others—are given short shrift by Leahy. He suggests that even if we were to replace meat with grains, the benefits from the reduction of world hunger in underdeveloped countries would be outweighed by the chilling prospect of the "demographic and political implications" of a dietary revolution (1991:213) by which he no doubt means overpopulation and global instability.

That meat eating is a health hazard is rejected by Leahy who claims "it is only necessary to show that a diet to which (meat) contributes can be no less healthy than one from which it is excluded". At this point Frey's (1983) book on moral vegetarianism is brought to the table, so to speak. Frey rejects Singer's claim that the costs to the meat industry as a consequence of a growth in vegetarianism are outweighed by the benefits to animals and goes on to list 21 instances which suggest that the opposite is true (1983:197-206). Leahy discusses just three of these issues— massive unemployment, forced dietary change and the demise of traditional cuisines and restaurants and the conversion of a bucolic countryside into an animal-free zone—and contends that the Regans and Singers of the world who attempt to play down the consequences of a vegetarian future are insensitive to human welfare. Leahy and Frey exaggerate what Leahy calls "the possible catastrophic consequences of widespread vegetarianism for human beings" (Leahy 1991:217) since all three of these consequences would diminish in severity within a generation or two. Intensive farming, on the other hand, appears to be becoming more intensive with ever increasing numbers of animals being killed in the process. It is difficult to see how under such conditions animal slaughter could become more humane or how any reasonable person would be convinced by Leahy's lame suggestion that thanatosis—a temporary paralysis or anaesthetic shock—could alleviate the suffering of factory-farmed animals as it evidently does for some accident victims.

Contrary to the anecdotal evidence of many animal watchers and people who work with animals, Leahy claims that animals, because they lack self-awareness do not experience the uniquely human fear of death (1991:219). We have already seen that Leahy and other opponents of animal liberation maintain that we do not know if animals have feelings or experience pain as we understand it. Leahy's "linguistic Cartesianism" comes unstuck at several places, for instance when referring to ritual slaughter as "an agonising and unsavoury procedure lasting between one and two minutes" (1991:219). There seems no better reason to raise this issue other than as an attempt to sanitise, by way of comparison, the treatment and conditions of animals in British abattoirs. Yet on the manner of their slaughter and the fear of death experienced by animals, Leahy is at odds with John Webster, a professor of animal husbandry. Webster contends that the difference between conventional and ritual slaughter is of minor importance, while the fear of death is the main problem facing animals in slaughterhouses (1994:106). Animals may not live in chronic fear of death as many humans do, but they do seem to know when their time is up. Under conditions of apparent cruelty, what can the humane individual do? A possible solution is offered by Frey whose more practical arguments are oddly omitted from Leahy's account.

Frey's (1983) *Rights, Killing and Suffering* is subtitled "moral vegetarianism and applied ethics". In this book Frey promotes the idea that it is not necessary to be a vegetarian in order to do something about the plight of animals. The "concerned individual" is the quintessential animal welfarist—one who campaigns against the worst abuses of factory farming or speaks out against cruelty to animals without giving up meat or using animals in ways that do not harm them. Vegetarianism is not the only tactic available to anyone who is disturbed by our treatment of animals. Frey believes a concerned individual should boycott meat produced cruelly but not meat that comes from a well-cared for animal. He is against the more strict moral vegetarianism advocated by Singer and Regan in favour of what might be called "semi-vegetarianism" (George 1994:405) For many people, these dietary regimes are preferable to the sacrifice or even "oral masochism" that is often associated with veganism and vegetarianism in predominantly meat-eating cultures. Semi-vegetarianism is popular also amongst animal activists (see Munro 1996) and is seen as a more realistic goal for women and others whose bodily needs are not the same as those of affluent, white males (George 1994). In proposing an alternative to moral vegetarianism, Frey offers a way out—purists would call it a convenient rationalisation—to those who want to eat meat with a conscience. His menu is therefore more palatable than what is offered by the militant school of vegetarians, vegans and fruitarians whose practice of ethical eating seems beyond the capacity of most people.

Experimenting on Animals

Leahy's discussion of animal experimentation begins by noting the uncertainties surrounding the practice within the science fraternity itself and the way both sides present their respective moral and scientific claims to the general public. Wittgenstein's language-games again reduce Leahy's arguments to little more than linguistic Cartesianism when he comes to discuss the concepts of pain, suffering, distress and anxiety. Rowan's (1989:97) definition of animal suffering—"the unpleasant emotional response to more than minimal pain and distress"—is described by Leahy as "hopeless" because it ignores unwitting suffering (e.g. when plants suffer from too much sun) and is improperly anthropomorphic (when it covertly seeks our sympathy by reference to the animal's unpleasant emotional response to suffering). Who are we to believe on animal behaviour, the philosopher Leahy, who is opposed to animal liberation, or the biochemist Rowan, who has both experimented on animals and enjoyed good relations with the animal movement? Cautious readers might seek the views of an independent expert when confronted with doubts about such a choice.

John Webster's credentials as professor of animal husbandry stand him in good stead to answer some of these questions. Webster seems to be in no doubt that animals are capable of both suffering pain, distress and anxiety and experiencing emotional states. His professional judgement explicitly contradicts the line taken by Leahy and the neo-Cartesians:

> Many animals, including those species whose lives we control the most demonstrate properties of mind which may be far less complex than ours but are sufficiently advanced to feel suffering and pleasure. Suffering occurs when the intensity or complexity of stresses exceeds or exhausts the capacity of the animal to cope, or when the animal is prevented from taking constructive action. Prolonged exposure to sources of suffering may induce abnormal behaviour patterns such as stereotypies or profound changes of mood, including the development of a sense of hopelessness (Webster, 1994:38).

Leahy may be wrong about nonhuman animal behaviour, but his views are in accord with moral orthodoxy. He notes that rats and mice (among the least loved animals) vastly outnumber all other species as laboratory animals and concedes that there is a strong case for banning the use of endangered chimpanzees (among the most charismatic of animals) in experiments despite the pressure of the AIDS lobby. The related issue of product testing puts rodents in a different light. Is it right to inflict pain and suffering on thousands of rats to test the safety of a new shoe polish or a more fragrant disinfectant? Leahy seems to put consumer interests before those of the animals when he expresses hostility to Regan's claim that the risk takers' interests should not be allowed to override the interests of animals to avoid pain and suffering. He does concede however that many pharmaceuticals, preservatives, insecticides and so on are harmful to both human and nonhuman animals and that it would be in our mutual interest to reduce the number of toxic materials that come onto the market every week.

Hunting Wild Animals

The third area covered by Leahy—zoos, field sports and furs—contains some of the remaining concerns of animal liberationists. Since zoos are not at the top of the list of grievances that concern animal protectionists, and hunting and trapping for furs are, I will focus on the latter, particularly blood sports which along with intensive farming and vivisection represent the trio of campaigns described in this book. Leahy is at his most contemptuous when it comes to protests against hunting, shooting and fishing. He claims that "much of the sound and fury seems to be generated more by a basic antipathy to the sorts of people who like to hunt and shoot and, in particular, by the fact that they do so for pleasure" (1991:244). While there may be a trace of class antagonism in the opposition to fox hunting in England, it is by no means the main reason for the opposition to blood sports there or elsewhere. Based on interviews with hunting opponents in the three case study countries, cruelty remains their main grievance.

In his discussion of our treatment of wild animals, John Webster is at pains to point out that his primary interest is to ascertain the impact of hunting and shooting on the welfare of the animals, not to moralise on the rights and wrongs of our actions in either rescuing or killing animals in the wild. He is unequivocal in concluding that the chasing of deer and hunting foxes with hounds is cruel (1994:222).

Yet Leahy does not accept that the animal liberation movement's central grievance against hunting is the cruelty inflicted on wild animals. It is axiomatic that for anyone to be able to make a reliable statement about the motives of animal liberationists, the views of the activists themselves must be sought. As is very common on this and other issues discussed thus far, some philosophers tend to rely on abstract reasoning or worse, pure speculation devoid of any empirical data. At the very least, Leahy ought to have acquainted himself with the independent assessment of animal behaviorists, not all of whom necessarily would come down on the side of the liberationists. Leahy's view that hunting is a form of pest control is in fact supported by Webster on the issue of fox hunting although he thinks hunting them may no longer be necessary in these gentler times (Webster 1994:219).

Leahy claims further that traditional field sports are good for conservation and that many hunters are motivated towards "not only the conservation of the species they pursue, but the maintenance of the unspoiled countryside in which they have their natural habitats" (1991:247). For animal liberationists, however, cruelty inflicted against individual animals takes priority over conservation, which leads them into conflict with their otherwise kindred spirits in the environmental movement. Leahy is dismissive of animal liberationist cruelty talk since nature herself is red in tooth and claw. He suggests that it is futile to view nature "as a state to be remedied" and suggests that to condemn the hunters for inflicting "a certain amount of necessary pain in the otherwise justifiable cause of field sports" is akin to condemning nature for the suffering of animals in the predatory wild.

Animal liberationists would respond that humans are among the rarest of creatures who engage in recreational violence and must be condemned for doing so. And unlike the wild animal that preys upon its fellows out of necessity, we are moral animals who have a choice. Leahy seems to think that hunters kill animals for several reasons including pleasure and that this is legitimate especially if it is provided with a cloak of respectability on *other* grounds, such as conservation. The respected sociologist Alan Wolfe, whose thesis I discuss next, does not need any techniques of rationalisation to defend human exploitation of other animals.

Alan Wolfe and Human Exceptionalism

Alan Wolfe's (1993) *The Human Difference: Animals, Computers, and the Necessity of Social Science* takes a similar anti-liberationist stance to Leahy's but from a distinctively sociological perspective. Wolfe is a proud speciesist who unblushingly manages to defend the worst excesses of anthropocentrism against what he sees as a dangerous anti- humanistic cosmology in the form of social movements concerned with ecological issues and animal rights. Wolfe's concerns about animal rights are worth examining in some detail.

According to Wolfe, one essential difference remains between us and other animals and that is our capacity for interpretation and the production of meaning. What makes us different, he suggests, is our power to use mind to alter the rules that govern us. Unlike animals, we have the capacity to create meaning in our lives which Wolfe acknowledges, does not come without unfairness: "Just as we experiment on animals to keep humans alive, we are sometimes cruel to animals in order to give our lives meaning" (1993:91).

Not just animal liberationists, but ordinary fair-minded people would be alarmed by Wolfe's bluntness and unblushing speciesism. He goes on to explain how meaning-producing creatures need to exploit less complex species in order to sustain their standard of living. As a consequence, there will be conflict between living by the principle of doing no harm and the desire to live "an imaginative and richly rewarding life" (1993:87). Animal experimentation is of central importance here since we sometimes use animals to keep us alive. And since we are nothing without life, animals genetically engineered to provide us with life-saving organs become our spare parts. Our ability to imaginatively recast the animal in this way in order to prolong our own lives is perhaps the most dramatic illustration to date of our total domination of other animals. While Wolfe does not specifically condone this example of speciesism, he would not rule it out if it made our lives richer and more meaningful. As one of the movements engaged in *putting nature first*, he sees the animal rights movement as a threat to the good life, so defined:

> Animal rights theorists (he cites Singer and Regan) are thus correct to detect certain patterns of cruelty in the way we use other species to make our own lives more rich with meaning. At the same time, if we were to revise the ways in which humans make meaning out of the natural world in such a way as never to be cruel to other animal species, we would live in a world without *fantasy, excitement, and creativity*" (1993:87 emphasis added).

Fantasy

Zoos and circuses are singled out by Wolfe as fulfilling symbolic roles in the lives of ordinary people. Zoos, he suggests, are not unlike poets. We can ban zoos in the way that Plato banned poets from the republic, but we would not necessarily be less cruel for doing so. Wolfe claims that children learn to develop their powers of imagination and fantasy by a visit to the zoo, a claim that is strenuously refuted by animal liberationists who suggest that what children learn about wild animals is "false and dangerous" (Jamieson 1985). Zoos tend to be seen as more benign than circuses since the circus animal has to be "trained" to perform unnatural tricks. Animal liberationists claim that this is evidence of extreme cruelty and oppose circuses for this reason. At the time of writing, 21 local government councils throughout Australia have banned circuses as a result of lobbying from the RSPCA and other animal welfarists.

Wolfe would view these developments as unwelcome since they strip the child "of one of the many symbols of the interpretative life that children have always experienced, and the likelihood is that, as adults, they will be more unfeeling rather than less" (1993: 88-9). A page later he is dismissive of animal rights advocates for believing that if we treat other animals with more respect, we might treat our fellow humans more respectfully. According to Wolfe, the opposite may well be true, although he omits to say how and appears to contradict himself when he recycles an old and unproven cliche that "those who love animals have problems with humans" (1993:85). Wolfe could be thinking here of some of the prominent Nazis, but it would be unreasonable to include most animal liberationists or people who keep pets or enjoy visiting animals in zoos and circuses in this rebuke.

Excitement

For many humans, especially those who live in big cities, the ultimate fantasy is to see animals in the wild. For many men and boys, however, the ultimate excitement is to hunt and kill wild animals. Were they to fantasise about killing their fellows, we would regard them as evil; on the other hand, the desire to hunt foxes or ducks or deer is viewed by many adults as deviant, but by no means criminal. Thus Wolfe is dismissive of Regan's (1983) observation that the oft-stated pleasures of hunting—

exercise, communication with nature, camaraderie, and the satisfaction of the well-aimed shot—could be satisfactorily replaced by the more gentle pursuit of bushwalking with a friend whose only weapon is a camera. What hunters seek, says Wolfe, are "the sensual pleasures of violent sport" (1993:89), a claim ominously echoed in Jack Katz's (1988) book *Seductions of Crime: The Moral and Sensual Attractions of Doing Evil.*

Creativity

Consider two ideas (1) because we are human, we are capable of creating our own worlds; and (2) human beings have always fantasised about living to a ripe old age without the inconvenience of illness or infirmity. Wolfe would no doubt approve of experimenting on animals if this was to help us combine these two ideas. Since animals are unable to think creatively, suggests Wolfe, and humans can, we are therefore entitled to use nature for our own pleasure and well-being. Wolfe fears that the animal rights and environmental movements represent "one more nail in the coffin of anthropocentrism" (1993:11). He makes no pretense of disguising his hostility towards animal rights and the kind of society the movement would spawn: "a society poor in imagination, imprisoned by logic, censorial toward evil, puritanical in outlook, and populated by those as lacking in appreciation of themselves as they are sensitive to the pains of others" (1993:91). This is not a description of Nazi Germany or of anti-Semitism, but of animal liberationists using their minds to eliminate the worst excesses of speciesism and anthropocentrism! This intemperate attack on animal rights by an anthropocentric leading sociologist is a good way to clear the air for the accounts of animal rights activism and advocacy in the remaining chapters.

REFERENCES

Appleyard, B. (1995) 'A Moral Life in this Godless World', *The Independent* 13 November: 19.

Barraclough, N., Neales, S. and Brew-Bevan, P. (1997) 'A Case of Neglect?', *Good Weekend, The Age* December 13, pp 16-23.

Benton, T.`(1992) ' Animal Rights and Wrongs: Prolegomena to a Debate', *Capitalism, Nature, Socialism: A Journal of Socialist Ecology* 3 (2) No. 10 June: 79-82.

Benton, T., and Redfearn, R. (1996) 'The Politics of Animal Rights: Where is the Left?' *New Left Review* 215: 43-58.

Cox, P. (1992) *The New Why You Don't Need Meat.* London: Bloomsbury Publishing Ltd.

Fiddes, M. (1991) *Meat: A Natural Symbol.* London: Routledge.

Finsen, L. and Finsen, S. (1994) *The Animal Rights Movement in America: From Compassion to Respect.* New York, Twayne Publishers.

Frey, R.G. (1983) *Rights, Killing and Suffering: Moral Vegetarianism and Applied Ethics.* Oxford: Basil Blackwell.

Frey, R.G. (1980) *Interests and Rights: The Case Against Animals.* Oxford: Clarendon Press.

George, K.P. (1994) 'Should Feminists be Vegetarians? *Signs* Winter: 405-34.

Groves, J. M (1995) 'Learning to Feel: The Neglected Sociology of Social Movements', *The Sociological Review* 43(3), pp 435-461.

Groves, J. M. (1997) *Hearts and Minds: The Controversy over Laboratory Animals.* Philadelphia, Temple University Press.

Hill, L. (1996) *The Case for Vegetarianism: Philosophy for a Small Planet.* Lanham, MD: Rowan and Littlefield Publishers.

Jamieson, D. (1985) 'Against Zoos' in P. Singer (ed.). *In Defense of Animals.* New York: Harper and Row Publishers.

Jamison, W and Lunch, W (1992) 'Rights of Animals, Perceptions of Science, and Political Activism: Profile of American Animal Rights Activists', *Science, Technology and Human Values* 17(4), Autumn, pp 438-458.

Jasper, J. and Nelkin, D. (1992) *The Animal Rights Crusade: The Growth of a Moral Protest.* New York, The Free Press.

Jasper, J and Poulsen, J. (1995) 'Recruiting Strangers and Friends: Moral Shocks and Social Networks in Animal Rights and Anti-Nuclear Protests', *Social Problems* 42(4), pp 493-512.

Johnson, A (1993) 'Review of M.Leahy's 'Against Liberation', *Anzccart News* 6 (4).

Katz, J. (1988) *Seductions of Crime: Moral and Sensual Attractions of Doing Evil,* New York, Basic.

Kennedy, J. S. (1992) *The New Anthropomorphism,* Cambridge, Cambridge University Press.

Leahy, M. (1991) *Against Liberation: Putting Animals in Perspective,* London: Routledge.

Masson, J. and McCarthy, S. (1995) *When Elephants Weep: The Emotional Lives of Animals.* New York: Delacorte Press.

Munro, L. (1996) *Mapping the Animal Movement: A Survey of Animal Rights and Welfare Advocates in Australia.* Paper Presented at the International Society of Anthrozoology Conference, Cambridge, Downing College, 24-26 July.

Nicoll, C. Russell, S. and Lau, A. (1992) 'Animal Liberation: An Exchange', *The New York Review,* 5 Nov, pp 59.

Regan, T. (1984) *The Case for Animal Rights,* Berkeley, University of California.

Regan, T. (1985) 'The Case for Animal Rights', in P. Singer (eds.), *In Defence of Animals,* New York, Harper & Row Publishers,

Regan, T. (1986) *The Struggle for Animal Rights,* International Society for Animal Rights, PA, Clarks Summit PA.

Robbins, J. (1987) *Diet for a New America.* Walpole, NH: Stillpoint Publishing.

Rodd, R. (1992) *Biology, Ethics and Animals* Oxford: Oxford University Press.

Rose, S. (1991) 'Proud to be Speciesist', *New Statesman and Society,* 26 April, p 21.

Rowan, A. (1989) 'Ethical Dilemmas in Experimentation:' in D. Paterson and M. Palmer (eds.), *The Status of Animals: Ethics, Education and Welfare.* Wallingford: CAB International.

Singer, P. (1975) *Animal Liberation: A New Ethic for Our Treatment of Animals*, New York: Jonathan Cape.

Tester, K. (1991) *Animals and Society: The Humanity of Animal Rights*, London, Routledge.

Webster, J. (1994) *Animal Welfare: A Cool Eye Towards Eden*, Oxford, Blackwell Science Ltd.

Wolfe, A. (1993) *The Human Difference: Animals, Computers and the Necessity of Social Science*, Berkeley, University of California Press.

Chapter 5

Framing Cruelty:

The Construction of Duck Shooting as a Social Problem

For the last decade conservationists have been confronting duck hunters on the wetlands of Victoria, the home of duck shooting in Australia. In 1986, a handful of protesters took on 90,000 shooters in an attempt to draw media attention to the alleged indiscriminate slaughter of Australian wildlife. In 1994, the number of shooters had fallen to 21,000 while the number of rescuers in the Coalition Against Duck Shooting (CADS) had risen to 300. The Coalition attributes the changing status of the duck-shooting fraternity to that of an endangered species to the success of its media campaign, particularly the television images which bring home to viewers every duck season the Coalition's anti-duck-shooting protest. This paper examines the way the Coalition's protest has been framed to attract media attention in ways that will promote its anti-duck-shooting cause.

Elsewhere (Munro, 1996) I have argued that the media both distort and reflect the Coalition's protest in ways which are, in the final analysis, advantageous to the anti-duck-shooting campaign. In this paper I want to explain how CADS, a small social movement organisation with limited financial resources, is able to mobilise public support against the much more powerful gun lobby. It does this by making its duck-rescue operation newsworthy and by shaping media discourse in ways which enhance its animal welfare/conservation message. This is a singular achievement given the central importance of media discourses in framing issues which can both help and hurt a social movement's campaign. Rootes succinctly explains the dilemma for social movement activists: "A movement may seek to exploit the media's insatiable appetite for novelty and spectacle, but no movement without a very broad social base and very considerable resources of power can hope to dictate the terms of the transaction or its outcome" (1984, p.6).

Nonetheless, some social movement organisations are more successful than others in shaping media discourse. As I show in this paper, CADS is one such activist group with a demonstrable record of success in influencing the media. How does it do this? According to Klandermans (1992, p.88), social movement organisations profoundly affect media discourse by framing the issues, defining the grievances and staging the collective actions that attract media attention. Coalition activists believe that this is how their relationship with the media works. Put simply, "man shoots duck" does not appeal to the media in the way that the metaphorical "duck (liberationist) shoots man" does. The Coalition has succeeded in making the images of duck rescue more compelling emotionally than the gun lobby's counter images of duck shooting as a manly, recreational outdoor sport. To understand how this is achieved, it is necessary to describe the protagonists and the background to what the media have dubbed the "Duck Wars".

Protagonists

There are three main protagonists in the "Duck Wars": Australia's native waterbirds, the shooters who hunt them and the animal liberationists and conservationists who seek to protect them.

The Rescuers

Before it officially formed in 1989, the Coalition's anti-duck-shooting campaign was conducted under the auspices of Animal Liberation Victoria which still serves as the Coalition's headquarters. Like Animal Liberation Victoria, CADS advocates non-violent direct action and is opposed to the more militant though non-violent tactics of its British and North American counterparts in the Hunt Saboteurs Association and the Coalition Against Sport Hunting. These animal liberation groups sabotage hunts and are often involved in confrontations with hunters. By contrast, the Victorian Coalition's tactics involve only minor harassment of duck shooters during duck-rescue operations; sabotage is limited to using whistles and sometimes light planes to frighten off the waterbirds and confiscating or retrieving injured birds but not attacking shooters or damaging their personal property.

In recent years, the Coalition has distanced itself organisationally from Animal Liberation Victoria, preferring its own loose, non-bureaucratic operational style to the latter's more formal committee structure. In this way it embodies the characteristics of "affinity groups" which are small groups of people, on average about 10, that autonomously decide the nature and extent of their participation in direct action (Sturgeon, 1995, p.39). Thus, while it is not affiliated with Animal Liberation Victoria, it subscribes to its philosophy as outlined by the latter's former President, Peter Singer (1975, 1990) and reflects the worldwide animal movement's focus as a "movement for social change based on issues of social justice and our moral duties to others" (Finsen and Finsen, 1994, p.281).

Native Waterbirds

Freckled Duck (Stictonetta naevosa) uniformly coloured with large (crested) head and dish-shaped bill. Male, uniform dark brown to black; head covered in small white or buff freckles. Female paler; obscure freckling (Simpson and Day, 1994: 58)

The freckled duck is one of the most endangered species of waterbird on the Victorian wetlands and a bird that features prominently in the Coalition's annual "casualty list" following the opening of the hunting season. It is also one of the 10 rarest waterfowl in the world and is therefore a suitable "representative" of the non-human animals in "Duck Wars".

In ancient times, ducks were seen as "prophets of the wind" an appropriate metaphor for the duck-rescue operation which has been described as the most action-packed, hands-on animal rights campaign in Australia (Action, 1994, p.10). The banning of duck shooting as a blood sport would be a major political and symbolic victory for animal liberationists in CADS who see the protection and rescue of wildlife as a social justice issue. Ducks, like other animals exploited by humans, represent "the suffering of innocents" (Jasper and Poulsen, 1995) which animal liberationists want to end.

The Hunters

Of the many pro-hunting groups that make up the gun lobby in Australia, the Sporting Shooters Association (SSA) is the most prominent in defending duck shooters. The SSA was first formed in 1948 and is Australia's largest firearms lobby group, with over 50,000 members. There are several other pro-gun and pro-hunting groups in Australia which claim the right to bear arms based on the conviction that hunting is a safe, legitimate and socially acceptable sport. About 80 per cent of Australia's estimated 132,000 licensed duck shooters live in Victoria, the home of Australian duck shooting.

But the image of hunting is clearly changing as one hunter lamented in the *Sporting Shooter* magazine:

> *Once we wore the White Hats and were heroes, a legacy perhaps of Hemingway and Ruark and the rest. (Today) we wear Black Hats, and our numbers are dwindling away. The pressure against us is unrelenting on every front. You'll try and avoid telling people about your hunting exploits. Years ago, people would listen enthralled; now you're a bloody disgrace, a social misfit who ought to be shot* (cited by Crook Ed. 1995, p.3).

In less dramatic terms the government in Western Australia banned duck shooting in 1990 and in Victoria, the government has recently extended the season. The *Age* newspaper's editorial in early 1993, much to the Coalition's delight, described duck shooting as an obscenity that should be outlawed.

Nonetheless, hunting devotees find occasional support in the published work of contemporary scholars and writers (see, for example, Ortega y Gasset, J, 1972; Leahy, 1991; Wolfe, 1993; Dizard, 1994). Of these defenders of the hunt, the sociologist Alan Wolfe argues the most provocative case. "Hunting", he acknowledges, "is no doubt cruel. But animal rights advocates lack appreciation for the symbolic meaning of human practices such as hunting. We are sometimes cruel to animals in order to give our lives meaning" (Wolfe, 1993, pp 89-91).

It is precisely hunting's association with societal violence involving firearms that is behind a growing community movement against violence. Yet for various reasons, the Coalition's campaign has not explicitly exploited the anti-gun sentiment. It has chosen to construct duck shooting as a social problem primarily because cruelty to animals is involved. While the hunters see ducks as mere objects, the rescuers regard them as "subjects who feel the world" to use Charles Birch's [1] apt description. A social constructionist approach will be used in this paper to explain how CADS constructs duck shooting as a social problem which has moral, legal and environmental implications for society.

The Social Construction of Duck Shooting as a Social Problem

Social constructionism has only recently been used as a theoretical framework for studying environmental and animal rights activists' claims in their defence of nature. Yearly (1992) and Hannigan (1995) used a social constructionist perspective to analyse environmental problems as social problems while Kunkel (1995) focused on factory farming as a case study in claims making by a social movement organisation.

These sociologists make a convincing case for studying the claims, the claims makers and the claims-making process in environmental and animal rights campaigns rather than the objective conditions of environmental degradation or animal exploitation per se. Social constructionists emphasise the subjective dimensions of social problems which put the claims people make, not the putative objective conditions, at the centre of the analysis.

According to Best (1995), contextual constructionists recognise that claims emerge at particular historical moments in particular societies. For example, (Kunkel 1995) shows how the Farm Animal Reform Movement (FARM) appealed to a wider audience by expanding the domain of the factory farming problem beyond animal suffering and cruelty to include issues of human health and the environment which appealed directly to people's self-interest. Social movement organisations in the animal rights movement like FARM and CADS may choose different strategies and tactics to achieve their goals but within the social constructionist perspective, the process of claims making is essentially the same.

According to Hannigan (1995), the process involves the three central tasks of assembling, presenting and contesting claims. Assembling claims involves discovering and naming the problem (e.g. duck shooting is morally, legally and environmentally reprehensible); presenting claims means that the campaigners have to command attention and legitimate their claims (e.g. CADS has promoted its media campaign as a duck-rescue operation which is more newsworthy than an anti-hunting protest); finally, contesting claims is about invoking action and mobilising support

---

[1] Charles Birch is an eminent Australian scientist and author of *Regaining compassion for humanity and nature* (1993) and *Feelings* (1995). He used the phrase in a radio broadcast to promote his latest book.

(e.g. CADS has used a rescue frame and dramatic television images to appeal to the better instincts of potential supporters).

Core Framing Tasks

Using a framework similar to Hannigan's, Snow and Benford (1988) identify three main tasks for social movement organisations: diagnostic, prognostic and motivational framing. Diagnostic framing identifies some condition or event as problematic; in the Coalition's case, the diagnosis that duck shooting is wrong, is based on the claim that it is morally, legally and environmentally unjust. The prognosis is closely linked to the diagnosis; the prognostic task is to spell out what is to be done to solve the problem. For the activists in CADS this means identifying strategies and tactics which will result in the banning of duck shooting.

Thus, in its diagnostic and prognostic framing work, the Coalition has to make a successful claim that duck shooting is wrong and then to do something about it. In the Snow and Benford model, the third task, motivational framing, involves the Coalition in mobilising support for its cause. Motivational framing is an "elaborate call to arms or a *rationale for action* that goes beyond the diagnosis and prognosis" (Snow and Benford, 1988, p. 202).

For CADS, the key mobilising strategy is to use the mass media, principally the electronic media, to promote its campaign as a rescue operation rather than a conventional animal rights/conservation protest. Television coverage is crucially important to the Coalition; CADS has hired the services of a media monitoring agency, Rehame Australia, which provides it with summary reports and video recordings of radio and television coverage of issues related to their campaign. Activists study these reports, particularly television footage, with a view to improving their campaign tactics. Likewise, their opponents in the Sporting Shooters Association are understood to make use of Rehame Australia's services. For the protagonists, the public relations battle is a respectability contest waged through the electronic media.

The Rehame news stories (n=46) and features (n=4) which tell the story of "Duck Wars" represent a visual record of the two duck shooting seasons in 1993 and 1994 [2]. For Coalition activists, television's representation of their protest is the most potent weapon they have in their campaign to outlaw duck shooting. What is important in this paper is to show how the Coalition constructs duck shooting as a social problem by attending to the framing tasks suggested by Snow and Benford (1988) and more recently by Hannigan (1995).

---

[2] There was no official duck hunting season in 1995 because of the effects of a prolonged drought.

Diagnostic Frame: Assembling Claims

The Coalition's campaign literature gives three main reasons for its anti-duck-shooting protest: (1) cruelty; (2) rare and protected birds are illegally shot; and (3) lead pollution damages the environment (Levy, 1989:6). It is unusual for an animal rights group to base its animal advocacy on mainly environmental grounds; in its opposition to duck shooting, only cruelty is explicitly an animal welfare issue, albeit the most important one in the Coalition's defence of wildlife. The Coalition claims that up to 30 per cent of the birds shot by hunters are crippled and die a slow and painful death.

The argument against cruelty makes it possible for the Coalition to base its diagnostic framing on moral grounds by calling upon widespread public sentiment in favour of kindness to animals. The environmental arguments against duck shooting broaden the Coalition's diagnostic frame to include conservation (of protected species) and ecological (lead pollution) concerns without diminishing its animal liberationist objective. Activists argue that lead pellets do not discriminate between game and protected birds, and even government authorities acknowledge that the birds die a painful death after digesting the pellets. Cruelty, therefore, remains the Coalition's central grievance against duck shooting and remains the single most important motivation for activism, as one activist explained:

> *people recognise cruelty as cruelty. There's no excuse for cruelty, I can't think of one. Our society and just about all religions don't accept cruelty. That's a good basis for an organisation* (Interview 9, 22 December 1994, p.3).

The Coalition's campaign director, Laurie Levy, argues that it is partly the reaction of the duck shooters' children to animal cruelty that has caused the average shooter to relinquish the gun:

> *I don't know how many duck shooters over the years have told me that: 'It wasn't you that stopped me, it was my kids.' And again, that's the power of the media at work* (Interview 4, 18 October 1994, p.6).

The Coalition's critique of duck shooting as "a cruel, cowardly, violent and anti-social act and very much a male macho activity" (Levy, 1989) strikes a responsive chord in a society weary of violence. Under these circumstances, it is not difficult for Coalition claims makers to convince potential supporters that compassion and non-violence are better alternatives to the cruelty towards animals and environmental damage that duck shooting represents. And television is the medium best suited to communicating this message for as Roshco (1975, p.101) points out, "a symbolic protest is news management by the socially invisible" (quoted in Kielbowicz and Scherer 1986).

Prognostic Frame: Presenting Claims

In prognostic framing, the social movement organisation specifies what is to be done about the grievance identified in the diagnosis. Snow and Benford (1988, p. 20) point out how prognostic framing is meant not only to suggest solutions, but to identify strategies, tactics and targets as well. To be successful in their claims making activities, social movement organisations depend heavily on the print and electronic media for publicising their grievances and keeping them visible (McCarthy, 1994). For the Coalition, the promotion of its cause via the media is part of its strategic thinking rather than one of its tactics. Media coverage is the Coalition's prognosis of how it can most effectively discredit duck shooting and literally disarm its adherents.

Rochon (1990) argues that a social movement's power is determined by its militancy, size and novelty while according to Koopmans (1993), militancy is the most direct power since radical protests, especially when they are violent, invariably attract media attention. The Coalition's strategy of non-violent opposition to duck shooting and its small size relative to the gun lobby suggest that without the novelty of "duck rescue", its campaign would have little appeal to the electronic media. One activist pointed out how

> *the visual pictures of what we do are far stronger than reading it in black and white or hearing about it on a radio; nothing could compare to those (television) pictures, particularly some of the media we've had where they'd be followed up with the wounded birds and shown them being rehabilitated. Things like that, it touches most people* (Interview 7, 15 November 1994, p.11).

And according to Gamson et al (1992, p.374), television images are a more subtle form of meaning construction than facts or information. Cottle (1993, p 131) also emphasises the importance of television news "at a deeper cultural level in which widespread, if rarely articulated, structures of feeling towards nature and the environment are mobilised". What people see and feel are typically more important than what they read or think. While the demands of concision (Herman and Chomsky, 1988) ensure that the complex arguments of animal rights are rarely or even superficially addressed in the media, the emotive issue of animal cruelty is nonetheless effectively conveyed in the graphic images of "Duck Wars". As Levy points out:

> *Two pictures come out of every season—a hunter dressed as a soldier carrying a semi-automatic and shooting at a defenceless bird. Or there is the single image of a rescuer coming out with a wounded bird. The second of concern and compassion will always beat an image of violence* (Levy, 1994).

In relying on the media as its main prognostic tool, the Coalition, in common with other interest groups which utilise the mass media in their causes, runs the risk of its message being distorted. Several theorists have warned activists of the dangers inherent in media-driven campaigns (Rootes, 1984; Herman and Chomsky, 1988; Gamson 1992; Tarrow, 1994). As a former television cameraman, Levy understands how the medium works as well as how to exploit the camera to the best advantage. In this, the Coalition is perhaps unique as a social movement organisation in that its leader is a former media professional adept at using the media.

As the main strategy in its anti-duck-shooting protest, the Coalition's objective is to use the media against the interests of the gun lobby. One very revealing result of the Coalition's success in "Duck Wars" is that in the 1993 and 1994 video coverage its representatives were responsible for 18 percent of the spoken lines compared to 8 per cent for the hunters and their spokespersons. The fact that the Coalition has achieved more than twice the air time available to its opponents suggests that it has been successful in framing its objection to duck shooting as a social justice issue— with moral, legal and environmental dimensions that have wide appeal for the viewing public. Gamson et al (1992) argue that the media are an arena for symbolic contests in which participants measure success or failure not by how the messages are read by the audience, but by their prominence in the news and how well media discourse tells the story they want told. The Coalition Against Duck Shooting believes its narrative of "Duck Wars" is favourably represented in news broadcasts and feature stories. In choosing to frame its collective action as a rescue operation rather than a conventional anti-hunting or animal rights protest (as with the Hunt Saboteurs), the Coalition has guaranteed media interest and hence the opportunity for mobilising support for its cause.

Motivational Frame: Contesting Claims

In Snow and Benford's (1988) model, the third task motivational framing is how the social movement organisation mobilises people to take action on behalf of its cause. Motivational framing is essentially "a call to arms". For the Coalition, the key mobilising strategy is to frame their campaign as a duck-rescue operation since the notion of rescue resonates well in a culture which values kindness to animals and where the connotations of saving (animals') lives in the tradition of the Red Cross strikes a responsive chord. Levy frequently invokes the metaphor of a "war zone", especially during the pre-season build-up to the campaign:

> *We'll be in the water with the hunters at first light and we'll be going about our job of rescuing wounded birds. I see our role as being similar to the Red Cross; we go into a war zone to help the innocent victims* (Levy on camera, ABC National Television, 18 March 1994).

As a public relations exercise, duck rescue has an appeal which a conventional political protest, say against the gun lobby, does not. Furthermore, the idea of duck liberation is sufficiently novel to attract media and public attention. The task for the Coalition is to frame their anti-duck-shooting protest in a way that will motivate people to participate and not alienate potential sympathisers.

The motivation for participation in the campaign, as in the larger animal rights movement, is framed in terms of social justice and rights discourse. The animal rights movement is primarily a moral protest on behalf of animals (Jasper and Nelkin, 1992). Peter Singer's *Animal Liberation* (1975, 1990) provides many activists worldwide with an ethical basis for their non-violent, direct action against cruelty towards animals. The book is a clarion call for people, individually and collectively, to protest against the exploitation of animals specifically in factory farming and animal experimentation. *Animal Liberation* is both a philosophical treatise on and a practical guide to how we should treat animals. In the case of hunting, Singer (1995) elsewhere sees hunting as the ultimate form of speciesism in contrast to hunters who claim that it is essential for good conservation (Dizard, 1994). For the Coalition, the challenge is to produce motivational frames that will inspire people to speak out against duck shooting. Motivation is a prerequisite for action mobilisation:

> For people to take action to overcome a collectively perceived problem or 'injustice', they must develop a set of compelling reasons for doing so. Motivational framing addresses this need (and) entails the social construction and avowal of motives and identities of protagonists (Hunt, Benford and Snow, 1994, p.191).

Images of Duck Shooting in the Media

According to Snow and Benford (1988), motivational frames function as "prods to action". Jasper (1990) argues that animal rights activists use "moral shocks" to propel people into action on behalf of animals. As a moral protest, the animal rights movement must tread a delicate path for fear of alienating potential sympathisers who may not be up to occupying the high moral ground which a fully ethical treatment of animals demands. As a primarily hands-on, activist group, the Coalition is careful to avoid the moralistic language of their more radical colleagues in the movement and opts for a motivational frame based on dramatic images of duck rescue.

In a paper by Jasper and Poulsen (1995), the authors argue that Snow and Benford do not show in detail how framing occurs because they implicitly assume recruitment to movements is via personal networks of those who share the activists' underlying world views. Jasper and Poulsen (1995) claim that in the case of animal rights protests at least, this assumption may be unfounded. Their study suggests that moral shocks rather than pre-existing social networks are more salient in the recruitment of animal rights supporters. The most important single factor in their recruitment was found to be reading followed by a combined category which included reading, listening and watching television. According to Jasper and Poulsen (1995), animals have extraordinary potential as condensing symbols which they define as "verbal or visual images that neatly capture both cognitively and emotionally a range of meanings and convey a frame, a master frame, or theme". They point out how images such as caged puppies are presented by protest organisers as a "suffering of innocents" master frame in order to convey the "moral shock" needed for the first stage in the recruitment of strangers. Television news stories and features are well equipped to produce these kinds of images. It is for these reasons that the Coalition uses the electronic media as an indispensable resource in its recruitment of strangers.

For the Coalition, cruelty is the master frame which it believes resonates most with the media and the general public. This is clearly illustrated in some of the television footage following the opening of the duck season when the Coalition ritualistically and symbolically displays dead and injured birds as spectacles of suffering in public places. An example from a television news item which was the second story in the bulletin and ran for two minutes is included below:

Table 5.1
Excerpt of footage from a TV report on the "Duck Wars"

Laurie Levy (CADS): This is a very young signet and obviously it can't fly, yet it had been shot through the neck.	*Levy holds a dead bird to the camera while other protesters display dead birds outside the Victorian Premier's office. In the background are members of the public and camera crews are filming the scene.*
Reporter: Predictably the annual display of protected birds following the opening of duck season in the wake of last weekend's shoot-out, 115 birds including swans and rare freckled ducks were dumped outside the Premier's office. They were collected mainly from Lake Buloke just outside Donald in central Victoria where a surprisingly small number of hunters, perhaps no more than 2000, battled it out against an increasing number of protesters.	*Shot of dozens of dead birds on the footpath; some are held up to the camera by different protesters. The dead birds are carefully lined up in the fashion of the war dead and in keeping with the Coalition's designation of the wetlands as a "war zone". A large bloodstain is clearly visible on the footpath. Cross to a lake scene where a shooter carries a dead bird from the water, and another successfully downs a duck which skims across the water as it falls. The shooter wades out to collect the bird as three rescuers two female and one male follow in hot pursuit.*

Laurie Levy (CADS):	
Duck shooting is not a sport and that's why duck hunter numbers are dropping; the public perceives duck shooting now as being an anti-social, male, macho activity and duck shooting is coming to an end.	*Levy appears in close-up outside the Premier's office to invoke the image of duck shooting as a shameful activity.*

Source: Analysis (1994), Story 19, "Fine Fight", ATV10 TV News, 5.00 pm, 21 March. The left-hand column is taken from the news stories while the italicised comments on the right are the author's.

Snow and Benford (1988) argue that a successful campaign must be relevant to people's lived experience or "plausibility structures", to use Jasper and Poulsen's (1995) terminology. For these reasons the Coalition was particularly pleased with the favourable coverage it received in an early morning feature program (*Good Morning Australia*), which boasts an audience of many thousands. The story is unique in that the presenter is unashamedly on the side of the duck liberationists as her opening remarks indicate. As the report continues, the pro-animal slant gets stronger with an anthropomorphic reference to waterbirds who "talk to one another" and an anti-hunting stance made explicit with references to "this extraordinary assault" on "the unsuspecting victims of this bloody sport".

In this program the presenter (Michelle) interviews Claire, an animal activist who runs an animal shelter. It is the longest story (7 minutes, 15 seconds) in the entire 1993-94 coverage totalling 50 stories (46 news stories and four feature stories). This excerpt is worth quoting at length since it captures the message and images the Coalition seeks to promote in its relationship with the media:

Table 5.2
Excerpt of footage from a TV report on the "Duck Wars"

Michelle:	
Dawn, all over Victoria the wetlands resound with the noises of a ritual older than mankind itself. Waterbirds awake, talk to one another and reaffirm their territory before taking flight into the new day. One morning of the year, this peace and tranquillity is shattered in the name of sport, when thousands of shooters open fire, releasing several hundred tons of toxic lead into our environment whilst killing and maiming thousands of our native waterfowl. To be here and experience this extraordinary assault on our environment can be likened only to a war zone, except in this war, only one side is armed. For eight years now, animal welfare groups have been making their annual pilgrimage to the wetlands. Confrontations like this are a familiar sight, with rescuers tolerating the most extreme conditions in order to alleviate what pain and suffering they can for the unsuspecting victims of this bloody sport. While hundreds of rescuers are braving the elements out on the wetlands, people like Claire Davies are on call 24 hours a day to receive the injured and the shocked.	*Atmospheric music (not used in news bulletins) suggests a mood of tranquillity. The scene is of a golden sky at sunrise filled with water birds: the lake reflects the yellow sun as a flock of birds flies above in close formation. Gunshots ring out on the reporter's mention of "shattered" tranquillity. Shooters fire skywards as a bird falls to the ground. Rescuers look on from the shore. A shooter wrings the neck of one bird as heavily armed hunters and their dogs cruise the lake in their motor boats. A lone shooter dressed in battle fatigue and armed with a shotgun loaded with cartridges surveys "the war zone". Levy points angrily at one shooter and approaches him armed only with his walkie-talkie. He confronts a middle-aged shooter who challenges Levy's right to be on the water. The next image is of Levy loaded up with injured birds as he attempts to return to shore. He slips and falls as he does so. On shore, he displays several dead birds to the media. Cross to the animal shelter at Berwick, outside of Melbourne. The reporter, speaking in hushed tones, introduces Davies who is holding a small, injured bird which has an attractive white and brown head and black wings.*

Source: Analysis (1993), Story V, "Wildlife Rehabilitation", Good Morning Australia, 22 March. The left-hand column is taken from the feature story while the italicised comments on the right are the author's.

Feature stories of this kind are seen as instrumental in the Coalition's mobilisation campaigns. Activists claim that dozens of people phone their headquarters offering support following favourable television coverage of their protest. There can be no doubt that the mistreatment of animals domestic and wild strikes an emotional chord with most people.

Animal rights philosophers are aware of the importance of emotions in mobilising support for the movement. Tom Regan put it most succinctly when he wrote: "Philosophy can lead the mind to water but only emotion can make it drink" (1986, p40). And as I have argued, television is the quintessential medium for maximising emotion and therefore a powerful resource for social movement activists. Yet sociologists have tended to neglect the role of emotions in social movements (Groves, 1995).

In the Coalition's case, duck liberationists have successfully exploited a medium not available to earlier generations of animal liberators. Furthermore, they have used emotion in a way this is perhaps unique to the modern animal rights movement. According to Groves (1995, pp 458-9), in the animal rights movement today, the emotional rubric of justice and rights for animals represent a break from its nineteenth century counterpart in the humane tradition (since) emotions in the animal rights movement took on a different meaning when men, as opposed to women, adopted them; sympathy or caring for defenceless victims became objective, rational and legitimate.

Groves points out that men's participation was a useful resource for overcoming the emotional deviance experienced by most of the activists in his study.

There is an element of this in the Coalition's media campaign which has effectively deviantised duck shooting as an anti-social, "male, macho activity" thereby legitimating duck rescue as the compassionate alternative. Whether the changing meaning of emotions can be attributed to men's participation in the duck rescue operation is not clear since the majority of rescuers are women. And Laurie Levy is careful to avoid gender connotations when he describes the potent television images that he claims ensure the success of the Coalition's campaign:

> *Two pictures come out of every season a hunter dressed as a soldier carrying a semi-automatic weapon and shooting a defenceless bird. Or there is the simple image of a rescuer coming out with an injured bird* (Levy, 1994).

Here Levy identifies the three main protagonists in the "Duck Wars" without any specific reference to gender although the images themselves reveal that the duck shooters are all men, and the rescuers are mostly women.

I have argued that the CADS campaign is a case study in the management of emotions and emotions are explicit in the key tasks identified by Hannigan (1995) for constructing social problems. First, in assembling claims about duck shooting, the Coalition diagnosed the problem as primarily a moral issue involving the rights of sentient beings not to be cruelly slaughtered or injured. Cruelty, and its opposite, kindness, are clearly concepts which provoke emotional reactions in people. Second, in presenting its campaign largely via the media, the Coalition has succeeded in making "duck rescue by duck liberationists" newsworthy. Finally, in contesting the rights and wrongs of duck shooting, the motivational frame adopted by CADS centred on the idea of rescue with its specific appeal to compassion towards non-human beings.

As noted above, animals are unique in symbolising both cognitively and emotionally, a range of meanings for humans. For many people, however, television images of duck shooting as an anti-social, cruel sport strike an emotional chord. The moral shocks associated with the sight of injured and slaughtered birds ensure that attitude change takes place at an emotional rather than cognitive level which for the Coalition Against Duck Shooting makes television its most potent ally in the construction of duck shooting as a social problem.

REFERENCES

Action. (1994). Duck rescue: Saving lives and changing attitudes. *Animal Liberation Magazine, 47*, 10-11.

Analysis. (1993, 1994). Television news and current affairs on the 1993 and 1994 duck shooting season and the protests against it, Unpublished transcripts of the television coverage filmed by Rehame Australia, Melbourne.

Best, J. (1995). *Images of issues: Typifying contemporary social problems.* New York: Aldine de Gruyter.

Cottle, S. (1993). Mediating the environment: Modalities of TV news. In Anders Hansen (Ed) *The mass media and environmental issues*, Leicester: Leicester University.

Crook, J. (Ed) (1995). *Hunting: A critical perspective*, published by Gun Control Australia: Melbourne.

Dizard, J.E. (1994). *Going wild: Hunting, animal rights and the contested meaning of nature*, Amherst: University of Massachusetts.

Finsen, L. & Finsen, S. (1994). *The animal rights movement in America: From compassion to respect*, New York: Twayne Publishers.

Gamson, W. (1992). *Talking politics*, Cambridge: Cambridge University.

Gamson, W. Croteau, D. Hoynes, W. & Sasson, T. (1992). Media images and the social construction of reality. *Annual Review of Sociology, 18*; 373-393.

Groves, J. McAllister. (1995). Learning to feel: The neglected sociology of social movements. *The Sociological Review, 43*, 3, 435-461.

Hannigan, J. (1995). *Environmental sociology: A social constructionist perspective*, London: Routledge.

Herman, E. & Chomsky, N. (1988). *Manufacturing consent: The political economy of the mass media*, New York: Pantheon Books.

Hunt, S.A, Benford, R.D & Snow, D.A. (1994). Identity fields: Framing processes and the social construction of movement identities. In Enrique Larana, Hank Johnston and Joseph Gusfield (Eds)., *New social movements: From ideology to identity* (pp. 185-208). Philadelphia: Temple University.

Interviews. (1994). *Animal liberationists and their campaigns*. Transcripts of unpublished interviews with members of Animal Liberation Victoria: Melbourne, Australia.

Jasper, J. (1990). Moral dimensions of social movements. Paper presented at the *American Sociological Association* annual meeting, December 1990, 1-27.

Jasper, J. & Nelkin, D. (1992). *The animal rights crusade: The growth of a moral protest*, New York: The Free Press.

Jasper, J. & Poulsen, J. (1995). Recruiting strangers and friends: Moral shocks and social networks in animal rights and anti-nuclear protests. *Social Problems, 42*, No. 4, 493-512.

Katz, J. (1988). *Seductions of crime: Moral and sensual attractions of doing evil*, New York: Basic Books.

Kielbowicz, R.B. and Scherer, C. (1986). The role of the press in the dynamics of social movements. In K. Lang, G. Engel Lang and L. Kriesberg (Eds). *Research in Social Movements, Conflicts, and Change* (pp. 71-96). Connecticut: JAI Press Inc.

Klandermans, B. (1992). The social construction of protest and multi organisational fields. In A. D Morris and C. McClurg Mueller (Eds). *Frontiers in social movement theory* (pp. 77-103). New Haven: Yale University.

Koopmans, R. (1993). The dynamics of protest waves. *American Sociological Review, 58*, 637-658.

Kunkel, K. (1995). Down on the farm: Rationale expansion in the construction of factory farming as a social problem. In J. Best (Ed)., *Images of issues: Typifying contemporary social problems* (pp. 239-256). Aldine de Gruyter.

Leahy, M. (1991). *Against liberation: Putting animals in perspective*, London: Routledge.

Levy, L. (1989). *Weapons and violence in Australia: Towards an end to gun lobby violence against Australia's native waterbirds*. A submission to Gun Control Australia from the Director, Coalition Against Duck Shooting: Melbourne.

Levy, L. (1994). It's Laurie Levy season. *La Trobe University Newspaper*, feature interview with Laurie Levy, March 1994. Melbourne: La Trobe University.

Levy, L. (1994). *Interview 4*, Animal liberationists and their campaigns. Unpublished transcript of interviews with activists in Animal Liberation Victoria, 18 October: Melbourne.

McCarthy, J.D. (1994). Activists, authorities and media framing of drunk driving. In E. Larana, H. Johnston and J. Gusfield (Eds)., *New social movements: From ideology to identity* (pp. 133-167). Philadelphia: Temple University Press.

Munro, L. (1993-94). A decade of animal liberation. *Current affairs bulletin, 70*, No. 7, 12-19, Sydney: WEA of NSW in association with the University of Sydney.

Munro, L. (1996). Narratives of protest: Television's representation of an animal liberation campaign. *Media International Australia* (forthcoming).

Ortega y Gasset, J. (1972). *Meditations on hunting*, trans. Scribner's: New York: H B Wescot.

Regan, T. (1983). *The case for animal rights*, Berkeley: University of California.

Regan, T. (1986). *The struggle for animal rights*, International Society for Animal Rights, Inc, PA: Clarks Summit.

Rochon, T. R. (1990). The west European peace movement and the theory of new social movements. In R. Dalton and M. Kuechler (eds). *Challenging the political order: new social and political movements in western democracies* (pp. 105-121). Cambridge: Polity Press.

Rootes, C. (1984). Protest, social movements, revolution. *Social Alternatives, 4,* 1, 4-8.

Simpson, K. and Day, N. (1994). *Field guide to the birds of Australia*, London: Christopher Helm, Ltd.

Singer, P. (1975, 1990). *Animal liberation: a new ethic for our treatment of animals*, London: Jonathan Cape.

Singer, P. (1995). Guns and animals: An animal liberation perspective. In J. Crook (Ed). *Hunting: A critical perspective* (pp. 68-72). Melbourne: Gun Control Australia Inc.

Snow, D. A. and Benford, R. D. (1988). Ideology, frame resonance and participant mobilisation. In B. Klandermans, H. Kriesi and S. Tarrow (eds). *From structure to action: comparing social movement research across cultures* (pp. 197-217). International Social Movement Research, a Research Annual, Greenwich, Connecticut: JAI Press Inc, 197-217.

Sturgeon, N. (1995). Theorising movement: Direct action and direct theory. In M. Darnovsky, B. Epstein and R. Flacks (Eds). *Cultural politics and social movements*, Philadelphia: Temple University.

Tarrow, S. (1994). *Power in movement: social movements, collective action and politics*, Cambridge: Cambridge University.

Wolfe, A. (1993). *The human difference: Animals, computers and the necessity of social science*, Berkeley: University of California.

Yearley, S. (1992). *The green case: A sociology of environmental issues, arguments and politics*, London: Routledge.

Chapter 6

The Live Animal Export Controversy in Australia:
A Moral Crusade Made for the Mass Media

On 31 May 2011 the Australian Broadcasting Commission's (ABC) *Four Corners* programme broadcast 'A Bloody Business', a 45-minute exposé which revealed the brutal treatment of Australian cattle in a number of Indonesian abattoirs at the killing end of the live animal export trade. Lyn White (Animals Australia) provided the ABC with disturbing images of animal cruelty in a number of Indonesian slaughter houses which *Four Corners* corroborated with their own footage and reporting. The public's reaction of shock and outrage was so intense that the Australian government imposed a temporary ban on the trade to Indonesia.

Voiceovers in the *Four Corners* report described how the cattle in the abattoirs were forced to slip on the wet, faeces-covered cement floor, some breaking their legs while others had their eyes gouged out, their tails broken and their bodies kicked and beaten by frustrated workers. Industry representatives claimed to have been horrified by what they saw in the programme despite evidence of the trade's cruelty produced by animal activists for close on two decades and the meat industry's pledges to reform the trade and improve conditions for the animals.

The programme, watched by about 500,000 viewers, caused an unprecedented public reaction of anger accompanied by demands from animal protectionists in Animals Australia and the Royal Society for the Prevention of Cruelty to Animals (RSPCA) for an immediate ban on the trade. In the aftermath of the *Four Corners* report the long-running crusade led by Animals Australia and the RSPCA seemed to be on the verge of success; however, after just a few weeks, media and public interest in the issue gradually declined with the government lifting the ban on 6 July.

The stalled campaign was due to a number of factors including (1) the indignant backlash from a mainly rural constituency supported by sections of the conservative print media, (2) the capitulation of the Australian government to these pressures and (3) the activists' inability to strike the right balance between emotion and persuasive argumentation in this classic 'hot cognition' (Gamson, 1992) protest. The last point is especially important; it is the major weakness in the activists' strategy that the article describes and for which social movement theory offers a solution via the idea of academic and activist collaboration.

My position on animal protection is as an academic advocate for animal rights rather than as an activist. I have described the animal protection movement as consisting of four main strands: the mainstream animal welfare, liberation and rights groups and outsiders in the Radical Animal Liberation Movement (RALM) (see Munro, 2012). These distinctions are important and are usually not recognised by the movement's critics who denounce 'animal people' as social deviants and misfits (Kew, 1999). The issue of animal rights extremism was raised at various times during the live export controversy in an attempt to discredit those responsible for the *Four Corners* exposé. To the average citizen, however, Lyn White, the RSPCA's chief scientist Dr Bidda Jones and reporter Sarah Ferguson were more likely to have been perceived as 'caring sleuths' (Shapiro, 1994) rather than as extremists, a term that arguably should only be applied to RALM activists outside the mainstream movement.

My advocacy is along the lines of Singer's (1990) pragmatic notion of animal liberation which occupies the middle ground between the welfarist preference for regulation via legislation and the strict abolitionist goals of animal rights. I cannot claim to have the emotional involvement or the commitment of White and Jones, nor have I experienced in situ the horrors of the Indonesian slaughterhouses which Krien (2011) describes in her much-praised ethnography in the *Quarterly Essay*. However, I am in favour of activist/scholar collaboration along the lines suggested by Bevington & Dixon (2005) and have written this article with both an academic and activist audience in mind. In doing so, I have utilised both the electronic and print media including the *Four Corners* transcript (2011) and related timelines provided by the activist groups (Appendix 1) and an analysis of the public's response to the controversy (Appendix 2). The list of references also includes relevant academic sources on social movements, media communication studies and the animal protection movement. Email correspondence with Glenys Oogjes, Animal Australia's CEO, and the RSPCA's Dr Bidda Jones is also included in the paper.

In what follows, I analyse the risks and opportunities for social movements in their interactions with the mass media and how the activists in the present case study succeeded in having their gruesome images of animal suffering broadcast to a large viewing audience. I discuss the power of television images and how they affect the emotions of viewers along with an account of the emotions that typically drive activists and movement supporters in campaigns such as in the present case study. The live animal export trade is an emotive issue which I analyse using frameworks developed by Gamson & Wolfsfeld (1993). I describe how and why the initial success of the campaign against the trade quickly petered out despite the sympathetic television presentation of the activists' grievances and the public's strong support for the activists' campaign. The idea of scholar-activist collaboration is suggested as a way of enhancing a social movement theorist's appreciation of 'activist wisdom' (Maddison & Scalmer, 2006) and improving an activist's understanding and application of relevant social movement concepts and theory including the importance of winning the support of the mass media.

Taking the Lead in the Media's 'Dance of Death'

A common contention in the social movement literature is that movements are usually much more dependent on the mass media than the media are for the drama and spectacle often provided by protest movements (Gamson & Wolfsfeld, 1993); furthermore, several theorists have warned social movement activists that they have a lot to lose in any media driven campaign (Gamson, 1992; Herman & Chomsky, 1988; Rootes, 1984; Tarrow, 1994). Rootes succinctly sums up these risks as follows:

> A movement may seek to exploit the media's insatiable appetite for novelty and spectacle, but no movement without a very broad social base and very considerable resources of power can hope to dictate the terms of the transaction or its outcome. (1984, p. 6)

In Van Zoonen's (1996) apt phrase, social movements and the mass media engage in 'a dance of death', a dance where the media are the dominant partner. It is for this reason that social movement scholars at the Media Research and Action Project (MRAP) in Boston have assisted more than 200 social movement organisations (SMOs) in pressing their claims using frame analysis as a tool to promote their clients' causes (Ryan, Carragee, & Meinhofer, 2001).

Unlike prominent international SMOs such as Greenpeace, community and activist groups rarely have the cultural and economic resources to mount campaigns that capture the attention of the mass media, hence the importance of scholar-activists in organisations like MRAP. As is well known, Greenpeace activists produce their own dramatic footage which they pass on to mass media outlets that will then in many cases broadcast dramatic images to a large viewing or reading audience. In the present case study, the activists were successful, at least initially, in convincing some major media organisations in the print and electronic media to promote their campaign by broadcasting their footage and by reporting the scandal of animal cruelty.

As Klandermans (1992, p. 88) contends, SMOs have a profound effect on media discourse by defining and framing their grievances to attract media attention. Television stories, both visual and verbal, are seen as powerful ways to attract the viewer's attention (Patterson & McClure, 1976) and activists who understand media rituals and values are most likely to run successful campaigns (Kielbowicz & Scherer, 1986). Furthermore, social movement scholars have observed how animal images convey both cognitively and emotionally a range of meanings such as 'the suffering of innocents' intended to generate a 'moral shock' (Jasper & Poulsen, 1995) and thus to recruit ordinary people to the animal protection cause.

Making Animal Suffering Visible

For close on 20 years, Animals Australia and the RSPCA have been involved in many public and media presentations that drew attention to the cruelty of the live export trade. However, these appeals had not induced the industry to insist on their trading partners raising their animal welfare standards. As a consequence, the film-makers believed they had the responsibility to make their gruesome footage available to the ABC's *Four Corners* in the hope that broadcasting the 'bloody business' would motivate the public to demand a ban on the trade. That Australian animals were being gratuitously tortured by some of the abattoir workers was painfully obvious in the images and sound effects and predictably public outrage was immediate. However, according to Berger (1990), the shock and empathy viewers feel need to be converted to indignation, otherwise the feelings will soon dissipate: 'As we look at them, the moment of the other's suffering engulfs us. We are filled with either despair or indignation. Despair takes on some of the other's suffering to no purpose. Indignation demands action' (p. 42).

Kean (1998) argues that animal protection over the last two centuries has been influenced by the visibility and visualisation of animals, that is, by the act of 'seeing' animal suffering. Thus, 'shining a light' on animal cruelty is one of the animal movement's oldest protest tactics especially in exposing the hidden cruelties of the factory farm, the animal research laboratory, the hunting field and the slaughterhouse; the latter has been reported by Pachirat (2011) in his book *Every Twelve Seconds*, the subtitle of which echoes Kean's theme—industrialized slaughter and the politics of sight. By focusing on the invisibility of animal suffering behind closed doors, animal activists like Lyn White expose cruel practices that are otherwise invisible, denied, justified, forgotten or ignored.

According to Eldridge (1993, p. 4), television is an astonishing feat of social construction in how it organises information and implicitly or explicitly explains what is presented on the screen. Importantly, as Lewis (1991, p. 140) discovered, media insiders believe that television stories are seen rather than heard by audiences. This is confirmed in the present case study. As noted already, the pitiful vocalisations and images of animal suffering sparked immediate outrage in Australia and demands to end what Boltanski (1999) labels 'distant suffering'. Boltanski suggests what moral people can do about spectacles of suffering from the distant haven of their living rooms; the answer, he opines, is that they should become indignant, as the pity they naturally feel for the suffering of others is transformed to become indignation. He nonetheless concedes that 'the weapon of anger' is no substitute for action.

Mobilising Indignation

White's footage revealed the brutal torture and obvious suffering of animals in a number of traditional Indonesian slaughterhouses where, the ABC's Ferguson (2011) remarked, 'the smell of blood and fear is almost totally overwhelming'. Andrew Tyler from Animal Aid in the UK believes that activists 'have to shock and mesmerise and entice, tell powerful stories about the suffering of animals and what animals really are when they're not molested and confined' (personal correspondence, July 1996). His observations, recorded at the height of the UK's live export controversy in the mid-1990s, suggest the emotional tone and energy that he argues needs to be struck for mobilising the public against animal cruelty. Tyler's idea is supported by the theory of 'emotional contagion' (Collins, 1990) whereby a movement's collectively-felt mood (of anger in this case) and emotional energy sustain their activism.

Chouliaraki (2008) describes the effects of the media's 'exemplary stories' as moral education for the audience. By 'shining a light' on animal cruelty, animal protectionists have traditionally produced attitude change towards factory farming, blood sports, vivisection, and in other contexts where animal cruelty is hidden from view. Invariably in animal rights campaigns which expose cruelty to animals as individuals or *en masse* strong emotions are triggered by the images. Brown & Pickerill (2009) have emphasised the importance of emotion in sustaining social movements along the lines endorsed by Collins (1990), the theorist, and Tyler, the animal rights activist. Brown and Pickerill identify three roles for emotions: emotions mobilise activists; shape identities; and sometimes contribute to activist burnout. On the latter, Tyler's heartfelt declaration supports the emotional burden some activists experience, which he describes as "the tremendous toll this thing (cruelty) plays upon our physical and emotional health [...] it's not just a question of having to cope with these extraordinary scenes of violence and exploitation that we physically see and read about, but it's the fact that it's denied and that we are mocked, we are called extremists and mad people" (personal correspondence, July 1996).

Emotions Running High on Both Sides of the Controversy

The controversy that ensued in Australia provides a valuable case study of a social movement campaign's relationship to the mass media and the media's impact on public sentiment and political action. It also illustrates how the typical victim/villain couplet favoured in media stories is by no means clear-cut. A wide range of emotions was on display during the controversy when the various protagonists sought to 'deviantise' their respective opponents for their part in the controversy. Jasper (1998) has listed the classic emotions that are prevalent in social protests as indicated in Table 6.1. A cottage industry has developed on the role of emotions in social movement protests with Jasper as the most prominent and prolific writer on the topic. One of his early books, co-authored with Nelkin, *The Animal Rights Crusade: The Growth of a Moral Protest* (Jasper & Nelkin, 1992) included some of the emotions in Table 1. More recently, Rodgers (2010) has focused on anger as the seminal emotion that drives her informants. While anger has been a key emotion in recent protests against live animal exports both in Australia and the UK (in the case of the latter, see McLeod, 1998), the most dominant emotion in the mainstream animal movement remains compassion and its cousins pity, empathy and sympathy (Munro, 2001). Of relevance to the present controversy is a survey by Tiplady, Walsh, and Phillips (2012) completed by 157 adults in southeast Queensland who had some exposure to the controversy via various media immediately following the *Four Corners* story. Their overwhelming reaction to 'A Bloody Business' and the media reports which followed the broadcast was to feel pity for the cattle (85%), followed by sadness (72%), anger (68%) and respect for the investigators (66%).

Table 6.1: Emotions expressed in "A Bloody Business" on *Four Corners*

Primarily objective (in *Four Corners)*	Primarily reactive (on display in the public's reaction)	Moods expressed by industry reps (1,2) & animal activists (3,4,5)
Hostility, Suspicion, Trust (or lack of), Respect, Love	Anger, Grief, Sorrow, Outrage, Indignation, Shame	1. Defiance 2. Resistance 3. Compassion 4. Pity 5. Sympathy

Source: Adapted from Jasper (1998, Table 1, p. 406).

Compassion, as part of one's character, tends to last for most people unless of course compassion fatigue sets in; anger, on the other hand, is usually short-lived and dissipates quite quickly even in the context of collective action. This may partly explain the brief moment of outrage following the *Four Corners* story and the lack of effective government action in the second half of 2011.

Media-Movement Transactions

Gamson and Wolfsfeld's (1993) analysis of media-movement transactions suggests promising ways to test the risks to the animal rights cause in the context of the media's role in collaborating with the critics of the trade. They identify three services mass media outlets offer activists: (1) mobilization, (2) validation and (3) scope for enlargement; all three services benefitted Animal Australia's campaign against live exports. First, the public was mobilized to send thousands of angry emails and letters to politicians and such was the intensity of their indignation that the protest could not be ignored by the Australian government. The Minister for Agriculture was compelled by his own colleagues to place a temporary ban on animal exports to Indonesia. For a short time, the *Four Corners* exposé spawned front-page newspaper headlines, dozens of talkback radio sessions and online opinion pieces, thousands of tweets and passionate debate in the federal parliament.

Second, 'A Bloody Business' validated the activists' cause mainly because of the iconic status of the ABC's long-running current affairs programme *Four Corners*, a programme in its 50th year and recognised as Australia's leader in investigative television journalism. Confirming the programme's iconic status, a recent study found that there had been a decline in audiences watching current affairs in Australia between 1998 and 2007 with *Four Corners* as an exception to the trend; *Four Corners* was only one of eight television programmes that increased its audience size in the first decade of the twenty-first century (Young, 2009). And as noted earlier, about half a million viewers tuned to 'A Bloody Business'.

Third, mass media exposure provides a social movement campaign with an opportunity to massively increase public awareness of its grievances and, in the present case study, to contribute to raising the public's consciousness and achieving what Klandermans (1984) refers to as 'consensus mobilization'. As Gamson & Wolfsfeld (1993) note, 'it is not merely attention but the content of the media coverage that affects whether and in what ways third parties will enter the conflict' (p. 116). In the live animal export conflict, the initial response of the electronic and print media was to frame the conflict as a clash between innocent victims—inhumanely slaughtered animals—and the incompetent, uncaring villains who controlled the trade in Australia. As the conflict developed, however, the animal victim was largely forgotten in what became an ever-changing narrative of the decent versus the deviant in which the animal activists exchanged roles with their opponents in the meat industry; in the construction of this narrative, a 'halo/ horns' effect was evident where professional and private commentators in the media sought to impose these labels by valorising or demonising the protagonists. Such campaigns are often contests over moral capital, that is, which side is entitled to occupy the high moral ground (see Munro, 1999).

Although the *Four Corners* programme won a prestigious media award for its portrayal of the hidden cruelties in the trade, reporter Ferguson predicted the story would rarely be watched again, as the images and sounds of animal cruelty are for most people too distressing. Yet the initial impact of the programme was profound as Ferguson noted: 'Every politician I've spoken to has said the same thing: that they've never had such an impact from anything' (quoted in Molitorisz, 2011, p. 3); by this, they mean the constant flow of letters and emails from constituents condemning the trade and the government for not ensuring Australian animal welfare standards were upheld in Indonesia.

For a media-movement campaign to succeed, argue Gamson and Wolfsfeld (1993, p. 121), it must be characterised by three elements: first, the activists or social movement must have standing, that is, credibility and be worthy of support; the second characteristic is whether the movement's preferred frame is adopted by the media; finally, success depends on a social movement's capacity to garner sympathy for their cause. The *Four Corners* story aired by the national broadcaster in association with respected animal protectionists, generated widespread public condemnation of the trade and for an animal welfare issue, this was unprecedented in Australia. Yet it must be acknowledged that the non-human victims featured in *Four Corners* were soon to be replaced by their human counterparts in the farming sector; sections of the print media took up the grievances of dozens of individual farming families who had been hurt economically by the government's banning of the trade. How public and media interest in the crusade peaked early and then gradually declined is discussed next.

The Moral Crusade Takes Off

As indicated in the title of this paper, the live export trade was an issue made for the mass media. In relation to Gamson and Wolfsfeld's (1993) three points it is important to evaluate, if only subjectively, the impact of the *Four Corners* story on the activists and their campaign. First, did *Four Corners* influence for good or bad those who had standing in the controversy? As noted already, the animal protectionists featured in the story all had good standing in terms of their respectability and commitment to animal welfare and did not need the blessing of the media. In stark contrast, their opponents in the live export industry were more often than not unconvincing in their responses to the expose´. For example, Rowan Sullivan, the President of the Northern Territory Cattlemen's Association was lost for words in the following exchange:

> Ferguson: *You say you've got to have patience but why should the animals suffer while we help Indonesia get its act together on stunning?*
>
> Sullivan: *Because I think that um.* (long pause).
>
> Ferguson: *It's a tough question, isn't it?*
>
> Sullivan: *Yes, it is.*
>
> (Source: *Four Corners* transcript)

This was a revealing moment in the Four Corners story and one that Krien (2011) also quoted in her much-lauded *Quarterly Essay.*

Second, did *Four Corners* have any role in shaping the campaign's strategy or tactics? To all intents and purposes, the reverse was probably the case. The video camera has been a useful tool used by animal defenders to expose animal cruelty in many different contexts such as hunting, animal experimentation and factory farming (see Munro, 2001). White's footage of animal cruelty in the Indonesian abattoirs was corroborated by the footage obtained by the *Four Corners* camera team. White and Animals Australia had used this undercover strategy in earlier campaigns, a tactical repertoire that has been widely used by animal rights campaigners elsewhere. In the present case the activists took the initiative in filming animal cruelty and passing the footage on to the ABC

Third, did *Four Corners* influence how the activists' campaign message was delivered? From the discussion thus far, it is clear that the television network in this case study was simply the medium for transmitting the campaigners' revelation of distant animal suffering in foreign abattoirs. The words spoken by the animal protectionists, including the reporter Ferguson's, amounted to about 156 lines of transcript, more than half of which were delivered by Ferguson herself, whose purpose was to interview the main stakeholders in the controversy. The various representatives of the meat industry accounted for approximately 120 lines, most of which appeared to be reluctantly and cautiously delivered. These estimates indicate the spoken words favoured the animal rights cause; furthermore, the graphic images demonstrated more than anything the fidelity of the activists' claims. In fact, none of the six Australian representatives who appeared on camera for the live export industry sought to defend the practices depicted in the programme. Likewise, in the UK during the live export protests in the mid-1990s, Benton & Redfearn (1996) noted that there was a complete absence of a moral counterargument from the farming lobby which was forced to rely on free trade claims in defending their business.

When asked by Ferguson if he would rule out sending animals to slaughterhouses where cruelty was the norm, David Farley, the CEO of the Australian Agricultural Company (AACo) was awkwardly evasive:

> Farley: *That would be you know, it's a challenge in itself. We actually don't know what abattoirs our animals [are] going to.*
>
> Ferguson: *Don't you have enough power to say I won't accept an AACo animal being sold to these abattoirs?*
>
> Farley: *We're more on process and systems.*

(Source: *Four Corners* transcript)

The most bizarre comment, however, came from Professor Ivan Caple, a veterinary scientist, who stated 'the welfare conditions for Australian cattle in Indonesia is [sic] good'. Later in the transcript, he made the following puzzling observation particularly for a veterinarian in reference to the footage: 'A couple of the handlers were a little bit exuberant with the use of a goad and a very long pointed stick. Sometimes a finger was in an eye socket. That's not required'.

Widespread Initial Support for the Activists in the Court of Public Opinion

A story by Wilson (2011) in *The Australian* quoted veterinary surgeon Lloyd Reeve-Johnson's criticism of the way the live export industry is run. He had warned former agriculture minister Tony Burke that self-policing by the industry was untenable, a view supported by animal lawyer Malcolm Caulfield (2008) and quoted in the same article on 13 July 2011. *The Australian* editorial (2011) also criticised the then Minister for Agriculture, Joe Ludwig, for failing in his obligation to police the trade adequately. An editorial in *The Australian* on 1 June, one day after the *Four Corners* story, carried the headline 'Australia Must Stop Cruelty' and praised the programme and Animals Australia for exposing the brutal practices in the Indonesian slaughterhouses. The editorial called for the use of halal-approved stunning of the animals but warned against a total ban on the trade. Animal welfare supporters who read this editorial would no doubt have had mixed feelings as on the one hand the footage of animal cruelty had evidently shocked even this conservative newspaper; on the other hand, the broadsheet's call for halal-approved stunning rather than mandating Australian stunning methods would be read as a signal for doing nothing. Gamson (1992) tells us that

> participants in symbolic contests read their success or failure by how well their preferred meanings and interpretations are doing in various media arenas. Prominence in these arenas is taken as an outcome measure in its own right, independent of evidence on the degree to which the messages are being read by the public. (p. 385)

In this case, clearly, public opinion was strongly in favour of stopping the animal cruelty exposed by *Four Corners*. Animal welfare supporters were heartened by much of the commentary in various media such as the traditional print and electronic forms as well as online and in dozens of blogs and opinion pieces by ordinary citizens. Even the aforementioned editorial in *The Australian* appeared to be on the side of the animal protectionists.

The Crusade Waxes and Wanes

However, in less than a month, the public's outrage had cooled and new victims emerged in the form of beef producers who complained bitterly that the government's ban on the trade had caused enormous economic pain and social suffering to their families (Hedley, 2012); the chief villains were now the Labor government, its Minister for Agriculture and the 'animal people' who exposed the scandal. *The Australian* wasted no time in turning away from the animal welfare frame to focus on the failings of the Minister for Agriculture specifically in a front page article on 13 July and in its editorial that day (Rout, 2011). The newspaper's frequent attacks on the policies of the federal government now had a new issue to add to its list of alleged government deficiencies. The live export controversy for this newspaper at least, was no longer a moral issue as suggested in its editorial of 1 June, but rather a motive for a political attack on the federal Labor government. In this case, the government capitulated and in a rare agreement with the federal opposition parties, the Minister lifted the ban on 6 July and 'the bloody business' continued as usual.

The RSPCA's Dr Jones had earlier complained to the Minister about the suffering to the animals caused by the restraining boxes, but her concerns were ignored. Jones suggests the campaign did have a positive impact on animal welfare through the supply-chain assurance system: 'while stunning is not mandatory, its uptake has dramatically increased in Indonesia' (personal correspondence, 23 July 2012). Arguably, this is a small victory, which is not to deny the importance of 'the psychology of small wins' (Weick, 1984). But the campaign has not thus far succeeded in achieving 'cognitive liberation' (McAdam, 1982), whereby thousands of bystanders feel empowered and motivated to mount an unrelenting campaign against injustice. Based on the results of their online survey, Tiplady et al. (2012) report that only a quarter of their informants were prepared to take action to ban live animal exports; moreover, while almost two-thirds of those surveyed had 'talked' about the media coverage, fewer than 15% had chosen to take any of the two dozen or so actions—ranging from writing letters to politicians etc. to donating money to the RSPCA or Animals Australia—proposed by the researchers.

Animals Australia has not abandoned the campaign and has succeeded in mobilising sporadic protests in some capital cities against live exports, but these were small-scale compared to those in the immediate aftermath of the *Four Corners* expose'. A revealing timeline provided by Davidson (2011) shows how in early June 2011, immediately after the *Four Corners* report, the controversy attracted well over 1000 tweets which, and thereafter despite a few peaks, declined gradually to less than 100 by year's end (see Appendix 2).

Post-Mortem: Can Social Movement Theory Benefit Activists?

Why did this classic 'hot cognition' campaign with strong public support end with only incremental improvements to animal welfare? Social movement theory suggests how the outcome might have been otherwise. As in many emotion-laden protests, there is more heat than light and in cases involving allegations of animal abuse, the heat is intense, rendering any intellectual or philosophical arguments irrelevant as reason inevitably gets trumped by emotion, at least initially. For activists inspired by the cool rationality of Peter Singer, emotionalism is to be avoided. Thus, Groves (2001) discovered how animal activists campaigning against scientists who use animals in research eschewed emotionalism because they believe it trivialises animal rights and makes activists look amateurish; these activists preferred what Groves calls 'non-emotional' framing based on rational arguments. In the campaign described by Groves, it was important for the activists' claims against the scientists to be based on scientific evidence. However, as we have seen in the live animal export controversy, the public's ire was aroused, not by persuasive intellectual arguments, but rather by the moral shock of seeing animal suffering on television. Social movement frames will vary depending on the issue. In the live animal export protests, the symbolic power of animals as innocent victims did mobilise public sentiment against the trade, but not enough to end it. Could this have been otherwise? Entman's (1993) explanation of how social movement framing works offers a partial answer from the perspective of communication studies. In Table 6.2 we can see how framing in the *Four Corners* report matched Entman's criteria and what Klandermans (1984) refers to as 'consensus mobilization', that is, a supportive climate for mobilisation. A campaign's success also depends on Klanderman's (1984) related concept of 'action mobilization', that is, the 'call to action' which is missing in both Entman's definition and in the *Four Corners* programme.

Table 6.2: Entman's analysis and its application to the *Four Corners* Report

Entman's definition of frames	Application to the *Four Corners* frame
1.To frame is to select some aspects of a perceived reality and	1. Inhumane animal slaughter in Indonesian abattoirs
2. make them more salient in a communicating text	2. TV footage of graphic images of animal suffering
3. in such a way as to promote a particular problem definition,	3. The absence of any effective stunning practice to diminish suffering
4. causal interpretation,	4. The failure of Australian authorities to ensure satisfactory animal welfare standards are met
5. moral evaluation and /or	5. This is implied in the programme's title: "A Bloody Business" and in the report itself
6.treatment recommendation	6. Ban the live animal export trade

Source: Left column is adapted from Entman (1993).

Snow and Benford's (1988) model provides a more comprehensive account of framing that includes 'action mobilization' and provides a practical methodology for animal protectionists like Lyn White and Animals Australia to be more effective in pressing their claims. It is important for social movement entrepreneurs to construct their campaigns in ways that balance short-lived, emotion-charged rhetoric and the more enduring cognitive dimension whereby animal rights is seen as a philosophical movement of justice for all creatures. In the live export campaign, in common with most social protests, a movement's effectiveness depends on the accomplishment of three essential tasks first identified by Wilson (1973) as the movement's diagnosis, prognosis and motivation or mobilising potential. Snow and Benford (1988) have described these tasks as diagnostic, prognostic and motivational framing, concepts which closely resemble Hannigan's (1995) social constructionist model of claims making as depicted in Table 6.3.

Table 6.3: Tasks needed to be accomplished for a social movement or a social movement organisation (SMO) to be successful.

SM analysts/activists	Task 1	Task 2	Task 3
Wilson (1973)	Diagnosis	Prognosis	Motivation/mobilisation
Hannigan (1995)	Assemble claims	Present claims	Contest claims
Snow & Benford (1988)	Diagnostic frame	Prognostic frame	Motivational frame
Gamson (1992)	Emotional domain Injustice frame	Cognitive domain Agency frame	Cognitive-emotional domains Identity frame
Animals Australia & the RSPCA	YES (to all of the above)	YES/NO (No to the cognitive domain; Yes to the prognosis	YES/NO (No to cognitive mobilization; Yes to emotional motivation

*Source: **Author** 2012. Reproduced from Table3, p.11 with a minor addition. Thanks to Social Movement Studies, http://dx.doi.org/10.1080/14742837.2013.874524*

As indicated in Table 6.3, the third task of a social movement is to defend its cause and philosophy against the arguments and tactics of counter movements. Animals Australia, the RSPCA and *Four Corners* collaborated in assembling and presenting their claims successfully in a television programme that reinvigorated the long-running crusade. There is no denying that the prognostic frame and presentation of the activists' claims via the programme's powerful images and sound effects succeeded in making a large number of viewers aware of animal cruelty link Indonesia. However, the diagnosis and prognosis failed to put the issue of inhumane cattle slaughter in the wider context of 'the animal-industrial complex' (Noske, 1989) where sentient creatures are 'processed' for their meat and other products. In the case of cattle, it is often observed, only the 'moo' escapes processing. The opportunity to develop the intellectual or cognitive dimension of the protest was not exploited, understandably perhaps, given television's emphasis on visualisation to the virtual exclusion of sustained argument. Thus, most of the comments from the *Four Corners* transcript consisted of no more than a few lines per speaker. One such strategy to engage the public in a sustained conversation about a social movement issue has been suggested by Pickerill (2006) who refers to online activities as 'symbolic crusades' aimed at convincing the public of the legitimacy of a cause by 'argument at a distance' (p. 275).

Conclusion

In order to mobilise sustained support for its cause, an SM or SMO needs to find a balance in the hot/cognition couplet. Motivating sympathetic bystanders using only powerful imagery or rhetorical devices will not succeed in the long term as motivation to join a movement and become committed to its cause needs to be based on compelling moral and philosophical grounds. Klandermans' (1984) concepts of consensus and action mobilization support this analysis; the mass media may provide a supportive mobilisation climate (consensus mobilisation) but action mobilisation—the call to action—is the responsibility of the SMO. As we have seen, there was widespread consensus that an injustice had been perpetrated against innocent animals subjected to abuse in unregulated Indonesian abattoirs. Gamson (1992) has stressed the importance of emotions in the construction of an injustice frame, particularly in the early stages of a campaign. This was the case in the live export controversy where the visceral impact of 'A Bloody Business' was profound, albeit short-lived.

I have argued that 'the call to action' by Animals Australia, the RSPCA and other critics of the trade was based on an emotional appeal that could not be sustained in the absence of a strategy of persuasive, philosophical and ethical argumentation. Animal activists and their supporters frequently burn out emotionally if they are not intellectually engaged. King (2005) supports the notion of activist burnout in performing the hard work of social change. She advises activists to practise 'emotional reflexivity', a process in which they are encouraged to balance 'emotional and cognitive aspects of the framing process' (p. 154). Reason and emotion are the two sides of a social movement's mobilisation potential and both must be utilised effectively if the movement is to be successful.

For this to happen in the live export protests, the moral education of the public will need to focus on the obvious cruelty of the trade as just one of many instances of problems associated with the 'animal industrial complex' (Noske, 1989) and 'animal-using consensus' (Kew, 1999) but also on the alternatives which might include strategies and tactics ranging from the promotion of a meat-free or meat-reduced diet (or eating only humanely produced meat along the lines suggested by Safran Foer, 2009) to the more basic requirements of humane slaughter such as mandatory stunning. It would seem that the latter could be easily and economically achieved if the Australian government heeded the eminently reasonable recommendations of Animals Australia and the RSPCA locally and Compassion in World Farming internationally. For example, the RSPCA's chief scientist believes that with sufficient investment in abattoirs in northern Australia and the marketing of meat exports instead of live animal exports, the problem would be resolved (personal correspondence, July 2012). While such a strategy would be welcomed by Australia's meat workers and their union, it may not satisfy the religious consumers in Indonesia and in other predominantly Muslim countries.

Only strong ethical arguments and public pressure will resolve this particular obstacle. Bagaric (2007) offers a number of cogent reasons for banning the trade and argues that what is at stake is the reputation of Australia and 'the collective conscience of a community' by which he means its stance on the pain and suffering of animals. For the religious consumers too, the activists' dilemma posed by the hot/cognition couple means a balance has to be found between the passion of religious and cultural beliefs and the politics of reason and compassion. Social movement scholars are well placed to take the lead on this and similar conflicts (for example Bevington & Dixon, 2005; Croteau, Hoynes, & Ryan, 2005; Eyal & Buchholz, 2010; Maddison & Scalmer, 2006; Valocchi, 2009); importantly, however, mass media outlets need to be on side and involved in a sustained campaign if the conflict is to be resolved in the activists' favour.

Acknowledgements

I thank the three referees for their useful suggestions and Glenys Oogjes, the Director of Animals Australia and Bidda Jones, the RSPCA's chief scientist for answering some questions helpfully suggested by one of the referees.

REFERENCES

Australian Broadcasting Commission. (2011, May 31). A Bloody Business. Four Corners. Sydney: ABC.

Bagaric, M. (2007, March 2). Much more than the economy at stake.

The Age. Benton, T., & Redfearn, S. (1996). The politics of animal rights: where is the Left? New Left Review, 215(Jan./ Feb.), 43 –58.

Berger, J. (1990). Photographs of agony. About looking. New York, NY: Vintage International, Vintage Books. Retrieved from http:/www.farmonline.com.au

Bevington, D., & Dixon, C. (2005). Movement relevant theory: Rethinking social movement scholarship and activism. Social Movement Studies, 4, 185–208.

Boltanski, L. (1999). Distant suffering: Morality, media, and politics. Cambridge: Cambridge University Press.

Brown, G., & Pickerill, J. (2009). Space for emotion in the spaces of activism. Emotion, Space and Society, 2, 24–35. doi: 10.1016/j.emospa.2009.03.004

Caulfield, M. (2008). Handbook of Australian animal cruelty law. North Melbourne: Animals Australia.

Chouliaraki, L. (2008). The media as moral education: Mediation and action. Media, Culture & Society, 30, 831–852.

Collins, R. (1990). Stratification, emotional energy, and transient emotions. In T. Kemper (Ed.), Research agendas in the sociology of emotions (pp. 25 –57). New York: State University of New York Press.

Croteau, D., Hoynes, W., & Ryan, C. (2005). Rhyming hope and history: Activists, academics, and social movement scholarship. Minneapolis: University of Minnesota Press.

Davidson, H. (2011, December 19). Care factor: after live exports have left the front pages. The Telegraph. Retrieved September 30, 2013, from www.news.com.au

Editorial. (2011, July 13). Canberra cannot hide on cattle: Agriculture minister had plenty of warning on cruelty issue. The Australian, p.12.

Eldridge, J. (Ed.). (1993). Getting the message: News, truth, and power. New York, NY: Routledge.

Entman, R. (1993). Framing: Towards clarification of a fractured paradigm. Journal of Communication, 43, 51 –58.

Eyal, G., & Buchholz, L. (2010). From the sociology of intellectuals to the sociology of interventions. Annual Review of Sociology, 36, 117– 137.

Ferguson, S. (2011). Four Corners transcript (2011) A Bloody Business, Australian Broadcasting Commission. Retrieved July 1, 2011. http://www.abc.net.au/4corners/content/S3228880.htm

Gamson, W. (1992). Talking politics. Cambridge: Cambridge University Press.

Gamson, W., & Wolfsfeld, G. (1993). Movements and media as interacting systems. Annals of the American Academy of Political and Social Science, 528(Jul.), 114– 125.

Groves, McAllister J. (2001). Animal rights and the politics of emotion. In J. Goodwin, J. Jasper, & F. Polletta (Eds.), Passionate politics: Emotions and social movements (pp. 212–229). Chicago, IL, and London: University of Chicago Press.

Hannigan, J. (1995). Environmental sociology: A social constructionist perspective. London: Routledge.

Hedley, T. (2012, June 2–3). Farmers feeling hung out to dry. The Weekend Australian, 15.

Herman, E., & Chomsky, N. (1988). Manufacturing consent: The political economy of the mass media. New York, NY: Pantheon Books.

Jasper, J. (1998). The emotions of protest: Affective and reactive emotions in and around social movements. Sociological Forum, 13, 397–424.

Jasper, J., & Nelkin, D. (1992). The animal rights crusade: The growth of a moral protest. New York, NY: The Free Press.

Jasper, J., & Poulsen, J. (1995). Recruiting strangers and friends: Moral shocks and social networks in animal rights and anti-nuclear protests. Social Problems, 42, 493–512.

Kean, H. (1998). Animal rights: Political and social change in Britain since 1800. London: Reaktion Books.

Kew, B. (1999). Fearsome truths: The challenge of animal liberation. (Unpublished doctoral dissertation in Sociology). University of Durham, Durham.

Kielbowicz, R. B., & Scherer, C. (1986). The role of the press in the dynamics of social movements. In K. Lang, G. Engel Lang, & L. Kriesberg (Eds.), Research in social movements, conflicts, and change (pp. 71–96). Greenwich, CT: JAI Press.

King, D. (2005). Sustaining activism through emotional reflexivity. In H. Flam & D. King (Eds.), Emotions and social movements (pp. 150– 169). London: Routledge.

Klandermans, B. (1984). Mobilization and participation: Social-psychological expansions of resource mobilization theory. American Sociological Review, 49(Oct.), 583 –600.

Klandermans, B. (1992). The social construction of protest and multi organisational fields. In A. D. Morris & C. McClurg Mueller (Eds.), Frontiers in social movement theory (pp. 77 –103). New Haven, CT: Yale University.

Krien, A. (2011). Us and them: On the importance of animals. Quarterly Essay, 45.

Lewis, J. (1991). Ideological octopus: An exploration of television and its audiences. New York, NY: Routledge.

Maddison, S., & Scalmer, S. (2006). Activist wisdom: Practical knowledge and creative tension in social movements. Sydney: UNSW Press.

McAdam, D. (1982). Political process and the development of black insurgency. Chicago, IL: University of Chicago Press.

McLeod, R. (1998). Calf exports at Brightlingsea. Parliamentary Affairs, 51, 345–357. Oxford: Oxford University Press.

Molitorisz, S. (2011, August 18). Witness from the back seat. Green Guide. The Age, 3.

Munro, L. (1999). Contesting moral capital in campaigns against animal liberation. Society & Animals, 7(1), 35 –53.

Munro, L. (2001). Compassionate beasts: The quest for animal rights. Westport, CT: Praeger.

Munro, L. (2012). The animal rights movement in theory and practice: A review of the sociological literature. Sociology Compass, 6, 166 –181.

Noske, B. (1989). Humans and other animals: Beyond the boundaries of anthropology. London: Pluto Press.

Pachirat, T. (2011). Every twelve seconds: Industrialized slaughter and the politics of sight. New Haven, CT: Yale University Press.

Patterson, T., & McClure, R. (1976). The unseeing eye: The myth of television power in national elections. New York, NY: Putnam.

Pickerill, J. (2006, April). Radical politics on the net. Parliamentary Affairs, 59, 283 –298. Live animal export controversy in Australia 227

Rodgers, K. (2010). 'Anger is why we're all here': Mobilizing and managing emotions in a professional activist organization. Social Movement Studies, 9, 273 –291.

Rootes, C. (1984). Protest, social movements, revolution. Social Alternatives, 4, 4 –8.

Rout, M. (2011). Ludwig warned on abuse of cattle. The Australian, 1.

Ryan, C., Carragee, K., & Meinhofer, W. (2001). Theory into practice: Framing, the news media, and collective action. Journal of Broadcasting and Electronic Media, 45(1), 175–182.

Safran Foer, J. (2009). Eating animals. New York, NY: Little, Brown.

Shapiro, K. (1994). The caring sleuth: Portrait of an animal rights activist. Society & Animals, 2(2), 145–165.

Singer, P. (1990). Animal liberation (2nd ed.). London: Jonathon Cape.

Snow, D. A., & Benford, R. D. (1988). Ideology, frame resonance and participant mobilisation. In B. Klandermans, H. Krisi, & S. Tarrow (Eds.), From structure to action: Comparing social movement research across cultures, International Social Movement Research, a Research Annual (pp. 197 –217). Greenwich, CT: JAI Press

Tarrow, S. (1994). Power in movement: Social movements and contentious politics (2nd ed.). Cambridge: Cambridge University Press.

Tiplady, C., Walsh, D-A, & Phillips, C. (2012, July 14). Public response to media coverage of animal cruelty. *Journal of Agricultural and Environmental Ethics*, 26, 869– 885. doi:10.1007/s10806-012-9412-0

Valocchi, S. (2009). Social movements and activism in the USA. Hobboken, NJ: Routledge.

Van Zoonen, L. (1996). A dance of death: New social movements and the mass media. In D. Paletz (Ed.), Political communication in action (pp. 201 –222). Cress Hill, NJ: Hampton Press.

Weick, K. (1984). Small wins: Redefining the scale of social problems. American Psychologist, 39, 40 – 49.Wilson, J. (1973). Introduction to social movements. New York, NY: Basic Books.

Wilson, L. (2011, July 13). Vet worried about 'dodgy' inspections of live exports. The Australian, 3.

Young, S. (2009). The decline of traditional news and current affairs and audiences in Australia. Media International Australia, 131(May), 147–159.

Appendix 1

Animals Australia and the RSPCA listed the main events following the *Four Corners* programme on 30 May up to 16 December 2011. The shorter, adapted version of the events of 2011 downloaded on 26 June 2012 outlined below is no longer available as the list was recorded on the (former) Ban Live Export website before Animals Australia took it over from the RSPCA. A similar list summarizing a monthly record of events is on Animal Australia's website which also includes other activities in addition to the live export campaign. The list can be found under the SMO's Track Record (2011) for the months from May to December. and at
http://www.animalsaustralia.org/ about/track_record. php

30 May 2011: *Four Corners* airs 'A Bloody Business' on their investigation of Indonesian abattoirs; the websites of Animals Australia, the RSPCA and GetUp! crash due to the massive response from the public.

2 June: An online petition calling for a ban on the trade presented to the Australian Parliament approaches 200,000 signatures.

8 June: Protest emails and letters sent to Julia Gillard, PM, via BanLiveExport.com exceed 100,000 and the PM responds by placing a temporary suspension on the live export trade to Indonesia.

6 July: Live export to Indonesia resumes. 7 July: The decision to resume the trade causes a backlash from government MPs.

14 August: 20,000 Australians rally throughout the country to call for an end to the trade.

18 August: Bills to end the trade are voted down. Brutal images of animal cruelty in Turkey revealed to the public.

25 August: Shocking footage of cruelty to Australian cattle in Israel revealed.

11 October: Labor's caucus fails to mandate stunning on animals exported live overseas.

21 October: An independent review of the trade neglects to address non-stunning, the cruellest aspect of the trade. (There were about 500 submissions which divided roughly equally between individuals and organisations both for and against banning the trade.)

28 November: *Four Corners* is awarded the prestigious Gold Walkley award for excellence in journalism demonstrated in 'A Bloody Business'.

16 December: News reports indicate the Indonesian government plans a dramatic reduction in the number of cattle imports from Australia.

Appendix 2: Care Factor: After Live Exports Left the Front Pages

This analysis by Helen Davidson is part of the Care Factor series which tracks significant issues in the media before and after the 'furore' dies down. The timeline of events following the *Four Corners* programme shows more than 1100 tweets reacting to the story in the first fortnight. The number then declined sharply to only a few hundred and peaked again in late July to about 700 when government MPs raised concerns over the government's lifting of the ban; from then, the numbers again slumped to only a few hundred in each of the last three months of 2011. The timeline can be viewed at www.news.com.au/national-news/care-factor-after-live-exports have left-the-front-pages, downloaded on 30 September 2013.

Activism

Chapter 7

Strategies, Action Repertoires and DIY Activism in the Animal Rights Movement

On 6 May 2002, Pim Fortuyn, a right-wing Dutch politician, was assassinated in the Netherlands by Volkert van der Graaf, a thirty-four-year-old vegan animal rights extremist who apparently was angry with Fortuyn over his support of intensive farming and his promise to repeal a ban on fur farming. This was the first political assassination in the Netherlands for over 400 years and the first ever documented murder by an animal rights activist. Yet even before this incident, animal rights supporters had been denounced in the media as violent extremists, particularly in America, the UK and Australia where animal activism has been most prominent in the movement's recent history. For example, Kew's (1999) doctoral dissertation contains two long chapters on the role of the media in the UK during the live animal export campaign from 1994 to 1996 and concludes that the quality media were overwhelmingly hostile to the movement, portraying supporters as 'misguided, dubious, irrational, heretical, sinister, dishonest, totalitarian, murderous and treacherous' (1999, pp. 261–262). If these labels are used in a country which pioneered animal protection, then they are most certainly more widespread in less animal-friendly countries. The purpose of the present paper is to show—in contrast to media images and public perception—how the animal movement is overwhelmingly non-violent and that its strategies and tactical repertoires are in the main the conventional, legal tactics used by non-violent movements.

In line with Tilly (1985), the paper takes the view that a social movement is what it does, as much as why it does it. Thus while the focus will be on the movement's strategies and tactics which have been developed during the long history of animal protection from the RSPCA to People for the Ethical Treatment of Animals (PETA), it is important to include the motives of the activists behind the various campaigns since it is people who have objectives, rather than organizations per se. I argue that the animal movement is dedicated to nonviolent direct action which incorporates the two broad strategies of gaining publicity for the movement and disturbing the status quo in the way we treat other animals. These approaches correspond to what Newell (2000) calls liberal governance strategies and critical governance strategies; the former refers to strategies which seek reforms within the system while the latter 'tend not to compromise' (Newell, 2000, p. 127). The paper also explains why movement insiders reject violence in campaigning for the ethical treatment of animals; instead, activists draw on a variety of non-violent tactics borrowed from the repertoire of the nineteenth-century humane movement as well as from more recent social movements.

During the late 1990s I observed animal activists in Australia, the UK and the USA as they prosecuted their campaigns collectively and as individuals in what can be described as DIY activism. DIY activism included many different tactical repertoires which were familiar and available to activists, as well as ones which were designed to gain a response from the targets. According to Harding (1998, p. 80), DIY came out of the Direct-Action movement of the 1990s and follows in the tradition of non-violent direct action espoused by the radical environmentalist group Earth First! (EF!). One of the slogans of EF! activists is 'DIY! if not you, who?' McKay (1998, p. 3) describes a broader social formation he labels DIY culture, which includes a form of activism characterized by immediacy, spontaneity and direct action. This 'definition' is in line with Shapiro's (1994, p. 148) description of animal rights activists as 'caring sleuths' whose DIY activism is characterized by an aggressive, investigative style of direct action that is enacted as soon as animal suffering is encountered.

According to Doherty (2000, p. 62), tactical repertoires as learned and shared understandings of how to protest are shaped by the values of the movement. The power in movement (Tarrow, 1994, 1998) for animal protectors is the capacity to combine various forms of collective action from direct mail to direct action. Tactics highlighted in the paper are pamphleteering and demonstrations (publicity strategies), and hunger strikes, ethical vegetarianism and undercover surveillance (interference strategies). Clearly, there is some overlap in the objectives of publicizing an issue and how it might subvert the status quo; a hunger strike, for example, is at first glance a classic illustration of a publicity stunt yet it is highly subversive in intent. Similarly, a demonstration, depending on its size, is used by activists to publicize an issue as well as to disrupt life in its immediate vicinity. These particular tactics will be highlighted in this paper because they were popular among the activists and because, as I suggest below, they are representative of the tactical repertoires I observed in various movement campaigns.

According to Rucht, the difference between strategy and tactics is stressed more in Europe than in the USA. Rucht notes that tactics may change from one situation to another and are not necessarily part of a general strategic concept (1990, p. 174). It is perhaps useful to think of strategy as the 'broad organizing plans' for acquiring and using resources to achieve the movement's goals (Turner and Killian, 1987, p. 286), while tactics refer to the specific techniques for implementing the strategy. Tactics are sometimes referred to as 'forms of action' (Rucht, 1990), 'action technologies' (Oliver and Marwell, 1992), 'claim-making repertoires' (Tilly, 1993/94), 'action repertoires', 'repertoires of contention' or as a 'tactical repertoire' (Tarrow, 1994). Rucht defines the action repertoire as 'the range of specific kinds of action carried out by a given collective actor in a cycle of conflict, usually lasting from some years to some decades' (1990, p. 164) while Tilly sees social movements as 'a cluster of performances' (1993/94, p. 3) which include the kinds of action repertoires listed in Table 7.1.

Animal Protection Praxis: Strategies and Tactics

Never doubt that a small group of thoughtful, committed citizens can change the world. Indeed, it's the only thing that ever has.

—Attributed to Margaret Mead

It's challenging. I like the strategy. I absolutely love the strategy of figuring out how to do something. I guess I like the politics of it.

—Adele Douglass, American Humane Association

Turner and Killian (1987) have identified four tactical mechanisms—persuasion, facilitation, bargaining, and coercion—which have been used at one time or another by activists and advocates in their campaigns on behalf of animals. These tactical mechanisms can best be thought of as a continuum, with persuasion as the most moderate tactic at one end and the more direct confrontational tactic of coercion at the other end. I have selected a representative sample of these tactics as space does not permit an account of more than a few iconic tactics from the animal movement's DIY toolkit.

Persuasion (e.g. pamphleteering, demonstrations) and facilitation (e.g. ethical vegetarianism) tend to be the preferred tactics of organizational advocates in the suites while bargaining (e.g. hunger strikes) and coercive tactics (e.g. undercover surveillance) are usually more commonly observed in grassroots activist campaigns. The tactics shown in parentheses above have been selected from Table 7.1 as representative of Turner and Killian's tactical continuum. Persuasion, involving the use of strictly symbolic manipulation and the raising of issue consciousness, is one of the most important ways in which ideology is produced and continuously modified (Turner and Killian, 1987, pp. 297–298). Although consciousness raising has been derided as 'social change through banner hanging' (Wapner, 1995), it is nonetheless an important tactic in the animal movement for changing the way people think about animals. Close relatives of persuasion—facilitation and bargaining—had been famously used by the late animal activist Henry Spira, although not without criticism from more radical elements in the animal movement (Munro, 2002). Nonetheless, persuasion, facilitation and bargaining remain the staple approaches of the mainstream movement.

There are also many instances in which coercive tactics of various kinds have been deployed, particularly by grassroots activists to achieve improvements in animal welfare.

Table 7.1: Strategies and tactics of nonviolent action by animal protectors

Publicity Strategies		Interference Strategies	
Persuasion strategy	**Protest strategy**	**Non-cooperation strategy**	**Intervention Strategy**
Petitions	***Demonstrations***	*Civil disobedience*	*Animal rescue*
(Celebrity) speeches	*Picketing*	*Boycotts*	*Sit-ins*
Direct mail	*Vigils*	*Legal obstructions*	*Blockades*
Publicising surveys, opinion polls	*Parades, marches and rallies*	*Occupations* *Ethical vegetarianism	***Undercover surveillance***
Information stands	Mock awards	Animal sanctuaries	*Nonviolent sabotage*
Displaying symbols and caricatures	Street theatre etc	*Seeking imprisonment	Exposure of animal abuser's identity
Posters and banner hanging	Mock funerals	*Hunger strikes	Litigation
*Pamphleteering	Burning effigies		Lobbying
*Writing books, articles, poems	*Renouncing honors		*Ethical investments
*Art exhibitions, media presentations			
*Submissions and reports to inquiries			
* Writing letters			
*Bearing witness			

*Source: Adapted from Ackerman and Kruegler (1994:6) as cited in Lofland (1996: 271; Figure 9.2) * denotes mainly actions by individuals and words in italics represent direct action activities. Tactics in **bold** are described in detail below.*

Nonviolent Actions by Animal Protectors

These range from the use of 'nuisance' tactics to more disruptive tactics including the violent actions of radical animal rights activists. Coercion, then, can be thought of as a continuum ranging from the mild forms of coercion used by activists like Spira to the threats and acts of violence made by extremist groups such as the Animal Liberation Front, the Animal Rights Militia and the Band of Mercy (see Tester & Walls, 1996). Violence is eschewed by the mainstream movement, and very few of the fifty activists I interviewed favoured extreme or violent action under any circumstances. This was even more evident in the results of a larger sample of animal rights supporters who overwhelmingly favoured legal, moderate protest actions over illegal, violent ones (Richards, 1990; Munro, 1995).

Non-violent movement strategies are represented in the four—protest, persuasion, non-cooperation and intervention—and related forms of action in Table 7.1 The publicity strategies are the legal, mostly non-violent institutionalized strategies which Newell (2000) calls 'liberal governance' strategies and Tarrow (1994) labels as 'conventional' social movement action repertoires. I qualify the tactics as 'mostly nonviolent' as demonstrations, for example, can often turn violent. Interference strategies correspond to Newell's concept of 'critical governance' and what Tarrow refers to as 'disruption'; these are non-institutionalized, unconventional tactics which are again mostly non-violent forms of direct action. All of these action repertoires and the related strategies—protest, persuasion, non-cooperation and intervention—have been deployed in recent animal rights campaigns that I observed in three different continents during the 1990s.

Media coverage is essential in many animal rights campaigns for giving the movement legitimacy and publicity. As Glenys Oogjes of Animals Australia explained: 'I'd have to say that the most successful strategy, if you can call it that, was when we've had successful media coverage of an issue' (Interview, 1997). Some of the tactics highlighted in this paper—demonstrations, hunger strikes, undercover surveillance—were chosen by activists for their headline potential while the remainder, ethical vegetarianism and pamphleteering were adopted with complete indifference to whether or not 'the whole world is watching' (Gitlin, 1980). DIY activism may not always be the best way to attract media attention in that the actions are typically enacted by small groups of individuals in isolation. Yet the media are always interested in dramatic news stories which many direct-action campaigns provide. Rochon (1990) claims that the power of a movement resides in its militancy, size and novelty, while Koopmans (1993) suggests that it is violence which attracts the media's attention. It is for this reason that the media-movement relationship is accurately summed up by Van Zoonen's apt term 'a dance of death' (1996). On the one hand, animal rights activists need the media to promote their call for the compassionate treatment of animals; on the other, the media need dramatic footage and headlines which violence and threats of violence provide, albeit, as we will see below, at a moral cost to the movement.

Extremism and Violence in Animal Activism

Animal rights and anti-roads protesters, according to one writer cited by McKay (1998, p. 3), were the main dissenters in the UK during the 1990s. While many of these protests were militant rather than violent, the representation of the activism in the mass media was of violence and extremism (Kew, 1999). In the case of the animal rights protests against the live export of animals, a single incident involving a brick through a lorry window provoked a moral panic about 'the loopy and violent Animal Rights Militia' (*The Economist*, 1995), IRA-style urban terrorists and the like. Activists I interviewed often used the language of war when describing their campaign strategies in Brightlingsea and Dover, but none supported the violence favoured by some extremist groups. Tilly (1978, p. 55) has provided some insights into why activists in new social movements eschew violence. There are essentially three factors which activists and bystanders consider, namely success, repression and facilitation. In the case of the success factor, many people now believe violence is counterproductive and indeed will invite repression from the authorities. As John Bryant claimed, 'the one thing the state can do better than anyone else is violence' (Interview, 1996). Finally, social movement goals will be facilitated by elites in government and the media only if they are non-violent. For these reasons, then, social movement activists, including the majority of animal activists, favour non-violent means to achieve their goals. Kitschelt (1986, p. 61) also argues that movements need to appeal to widely held norms if they are to succeed and that the strategy of non-violence is crucial for the emergence of protest and the building of broad mobilizations in Western democracies.

Gurr (2000, p. 156) supports this view and notes how non-violent movements of the late twentieth century differed in at least three ways from previous movements. First, nonviolent resistance gives protesters a moral advantage, a point frequently made by Peter Singer and other leaders of the mainstream animal movement. Second, because the tactics often proved to be creatively disruptive of public order and economic activity, authorities were compelled to respond in ways that put them at a moral and political disadvantage to the protesters. The large-scale protests in England in the mid-1990s against live animal exports are a good illustration of the effectiveness of nonviolent civil disobedience. Third, recent non-violent protests have used the mass media to send their images and messages well beyond the immediate sites of conflict to 'a distant but potentially sympathetic public composed of people who might be enlisted as allies and agents of reform' (Gurr, 2000, p. 156). Gurr argues that this outreach was not available to the nineteenth-century activists.

Given these arguments for non-violence and against violence, it is therefore not surprising that Rucht has identified a decline in violence in contemporary new social movements and a corresponding increase in civil disobedience (1990, p. 159). Doherty also claims that there has been an increase in non-violent direct action in the twentieth century (2002, p. 180). He identifies a number of factors which explain why violence is not popular in small environmental and animal rights groups: an expanded repertoire of nonviolent tactics; much greater access to the mass media; and lack of public support for violence. In the case of animal rights, however, there is at least a perception in some sections of the media that violence has been increasing in the last decade or so. These media reports followed an admission from an animal rights extremist in 1994 that he had sent six letter bombs to companies involved in the live animal export trade in the UK (Jordan, 2002, p. 68).

Jordan distinguishes between activism! and activism, noting that the Animal Liberation Front (ALF) has become emblematic of the former. He points out that the ALF's 'terrorist' actions are a component of the mainstream animal liberation movement which uses primarily nonviolent direct action in its campaigns (Jordan, 2002, pp. 67–68). Not surprisingly, then, in the public mind the animal rights movement is often associated with violence, especially in the UK where the ALF has been most active. Even in Australia, the birthplace of the leading advocate of nonviolent animal liberation, Peter Singer, peaceful animal activists have been unfairly labelled 'terrorists' and 'extremists' and their campaigns linked to those of the ALF.

That there are violent and extreme elements on the fringes of the mainstream movement cannot be denied; yet they are a minority who evidently do not accept the non-violent stance of the mainstream movement. Turner and Killian (1987, pp. 303–304) note how non-violence is often found alongside terrorism rather than in association with the more conventional persuasive and bargaining tactics, an idea which at first blush seems counterintuitive. However, as they explain it, terrorism requires only a small group of well-disciplined participants to prevail, while nonviolence cannot be sustained without a mobilizable amount of sympathy for the cause and the presence in the constituency of an ethos that values both non-violence and self-sacrifice. In line with Merton's (1968, p. 140) famous typology, there is sometimes a tension between the compassionate goals of the animal movement and the means to achieve these goals which is resolved by deviant means. When peaceful animal rights protests fail, activists become frustrated and are tempted to turn to more aggressive tactics. Thus, while the vast majority of respondents to ASIS (Munro, 1995) favour peaceful and legal means to achieve improvements in the treatment of animals, many activists become disgruntled when their conventional lobbying and years of campaigning fall on deaf ears. Violence and extremism are then rationalized by some perpetrators as necessary evils, with both positive and negative unintended consequences.

When activists engage in more extreme actions, their more moderate colleagues are sometimes accorded more respect by policy makers. In practice, this means that radical actions in the movement often have the effect of creating a niche for more moderate voices. This phenomenon was first identified by Haines (1984) as 'the radical flank effect' which is concerned with how radical groups affect the bargaining chances of moderates. According to Haines, this can either be negative or positive. When there is a negative radical flank effect, the moderates get tainted with the same brush as the radicals; this was the media's reaction to the peaceful protests associated with the live animal export trade in the UK in the mid-1990s. An example of a 'positive radical flank effect' has been noted in the US Congress where the radical and dramatic tactics of People for the Ethical Treatment of Animals (PETA) have made the moderates in the animal movement a more congenial group with which to bargain. This was the experience of at least one movement leader, Adele Douglass, of the American Humane Association:

> *I know for a fact that the 1985 amendments to the Animal Welfare Act would never have been passed without the PETA protests and all the stuff that they were doing. Because then—and it helps us I have to say from the perspective that we're at—when you have extremists and then we come in and where the extremists say 'we want research ended this afternoon,' and we say 'we want the animals treated humanely,' they pay attention to us because that's the other option. I don't think the laws since at least the 1980s would ever have gotten this far without those organizations.* (Interview, 1996)

A similar case was made by Haines, who argued that moderate civil rights groups in the USA in the 1960s were the beneficiaries of a positive radical flank effect when elite white groups were prepared to financially support moderates in order to neutralize the extremists. Haines's findings are supported by a number of contemporary movement watchers who have suggested that the extreme actions of radicals can have the effect of legitimating and strengthening the bargaining position of the moderates (McAdam, 1988, pp. 718–719; Scarce, 1990, pp. 6–7; Dalton, 1994, p. 211). On the other hand, at least one writer (Godwin, 1988, p. 48) has argued that Greenpeace's dramatic actions mobilize financial and moral support from people who 'vicariously' participate in the actions by responding to Greenpeace's direct marketing campaigns. He also points out that threats on the lives of Christian Right leaders have also encouraged people to send money to the evangelicals in the hope of discrediting their extremist enemies. People therefore seem prepared to support dramatic, non-violent actions as in the case of Greenpeace and to register their disapproval of violence and threats of violence as in the case of the Christian Right.

Violent actions by animal rights extremists such as damaging property, sabotage, sending letter and parcel bombs, planting car bombs, making violent threats and engaging in intimidation (see Tester and Walls, 1996) make the actions listed in Table 7.1 seem moderate. For most of the informants in this study, then, violence is seen as counterproductive to the goals of the movement. For John Bryant and the League Against Cruel Sports (LACS), violence is a tactical disaster as well:

> *We're supposed to be a humanitarian cause and in a democracy we have a duty to use every militant but peaceful avenue up to the level of and including the level of civil disobedience but any violence, intimidation, threats, abuse, particularly when it's targeted at individual researchers or*

individual huntsmen and people like that, then if we go down that way there's no way back. (Interview, 1996)

Finally, according to Tarrow, violence can 'chill the blood of bystanders, give pause to prospective allies and cause (early enthusiasts) to defect' (1994, p. 112). Tarrow also makes the point that conventional forms of collective action are advantageous in that they are familiar, easy to employ and enjoy cultural resonance. Indeed, for some activists, the use of militant, confrontational tactics is unattractive. Patty Mark of Animal Liberation Victoria, for example, speaks for many activists when she describes the frustration of being forced into militant forms of direct action as a consequence of official indifference to their more moderate claims:

> *What do you do? You've gone to the police, you've gone to the Minister, you've gone to the RSPCA, you've done everything legally viable, and nobody does anything. Then I think I have a moral responsibility to individually go in and help those animals. And, so I'll be straight, at the same time, I don't want to do that, I don't like to do that, it's nerve-racking!* (Interview, 1994)

Thus, some prominent social movement analysts (Doherty, Gurr, Kitschelt, Tarrow and Tilly, among others), as well as leading activists like John Bryant in the UK and Patty Mark in Australia, see violence as counterproductive as a social movement strategy. This was the view of virtually all of the 53 advocates and activists interviewed for this book; furthermore, it is the overwhelming belief of animal defenders surveyed in the USA and Australia that legal, non-violent protests are both more justified and effective than illegal, violent activities.

The Power in DIY Direct Action

Tarrow (1994) has identified three major types of publicly mounted collective action: violence, disruption caused by non-violent direct action and convention via primarily organized public demonstrations. In Table 7.1, I have labelled the strategies of disruption and convention 'interference' and 'publicity', respectively, in the case of the animal movement's strategic praxis. All three forms of collective action— publicity, interference and violence—have been enacted by the animal movement, although violence is a strategy only of groups outside the mainstream movement. For the supporters of Singer and Regan in the animal welfare and liberation/rights strands of the movement, the strategies of conventional lobbying and non-violent direct action are used in preference to violence (Garner, 1993). Tarrow points out that one of the major powers of the modern social movement is its capacity to combine various forms of collective action. Tilly supports the idea that action repertoires are enacted 'cumulatively over many simultaneous and/or repeated meetings, demonstrations, marches, petitions, statements, and other interactions with objects of claims' (1999, p. 262)

Virtually every informant interviewed for this paper acknowledged the importance of getting favourable publicity via the media for their different campaigns and many believed that the best way of attracting the media was by provocative, dramatic actions such as hunger strikes, animal rescue operations and other 'interference' tactics. Most of the tactics shown in Table 7.1 are usually deployed collectively although some like those denoted with an asterisk lend themselves more to individual or DIY actions. Tilly (1978) has pointed out that social movements use quite a small number of tactics considering the vast number that have been used throughout history. Thus, in a series of books on nonviolent protest, Sharp (1973) describes approximately 200 such activities. How do activists choose from the available repertoire? Jasper (1997) suggests that activists exhibit 'tactical tastes', that is, they choose the tactics that match their habitus or disposition to act in a particular way. Thus, trade unionists tend to go on strike, students 'sit in' and so on. Jasper also argues that tactics express protesters' political identities and moral visions (1997, p. 237). To go on a hunger strike or to raid a battery farm says different things about personal identity. The identity of an animal activist might be as a radical vegan, an animal rescuer, a conservationist or as someone who goes on marches or writes letters to the editor. 'A taste in tactics persists partly because it shapes one's sense of self' (1997, p. 246).

DIY Activism at the League Against Cruel Sports

DIY activism is in accord with Margaret Mead's epigraph quoted above (on p. 122). Most of the tactics discussed in the remainder of the paper are examples of DIY activism which many animal activists favour. In the case of the League Against Cruel Sports (LACS), DIY activism is a philosophy which successfully combines the grassroots activities of activists equipped with cameras and the political skills of the organizational advocates who spend their time drafting animal welfare legislation. Thus, Mike Huskisson's Animal Cruelty Investigation Group (ACIG) has formed an alliance with LACS so as to engage in lawful, covert operations designed to break the back of the hunting fraternity. Huskisson's grassroots, anti-cruelty surveillance work with the League is a good example of effective advocacy/activist cooperation in animal protection. The ACIG was founded by Huskisson, a former hunt saboteur who now works alongside John Bryant to expose animal cruelty, lawfully and by non-violent means. The ACIG provides detailed tips to its 1,700 supporters throughout the country on DIY activism in which people are encouraged to video violations of the Animal Welfare Act and expose the cruelty of hunting.

Huskisson is a legend in the UK animal movement for his undercover work in the Feldberg case (McDonald, 1994). He maintains that video activism is more effective in reforming animal abusers than violent and illegal activities which, he says, 'led to people like myself and others ending up in prison because there wasn't any other outlet' (Interview, 1996). The DIY actions listed in Table 7.1 are preferred by 'caring sleuths' like Huskisson because they are legal, non-violent forms of direct action. Melucci defines direct action as a

> form of resistance or collective intervention which possesses a minimum of organisation; which breaks the rules of the political game and/or the norms of the organisation without, however, undermining the foundations of the system of domination; which does not involve the deliberate use of violence; and which seeks to change the rules of the political game and/or to intervene in the political system. (1996, p. 378)

As space does not permit an analysis of each of the tactics listed in Table 7.1, I have selected a sample (shown in bold in the table) of the most commonly used and representative action repertoires—in the context of Turner and Killian's (1987) typology—in the contemporary animal movement. The tactics of DIY direct action, the demonstration (publicity strategies) and the hunger strike, ethical vegetarianism and undercover surveillance (interference strategies) are described below.

Publicity Strategies in Animal Protection

> *I mean sitting chained up to a pig stall for seven hours is very tiring and there's not a great deal of excitement in it.*

> —Australian animal activist

Demonstrations

The demonstration is the most widely used protest strategy in the social movement's repertoire. Demonstrations have become institutionalized and constitute 'the classical modular form of collective action' (Tarrow, 1994, p. 107). While Melucci implies that demonstrations require a minimum of organization, organizers themselves claim otherwise (Mondros & Wilson, 1994, pp. 165–166).

Tarrow notes that demonstrations can be used to express the existence of a group or its solidarity with another group or to celebrate a victory or mourn the passage of a leader (1994, p. 100). Yet for many animal movement leaders, the demonstration is seen as a risky venture. For example, John Bryant, the co-chair of LACS, cautions against its use as it can prove to be counterproductive: 'If the demonstration turns violent, and somebody puts a brick through a window, then it becomes a tactical disaster' (Interview, 1996). Compassion in World Farming (CIWF) experienced this when one of its peaceful demonstrations was hijacked by extremists who smashed the window of a lorry carrying live animals for overseas export. The media ignored the animal welfare issue behind the demonstration and focused on 'the brick through a window' story which featured pictures of men in balaclavas smashing the window of a lorry (Erlichman, 1995). Yet demonstrations remain the quintessential form of protest for social movement activists who as individuals or as members of collectivities can enact the several kinds of demonstrations listed in Table 7.1 under protest strategies. These include a large number of options ranging from the collective actions of parades, marches, rallies, etc. to the DIY activism of renouncing honours.

Pamphleteering

And then somebody handed me a leaflet.

—English animal activist

John Bryant advocates social change via leafleting and notes in his *Fettered Kingdoms* (1982) that the great strength of the animal rights movement lies with the supporters who hand out leaflets every week: 'The leaflet is our media. In nearly twenty years in animal welfare and rights I have rarely found a campaigner who did not join the movement after being handed a leaflet usually in the street' (Bryant, 1982, p. 88). Time and again in this study, when I asked what it was that got informants started in the movement, the response was that it came in the form of a leaflet, advertisement or in an arresting image. Tarrow claims that it was in the form of the pamphlet that the democratic implications of print first became known (1998, p. 45). The leaflet is therefore one of the oldest tactics in the social movement's repertoire. For many activists like John Bryant, it is the medium of the animal movement. The political potency of the leaflet can be gauged by its impact in the McLibel episode when vegetarian, animal rights activists distributed a short critique of McDonald's in the form of a leaflet which subsequently led to the widely publicized libel trial in London's High Court in 1996.

In the above section I have outlined two of the liberal governance strategies associated with getting publicity for the movement via persuasive communication; in the next section, the critical governance strategies of hunger strikes (bargaining strategy), ethical vegetarianism (facilitation strategy) and undercover surveillance (coercion strategy) will be discussed. Each of these repertoires are further examples of DIY activism which have the potential to subvert, if not disrupt, the status quo. According to Tarrow (1994, p. 108) in its contemporary form, disruptive tactics have three main purposes; first, disruption concretely expresses a movement's determination (e.g. sit-ins); second, it obstructs the routine activities of opponents, bystanders and authorities (e.g. blockades); and third, disruption broadens the field of conflict by posing a risk to law and order and drawing the state into the conflict (e.g. Brightlingsea Against Animal Exports (BALE's) street demonstrations discussed below). Yet despite frequent reference in the literature to direct action, the animal movement, like the environmental movement, tends to avoid direct action in the strong sense of forced entry, occupations and the like (Tilly, 1999, p. 267).

Interference Strategies in Animal Protection

The Save-Our-Sheep Hunger Strike

English ports used in the live export trade in the mid-1990s became the scene for some of the biggest demonstrations seen in the UK since the miners' strike a decade earlier. The new year in 1995 began with British newspapers trumpeting a moral panic with headlines about 'animal rights siege', 'single issue hooligans' and 'bunny-huggers do battle'. An editorial in *The Times*, headed 'Cuddly Terrorism', described the animal liberation protesters as 'on a par with the IRA' (*The Times*, 8 February 1995), a claim that was often repeated in the media during the mass protests that year. To be sure, other themes also featured in the mainstream press although the law and order story was the predominant frame for most of the time. Under these conditions, the idea of a hunger strike was certain to invite further derision, or indifference, from a cynical mass media. However, one regional newspaper at least seemed to have a grudging respect for the willingness of the activists to bear witness. In the lead-up to the hunger strike in London, the *Cambridge Evening News* (22 July 1996) wrote:

> The usual Cambridge cranks will be among the loonies in a hunger strike next week. True, history will eventually recognise these cranks and loonies as heroes in the long struggle against cruelty to exported farm animals. History will see their dotty little gesture outside the Ministry of Agriculture as one of the few significant steps towards real civilisation in an otherwise benighted age.

Activists from Animal Rights Cambridge proudly displayed this clipping on their noticeboard at their regular meetings and at BALE's post-mortem of the hunger strike I attended in the Brightlingsea community hall. With this 'dotty little gesture', the hunger strikers hoped to shame authorities into bargaining over, if not banning, the animal export trade.

The campaign against live exports in England was motivated primarily by anger over the cruelty involved in transporting animals long distances by road and sea. It was an animal welfare protest, not a strict animal rights campaign in which the rights of animals not to be slaughtered for food was prominent. While most of the leaders of the grassroots groups like BALE and the more structured advocacy organizations such as Compassion in World Farming (CIWF) were vegetarians or vegans, most of the rank-and-file protesters were not. Indeed, a large placard hanging from a Colchester pub explained: 'You Don't Have to Stop Eating Meat to Care—Ban Live Exports'. Even so, inside the animal movement, the distinction is made between those who eat meat and those who do not. While meat avoidance is not a high priority for just over half of the movement's supporters in the Animals and Social Issues Survey (Munro, 1995), it is seen by many inside the movement as the measure of one's commitment to the cause of animals. Vegetarianism, as the quintessential form of DIY activism, is taken up in the next section.

Ethical Vegetarianism at FARM and MRAR

When we ask what drives the contemporary vegetarian movement, the only consistent reply is compassion for animal suffering. (Douglas, 2000) The Farm Animal Reform Movement (FARM) in the USA seeks to promote vegetarianism in a climate in which the American media have not been sympathetic to animal rights and anti-cruelty issues for most of the twentieth century (Jones, 1996). The activists at FARM have used innovative strategies and tactics to publicize a health education message that the US press finds difficult to ignore. When FARM began its animal advocacy in 1976 it was called the Vegetarian Information Service; five years later it focused more on cruelty issues associated with factory farming. FARM's most prominent campaign, The Great American Meatout, tends to downplay the cruelty issues in preference to the positive message of a vegetarian lifestyle. Jones (1996) believes that this, along with FARM's potential as an ally of environmental groups, explains its recent success in the media. For example, it has been very effective in the strategy of 'mobilizing information' (Lemert, 1984) whereby its issues and campaigns are advertised free of charge in the mass media.

Its campaigns give activists hands-on, practical ways to get FARM's message across. World Farm Animals' Day (WFAD) on Gandhi's birthday, 2 October is promoted as a non-violent educational event. In the WFAD campaign, bearing witness by the observance of this tradition appears to be more important than getting media attention, although a media kit is available to activists who want to issue press releases and the like.

Similarly, a kindred organization in Australia, Mountain Residents for Animal Rights (MRAR) has used unconventional, eccentric and exhibitionist tactics to attract the media's attention. Like FARM's success in the national media, MRAR has been successful in 'mobilizing information' in the local media. It has achieved this by dramatic, eco-friendly tactics and messages that appeal to the media as well as animal protectors, environmentalists and vegetarians. Unlike FARM's strident 'Meat or Murder' rhetoric, MRAR has adopted a 'Transforming McDonald's' campaign in which the fast-food giant has been asked (unsuccessfully) to convert to a vegetarian diet. MRAR used street theatre and 'the world's biggest veggie burger' to promote its campaign to transform McDonald's; a 'non-sexist, eco-friendly clown' in the form of Regie McVeggie was created as an alternative to Ronald McDonald. While the campaign did not achieve the publicity of the McLibel trial in the UK, for a brief time it did put vegetarianism on the public agenda in the Sydney-Blue Mountains area.

In their different ways, these animal SMOs have utilized various media to promote the cause of farm animals by using the positive message of a vegetarian lifestyle. For many animal activists, the ultimate boycott is to live a vegan or vegetarian lifestyle. In Singer's view, vegetarianism is a prerequisite to effective animal activism for 'the moral obligation to boycott the meat available in butchers' shops and supermarkets today is inescapable' (Singer, 1992, p. 174). There is, however, much ambivalence in the animal movement associated with ethical vegetarianism as revealed in ASIS (Munro, 1995). Nonetheless, many people inside the movement would agree with Adams (1990) that meat eating is the most extensive and institutionalized form of violence against animals. FARM's Scott Williams, for example, points out that 'if you can eat them, what can't you justify?' (Interview, 1996).

Joan Court from Animal Rights Cambridge explained what she believes is the trend in the UK:

> *People use the word 'obscene' all the time, so it seems to be dreadful to eat animals. Everybody I know in the movement is vegetarian drifting towards veganism. The young people can't understand why everybody's not a vegan but we're now attracting a lot of older women and men who have had a lifetime of course of eating dairy products and it's more difficult [for them].* (Interview, 1996)

One of the factors identified in ASIS (Munro, 1995) which distinguished animal rights activists from advocates and supporters of animal welfare was the respondents' dietary habits. As expected, only a small percentage of activists were meat eaters. At the other dietary extreme, vegans were much more prolific among activists (32 per cent) than among either advocates (12 per cent) or supporters (3 percent). Respondents with weaker attachments to the animal movement were much more likely to eat meat; supporters were four times more likely than activists to be meat eaters while the percentage of meat-eating advocates was double the percentage for activists.

The conclusion we can draw from these data is that the more active members (according to their self-designation as activist, advocate or supporter) practise meat avoidance. Thus, the habit of meat avoidance is for many animal protectionists the single most important thing an individual can do for animals. For many activists, animal rights and vegetarianism are different sides of the same coin. Committed animal rights activists believe that eating meat devalues the movement's philosophy that animals should be left alone. For them, the avoidance of meat is the most basic prerequisite to movement commitment and credibility even if this involves personal sacrifice.

Vegetarianism, whether motivated by gustatory, health, environmental or animal welfare concerns, is a profoundly radical tactic for a social movement to practise since it disrupts and challenges society's predominant construction of animals as meat to be eaten. It is also a tactic that individuals adopt to demonstrate their commitment to the animal rights cause, 'to attest personally to the sincerity of our concern for non-human animals' (Singer, 1975, p. 175). Seen in this way, it is the quintessential form of DIY activism.

Undercover Surveillance

While vegetarianism involves increasing numbers of people in what is a mild form of direct action in the private sphere, a more assertive form of DIY activism is undercover surveillance which is typically enacted by one or two committed individuals. Undercover surveillance is one of the oldest tactics in the animal movement's repertoire.

The most famous case of undercover surveillance in the animal movement's history was the expose´ of animal experimenter Edward Taub by Alex Pacheco in Silver Spring in 1981. The police raid on the Institute of Behavioral Research was televised, thus giving maximum publicity to the animal movement. This episode—which involved exposing experiments on surgically crippled monkeys—is one of the most well documented in the movement's history (see Fraser, 1993; Orlans, 1993, pp. 176–179; Blum, 1994, chapter 5; Rudacille, 2001).

The English equivalent to the Silver Spring's episode was initiated by the ACIG undercover operation in 1990 when its founder Mike Huskisson and another animal rights activist, Melody McDonald, gained access to the laboratories of Professor Wilhelm Feldberg and for a period of five months videoed the 89-year-old researcher at work. The tapes, which ran to over 30 hours, revealed breaches of the 1986 Act concerning animal experimentation. A subsequent governmental inquiry confirmed that apart from failing to anaesthetize experimental animals properly, Feldberg had broken the law by continuing with experiments he had been told to terminate. Once the video-taped evidence was made public, Feldberg's experiments were ended within twenty-four hours by the Home Office.

From the perspective of vivisectors, the expose´ would no doubt be seen as a colossal deception since Huskisson and his accomplice had posed as researcher and biographer, respectively, thus duping Feldberg into believing they had no ulterior motives. Undercover surveillance raises some interesting ethical questions for a movement that promotes the ethical treatment of animals. Is it ethical to use deception to gain access to an organization for the purpose of exposing wrongdoing in that organization? Most animal activists believe that they are morally obliged to do whatever they can within the law to save animals' lives. In the Feldberg case, activists would claim that the deception involved was justified given the apparent laxity of government controls over scientists like Feldberg. Deception was necessary if the activists were to expose what they saw as a greater evil—cruelty to animals—perpetrated by scientists funded by taxpayers, most of whom would object to the research if they knew the facts. Huskisson claims the ACIG had the public's support for what they did and argues that undercover surveillance is lawful, justified and non-violent as opposed to more extreme forms of animal rights activism which he condemns:

> *We secured the film and within a day of showing it to the Home Office that experiment was ended. The man's licence to experiment was taken away; the*

Medical Research Council had an investigation and if he'd been a younger man he'd have been prosecuted. That ended that experiment dead. Now we did that, and we had public support and there was anger directed against the laboratory. If someone had parked a vehicle outside and blown the place to smithereens it would have been the same result, but the public would have said 'How could they do that? That's an outrage, there's that man doing his work, his lifetime work to end suffering to humans and these cowardly scum come out of the dark and they destroy a laboratory.' Same effect, but public anger would have been rightly directed against our side, so we have to use our brains to get in amongst the opponents and put an end to it lawfully. That's what we do. (Interview, 1996)

Like the Silver Spring case, the Feldberg expose´ has become one of the most celebrated in the movement. Huskisson uses it to promote the virtues of undercover surveillance. He advises young people attracted to animal protection to:

Get a video camera, get yourself a job in a research place, get yourself a job in a hunt kennel, go out there and get the film and you're not breaking the law, but you're breaking the back of the opponents. (Interview, 1996)

Conclusion

This paper has focused on how the animal rights movement strategizes its various campaigns. It does this via the non-violent DIY strategies of publicity and interference in campaigns to save animals' lives. Only a small number of publicity strategies (demonstrations and pamphleteering) and interference strategies (hunger strikes, ethical vegetarianism and undercover surveillance) have been described in this paper. They were chosen because they are among the most common in the animal movement; moreover, they are newsworthy (e.g. demonstrations) and appeal also to DIY activists ranging from the moderate (e.g. pamphleteering) to the more radical (e.g. ethical vegetarianism, hunger strikes and undercover surveillance). These tactics are also representative of Turner and Killian's (1987) typology of tactical mechanisms deployed by social movements: persuasion (pamphleteering, demonstrations), bargaining (hunger strikes), facilitation (ethical vegetarianism) and coercion (undercover surveillance). Furthermore, they are in accord with Turner and Killian's claim that social movement activists choose tactics that are familiar, available and likely to guarantee a (positive) response from their targets. Various theorists have argued that non-violence is the most effective mobilization strategy in Western democracies for social movements to adopt (Doherty, Gurr, Kitschelt, Tarrow and Tilly). For mainstream animal activists, too, violence is seen as counterproductive to the movement's goal in promoting the compassionate treatment of non-human animals.

REFERENCES

Adams, C. (1990) *The Sexual Politics of Meat: A Feminist-Vegetarian Critical Theory* (Cambridge: Polity).

Blum, D. (1994) *The Monkey Wars* (New York: Oxford University Press).

Bryant, J. (1982) *Fettered Kingdoms* (Manchester: Fox Press).

Dalton, R. (1994) *The Green Rainbow: Environmental Groups in Western Europe* (New Haven: Yale University Press).

Doherty, B. (2000) "Manufactured vulnerability: protest campaign tactics," in: B. Seel, M. Paterson & B. Doherty (Eds) *Direct Action in British Environmentalism* (London and New York: Routledge).

Doherty, B. (2002) *Ideas and Actions in the Green Movement* (London and New York: Routledge).

Douglas, M. (2000) 'The flesh is weak', a review of ethical vegetarianism: from Pythagoras to Peter Singer," *Times Literary Supplement*, 8.

Erlichman, J. (1995) "Rent-a-mob forces end to animal welfare protests," *The Guardian*, 5 January.

Fraser, C. (1993) "The Raid at Silver Spring" *The New Yorker*, pp. 66–84, 19 April.

Garner, R. (1993) *Animals, Politics and Morality* (Manchester: Manchester University Press).

Gitlin, T. (1980) *The Whole World is Watching: Mass Media in the Making or Unmaking of the New Left* (Berkeley and Los Angeles: University of California Press).

Godwin, R. K. (1988) *One Billion Dollars of Influence: The Direct Marketing of Politics* (Chatham, NJ: Chatham House), [Cited in Shaiko, R.G. (1993) Greenpeace USA: "Something old, new, borrowed," *Annals of the American Academy of Political and Social Science*, 528, July, p. 93.].

Gurr, T. (2000) "Nonviolence in ethnopolitics: strategies for the attainment of group rights and autonomy," *PS: Political Science*, XXIII (2), pp. 155–160.

Haines, H. (1984) "Black radicalization and the funding of civil rights: 1957–1970," *Social Problems*, 32(1), pp. 31–43.

Harding, T. (1998) "Viva camcordistas! Video activism and the protest movement," in: G. McKay (Ed.) *DIY Culture: Party and Protest in Nineties Britain* (London: Verso).

Jasper, J. (1997) *The Art of Moral Protest: Culture, Biography and Creativity in Social Movements* (Chicago, IL: University of Chicago Press).

Jones, D. (1996) "The Media's Response to Animal Rights Activism: Tracking Print Coverage for Three Annual Events," pp. 1–24 (North Grafton, MA: Centre for Animals and Public Policy, Tufts University, School of Veterinary Medicine).

Jordan, T. (2002) *Activism! Direct Action, Hacktivism and the Future of Society* (London: Reaktion Books).

Kew, B. (1999) "Fearsome Truths: The Challenge of Animal Liberation," Unpublished PhD Thesis in Sociology, University of Durham, Durham.

Kitschelt, H. (1986) "Political opportunity structures and political protest: anti-nuclear movements in four democracies," *British Journal of Political Science*, 16, pp. 57–85.

Koopmans, R. (1993) "The dynamics of protest waves," *American Sociological Review*, 58, pp. 637–658.

Lemert, J. B. (1984) "News context and the elimination of mobilizing information: an experiment," *Journalism Quarterly*, Summer, pp. 243–249.

Lofland, J. (1996) *Social Movement Organisations: Guide to Research in Insurgent Realities* (New York: Aldine de Gruyter).

McAdam, D. (1988) "Micromobilization contexts and recruitment to activism," *International Social Movement Research*, I, pp. 125–154 (Greenwich, CT: JAI Press).

McDonald, M. (1994) Caught in the Act: The Feldberg Investigation (Oxford: Jon Carpenter Publishing).

McKay, G. (Ed.) (1998) *DIY Culture: Party and Protest in Nineties Britain* (London: Verso).

Melucci, A. (1996) *Challenging Codes: Collective Action in the Information Age* (Cambridge: Cambridge University Press).

Merton, R. (1968) *Social Theory and Social Structure* (New York: The Free Press).

Mondros, J. & Wilson, S. (1994) *Organizing for Power and Empowerment* (New York: Columbia University Press).

Munro, L. (1995) "Animals and Social Issues Survey (ASIS)": a questionnaire used in unpublished PhD thesis.

Munro, L. (2002) "The animal activism of Henry Spira 1927–1998," *Society and Animals*, 10(2), pp. 61–79.

Newell, P. (2000) "Environmental NGOs and globalization: the governance of TNCs", in: R. Cohen & S. Rai (Eds) *Global Social Movements* (London and New Brunswick, NJ: Athlone Press).

Oliver, P. & Marwell, G. (1992) "Mobilizing technologies for collective action," in: A. D. Morris & C. McClurgMueller (Eds) *Frontiers of Social Movement Theory* (New Haven, CT: Yale University Press).

Orlans, F. B. (1993) *In the Name of Science: Issues in Responsible Animal Experimentation* (Oxford: Oxford University Press)

Richards, R. (1990) "Consensus mobilization through ideology, networks, and grievances: a study of the contemporary animal rights movement," PhD Dissertation, Ann Arbor.

Rochon, T. R. (1990) "The West European peace movement and the theory of new social movements," in: R. Dalton & M. Kuechler (Eds) *Challenging the Political Order: New Social and Political Movements in Western Democracies*, pp. 105–121 (Cambridge: Polity Press).

Rucht, D. (1990) "The strategies and action repertoires of new movements," in: R. Dalton & M. Kuechler (Eds) *Challenging the Political Order: New Social and Political Movements in Western Democracies* (Cambridge: Polity Press).

Rudacille, D. (2001) *The Scalpel and the Butterfly: The Conflict between Animal Research and Animal Protection* (Berkeley: University of California Press).

Scarce, R. (1990) *Eco-Warriors: Understanding the Radical Environmental Movement* (Chicago: Noble Press).

Shapiro, K. (1994) "The caring sleuth: portrait of an animal rights activist," *Society & Animals*, 2(2), pp. 145–165.

Sharp, G. (1973) *The Politics of Nonviolent Action* (Boston, MA: P. Sargent).

Singer, P. (1975) *Animal Liberation: A New Ethic for Our Treatment of Animals* (New York: New York Review and Random House).

Singer, P. (1992) "Becoming a vegetarian," in: D. W. Curtin & L. M. Heldke (Eds) *Cooking, Eating, Thinking: Transformative Philosophies of Food* (Bloomington: Indiana University Press).

Tarrow, S. (1994) *Power in Movement: Social Movements, Collective Action and Politics* (Cambridge: Cambridge University Press).

Tarrow, S. (1998) *Power in Movement: Social Movements and Contentious Politics*, 2nd edition (Cambridge: Cambridge University Press).

Tester, K. & Walls, G. (1996) "The ideology and current activities of the Animal Liberation Front," *Contemporary Politics*, 2(2), pp. 79–91.

The Economist (1995) The meat of the matter, 21 January, p. 62.

Tilly, C. (1978) *From Mobilization to Revolution* (Reading, MA: Addison-Wesley).

Tilly, C. (1985) "Models and realities of popular collective action," *Social Research*, 52, Winter, pp. 717–747.

Tilly, C. (1993/1994) "Social movements as historically specific clusters of political performances," Berkeley *Journal of Sociology*, 38, pp. 1–29.

Tilly, C. (1999) "Conclusion: from interactions to outcomes in social movements," in: M. Giugni, D. McAdam & C. Tilly (Eds) *How Social Movements Matter* (Minneapolis: University of Minnesota Press).

Turner, R. & Killian, L. (1987) *Collective Behavior*, 3rd edition (Englewood Cliffs, NJ: Prentice-Hall).

Van Zoonen, L. (1996) "A dance of death: new social movements and the mass media," in: D. Paletz (Ed.) *Political Communication in Action: States, Institutions, Movement, Audiences* (Cresshill, NJ: Hampton Press).

Wapner, P. (1995) In defense of banner hangers: the dark green politics of Greenpeace, in: B. Taylor (Ed.) *Ecological Resistance Movements: The Global Emergence of Radical and Popular Environmentalism* (New York: State University of New York Press).

Chapter 8

Grassroots Animal Rights Activism:
The Case of Mountain Residents for Animal Rights

Mountain Residents for Animal Rights (MRAR)

MRAR is a grassroots animal activist group made up of about a dozen activists operating in the Blue Mountains (population 66,000) west of Sydney. The group has chosen to remain small and close-knit so as to avoid the inevitable bureaucracy that characterises most large organizations (Interview, 1993). It was founded in 1984 by Anne Elliott who until then had been involved in working for animals for about eight years. During the past ten years MRAR has lobbied local politicians and used the local media in its campaigns on behalf of animals and in doing so, it has put animals on the political agenda in the Blue Mountains. An analysis of these campaigns in the context of animal rights as a New Social Movement (NSM) will show how effective a small grassroots lobby group can be in achieving the goals of the wider movement. For as Rucht (1990:158) points out, NSMs "do not necessarily focus on the national level. They emphasize the role of independent and small groups and the importance of local activities, and they promote grassroots politics".

Grassroots activism in MRAR is driven by its philosophy of "saving animals' lives, saving finite resources, and promoting a more gentle way of living" (MRAR, 1992:15). In common with other new SMOs, MRAR's approach is didactic and the tactics "unorthodox, informal and above all, critical and value-infused" (Crook et al, 1992:155). Because of MRAR's lack of material resources, it relies heavily on the local media to publicize its campaigns and promote its causes. What MRAR lacks in material resources is more than compensated for by its energetic and innovative campaigns which, according to Crook et al, are characteristic of grassroots activism: "Action which stresses grassroots involvement, commitment and spontaneity and unselfish dedication contrasts sharply with a formalized corporatist-bureaucratic idiom" (Crook et al, 1992:155). In identifying what is new in the NSMs, Crook et al, (1992:148) single out their specific orientations combined with international mass media exposure. They identify five features of the distinctive orientation of NSMs which are generally applicable to the animal rights movement. 1. movement politics is driven by moral rather than instrumental considerations; 2. NSMs are anti-bureaucratic and rely on self-organisation; 3. key activists are suspicious of conventional party politics and established elites; 4. they combine leisure activities such as street theatre with protest; and 5. NSMs are highly dependent on the mass media for getting their messages across to the public.

Anne Elliott: MRAR's Founder

To be successful, a SMO depends on visionaries and a comprehensive agenda based on scholarly research (Spencer, 1991). For MRAR this means having a strong ethical foundation on which to base its campaigns. Elliott is a "moral reformer" with a vision of a better world built on a gentler relationship with nature; "harmony", "social justice", "ethical behaviour" and "reverence for nature" are concepts she uses frequently in explaining her philosophy of deep-ecology and ethical vegetarianism. She is widely read on these issues as well as on feminism and animal rights. She gave up her full-time job as a special education teacher so as "to be able to devote more time to animal welfare issues" (Interview, 1993). Elliot believes in "thinking globally and acting locally", for her, "grassroots action is the most powerful tool of all" (MRAR, 1992:16). She sought to promote the Blue Mountains as a "cruelty-free zone" by adopting the slogan used internationally in 1985 by animal welfare/rights groups—Phase Out 2000—working towards the phasing out of meat eating, vivisection, factory farming, zoos and circuses and other forms of animal abuse by the year 2000. In its campaigns on behalf of animals, MRAR has focussed creatively on four main issues which have global relevance for the animal rights movement and its general objectives. The campaigns are:

1. transforming the fast-food chain McDonald's.

2. promoting eco-friendly eating (vegetarianism).

3. opposing zoos and circuses.

4. opposing the use of stray dogs in vivisection.

Data for the case study reported here are based on interviews with Anne Elliott, articles and letters to the editors which appeared in local newspapers about each of the campaigns, various brochures, press releases, posters, and advertisements used by MRAR activists as well as correspondence from the group's file. Six newspapers in the Blue Mountains region regularly featured stories about MRAR campaigns. Some of these were of a substantial length providing valuable descriptive detail, if not analysis, of the campaigns. Because the issues targeted by MRAR were framed as social justice issues, the local council could not ignore them; moreover, the campaigns were organised as "events", typically with a dramatic or humorous theme which the local media found difficult to resist.

The Transforming Mc Donald's Campaign

According to Elliott, MRAR's McDonald's Campaign "highlights the link between meat-eating and the destruction of our planet" (MRAR, 1992:14). In making the link between animal rights and the rights of nature, MRAR is stating its basic philosophy of saving animals' lives and saving finite resources. The McDonald's campaign is important for this reason. In 1987, MRAR asked candidates in the local council election if they were in favour of the fast-food giant setting up a restaurant in the Blue Mountains township of Blaxland; the results were published in the local press giving details of "the candidates" views on animal rights and the McDonald's restaurant proposal. *The Blue Mountains Gazette* reported that about 150 residents had met at a public meeting to voice their support for McDonald's in Blaxland; the newspaper later carried the headline "McDonald's face strong opposition" (1 June, 1988:7). The Blaxland Residents' Action Group (BRAG) was evidently opposed to the proposed location because of the traffic congestion the restaurant would cause; no mention was made of animal rights or the meat-eating issue which was the basis of the MRAR's protest. As environmental activists, BRAG's anti-development stance saw McDonald's as an affront to the aesthetic sensibilities of its members; consequently, their primary objective was to defend (their) human right to enjoy nature, rather than to defend the interests of animals not to be eaten.

The activists in BRAG and MRAR kept the multi-national at bay for over two years; however, in September 1990, a McDonald's outlet was finally opened in Blaxland in the Blue Mountains. MRAR then began to "target" McDonald's with its "Transforming McDonald's Campaign". It began on the day the Blaxland outlet opened with the launching of "the world's biggest veggie burger" by Regie McVegie, the eco-friendly, non-sexist clown who has continued publicising the virtues of a vegetarian burger ever since. MRAR has written to McDonald's and has initiated an international "Telephone McDonald's Month" requesting the fast-food chain to introduce a veggie burger in all of their outlets for ethical and environmental reasons. The idea of telephoning McDonald's at its US headquarters is a world first for MRAR. Information about the "Transforming McDonald's Campaign" was circulated to over 200 environmental, animal rights and humanitarian organisations throughout the world; many of these advertised the campaign in their regions and several prominent people (including the well-known American animal rights activist Henry Spiral contacted MRAR about joining the campaign. In a press release late in 1993, MRAR reported that McDonald's Quality Assurance Manager in Australia "has been exploring vegetarian burger alternatives, but at this stage feels there is not a formula quite suited to McDonald's unique conditions" (MRAR Press Release, September, 1993).

The fact that McDonald's is at least exploring a vegetarian alternative is a sign of the campaign's potential success. Goode (1992:458), in the context of discussing the animal rights movement, argues that successful protest movements focus on "vulnerable" targets. McDonald's, in spite of its size and power, is very vulnerable and highly sensitive to adverse publicity. Gunn and Gunn (1991), for example, sum up the main objections (and sources of vulnerability) to the spread of McDonald's outlets as:

1. environmental degradation (destruction of tropical areas for raising beef cattle).

2. proliferation of dead-end jobs.

3. the nature of the food they serve (high fat and high salt content); and

4. the forcing of local competitors out of business (1991:36).

MRAR has "targeted" McDonald's using humour and street theatre in order to encourage the organisation to transform itself. In this way MRAR has avoided litigation since it believes McDonald's would be reluctant to take action against a group running a good-humoured campaign against it (Interview, 1993).

The creative use of humour ensured wide publicity in the McDonald's campaign. MRAR's strategy was evidently inspired by the success of the Great American Meat-Out in 1986 sponsored by the Farm Animal Reform Movement (FARM). It conducted about seventy Meat-Out events and "publicity stunts to induce media coverage of meat-eating issues" (The Animals' Agenda, 1986:2) These events resulted in some 200 news stories in the American media including a front page report in *The Boston Globe* and stories on national network radio news. One newspaper featured a photograph of campaigners outside a McDonald's outlet holding placards reading: "Farm animals never have a nice day"; "McDonalds = Mc Death to the rain-forests"; "Try a food revolution go veggie". MRAR preferred more diplomatic language. Elliott told a local journalist that "it would be a nice gesture if McDonald's introduced a veggie burger as its contribution to the International Year of the Peace" (*Penrith Press*, 22 October 1986).

The Eco-Friendly Eating Campaign

Related to the McDonald's campaign is the MRAR quest to encourage people in the Blue Mountains to convert from meat to a vegetarian diet. The organisation so far has been unsuccessful in convincing McDonald's to follow the example of their outlets in Amsterdam which now offer a vegetarian menu; however, Mc Salad rolls have been introduced in some Sydney outlets and MRAR sees this as a good omen. In the Blue Mountains about a dozen restaurants now offer vegetarian and vegan food as a result of MRAR's urging, and the organisation coordinates a" Yulefest" Vegetarian Dinner as a yearly service to the community, the idea being to help people "celebrate Christmas in a more thoughtful way" (MRAR, 1992:15). In his analysis of the efficacy of symbols in the mass media, Schudson (1989:163) emphasises the importance of the yearly calendar as a storage device for cultural symbols; by getting its "Yulefest" alternative permanently fixed as a yearly event in the Blue Mountains, MRAR has effectively institutionalised the event.

Whilst not all animal liberationists are vegetarians, some believe "meat eating is the most oppressive and extensive institutionalised violence against animals" (Adams, 1990:70). MRAR believes that the best chance for animals to be liberated from human exploitation is through successful appeals to our consciences; if we think about what we eat when we dine out on a Big Mac or a pork chop, our appetite for animals might be curbed. For MRAR, meat eating is both an animal rights issue and an environmental one. "With less than ten years in which to turn the tide against the destruction of the earth, the promotion of vegetarianism and vegetarian food is perhaps the single most important environmental and ethical issue of all" (MRAR 1992:15). The non-violent, non-sexist vegetarian Regie McVegie was created as the symbol of a "gentler way of living" and eating. Schudson (1989:165) notes that a cultural object, be it a ritual, advertisement or a piece of street-theatre, has rhetorical force as either a positive or negative appeal; whether humour attracts attention to the seriousness of the appeal or only trivialises it, is always a dilemma for those engaged in the art of persuasion. The balance between humour and the message of harmony has been carefully struck by MRAR and as a result the campaign attracted a good deal of media attention with "photo opportunities" for Regie McVeggie and headlines such as: "Reggie to hand out 'eco' awards" (*BMG*, 26 June, 1991); "Reggie pushes for eco-friendly burger" (*BMG*, 8 September, 1993); "Offer for Reggie to replace Ronald" (*BMG*, 6 October, 1993) and even "Reggie McVeggie for Mayor" (*Blue Mountains Whisper*, October 1990). As surrogate mayor of the Blue Mountains or Resident of McDonald's, Regie Mc Veggie is portrayed as an eco-friendly alternative to meat eating. During the three-year campaign MRAR produced a *McDonald's Campaign Pack* which was sent to dozens of interested groups and media outlets. The campaign attracted international attention and was reported in a major American publication. Related activities included the presentation of Eco-Awards to individuals and organizations who are "doing the right thing by the earth", an *Animal Aware Fair* and a *Festive Vegetarian Banquet* as "a more thoughtful way of celebrating Christmas without exploiting animals" (MRAR Transforming McDonald's Flyer, July 1992).

Both the McDonald's campaign and the eco- friendly eating campaign were unconventional, eccentric and exhibitionist—in short, designed to attract media attention. In order to maximize media exposure, the content of the campaigns was contextualized and linked to global issues and universal values—peace, social justice, harmony with nature and reverence for life. In common with other kindred NSMs, MRAR used the media "for informing, educating, converting and mobilizing" (Crook et al, 1992:156).

Campaign Against Zoos and Circuses

Circuses were first banned in the Blue Mountains in 1983 when the Royal Society for the Prevention of Cruelty to Animals (RSPCA) successfully prosecuted Sole Brothers for "an act of cruelty against a camel" (*BMG*, 5 February, 1986). Other circuses sought council approval to operate in the region and complained through the Circus Federation of Australia (CFA) that the Blue Mountains council was responding to "backroom pressure by liberation groups" (*Daily Mirror*, 31 January, 1986). Like the McDonald's campaign, the issue of circuses using wild animals was hotly debated in the local press: "Ratbags win big top debate" (*Penrith Press*, 5 February 1986:5) and later, "More salvos fired in circus battle" (*BMG*, 18 September 1991:3).

In the circus campaign, MRAR has worked with the local RSPCA in a long struggle to convince the Blue Mountains City Council (BMCC) to resist the pro-circus lobby. Several letters appeared in the *Blue Mountains Gazette* congratulating council members on their decision to ban circuses in 1986. Two years later the ban was lifted with Ferry Brothers gaining access to private land to stage the circus. MRAR called for a boycott on any businesses supporting the circus, and with a large photo-ad of a caged lion, with the caption—"Please Help Him"—the RSPCA sought to mobilize public opinion against the circus (*BMG*, 13 April, 1988). The advertisement included details of how people could protest against the use of animals in circuses with petitions, donations and boycotts of businesses supporting the circus. Yet a successful outcome for the protesters would pose the dilemma of what would happen to circus animals once the circus closes down. Unlike circus people, circus animals cannot be redeployed except where they might be bought by zoos. Since for many animal rights activists zoos are less objectionable than circuses this may be the only short-term solution to the dilemma.

In the anti-circus campaign, a petition of over 1,000 signatures was presented to the BMCC. When this did not work, MRAR set up an alternative ticket box which promoted "the greatest show on earth"—animals in the wild as opposed to captive animals in "the saddest show on earth". The tactic outraged the circus proprietor and his workers who engaged in public altercations outside Katoomba's RSPCA with what they referred to as "the animal libbers". Ferry Brothers were given considerable space to air their pro-circus views in *The Blue Mountains Gazette*. A council alderman was heckled when he argued that the 5,000 people who wanted the circus also had "rights". When in 1991 the BMCC extended circus rights to include the use of its own land, MRAR set up "a circus animal information van" and toured Blue Mountains townships to dramatise the plight of circus animals. RSPCA volunteers who supported the action received obscene phone calls and unwanted perishable goods were delivered to their homes. Unlike the good-natured McDonald's campaign, the anti-circus action had a decidedly nasty edge, since many of the circus workers felt that they were becoming an endangered species as a result of the "minority ratbags, scum and do-gooders" in the RSPCA and MRAR. Anne Elliott was aware of the physical dangers the circus campaign posed for her campaigners: "Circus workers led by Mr.

Ferry are quite willing to get abusive and physical" (Interview, 1992). Yet there was a humorous moment in the campaign when the administrator of the RSPCA in the Blue Mountains dismissed the charge that she was running a personal vendetta against the circus owner Robert Ferry: "He's a nice guy. I told him that if he wasn't married I'd marry him. I admire him, he's a streetwise little devil" (*BMG*, 18 September 1991). It is unlikely that this would placate the circus fraternity who see their livelihoods threatened by the anti-circus lobby which, in early 1992, again succeeded in convincing a new BMCC to ban circuses from using council land.

As council membership changes, so too will the fortunes of MRAR, the RSPCA and the CFA. In the short-term the anti-circus lobby led by MRAR has triumphed not least because it has established the circus campaign as a political issue in the BMCC elections. Prior to local, State and Federal elections, MRAR runs half-page Political Animal advertisements featuring questions and answers from aspiring candidates about their views on animal rights. For example, in the 1991 NSW State election, all candidates for the seat of Blue Mountains were invited to respond to four questions concerning:

1. the proposed fauna zoo.

2. the de-sexing of dogs and cats.

3. beef cattle feedlots

4. duck shooting.

The candidates' responses to each question were published "as a service to the community" in a half-page advertisement (cost $350) prior to the election in *The Blue Mountains Gazette* (22 May 1991:8). The Political Animal advertisement identified each candidate's name, party and response to the MRAR's related campaign against zoos:

> Question1: Bearing in mind the controversy surrounding the proposed zoo at Boddington Hill, Wentworth Falls, what is your opinion of privately-owned zoos?

Candidates' answers followed and voters were called upon to Vote (1) for Animal Rights.

The anti-zoo campaign began in 1987 when the BMCC rezoned some land in the Blue Mountains for the purpose of building a $2.5 million flora and fauna park. The following year the Bullaburra Residents' Action Group (BRAG) "occupied" the council's chamber effectively disrupting the meeting and forcing the council to close. Local newspapers gave the story front-page prominence with headlines like "No guarantee it won't happen again—Council take-over by mob" (*The Echo*, 20

September 1988) and "Objectors take over BMCC" (BMG, 21 September 1988). The protesters in BRAG represent a number of groups opposed to the zoo including MRAR, the Wilderness Society, Animal Liberation and Freedom from Hunger. In the township of Katoomba where protests of this kind are rare, there were the charges of "mindless mob" and "communist rabble" which the local press duly reported.

Opposition to the zoo was based on environmental objections—traffic congestion and the notion that a flora and fauna park was "out of character" for the region; the initial protest did not mention animal welfare which was added to the list of objections by MRAR. In several letters to the editor, Anne Elliott put the anti-zoo case on behalf of animals and a number of articles quoted her views: "Can we truly say we are a civilised society if we allow even more animals to be confined for our supposed 'benefit' in the park? Death and disease are synonymous with zoos" (letter to the editor *BMG*, 30 August 1989). Elliott used the tactic of invoking the names of well-known people Gandhi, Einstein, da Vinci and so on—suggesting that to be an "animal liberationist" was to be in good company.

While circuses will no doubt come and go, the idea of a $2.5m zoo as a permanent part of the Blue Mountains is anathema to MRAR and other anti-zoo groups. They have recently formed a Coalition of Residents for the Environment (CORE) to defend the Blue Mountains against what they see as an "out of character" development. For MRAR and Anne Elliott, the zoo represents another atrocity against animals by human beings; for others in CORE, the zoo is perceived as an environmental blot on the landscape and is opposed for aesthetic and ecological reasons. Nonetheless, MRAR has been able to add an animal rights dimension to what at the moment has been a successful anti- development campaign. As in the case of the McDonald's campaign, the media's role was crucial to its success. As Gamson (1992:71) correctly observes, the media can either help or hurt a social movement. In the circus saga and in the zoo campaign MRAR was helped by the free publicity it got for its actions and most importantly by the pressure of media attention on candidates holding, or aspiring to hold, political office.

In its campaigns, MRAR has successfully attracted media attention by the novelty of its approach and the newsworthiness of the campaign issues. It has also made effective use of paid advertisements, letters to the editor and what Lemert (1984) calls "mobilizing information" wherein the reader is given details of an action—what it means, where it is and how one can participate in it. As a matter of policy, large media organizations do not publicize "mobilizing information" which they correctly see as surrogate commercial advertisements. MRAR and the other SMOs in the Blue Mountains have been fortunate in that their campaigns—including the what, where and how details—are seen as newsworthy by the small regional newspapers. In these circumstances then, the media are the message. This is clearly evident in the anti-vivisection campaign, the final example of MRAR's involvement in animal rights activism outlined below.

The Anti-Vivisection Campaign

For many animal liberationists, vivisection is the worst atrocity perpetrated by humans against non-human animals. Modern animal liberationists, like their anti-vivisectionist predecessors in the nineteenth century perceive the abuse of animals as the central moral dilemma facing society. "The animal as victim has become a symbol of both humanity and nature besieged (in the) vivisection of our planet" (Sperling, 1988:39).

Early in 1985 a large Sydney newspaper carried a story under the headline "Dogs sold for secret research" with an accompanying picture of a "dog lover" and one of her rescued strays, Barney (*Daily Mirror*, 1 February 1985). The "dog lover", Phyllis Owen of the Domestic Animals Birth Control Society, had been campaigning for several years against dog pounds in the Blue Mountains which were selling strays to Sydney University for research and medical experimentation. What outraged many readers was the token price of one cent per dog the pounds received in the deal with Australia's oldest university. Because Sydney University was involved, this issue, more than the other MRAR campaigns, attracted the attention of Sydney's media.

A number of animal welfare groups mobilized after the "Barney" story appeared in the press. The Australian Association for Humane Research (AAHR) placed a large advertisement in the BMG (27 February 1985) featuring "Mary—a tiny terrier who served time in Penrith Pound" under the caption "This is a Laboratory Tool!" The advertisement was aimed at stopping Penrith Pound from selling stray dogs for vivisection and asked in bold letters—"Do You Care?" The advertisement called for donations and active involvement in the campaign and offered further information about the AAHR's work (Anne Elliott was at the time Vice-President of AAHR; the $164 ad was paid by MRAR).

MRAR and members of the AAHR mounted a vigil in Penrith highlighting the fate of stray dogs at the local pound. The *BMG* gave "mobilizing information" about the vigil when, how, where and why details—and quoted a spokesperson from MRAR: "If you care, why not come along and be entertained by the street theatre, participate in a meditation for peace for animals and sign the Scroll of Shame to be presented to the Mayor of Penrith" (*BMG*, 6 March, 1985). In addition, the story advertised a market stall to be run as a fund-raiser by MRAR as well as the group's next meeting. Here was free publicity, which as an advertisement would have been the equivalent in cost to the "Do You Care?" appeal a few days before. Publicity of a different kind was achieved by several letters to the editor by "dog lovers" protesting against the sale of dogs for vivisection. MRAR collected over 1,000 signatures on its Scroll of Shame which, along with its mascot, "Mr. Beagle", succeeded in drawing the public's attention to the practices of the Penrith Pound. After a few months of campaigning, the Penrith Council bowed to public pressure and agreed to end the practice. A Sydney daily newspaper announced the decision with the headline— "Animal Lovers Claim Victory—stray dogs to be sold to the public" (*Daily Mirror*, 4 June 1985). While this victory did not guarantee that the animals would not be abused, to the campaigners, pet owners are seen as offering a more humane prospect for the dogs than the vivisector's laboratory.

MRAR and the AAHR then turned their attention to the Blacktown Council which had refused to follow Penrith's example arguing that Sydney University's research unit treats the (approximately 3,000) dogs humanely, adding that to stop the practice would be wasteful considering the great benefits from the research (*Blacktown City Star*, 14 May 1986). Members of MRAR and the AAHR, along with "Mr. Beagle", protested outside Blacktown's shopping centre. The idea was to shame Blacktown Council into changing its policy since Sydney University had refused access to the AAHR for the purpose of inspecting its facilities. Anne Ellott used a moralizing strategy advocated by criminologist John Braithwaite (1989) when she praised the Penrith Council for having "the good grace to bow to public pressure" as opposed to Blacktown Council's shameful treatment of stray dogs. In Braithwaite's shaming theory, rituals of acceptance and community approval are as important as the stigmatization of offensive conduct. In a small community like the Blue Mountains, shaming can be a powerful catalyst for change. After nearly five years of MRAR campaigning, a Penrith Council spokesperson told the local press that it had seen the light: "We are well aware Blacktown Council sells some dogs for research but we would not allow this to happen to our dogs" (*Penrith Press*, 15 January, 1991). Penrith Council had been shamed and reintegrated into the moral community along the lines advocated in Braithwaite's (1989) theory. It was now described as having done the "humane thing" and was praised for demonstrating an "enlightened attitude" (*Penrith Press*, June 1985).

Since the AAHR has been unsuccessful in drawing Sydney University into a debate over vivisection, MRAR has focused its campaign on the local councils which supply dogs to the university. As noted already, Penrith Council succumbed to "Mr. Beagle and his Scroll of Shame" (*Penrith Press* front page headline, 22 May 1991). Blacktown Council has been more resistant to MRAR's shaming strategy, and it was feared that the Penrith Council might reverse its more humane policy on stray dogs following a change in the membership in late 1991. Anne Elliott met the challenge with a warning:

> The animal vote is a powerful one. It can only be hoped that as there are council elections in September candidates for council will be "animal aware" and see that for too long organisations such as the RSPCA have had to carry the too hard basket on their own" (letter to the editor *BMG*, 9 January, 1991).

She was in effect announcing to aspiring political candidates that animal welfare was a political issue in the Blue Mountains which no future council could ignore.

In framing animal rights as a social justice issue, MRAR has used many of the grassroots tactics of its umbrella organization, Animal Liberation. It has also been successful in its use of political tactics favoured by women, peace activists and environmentalists in the new social movements. These tactics include injecting their issues into electoral campaigns, getting their points of view in the local media (particularly the print media in the MRAR's case), organizing promotional activities, and generally by persuading people to support the movement (McFarland 1984:205). While it is difficult to assess the success of MRAR's four campaigns quantitatively, it can be confidently asserted that many people in the Blue Mountains now see a hamburger, a caged or captive animal and a stray dog in a different light than before MRAR's activism on behalf of animals. It is this recognition that animals are deserving of moral consideration, not philosophical doctrine as such, which one philosopher recently argued is what animal liberation is all about (Weston, 1992).

Note: The author would like to acknowledge the generous assistance of Anne Elliott of Mountain Residents for Animal Rights in providing background material for this article. Sincere thanks also to Elaine Stratford for her helpful comments on an earlier draft of this paper.

REFERENCES

Adams, C. (1990) *The Sexual Politics of Meat : A Feminist--Vegetarian Critical Theory*, Polity Press, UK.
Benton, T. (1993) *Natural Relations: Ecology, Animal Rights and Social Justice*, Verse, London.
Blacktown Advocate, "Council stays firm on strays", 13 May 1986.
Blacktown City Star, "Group takes on council over vivisection", May 14, 1986.
Blue Mountains Gazette (BMG), "This is a Laboratory Tool" (advertisement), 27 February 1985.
BMG, "Vigil to obtain better treatment for dogs", 6 March 1985.
BMG, "McDonald's face strong opposition", 1 June 1988.
BMG, "Please Help Him" (advertisement), 13 April 1988.
BMG, "Objectors take over BMCC", 21 September 1988.
BMG, "Parting shot at circus", 13 December 1989.
BMG, "Reggie to hand out eco-awards", 26 June 1991.
BMG, "More salves fired in circus battle", 18 September 1991.
BMG, "Reggie pushes for eco-friendly burgers", 8 September 1993.
BMG, "Offer for Reggie to replace Ronald", 6 October 1993.
Blue Mountains Whisper, "Reggie Mcveggie for Mayor", October 1990.
Braithwaite, J. (1989) *Crime, Shame and Reintegration*, Cambridge University Press, Cambridge.
Crooke, S., Pakulski, J. and Waters, M. (1992) *Post modernization: Change in Advanced Society*, Sage Publications, London.
Daily Mirror, "Circus blows big top on ban", 31January, 1986.
Daily Mirror, "Dogs sold for secret research, 1 February 1985.
Daily Mirror, "Animal Lovers Claim Victory-stray dogs to be sold to the public", 4 June 1985.
Elias, N. (1978) *The Civilising Process, Vol I, The History of Manners*, Basil Blackwell, Oxford.
Gamson, W. (1992) 'The Social Psychology of Collective Action' in A.D. Morris and C. McClurg Mueller (eds.) *Frontiers in Social Movement Theory*, Yale University Press, New Haven.
Gunn, C. and Gunn, H. (1991) *Reclining Capital: Democratic Initiatives and Community Development*, Cornell University Press, New York.
Interview (1992) with Anne Elliott by the author in Katoomba, 29 November.
Interview (1993) with Anne Elliott by the author in Katoomba, 12 December.
Lemert, J.B. (1984) "News Context and the Elimination of Mobilizing Information: An Experiment" in *Journalism Quarterly* Summer, pp. 243-249.
McFarland, A.S. (1984) *Common Cause: Lobbying in the Public Interest*, Chatham House Publishers, Inc. Chatham, New Jersey.
MRAR (1992) 'People Working for Animals' in *Animal Liberation Magazine*, October-December, pp. 14-16.
Penrith Press, "Stray dogs sell for 1 cent each--no more sales to Sydney University", June 1985.
Penrith Press, "Ratbags win big top debate", 5 February 1986.
Penrith Press, "Dog pound crisis", 15 January 1991.
Penrith Press, "Mr. Beagle and his Scroll of Shame", 22 May 1991.
Regan, T. (1985) 'The Case for Animal Rights' in P. Singer (ed.) *In Defence of Animals*, Harper & row Publishers, New York.
Rucht, D. (1990) 'The political action of new movements: an historical perspective' in *Challenging the Political Order*, R.J. Dalton and M. Kuechler (eds.), Polity Press, Cambridge.
Schudson, M. (1989) 'How culture works: Perspectives from media studies on the efficacy of symbols' in *Theory and Society*, 18, pp. 153-180.
Spencer, C. (1993) *The Heretic's Feast: A History of Vegetarianism*, Fourth Estate, London.
Spencer, M. (1991) 'Advocating Peace' in Peter Harries-Jones (ed) *Making Knowledge Count: Advocacy and Social Science,* McGill Queen's University Press, Montreal.
The Echo, "No guarantee it won't happen again-Council take-over by mob", 20 September 1988.
Weston, A. (1992) *Toward Better Problems: New Perspectives on Abortion, Animal Rights, the Environment, and Justice,* Temple University Press, Philadelphia.

Chapter 9

The Animal Activism of Henry Spira (1927-1998)

Henry Spira is a classic example of an issue entrepreneur who used a variety of legal tactics, both conventional and unconventional, to achieve his nonhuman animal welfare goals. His strategy was unusual for an animal protectionist in that he sought to make instances of animal cruelty public only as a last resort. Ever the pragmatist, his primary goal was to reduce the level of suffering and cruelty to animals, preferably by persuasive communication and only when that failed, by coercion. Sometimes Spira worked alone, and sometimes he formed social movement organizations from existing animal rights groups to achieve his ends. His tactics always were designed to achieve maximum benefits in terms of saving animals' lives and ranged across the spectrum of tactical mechanisms identified by Turner and Killian (1987).

Activists and advocates, at one time or another, have used all four mechanisms—persuasion, facilitation, bargaining, and coercion—in their campaigns on behalf of animals. These tactical mechanisms can best be thought of as a continuum with persuasion as the most moderate tactic at one end and the more direct confrontational tactic of coercion at the other end. Not surprisingly, persuasion, facilitation, and bargaining tend to be the preferred tactics of organizational advocates in the suites while coercive tactics are usually more commonly observed in grassroots activist campaigns.

Persuasion, involving the use of strictly symbolic manipulation and the raising of issue consciousness, is one of the most important ways in which ideology is produced and continuously modified (Turner & Killian, 1987, pp. 297-298). For organizational advocates, persuasion usually takes the form of education campaigns, typically via their own print media (brochures, glossy magazines, and the like). Although consciousness-raising in the environmental movement has been derided as "social change through banner hanging" (Wapner, 1995), it is an important tactic in the animal movement for changing the way people think about animals. As described below, the use of persuasive communication as a tactic for changing people's sensibilities is exemplified in the various campaigns organized by Henry Spira.

In many instances, grassroots activists, in particular, have deployed coercive tactics of various kinds to achieve improvements in animal welfare. These range from the use of "nuisance" tactics to more disruptive tactics including the violent actions of extreme animal rights activists. Coercion, then, can be thought of as a continuum ranging from the mild forms of persuasive communication used by Spira to the threats of violence made by extremist groups such as the Animal Liberation Front. Spira used coercive shaming only as a last resort and only when his targets failed to respond to his animal welfare proposals. Put differently, he preferred liberal governance strategies to critical governance strategies (Newell, 2000). Newell describes liberal governance strategies as those that seek reforms within the system while those engaged in critical governance "tend not to compromise and are less inclined to discuss ways in which (environmental) activists and company executives may be able to help one another" (p. 127).

Grassroots activists are more inclined to embrace the symbolic and expressive with little concern for the more pragmatic evaluation of long-term strategic planning favored by animal advocates and lobbyists. Turner and Killian (1987, p. 301) note that an undisciplined grassroots movement employs many tactics more expressively than strategically. These distinctions are never cut and dried. For example, in forming coalitions with other groups or in facilitating common cause alliances, grassroots activists sometimes employ the tactical mechanisms of persuasion, bargaining, and facilitation that, in theory, belong in the suites and offices of the professional lobbyist. As I will show, Spira's style of activism used all these conventional tactics, including coercion, albeit with a different twist.

Spira's Animal Activism in Theory and Practice

In common with other social change advocates and activists in social movement organizations, Spira's campaigns consisted of three essential frames: diagnosis, prognosis, and a call to action (Wilson, 1973; Snow & Benford, 1988). I describe Spira's diagnostic and prognostic frames as belonging to the conventional animal protectionist's techniques of seeing and exposing cruel practices. His "call to action"—the frame that constitutes the third prong of a social movement's framing repertoire—was more unconventional. It was used (a) as a weapon of last resort to shame recalcitrant animal abusers and (b), in a reformatory, reintegrative sense along the lines advocated by the criminologist Braithwaite (1989), for controlling crime. Spira was unusual as an activist in that he hoped to avoid the disintegrative or dysfunctional shaming that characterized the rhetoric of vilification used by antivivisectionists in the nineteenth century and the "them versus us" stance of many contemporary animal rights fundamentalists. Thus, in stark contrast to Spira's approach, People for the Ethical Treatment of Animals (PETA) has used consumer boycotts to attack directly the interests of alleged animal abusers. Friedman (1999) found that in recent years 11 of 12 PETA boycott campaigns focused on using the media to dramatize the actions. In half these boycotts, PETA made no effort to communicate with its targets either before or after the actions took place (p. 190).

In contrast to the hard-line tactics of PETA and similar groups, Spira's strategy in all of his most widely publicized campaigns that are discussed below— the American Museum of Natural History's cat campaign, the targeting of Revlon, Procter & Gamble, Perdue Farms Inc., and the U. S. Department of Agriculture (USDA)— included the novel strategy of attempting to identify common interests between the targeted organization and the animal lobby rather than the "them and us" stalemate that characterizes most animal rights campaigns (Munro, 1999). Working with, rather than against, animal industries made Spira a target for criticism from some sections of the animal rights movement. When Spira exposed institutional cruelty toward animals, he used the threat of coercive shaming only as a last resort. His primary objective was instrumental, not expressive. His strategy was unusual in social movement activism in that he would prefer to avoid the call to action—the last of the three framing processes used by social movements—because his preferred outcome was to resolve the movement's grievance during the second stage of the process, that is, during the prognosis.

His strategy was to work through the processes identified by Turner and Killian (1987) as persuasion, facilitation, bargaining, and identifying the interests of the movement's opponents that were compatible with the ethical treatment of animals. Spira sought to engage in reformatory or reintegrative work with his adversaries to find more humane ways of using animals to reduce their suffering and still preserve the legitimate interests of his targets. As we will see, this typically meant initially applying mild coercion to corporations and individuals in the form of an offer they were reluctant to refuse. Although Spira politely suggested that it was in the interests of an organization not to be subjected to negative publicity, which could threaten the reputation of the enterprise, not all his targets were prepared to cooperate with what they saw as blatant extortion. Spira's style of animal advocacy / activism, while unique in many ways, had much in common with some of the tactics of the nineteenth century animal protection pioneers. The characteristics of Spira's work are described in the remainder of the paper.

Diagnosing Oppression: Ways of Seeing Animal Suffering

According to Shapiro (1996), there are different styles of seeing or different levels of perception (one woman's elegant fur coat is another woman's dead animal) that involve taking in or fully grasping the meaning of the object of perception—in this case the animal reduced to a commodity. The feminist philosopher Rosemary Tong has noted that Aristotle claimed the basis for making ethical decisions was "in the act of perceiving, in *seeing through one's experience* [italics added], to the moral truth beneath appearances" (cited in Donovan, 1996, p. 165). Donovan argues, however, that philosophers in the Western tradition have not lived up to the Aristotelian model. "Not seeing the oppression that surrounded them, they shaped an abstract ethics that may have served to protect the interests of those in power" (p. 165). Thus, while moral philosophers Peter Singer and Tom Regan have served as midwives to the animal movement, ordinary citizens have been responsible for translating "ethics into action" as the title of Singer 's (1998) book on Spira acknowledges.

Kean's (1998) history of the animal rights movement in England from 1800 to the present highlights the act of "seeing" animal suffering in the streets of London as the most important factor in the development of the movement in that country. Lansbury (1985), also notes that in the city at least, cruelty towards horses "was under the *supervision* of a *watchful* [italics added] populace, but in the country the old barbarities persisted" (p. 35). Kean criticizes fellow historian Thomas for not recognizing the importance of the sheer number and visibility of England's working animals in the development of what Thomas (1984) called "the new sensibilities" in our treatment of animals in the early modern period (p. 303). Then as now, she argues, it was the sight of suffering animals—for example, animals in transit under the control of drovers in the nineteenth century or lorry drivers as recently as 1995—that inspired public protests against the injustice of animal cruelty in England. For Kean, animal rights sensibilities during the past two centuries were affected primarily by the visibility and the visualization of animals. "Paradoxically," writes Shapiro (1996) about cruelty toward animals in the late twentieth century, "what is everywhere hidden, forgotten, denied, erased, transmuted, manufactured is yet everywhere present. The shopping mall, the restaurant, the city, but not less the woods and the sea—each has its own network of bloody trails" (p. 140). Both animal visibility and the way animals are visualized or represented are important in Spira's diagnosis of cruelty. By focusing on the "invisibility" of animal suffering behind the closed doors of the research laboratory and the factory farm, he has attempted to make these hidden worlds more visible so that as in the case of the working animals of the nineteenth century, a watchful populace can condemn cruel practices. In the visualization of animal suffering, parallels can be drawn with some of Spira's campaigns and those of the early animal protectionists described by Kean (1998). There are differences, however, in the way the antivivisectionists and Spira's supporters dealt with their opponents. In Chapter 14, I describe this as a difference between the rhetoric of vilification and a policy of accommodation.

Spira focused on institutionalized cruelty, on systems of oppression as represented by corporations involved in animal exploitation rather than individual abusers of animals although they too have been targeted, as we will see. Shapiro (1996) suggests that terms like systems of oppression, injustice, and speciesism are examples of abstract seeing that protagonists on both sides of the movement use to deflect or soften the reality of individual animal suffering (p. 136). In Spira's case, the abstraction served as a tactical mechanism for encouraging oppressed workers, migrants, women, and other down trodden groups to see animal suffering as an extension of their own oppression. More than most animal rights leaders, Spira was conscious of the interconnectedness of speciesism, racism, and sexism as social injustices. For him, the treatment of nonhuman animals was bound up with our treatment of downtrodden workers, blacks, and women. Nonetheless, Spira was first and foremost an animal rights activist. These other causes were important only in so far as they contributed to an understanding of the plight of animals. Strategically, he reflected: 'We knew that we must focus sharply on a single significant injustice, on one clearly limited goal. Moreover, that goal must be achievable' (Spira, 1985, p. 197).

Spira's Prognostic Frame: Visualizing and Exposing Cruelty

That goal was a ban on the use of cats at the American Museum of Natural History (AMNH) for sex experiments, a practice that would not be exposed by recourse to "abstract seeing" but rather by visualizing vivisection at its worst. Spira first came across the "cat torture experiments" in a report published by the antivivisectionist organization, United Action for Animals. The first step in his prognosis—that is, what to do about the grievance—was to seek more details about the nature and funding sources of the experiments by using the Freedom of Information (FOI) Act (Singer, 1998, p. 54). The evidence in the documents obtained via FOI indicated to Spira that the experiments were both cruel and useless. These bizarre sex procedures on cats made the AMNH in New York City a vulnerable target for his first public campaign in 1976 on behalf of nonhuman animals (Singer, p. 55). Seeking an opportunity to discuss the future of the cat sex experiments with the researchers, Spira sent requests to the museum, but the letters and calls were ignored. A radio station and a Manhattan weekly newspaper sympathetic to the cause gave the campaigners some publicity, which then was followed by public demonstrations outside the museum (Singer, pp. 56, 57). These continued every weekend for more than a year but there was still no dialogue with the museum (Singer, pp. 57-59).

In May 1977, "Stop the cat-torture at the Museum of Natural History"—a full-page advertisement—appeared in *The New York Times*. It featured a graphic picture and headline—along with an explanatory text that detailed the cruelty to cats performed at public expense in the name of science. The picture and the accompanying text are reminiscent of "Shedding light on professional cruelty" (1909-1910) featured in Kean (1998), which depicts a guilt- ridden vivisector caught in the act of experimenting on a small dog. At about the same time, in 1907, moral reformers in the National Council of Women of Canada called for "the searchlight of knowledge and truth" to be turned on the "social evil" of female prostitution (Valverde, 1990, p. 68). Valverde gives a number of examples where light was used as a metaphor in various social purity campaigns; in contrast to Kean's example, in this campaign the authority figure holding the searchlight of surveillance is a doctor responsible for "cleansing and healing" the impure. The "Stop the Cat Torture" (1977) text in small print claims that "Behind locked doors, in sound-proof labs, hid-den from an unknowing public" doctors and scientists are perpetrating unspeakable cruelties. These are then graphically described, and the chief scientist named, along with advice on how readers can assist the campaign to ban the cat-torture. Independent of this publicity, the chief scientist was harassed when activists distributed fliers asking, "Do you know this man?"—and outlining details of his experiments to his residential neighbours. Although Spira was not involved directly in the intimidation of the individual, he managed to encourage thousands of scientists to believe that they too could be exposed and shamed if they were involved in cruel animal experiments (Singer, 1998, p. 71).

When the museum eventually discontinued the cat experiments, Spira had succeeded where the antivivisectionists a century earlier repeatedly had failed. How can this be explained, given that similar tactics of exposing and vilifying vivisectionists for inflicting unnecessary cruelty on animals had failed in the campaigns of the nineteenth century? The most plausible explanation is that in the mid-1970s a much larger public was receptive to the influence of a much more extensive network of print and electronic media than was available to animal protectionists in the mid-1870s. In addition, with the publication of Singer 's *Animal Liberation*, the various liberation movements of the twentieth century involving blacks, women, and—in 1975—animals all contributed to the mood of social change that Spira and others were promoting in their advocacy of social justice. As Spira (1985) explained: "We wanted to adapt to the animal movement the traditions of struggle which had proven effective in the civil rights movement, the union movement and the women's movement" (p. 197).

Yet, the systems of oppression that Spira (1985) identified were not unlike those that Lansbury (1985) described. Lansbury recounts a turn of-the-century controversy in Battersea, when suffragettes, antivivisectionists, and working-class men defended the statue of an old, brown dog as a symbol of oppression by the "New Priesthood" of doctors and medical students. Citing Patrick White's *The Vivisector*, Lansbury (p. 24) explains how— according to a Battersea resident who remembered the riots—the dog became "an advertising story in the Anti-Vivisection Council's shop-front display in Oxford Street. Shop-front displays, exhibits in shopping malls, and week- end markets are still popular with animal protectionists in welfare groups like the Royal Society for the Prevention of Cruelty to Animals (RSPCA) as well as with more radical activists in animal liberation branches—at least in Australia.

The difference in the visualizing of cruelty in the two eras lay in the media available to the activists. Thus, whereas the early antivivisectionists relied on popular fiction, in-house journals, and shop window displays to press their claims, contemporary animal protectionists like Spira have a potentially more effective medium for propagating their issues to a much larger audience in the form of the electronic and print mass media. The 1977 campaign advertisement in the *New York Times* was read by thousands of readers, many of whom responded to the call to action. The early antivivisectionists' propaganda against animal experimentation was published in animal protection tracts, fliers, and posters read mainly by the converted. Reaching a wider audience was achieved through the medium of fiction in popular novels like *Black Beauty* (1877), which became a school text and a regular prize at Sunday schools (Lansbury, 1985, p. 5). According to Lansbury, what people said and did at the turn of the century "was shaped as much by literature as by history." Hogarth's (1750) *Four Stages of Cruelty* provided a recurring theme used by novelists more than a century after the work first appeared and suggested to the working class that the natural order of things was that cruelty to animals led to the murder of women and the offender 's own dissection by experimentalists.

It is not possible to say whether the more sophisticated electronic media of the late twentieth century are a more effective mobilizing force than the print- based propaganda used in the nineteenth century. Yet, in reading Lansbury (1985), one is struck by the number of "advertising stories" about animals— in addition to the posters, pamphlets, and essays on the subject—in which novelists used "the truths of fiction" to move the hearts of their readers (130- 131). Vivisectors became "a recurring figure in pornography and in women's fiction" and were portrayed as the ultimate in evil. Consequently, both sides used the rhetoric of vilification to mobilize support for their respective causes. Using a tactic that would be repeated 75 years later by the defenders of animal experimentation in a *Newsweek* cover story (The battle over, 1988), the Research Defence Society in 1912 challenged Hogarth's prints with a morality tale of its own—a picture of a smiling woman and her child with the caption: "which will you save—your child or a guinea-pig?" (Lansbury, 1985, p.169)[1]

Prodding Action Through Motivational Shaming

As noted at the beginning of this paper, when Spira exposed institutional cruelty in the treatment of animals, he employed the threat of coercive shaming, but only as a last resort. His primary objective was to achieve animal welfare goals through persuasion, bargaining, and facilitation, and without the mobilizing frame or call to action that social movements use to coerce their opponents. Just as the early pioneers in the animal movement used fictional literature as advertising stories to inspire compassion, Spira's coalition of activist groups in Animal Rights International (ARI), reminded its adversaries of the animal lobby's version of successful advertising stories, namely those featured in the *New York Times.* Although some animal exploiters have seen this as a not so subtle threat, most have accepted the tactic as legitimate. By offering to work with his adversaries to find a mutually beneficial outcome, Spira was seen to be acting in good faith.

Spira's animal rights campaigns were unique in that they sought to replace vilification with accommodation by identifying the common interests of animal protectionists and animal exploiters (Munro, 1999). Unlike the nineteenth century antivivisectionists who demanded the abolition of animal experimentation and whose arguments were used to deviantize the vivisectors, Spira was prepared to work with animal users to achieve improvements in animal welfare. Just as the campaigners of the nineteenth century used access to fresh water as an incentive for people to be kind to animals, contemporary animal protectionists like Spira appeal to the self-interest of people who work with animals (Kean, 1998). Business and scientific fraternities that use animals for commercial and research purposes cannot afford to have their reputations damaged by charges of animal cruelty or indifference to animal suffering. Spira and his supporters have effectively employed the motivational power of shame and its converse pride in their campaigns against major companies and institutions in the United States.

---

[1] Similarly, contemporary animal experimenters have framed the issue in the language of a stark choice between saving a child's or an animal's life or as the title of a *Newsweek* cover story (December, 1988) proclaimed, a choice over "suffering versus science." Thus, the different ways of representing cruelty by these generations of animal protectionists has been one of degree rather than of kind.

One of Spira's most successful campaigns, the Revlon campaign which began in September 1978, illustrates this point, and demonstrates his use of persuasive communication and coercion. A letter was sent to Revlon suggesting an alternative to the Draize test, which involves the application of toxic or irritant substances to the eyes of rabbits to test levels of safety. According to ARI, replacing Draize, in cosmetics testing alone, with a more humane alternative might spare 10,000 rabbits needless suffering and death. As in other campaigns, Spira sought to identify the overlapping interests of the company and the animals. In the letter to Revlon, Spira's scientific adviser Leonard Rack suggested that alternative methods to the Draize test would "be faster, more economic, and more efficiently protective of the cosmetics user than current methods" (Singer, 1998, p. 92). In June 1979, a meeting between Spira and Revlon's vice president for public affairs ended without any meaningful dialogue between the two and no indication of any willingness by Revlon to use a more humane alternative to Draize.

Spira then set up a new group of alliances, the Coalition to Stop Draize Rabbit Blinding Tests, consisting of more than 400 organizations with a membership in the millions (Singer, 1998, p. 93). News of the Coalition's Revlon campaign and the cruelty of the Draize test began to appear in the popular press, but Revlon was unmoved. When a further meeting in January 1980 with Coalition members and Revlon's vice president proved fruitless, Spira arranged for a full-page advertisement to be run in the *New York Times* on April 15, 1980 (Singer, p. 96). As the words in large print—and the accompanying mobilizing information made clear—this was a call to action that could be disastrous to Revlon's reputation as "the General Motors of beauty". Revlon denied the claims, but a new, more conciliatory vice president was convinced the company was in trouble when "an enormous demonstration on Fifth Avenue" took place with dozens of reporters and science writers in attendance (Singer, 1997). The Coalition continued the pressure on Revlon with representations to different levels of government and a new full-page advertisement in the *New York Times* (October 7, 1980), which observed that, "There must be a less ugly way for Revlon to test beauty products."

More public demonstrations against Revlon induced the company to agree to fund research for an alternative to Draize, and—in the spirit of reintegrative shaming—Spira praised the industry leader for "linking imaginative, elegant science with effective and efficient safety testing" and for providing $750,000 over three years for the research. The Revlon chairman and chief executive described the grant as "proof of Revlon's social conscience" (Singer, 1998, pp. 103-104), a phrase Spira used to encourage other cosmetic companies to support Revlon's initiative. Revlon's vice president was gratified by the company's new image as a good corporate citizen and noted, "a great pride in what we were doing. Everybody in our company felt good when they went home that night because their kids would no longer look at them cockeyed as being someone who does untoward things to rabbits" (Singer, p. 105). The Coalition to Stop Draize Rabbit Blinding Tests described the outcome as an historic breakthrough in "imaginative, humane science" rather than a victory *per se*.

Accommodation had replaced vilification in the repertoire of animal activist strategies.

Spira's next major campaign focused on the notorious LD50 in which animals are used to test the "Lethal Dose" of household products like shoe polish and shampoo. A newspaper advertisement explained that the Lethal Dose 50% was the amount of any substance, from cosmetics to cleaning products, sufficient to kill exactly half a group of laboratory animals. The advertisement targeted regulatory agencies in the United States and led to admissions by the authorities that LD50 was of limited use (Would you pay, 1983).

Spira's stance on LD50 was, however, not for its abolition but for reduction and refinement; he argued that six animals, rather than 600, could provide sufficient data for the safety tests to be valid. Although this was heresy to the fundamentalists in the movement, Spira knew that years of campaigning by abolitionists had not reduced the numbers of animals used in such experiments. His strategy was to approach a large company that used the LD50, Procter & Gamble, and suggest a plan that would serve the interests of the company. He made it clear to Procter & Gamble that they were not being asked for money to fund research for alternatives but rather to save money by reducing the number of animals used for product safety tests. After some persistence on Spira's part—including attendance at an annual meeting made possible by the purchase of a single share in the company—Procter & Gamble agreed that they had an interest in avoiding unwanted publicity and could benefit financially and ethically by "Taking Animals Out of the Laboratory," (Singer, 1998, p. 145) as one of its in-house journals proclaimed. It was in this journal that Spira took the opportunity to congratulate the company for its "serious initiatives and commitment to replace and reduce the use and suffering of lab animals [which was] both visionary and practical" (Singer, 1998, p. 126). Here then was an example of how the tactical mechanisms identified by Turner and Killian (1987) actually worked.

More radical animal rights groups like PETA were appalled by Spira's support of companies that had a history of exploiting animals. Spira's response is that his strategy of accommodation is more effective than the vilification and stigmatization of opponents:

> *I do not support PETA's campaign which attempts to portray Procter & Gamble as villain when, in fact, P&G has the best record to date in developing [alternatives]. It seems to me that when a corporation is responsive to our concerns, it makes no sense to clobber them over the head. Rather, we want to encourage them to continue to be responsive and use their responsiveness as an example to others.* (Singer, 1998, p. 131)

According to Singer who clearly prefers Spira's style of activism to PETA's more aggressive campaigns, the complete abolition of Draize and LD50 remains elusive. Even so, PETA's worldwide campaign against Avon, in which millions of door-hangers labeled "Avon killing" were distributed, caused the company to discontinue animal tests within a month of the boycott on its products. PETA's campaign had all the ingredients of successful social movement campaigns that Rochon (1990) has identified as "size, militancy and novelty." The question, therefore, is raised as to the effectiveness of Spira's campaign tactics, which, though novel, rely less on size and not at all on militancy. Is the strategy of accommodating opponents less effective than their outright defeat?

According to Braithwaite's (1989) theory of reintegrative shaming, stigmatizing white-collar offenders as "criminals" is less effective than moralizing with them and encouraging them to mend their ways. Reintegrative shaming focuses on the offence rather than the offender. Spira appears to have used this strategy long before Braithwaite coined the term "reintegrative shaming" as a theory of crime control. Braithwaite argues that white-collar offenders are more susceptible to shaming than their blue-collar counterparts. This is confirmed by Spira's targeting of corporations that likewise are interested in protecting their reputations and profits from the negative consequences of bad publicity alleging cruelty to innocent animals.

Not everyone, however, is responsive to the moralizing efforts of social movement entrepreneurs. One such individual who seemed impervious to Spira's moralizing efforts on behalf of farm animals is the chicken mogul Frank Perdue, who was unsuccessfully targeted in at least two major campaigns (Singer, p. 145). In the *New York Times* advertisement (Frank, are you telling, 1989), Spira's ARI targeted Perdue after efforts to liaise with Perdue Farms Inc., failed. Unlike the Revlon campaign, this did not have the desired effect, and a new slant was put on the anti-Perdue publicity. In one campaign, the ARI used the novel and eye-catching image of a chicken in a condom to highlight the message that "there's no such thing as a safe chicken." Like other groups such as the Farm Animal Reform Movement that in recent years have expanded their rationale against factory farming (Kunkel, 1995), Spira had dropped the cruelty frame in the advertisement in favor of a health frame in the hope of mobilizing more supporters by appealing to their self-interest. This also had no effect on Perdue, although Spira claims the campaign worked well despite getting "absolutely nothing from him"). Some individuals, as Braithwaite (1989) readily acknowledges, are beyond shaming.

The Effectiveness of Spira-Style Animal Activism

In an age of visual overload, pictures that startle, shock, or otherwise attract people's attention are widely believed to be more useful to the movement in changing people's attitudes about animals than the cute clichés of the coffee table variety. On the other hand, a number of animal movement leaders told me that some of their members refuse to read in-house magazines if they picture injured, suffering, or dead animals. Most of the animal images used in Spira's campaigns have been neither obnoxious nor nice. Rather, his way of "picturing the beast" is to use representations of animals that are realistic rather than sensationalist, which in the case of the campaigns described thus far—and with the notable exception of the "condom chicken"—have been fairly innocuous. An advertisement published in the *New York Times* (This is what USDA, 1994), however, which depicts the cruelty involved in face branding cattle, is one of the most disturbing and dramatic images used by ARI.

Here, the target was the U. S. Department of Agriculture (USDA) that cancelled a meeting Spira had requested to discuss finding an alternative to the painful and unnecessary procedure of face branding. Berger (1990) describes violent war pictures as arresting—we are seized by them. It is no exaggeration to say that Berger's comments apply equally well to the images of face branding in the ARI advertisement: "As we look at them, the moment of the other's suffering engulfs us. We are filled with either despair or indignation. Despair takes on some of the other's suffering to no purpose. Indignation demands action" (Berger, 1990, p. 42). For the "caring sleuth" (Shapiro, 1996) for whom animal rights activism is a way of life, there is both sorrow and anger in these images of agony. But the purpose of the face-branding image was not to engender despair among the movement's membership but to mobilize the indignation of those outside the movement and to demand action. The call to action was explicit in the caption: "This is what USDA policy looks like. Can you imagine what it feels like?" This is a classic instance of the use of "moral shocks" to prod people into action (Jasper, 1997; Jasper & Poulsen, 1995). According to Singer (1998, p. 162), 1,000 readers had called the USDA in the two days following the appearance of the advertisement. By December of that year, the USDA was forced to discontinue the practice as a result of public pressure. Typically, Spira did not gloat or claim a victory for ARI. Instead, a follow-up full-page advertisement picturing a more contented steer asked— "Who is listening? The USDA is listening!" In the spirit of reintegrative shaming, the advertisement—later hung in the department's offices— went on to thank the USDA for its change of heart.

Many animal activists are offended by Spira's willingness "to work with the devil himself," to use the phrase of Adele Douglass of the American Humane Association (personal communication, 1996) who would wholeheartedly agree with Spira's strategy. On the other hand, Spira's policy of accommodating opponents to achieve animal welfare reforms has been denounced by some rights proponents, including the president of the International Society for Animal Rights, Helen Jones, who has sought to dismiss Spira's activism as belonging to "the old humane movement" (Feder, 1989, p. 60). According to her, Spira's methods are ineffectual because they promote animal welfarist incrementalism (lengthening the chains on the animal slaves) as opposed to animal rights abolitionism (banning animal slavery outright). Yet this criticism misses what was unique about Spira's animal activism. Unlike the abolitionists and his critics in the contemporary animal rights movement, Spira relied on what has proved to be a very effective form of "reintegrative shaming" (Braithwaite, 1989) as a strategy to achieve improvements in institutional practices involving nonhuman animals.

A different view is taken by New York writer and activist Fano (1997) who believes there are two strategies available to activists. The first is to work within the current system to achieve incremental change, which critics deride as animal welfare conservatism. The second, which she advocates, is to work outside the system for radical change (p. 209). These strategies correspond to Newell's (2000) liberal and critical governance strategies noted in the early part of this paper. Spira's approach was to work, at least initially with, rather than against, companies like Procter & Gamble, Revlon, and Gillette as well as with the National Institutes of Health (NIH), the organizational center of U. S. bio-logical research. Fano suggests that although this approach might be expected to work in banning cosmetics testing, more radical, "grassroots" activism will be needed if systems of oppression are to be effectively challenged.

Although it is true that fundamental change will be achieved only by reforming the structures underpinning the institutionalized exploitation of animals, both the strategies of grassroots activism and organizational advocacy are needed to achieve this goal. Fano (1997) acknowledges as much when she cites approvingly the repertoire of tactics used by an American animal advocacy group that pressures companies in much the same way that Spira did. The repertoire of tactics cited by Fano—which could have been borrowed from "An Animal Activist's Handbook," devised by Spira himself—include the key ideas of pressure group politics; the promotion of alternatives; and the use of international coalitions, advertising, public information, and education as well as the accommodation of the interests of compassionate companies (pp. 217-218).

I have suggested that Spira's style of animal activism incorporated many of the tactics used by the pioneering animal protectionists in the nineteenth century but not the "them versus us", anti-science stance of the early antivivisectionists. Spira's diagnosis of the institutionalized oppression of animals as a social problem is in accord with Singer's (1975) critique that sees sexism, racism, and speciesism as interconnected systems of oppression. In attempting to do something about cruelty to animals, Spira's prognostic frame was unique in that he sought to work with corporations and individuals who harm animals in the hope of reducing the total amount of animal suffering. His reformatory and reintegrative work with animal industries has led the leaders of some animal rights groups to condemn his style of activism as ineffectual. Although Spira preferred to accommodate the legitimate interests of his opponents, he was, nonetheless, not averse to exposing their cruel practices if they refused to consider using more humane, non-animal alternatives. Although he was not the only moral entrepreneur to have used the threat of coercion to achieve movement goals, he was unique in that the tactic was used only as a last resort and then in the spirit of reintegrative shaming. As an activist of long standing, working with his adversaries, rather than against them, may not have been his natural inclination but it was the strategy that he believed achieved most for the animals.

Note: I would like to thank Ken Shapiro and three anonymous reviewers for helpful comments on an earlier version of this paper.

REFERENCES

Berger, J. (1990). "Photographs of agony" in *About looking*. New York: Vintage Books. Braithwaite, J. (1989). *Crime, shame, and reintegration*. Cambridge: Cambridge University Press.

Braithwaite, J. (1989) *Crime, shame and reinegration*, Cambridge: Cambridge University Press.

Donovan, J. (1996). Attention to suffering: Sympathy as a basis for ethical treatment of animals. In J. Donovan & C. J. Adams (Eds.). *Beyond animal rights: A feminist caring ethic for the treatment of animals*. New York: Continuum.

Feder, B. J. (November 26, 1989). Pressuring Perdue. *New York Times Magazine*, pp. 32, 33, 60, 72.

Fano, A. (1997). *Lethal laws: Animal testing, human health, and environmental policy*. New York: Zed Books Ltd.

Frank, are you telling the truth about your chickens? (1989, October 20), *New York Times*.

Friedman, M. (1999). *Consumer boycotts: Effecting change through the marketplace and the media*. New York: Routledge.

Jasper, J. (1997). *The art of moral protest: Culture, biography & creativity in social movements*. Chicago: University of Chicago Press.

Jasper, J. & Poulsen, J. (1995). Recruiting strangers and friends: Moral shocks and social networks in animal rights and anti-nuclear protests. *Social Problems, 42* (4), 493-512.

Kean, H. (1998). *Animal rights: Political and social change in Britain since 1800*. London: Reaktion Books.

Kunkel, K. (1995). Down on the farm: Rationale expansion in the construction of fac- tory farming as a social problem. In J. Best (Ed.). *Images of issues: Typifying contemporary social problems* (pp. 239-256). New York: Aldine de Gruyter.

Lansbury, C. (1985). *The old brown dog: Women, workers, and vivisection in Edwardian England*. Madison: The University of Wisconsin Press.

Munro, L. (1999, Winter). From vilification to accommodation: Making a common cause movement. *Cambridge Quarterly of Healthcare Ethics, 4* (1), pp. 46-57.

Newell, P. (2000) "Environmental NGOs and globalisation: The governance of TNCs." In R. Cohen & S. Rai (Eds.). *Global social movements*. London: The Athlone Press.

Rochon, T. (1990). The West European peace movement and the theory of new social movements. In R. Dalton & M. Kuechler (Eds.). *Challenging the political order: New social and political movements in western democracies* (pp. 105-121). Cambridge: Polity Press.

Shapiro, K. (1996). The caring sleuth: Portrait of an animal rights activist. In J. Donovan & C. J. Adams (Eds.). *Beyond animal rights: A feminist caring ethic for the treatment of animals*. New York: Continuum.

Singer, P. (1975). *Animal liberation: A new ethics for our treatment of animals*. London: Jonathan Cape.

Singer, P. (1997). *Henry: One man's way*, a film written and co-produced by Peter Singer.

Singer, P. (1998). *Ethics into action: Henry Spira and the animal rights movement*. Lanham, MD: Rowman & Littlefield Publishers Inc.

Snow, D. A. & Benford, R. D. (1988). Ideology, frame resonance and participant mobilisation. In B. Klandermans, H. Kriesi & S. Tarrow (Eds.). *From structure to action: Comparing social movement research across cultures* (pp. 197-217). Greenwich, CN: JAI Press Inc

Spira, H. (1985). Fighting to win. In P. Singer (Ed.). *In defense of animals*. New York: Harper & Row Publisher.

Stop the Cat Torture at the Museum of Natural History (1997, May 3). Advertisement. *The New York Times*.

The battle over animal rights: A question of suffering versus science. (1988, December 26). *Newsweek*, pp. 50-59.

This is what USDA policy looks like: Can you imagine what it feels like? (1994, March 15). *New York Times*.

Thomas, K. (1984). *Man and the natural world: Changing attitudes in England 1500-1800.* Middlesex: Penguin Books.

Turner, R. & Killian, L. (1987). *Collective behavior* (3rd ed.). Englewood Cliffs: Prentice- Hall, Inc.

Valverde, M. (1990). The rhetoric of reform: Tropes and the moral subject. *International Journal of the Sociology of the Law, 18,* 61-73.

Wapner, P. (1995). In defense of banner hangers: The dark green politics of Greenpeace, in B. Taylor (Ed.). *Ecological resistance movements: The global emergence of radical and popular environmentalism.* New York: State University of New York Press.

Would you pay someone to kill this animal? (1983, May 3). *New York Times.*

Chapter 10

Caring about Blood, Flesh, and Pain:
Women's Standing in the Animal Protection Movement

The animal rights movement in many ways is the kindred spirit of the environmental movement. Indeed Eckersley (1992) sees the former as an offshoot of the latter although in Australia the reverse appears to be true. In terms of membership and activism, women have played a pre-eminent role in both movements. Most notably, Rachel Carson's *Silent Spring* is widely understood to have launched the environmental movement in the United States in the 1960s. It is therefore surprising to read, "a good bit of feminist theory is either insensitive to environmental and animal rights issues or downright hostile toward them" (Slicer, 1994, p. 35). Partly for this reason, ecofeminism emerged in the 1970s as a new and separate field of research that would herald an era of new relationships between men and women and between people and nature (Instone, 1997, p. 136). Writing about the environmental movement in Australia, Instone claims that the majority of members and volunteers of the movement are women. She notes that women's numerical importance does not protect them from doing the low status paid work or from being locked into the majority of voluntary jobs in the movement. "The male public face of the movement," observes Instone, "contrasts sharply with the behind the scenes reality of women doing most of the jobs" (p.138). In this respect at least, the animal movement is different. From the nineteenth century on, women historically, have enjoyed high standing as protectors of nonhuman animals.

A Brief History of Animal Activism

Women have been conspicuous in the animal protection movement from the outset as pioneers in the early antivivisectionist and animal protectionist organizations that were active in Victorian and Edwardian England. The early antivivisectionist movement in Victorian England attracted many women because they drew connections between the abusive treatment of especially poor women as gynecological patients, women's portrayal in pornography, and male vivisectors' dissection of nonhuman animals (Lansbury, 1985). Despite their strength of numbers however, they were denied leadership positions in the early Royal Society for the Prevention of Cruelty to Animals (RSPCA), its counterpart, the American Society for the Prevention of Cruelty to Animals and local SPCAs.

The early history of the animal protection movement in Australia took a different route. According to MacCulloch (1993), the animal protection and conservation movements were irrevocably intertwined and culturally became feminized, which—at least organizationally—ironically led to the movement's gradual decline. MacCulloch's carefully researched thesis traces the history of both movements in Sydney between 1850 and 1930. The Animal Protection Society of New South Wales was established in 1873, a half-century after the SPCA had been founded in England. The Women's Society for the Prevention of Cruelty to Animals (was founded in 1886). MacCulloch argues that in the twentieth century women and a shift in ideology increasingly would dominate the animal protection movement.

From a moralizing, reformist body, the movement was transformed into a society of pet lovers with a consequent change in direction from a campaign against cruelty to the more genteel approach of promoting kindness to animals. "This loss of purpose both mirrored and was reinforced by the growing feminization of the cause. Increasingly, the cause of animal protection was given over to women, and subsequently, children" (MacCulloch, 1993, pp. 45-46). Although these changes diluted the strength of the early movement, MacCulloch's account acknowledges the social legacy of animal protection's female pioneers that by the early twentieth century "had effectively changed the moral make-up of society" (p. 46), and the emotions that cruelty evoked had "overflowed into the preservation movement and fused them together at a popular level" (p. 46).

This brief historical excursus suggests the organizational vulnerability of the modern animal protection movement with its predominantly female membership. The female of 1996 is altogether different from her 1886 counterpart, although to explain the fundamental changes affecting women's status over the past century is beyond the scope of this paper. At the end of the twentieth century, however, Western democracies no longer see women as a liability to animal protectionist and environmental causes. In the case of the animal movement, female animal protectionists at century's end can no longer be so easily dismissed as "dotty" cat lovers, or worse, diagnosed as suffering from "zoophil-psychosis" as they were both in the nineteenth and early twentieth centuries (Buettinger, 1993).

Even so, a movement predominantly female in membership is likely to attract criticism as being "emotional" (stereotypical feminine trait) as opposed to "rational" (the masculine opposite). Indeed, stereotypes associated with labels such as "crazed spinsters", "sob sisters", and "idle, muddle-headed women" who are dismissed as "too emotional" to understand the rational endeavors of science and agriculture continue to crop up in the rhetoric of vilification used by critics of the animal movement (Munro, 1999b). Yet, these enterprises are quick to use emotional appeals in their counter attacks against animal liberationists (Munro, 1999a).

Gender, Attitudes, and Women's Standing

Reviews of both feminist (Adams & Donovan, 1995) and ecofeminist (Vance, 1993) writings indicate that the large body of literature on the themes of women, nature, and animals support the argument that, when it comes to nature, there is a vast gender gap on attitudes and values. Much of the literature contains an implicit assumption that women and men vary fundamentally in the way they treat other life forms. There is ample empirical evidence in every context where humans use or abuse animals. It is evident that men, more than women, work or otherwise engage in animal-oriented occupations and leisure activities, in factory farms, abattoirs, science and veterinary practice, hunting, shooting, trapping and fishing, rodeos, horse and dog racing, and a host of similar pursuits. However, most studies of gender differences toward the treatment of animals focus on animal research rather than on other substantive areas such as hunting and farming (Pifer, 1996). Furthermore, many of those studies are based on comparisons between movement insiders and outsiders, animal rights supporters and animal researchers (Hills, 1993; Paul, 1995). In addition, the typical study of gender differences in our relations with other animals focuses on individual attitudes and behavior rather than on broader sociological issues. Virtually no studies look at the significance of the gender gap in relation to the preponderance of women within the animal movement.

It would seem plausible to argue that women are the primary actors within the animal protection movement since they make up close to 80% of the membership (Richards, 1990/1992; Jasper & Nelkin, 1992). Put differently, women have a pre-eminent standing and legitimacy in the movement that may eclipse that of their male colleagues. Yet, standing is not determined by sheer weight of numbers alone. Women have always constituted the army of grassroots activists in the animal movement, the handmaidens or "midwives" to the movement (Jasper & Nelkin, 1992, p. 90). Ironically, however, male philosophers, notably Tom Regan and Peter Singer, have predominated as the leading advocates of animal rights.

Indeed, a case can be made for describing the animal movement as "gender direct" rather than "non gender direct" or "indirect" (Beckwith, 1996). By gender direct, Beckwith means a social movement characterized by the primacy of women's gendered experiences, women's issues, and women's leadership and decision making in feminist and women's movements (p. 1038). Strictly speaking, animal rights issues are gender neutral, although, in practice, many women believe that especially in the predominantly male areas of science, hunting, and factory farming their oppression parallels that of animal exploitation by men. The president of Animal Liberation (Victoria) sees that organization with its 95% female membership as fulfilling the requirements of a gender direct movement:

> I think we need to look at the politics of animal rights to see how they do converge quite clearly with feminist politics. And they are issues of oppression, they're issues of abuse and the link is very easy to make for women because women have known what it is to live in patriarchies, to know what it is to confront that masculine scientific detachment that allows abuse to continue for abstract greater goals. I'd have to say that people who care about animals and are prepared to politicise that caring, care about blood, flesh, pain, care about a particular animal's suffering in this particular

situation now. So, they are situating their caring, they're not abstracting it. (R. Linden, personal communication, 1997)

Most studies of everyday attitudes toward animals confirm the general feminist/ecofeminist thesis Linden articulates that women, more than men, care about nonhuman animals, a claim dramatically underlined by the massive over-representation of women in her own organization. Yet, within the context of animal movement membership the gender gap takes on a different complexion. In comparing the attitudes of animal rights supporters, farmers, and the urban public, Hills (1993) notes that there were gender differences between all three groups, with animal rights supporters scoring highest on empathy and lowest on instrumentality. These results were a direct contrast to males in general and to farmers in particular. For our purpose, the most pertinent result was the similarity in responses between male and female animal rights supporters, which was not the case for farmers and the urban public where gender differences were marked.

McAdam (1992) points out that in the context of social movements, sociologists have perceived activism as gender neutral (p. 1214). My own study of the attitudes of animal welfare supporters toward animals generally confirmed the finding by Hills (1993) that little or no difference exists between the views of men and women committed to the animal welfare cause. Although this might seem self-evident, the finding has important theoretical implications for the analysis of gender relations in other social movement organizations. According to McAdam, gender is arguably the most important factor mediating the experience of social movement activism (p. 1213). While the worldviews of males and females may seem of a different order, when their attitudes and values are compared within a specific social movement con-text, there may be a degree of convergence within these movements and organizations that challenges conventional wisdom. More particularly, the convergence challenges the view, *pace* Gilligan (1982), that there is a different female voice in various moral contexts, such as within the animal protection movement. This argument about convergence is based on the results of my Animal and Social Issues Survey (ASIS) conducted among members of the Australian and New Zealand Federation of Animal Societies (ANZFAS) in late 1995.

About ANZFAS and ASIS

Widely representative of the animal protection lobby in Australia, ANZFAS covers the whole spectrum of animal protectionists from RSPCA welfarists and Australian Koala Foundation conservationists to the more radical animal liberationists, anti-vivisectionists, and animal rights advocates who belong to one of several campaigning groups such as Animal Liberation. ANZFAS is the umbrella organization for some 35 societies in Australia numbering about 33,000 members. An additional 500 individuals join as private rather than as affiliated members.

In late 1995, the ASIS, an eight-page questionnaire, was sent to these 500 private members throughout Australia. The response rate was 87% (n=437), well above the usual rate of around 30% for mail-out surveys (Fowler, 1988, p. 49). The survey was designed to elicit the following information about members: attitudes toward animals; involvement in animal issues; views about ways to improve the treatment of animals; lifestyle and social attitude as well as a personal profile of the ANZFAS membership, including how members defined themselves in the movement as animal activist, advocate or animal welfare supporter. Two demographic variables in ANZFAS stood out. In relation to age and sex, there were major discrepancies between ANZFAS members and the rest of the Australian population: There was a disproportionately large number of females in the sample (79%), and the age distribution of the sample did not conform to the national figures. For example, the median age for the population in 1994 was 33.4 years as compared to 51 years for the sample. Structural factors may also be important in explaining the preponderance of older people in the organization. Biographical availability may account for the high proportion of older women in ANZFAS, since people who are willing to support such organizations must have the time to do so. For example, in Oliver's (1983) study of voluntary activists in the neighborhood movement, discretionary time was seen as a critical resource. People who are employed full-time or have heavy marital and familial responsibilities are less likely than retired seniors to engage in social movement activism.

Thus, while discretionary time is important for a person's availability to a cause, age made little difference to the level of self-designated activism. That is, age was not important when people described themselves as activists, advocates, or supporters, at least when the cohorts were categorized broadly as young (under 39 years) and old (over 40 years). The unusually high number of middle-aged people in ANZFAS suggests that members might be unwilling to engage in the direct-action campaigns favored by younger activists. That this was not the case is supported by the evidence of the massive protests and militant actions of "middle England" where many of the activists were older people protesting against the United Kingdom's mid 1990s live animal export trade. In the Australian sample, however, age was a significant variable affecting respondents' dietary habits. Not surprisingly, as vegans and vegetarians, younger cohorts had stricter dietary regimens than the older persons who made up the bulk of carnivores in the sample. Therefore, except for diets where meat avoidance was strongest among the young, age was not a factor in determining the respondents' beliefs, attitudes, or behaviors toward animals.

Gender effects were only slightly more noticeable than age. The most striking feature about ANZFAS as an organization is its predominantly female membership (79%), a characteristic of the animal protection movement world-wide. In a sample taken from the readership of *Animals' Agenda,* Richards' (1990) study of a similar group of American animal welfare and rights supporters also reported a 79% female membership.

Wells & Hepper (1997) and Kruse (1999) report on greater female affinities with animal issues. Their studies demonstrate that women, more than men, express concern about the use of animals in research, are more likely to be members of animal welfare groups, are more inclined to abstain from eating meat or other selected animal products , hold anthropomorphic views regarding animals, and support animal rights. They also report that women are more likely than men to take action to promote animal welfare.

How can we explain why women, more so than men, are active in the animal protection movement? According to McAdam (1992), activists in social movements appear to be distinguishable from non-activists. Does this mean that high levels of consensus activists can characterize attitudes within the same social movement? At least in the case of the animal movement, the activists do share a common worldview for which there is a strong ideological consensus (Munro, 1997). In fact, McAdam points out that very little research exists about activists within the same movement, a fact most evident in the case of animal protection and one that this paper seeks to redress.

That women have good standing in the contemporary animal movement can be seen in the increasing number of women in animal protection organizations who are taking up leadership roles that were not available to them in the nineteenth century. Women led more than half of the 27 animal protection organizations I studied in Australia, Britain, and the United States (Munro, 2001), although only three of these were large, prominent organizations with relatively well-paid staff. These gendered work patterns are reflected in the staffing of anti-environmental/animal rights groups such as Put People First. A sample of the same number of these organizations (Deal, 1993) indicated that women headed only 7 of the 27 groups sampled and that men headed the remaining 20. This can be explained sociologically by the industries and interests represented by these anti-green organizations. Most are male oriented enterprises associated with the extractive industries (coal, gas, oil, timber), off-road vehicle manufacturers, hunting and fishing lobbies, chemical and pharmaceutical companies, and the cattle industry. There can be little doubt that leadership positions in these social movements and, especially, countermovement organizations reflect the structure of gendered employment opportunities in the wider society. Yet, leadership issues aside, this is where differentials cease to be important.

The ASIS data show a strong consensus among women and men on most of the issues covered in the survey. The ASIS findings suggest that the issue of animal cruelty blurs the differences between male and female protectionists and acts as a catalyst for bringing the two together. The moral standing of women in the movement is also strengthened by the movement's strong ideological consensus, specifically in what it condemns as the worst forms of animal exploitation (Munro, 1997). In the remainder of the paper, I outline the main findings in connection with the role of gender in animal protection.

Discussion

The sex of the survey respondents in ASIS made a significant difference to fewer than 20% of the issues surveyed. For more than 80% of the issues examined in the survey, there was a strong consensus between the male and female members of ANZFAS. Ideological consensus in the movement as a whole has been reported elsewhere (Munro, 1997). The purpose of the following discussion is to identify and explain the areas where there is a significant difference between women and men on the issues covered in the survey. Gender differences may have been relevant in four broad areas. As indicated in Table 10.1 below, there were only 12 instances where this was the case.

Table 10.1: Gender Effects on Animal and Social Issues

Survey Item		Number of Items	Significant Gender Effect
1 – 24	*Attitude towards animals*	*24*	*7*
25 – 38	*Involvement in animal issues*	*14*	*1*
39 – 57	*Improving the treatment of animals*	*18*	*0*
57 – 69	*Lifestyle and social attitudes*	*13*	*4*
		N = 69	*N = 12*

Source: ASIS (1995) in Munro (2005)

Given the importance of gender differences in the way men and women are said to perceive nature and other life forms, the gaps identified in this study are of particular interest. Why is it that both men and women reject some abuses of animals with equal vehemence but not others? Thus, while the respondents agree on how to improve the welfare of animals in general, there are significant gender differences when it comes to specific issues. (See Table10.2.) Respondents were asked to rate these issues on a scale from 1 (extremely wrong) to 7 (not at all wrong). There were seven such issues identified in the questions on which there was significant gender divergence.

Table 10.2: Gender Differences on Specific Issues

Items Significant Gender Difference on Seven Issues	*Females' Lower Mean and Tolerance*
1. *Hunting wild animals with guns*	*p<.015*
2. *Using horses for steeple/jump racing*	*p<.005*
3. *Exposing an animal to a disease as part of a medical experiment*	*p<.05*
4. *Using animals organs in human transplants*	*p<.0006*
5. *Killing kangaroos for their meat or skin*	*p<.03*
6. *Using poisons for feral animal control*	*p<.002*
7. *Performing operations on animals without anesthetics (eg. branding/de-horning)*	*p<.032*

Source: ASIS (1995) in Munro (2005).

On the remaining 17 uses to which animals are put, there were no significant differences between the sexes. So how can the gender effects for these seven practices be explained? The practices can be further divided into four categories as indicated below.

Hunting

Hunting wild animals with guns ranked 10th (very high level of concern with a mean of 1.32) in the list of 24 practices involving the human use of animals. That female respondents, rather than their male counterparts, see sport hunting as more morally objectionable is supported in the feminist and ecofeminist literature, specifically in papers by Comninou (1995), Kheel (1995), Adams and Donovan (1995), and Collard and Contruccis (1988). They explicitly define "man" as male to argue that hunting is man's oldest profession and that it is pursued for "pleasure, status, profit, power and masculine identity" (p. 52), a thesis challenged by Stange (1997). Stange's refutation of feminist discourse on women's estrangement from hunting is, however, a voice in the wilderness when measured against the empirical data on hunting that suggest that most forms of hunting remain primarily a male activity. Hunting wild animals with guns in Australia typically means men killing indigenous animals like kangaroos, wild pigs, and ducks. Unlike the United Kingdom where fox hunting includes a smattering of female hunters, almost all Australia's recreational and professional hunters are male. According to Stange, (1997), roughly 10% of all-American hunters are female and "these numbers seem to be growing exponentially (although) the precise number of female hunters nationally is impossible to determine" (p. 179).

Steeple/Jump Horse Racing

This particular practice, glamorized in Australia as the sport of kings, ranked 17th in terms of moral reprehensibility. Nonetheless, a mean score of 1.79 places it in the second division of perceived atrocities to animals; that is, it represents a high, rather than very high, level of concern for the respondents. Like hunting, but less so, horse racing in Australia is largely a male preoccupation. There are few female jockeys, bookmakers, or trainers, and a visit to any betting shop will confirm that gambling is predominantly, though not exclusively, a male phenomenon. Furthermore, females tend to have a special relationship with horses through their childhood experiences in pony clubs and the like. These reasons no doubt explain a significant difference in attitudes toward the sport among the survey respondents.

Animal Experimentation: Disease, Animal Organs, and Branding

Three uses of animals came under the heading of animal experimentation:

> (a) operations without anaesthetics (ranked 8, mean 1.20)

> (b) exposing an animal to a disease as part of a medical experiment (ranked 11, mean 1.33) and

> (c) using animal organs in human transplants (ranked 13, mean 1.73). Female respondents recorded lower means than their male counterparts.

Given the pioneering role of women in the early antivivisectionist movements discussed above, it is hardly surprising that more women than men should oppose animal experimentation. As we have seen, the term *animal experimentation* arouses the passions more of women than of men. That female respondents had a significantly lower mean and tolerance for animal research than their male counterparts was reinforced elsewhere in the survey with more women than men believing that scientists cause more harm than good.

Wild Animals: Kangaroos and Feral Animals

Males and females differed on an additional two questions that concerned the killing of kangaroos for their meat and skins and the poisoning of feral animals as a means of control. Both tied for 15th place in the list of 24 practices and were seen as being of great concern to the respondents (mean 1.76). Thorne (1998) suggests that killing kangaroos for commercial reasons, although perceived as less morally objectionable than recreational hunting, is pre-dominantly men's business:

> Four-wheel drive vehicles penetrate the darkness using light to freeze groups or individuals. A gunshot claps, echoing fear. Adult bodies fall to the dusty

ground, often dead on impact. Young-at-foot, hurtling into the blackness, die alone. Pouched young stunned, but not killed outright, expire with time. The shooter, most likely a part-timer, hangs each carcass—legs tied vertically, head swinging—on the truck. The shooter proceeds to the next target. (p. 174)

Cruelty seems to be the issue that explains the gender difference here. There is no need to refer to the sex of the part-time shooter in this passage, which focuses on the death of an Australian icon in the outback. The passage speaks for itself.

Movement Involvement, Lifestyle, and Social Attitudes

Gender differences also were significant in a number of other areas covered in the survey.

Involvement in animal issues. Female respondents belonged to significantly more animal welfare/rights organizations than their male counterparts (p=<.001). Apart from the ecofeminist claim that women are more in tune with nature than men and Gilligan's (1982) argument that women, more than men, seek a sense of inter-connectedness with others (including other animals), there is the historical fact concerning women's traditional involvement and standing in the animal protectionist movement. For many contemporary women, animal protection organizations still offer an outlet for social and professional development. This is particularly likely in the ANZFAS membership with its very high number of retired and elderly women. Similarly, of the 330 life members in the RSPCA, just over 80%—roughly the same proportions as in ANZFAS—are female. Although pro-active groups like hunting fraternities mainly attract male enthusiasts, reactive animal protection organizations like ANZFAS and the RSPCA appeal more to women. In the nineteenth century, animal protection societies provided a rare opportunity for women to work outside the home. At the end of the twentieth century in Australia, animal protection still manages to attract women, but typically only as voluntary workers or part-time employees. Although this does not augur well for the future of the movement, it does say a lot for the commitment of females to the cause. In 1994 and 1995, women contributed just over 60% of all donations to the RSPCA (Victoria) in excess of $500. In that period in Victoria alone, the RSPCA received more than $1 million in bequests and over $60 million in donations, most of which, it is safe to assume, came from female benefactors (RSPCA, 1994, 1995).

Lifestyle. In the western world, a high rate of pet ownership is a strong characteristic of animal rights supporters (Richards, 1990/1992; Jasper & Nelkin, 1992). In the ANZFAS sample, the rate was 81% compared to the national figure of 60%. Females (84%) are more likely than males (69%) to keep a companion animal, and the difference here is significant at the .0001 level. Although by no means an earth-shattering revelation, this may confirm the ecofeminist claim concerning female empathy with animals. In addition, companion animals function as honorary members in the family where women traditionally do much of the caring and nurturing, which may explain the discrepancy. Also, more divorced, separated, and widowed females than males comprise the ANZFAS membership. These women may have a greater need for companion animals. Although more male than female respondents were single at the time of the survey, this is not the same as a since-ended relationship.

Social Attitudes. The survey asked respondents to rate eight statements from strongly disagree to strongly agree (see Table 10.3). There was a significant gender gap in only three statements where females scored a higher mean than their male counterparts.

Table 10.3: Survey Respondent Statements on Social Attitudes –
Rated from Strongly Disagree to Strongly Agree

	Being Involved in the the Animal Movement is	**Gender Difference**
1.	**a way of life to me**	(p<.005)
2.	very satisfying to me	0
3.	**a personal sacrifice** **From my point of view:**	(p<.05)
4.	religion is very important in my life	0
5.	meat eating is the worst form of animal abuse	0
6.	**on the whole, scientists do more harm than good**	(p<.001)
7.	moral support is more important for the movement than financial support	0
8.	wide media coverage is important for the movement's success	0

Source: ASIS (1995) in Munro (2005)

The first two issues—belonging to the movement are a way of life and a personal sacrifice—may be idiosyncrasies of the survey respondents, many of whom are older women. Although animal welfare work in Australia does not provide daily bread, it does provide daily meaning for many people, especially older women. This is borne out in interviews with members of animal welfare organizations (Munro, personal communications, 1994, 1995, 1996). Therefore, it is not surprising that for many women this work involves a high degree of commitment and sacrifice. A commonly expressed sentiment in the open-ended section of the questionnaire was that being a member of so many animal welfare groups often was financially taxing, especially for females on a pension.

Finally, in the question concerning scientists, females had a significantly higher mean than males in agreeing with the proposition that scientists do more harm than good. Again, as in opposition to vivisection, there is a strong historical precedent for this negative view of the scientist's work. Modern animal protectionists, like their anti

-vivisection predecessors in the late nineteenth century, perceive the abuse of animals as a central moral dilemma confronting society. Sperling (1988) puts the contemporary position succinctly when she writes how for many animal activists "the animal as victim has become a symbol of both humanity and nature besieged (in the) vivisection of the planet" (p. 39). If gender differences in activities associated with hunting, wild animals, horse racing, and animal experimentation explain the divergence of attitudes of male and female animal supporters, converging attitudes logically would mean equal or minimal differences in male and female involvement in these activities. This seems to be the case in the majority of practices ranked by the respondents at either very high or high levels of concern. For most of these practices, either a roughly equal involvement of men and women or some other factor made the issue of gender involvement less important. Thus, in condemning the use of steel-jawed leghold traps ranked as the most morally objectionable practice in the entire list males and females are equally concerned by the sheer cruelty of the practice; that the relatively small number of trappers is predominantly male is of little importance.

Nor does gender involvement appear to be the most important factor in the relatively low condemnation of the commercial use of wildlife (ranked 14) or the raising of cattle on open ranges (ranked 20). In Australia at least, these practices are viewed as relatively benign, often carried out as small-scale, family enterprises in contrast to the industrialized mass production of animal products in factory farming. Even in raising animals in feedlots (ranked 12), the most important factor in shaping attitudes concerns the purpose of intensive farming, namely the production and consumption of meat. The ASIS questionnaire revealed much ambivalence about this. Both male and female respondents viewed meat eating (ranked 18) as only slightly more objectionable than containing animals in zoos (ranked 19). Because the sampled men and women consume meat equally, though perhaps not in the same quantities, we can expect that attitudes toward industries involving pig production (ranked 2), battery hens (ranked 4), and the live sheep trade (ranked 5) will share the same fate as raising cattle in feedlots. The equal numbers of males and females involved in the consumptive side outweigh the gender imbalance in the productive side of these industries. Similarly, for using animals in cosmetic/beauty product experiments and for fur coats the consumptive outweighs or equals the productive so that both males and females are equally involved in these activities.

For the purpose of breeding animals for research (ranked 9) and the use of unclaimed dogs in experiments (ranked 7) the respondents' convergence of attitudes calls for different explanations. One can only speculate that males and females equally see the use of unclaimed dogs as morally reprehensible because they associate dogs with companion animals. For purpose-bred animals, it may be that the gender involvement is about equal because both female animal technicians and male scientists perform this practice.

In the practices for which there are convergences of attitudes from the respondents, the relevance of gender involvement is either minimal or outweighed by some other factor. A strong male involvement and an almost complete absence of females characterize the seven practices (in Table 10.2) in which there is divergence of attitudes between the sexes.

Conclusion

I have tried to show in this paper that women have high standing in the animal protection movement because of their long-standing commitment to animals and deep involvement in animal issues. By focusing on activism within the animal movement, the paper reveals much more convergence (80%) than divergence (20%) of attitudes and actions by male and female animal protectors. This ideological consensus reflects the high standing of women as activists and advocates in the animal movement. It means that women's ideas are the prevailing ideas of the movement. Issues of divergence results indicate that stronger female opposition to hunting and allegedly cruel practices—steeple/jump horse racing, experiments on animals, and the commercial exploitation of wildlife—is contingent on early socialization, gendered work and leisure patterns, affinity with companion animals, ambivalence about science, and a history of opposition to animal abuse by generations of female activists and animal advocates. Outside the feminist and women's movements, it is rare to find a social movement in which the standing of women—their gendered experiences, their issues, and their roles—eclipses those of their male colleagues. Much more than in the environmental movement, animal protection remains a bastion of female activism and advocacy. Unlike previous generations of activists, today's female animal protectors are seen as an asset in the animal protection cause, and their standing in the movement is increasingly reflected in leadership positions and decision making.

Note: The author would like to thank Ken Shapiro and two anonymous reviewers for helpful comments on this paper.

REFERENCES

Adams, C. J. & Donovan, J. (1995). *Animals and women: Feminist theoretical explorations*. Durham & London: Duke University Press.

Beckwith, K. (1996, Summer). Lancashire women against pit closures: Women's standing in a man's movement. *Signs*, 1034-1068.

Buettinger, C. (1993, Winter). Anti-vivisection and the charge of zoophil-psychosis in the early twentieth century. *The Historian, 15* (2), 277-289.

Collard, A. & Contrucci, J. (1988). *Rape of the wild: Man's violence against animals and the earth*. London: The Women's Press.

Comninou, M. (1995). Speech, pornography, and hunting. In C. J. Adams & J. Donovan (Eds.), *Animals & women: Feminist theoretical explorations* (pp. 126-148). Durham & London: Duke University Press.

Deal, C. (1993). *The Greenpeace guide to anti-environmental organizations*. Berkeley, CA: Odonian Press.

Eckersley, R. (1992). *Environmentalism and political theory: Toward an ecocentric approach*, London: UCL Press.

Fowler, F. (1988). *Survey research methods*. Newbury Park: Sage Publications.

Gilligan, C. (1982). *In a different voice: Psychological theory and women's development*. Cambridge: Harvard University Press.

Hills, A. (1993). The motivational bases of attitudes towards animals. *Society & Animals, 1*, 111-128.

Instone, L. (1997). Denaturing women: Women, feminism, and the environment. In K. P. Hughes (Ed.), *Contemporary Australian feminism*. Melbourne: Longman.

Jasper, J. & Nelkin, D. (1992). *The animal rights crusade: The growth of a moral protest*. New York: The Free Press.

Kheel, M. (1995). License to kill: An ecofeminist critique of hunters discourse. In C. J. Adams & J. Donovan (Eds.), *Animals and women: Feminist theoretical explorations* (pp. 85-125). Durham & London: Duke University Press.

Kruse, C. R. (1999). Gender, views of nature, and support for animal rights. *Society & Animals, 7*, 179-198

Lansbury, C. (1985). Gynaecology, pornography and the antivivisection movement, *Victorian Studies, 28* (3), 413-437.

MacCulloch, J. (1993). *Creatures of culture: The Animal protection and preservation movements in Sydney 1880-1930*, Doctoral dissertation, University of Sydney, Sydney.

McAdam, D. (1992, Summer). Gender as a mediator of the activist experience: The case of freedom. *American Journal of Sociology, 97*, 1211-1240.

Munro, L. (1999a). Contesting moral capital in campaigns against animal liberation. *Society & Animals, 1* (7), 35-53.

Munro, L. (1999b). From Vilification to accommodation: Making a common cause movement, *Cambridge Quarterly of Healthcare Ethics, 8*, 46-57.

Munro, L. P. (1997). Animal rights/welfare down under, International Society for Anthrozoology, *ISAZ Newsletter, 14*, 15-19.

Munro, L. P. (2001). *Compassionate beasts: The quest for animal rights*. New York: Praeger.

Oliver, P. (1983). The mobilization of paid and volunteer activists in the neighbourhood movement. *Research in social movements: Conflict and change, 5*, 133-70.

Paul, E. (1995). Us and them: Scientists' and animal rights campaigners' views of the animal experimentation debate. *Society & Animals, 3*, 1-21.

Pifer, L. (1996). Exploring the gender gap in young adults' attitudes about animal research. *Society & Animals, 4*, 37-52.

Richards, R. (1990). *Consensus mobilization through ideology, networks, and grievances: A study of the contemporary animal rights involvement*. Doctoral dissertation, Printed by University Microfilms International in 1992, Ann Arbor.

RSPCA. (1994/1995). *12th Annual Report of the Royal Society for the Protection of Animals (Victoria) Incorporated*. Melbourne: Author.

Slicer, D. (1994). Wrongs of passage: Three challenges to the maturing of ecofeminism. In K. J. Warren (Ed.), *Ecological feminism*, London, and New York: Routledge.

Sperling, S. (1988). *Animal liberators: Research and morality.* Berkeley: University of California Press.

Stange, M. Z. (1997). *Woman the hunter.* Boston: Beacon Press.

Thorne, L. (1998). Kangaroos: The non-issue, *Society & Animals, 6,* 167-182Vance, L. (1993, June). Remapping the terrain: Books on ecofeminism. *Choice,* 1585- 1593.

Vance,L. (1993) Remapping the terrain: Books on ecofeminism. Choice, 1585-1593.

Wells, D. L. and Hepper, P. G. (1997). Pet ownership and adults' views on the use of animals. *Society & Animals, 5,* 45-63.

Perspectives

Chapter 11

The Animal Rights Movement in Theory and Practice:
A Review of the Sociological Literature

Introduction

A number of writers including Tovey (2003), Hobson-West (2007) and Irvine (2008) have recently drawn attention to the rare appearance of human-animal topics in social science texts. Work in the field of Human-Animal Studies (HAS) has mainly been confined to specialist journals and more recently to edited anthologies of previously published articles (Arluke and Sanders 2009; Flynn 2008; Wilkie and Inglis 2007). Of these tomes, the Arluke and Sanders collection pays the most attention to the sociology of the animal movement (four papers from a total of 35). That none of these papers is devoted exclusively to the sociology of the animal movement is a reflection of the literature more generally as few sociologists have focused on the movement's broad agenda or its grievances. For example, the seminal campaigns of the animal movement against the (ab)use of animals in animal experimentation, intensive farming and in a variety of entertainments and sports are rarely examined by social scientists. Notable exceptions include Beirne (1995, 1999, 2007) and Cazaux (1999) in criminology, Noske (1989) in anthropology , Garner (1993, 1998, 2006, 2010) in political science and Jasper and his colleagues (1992; 1995; 1997; 1999; 2004), Agnew (1998) , Einwohner (2002), Nibert (2002), Munro (2005) and Cherry (2010) in sociology. As suggested in the section which follows, the study of animal protectionism as a new social movement (NSM) is potentially rich in the range of theories and perspectives available to scholars.

Some Perspectives on the Animal Movement

According to Barnes (1995) unlike the older, class-based European movements that sought large-scale societal transformations, new social movements (NSMs)—he mentions gay rights and green issues including animal rights—focused on 'the piecemeal defence of particular threatened groups or lifestyles'. The animal movement is perceived by some social scientists as a political movement (Garner 1993; Wolfe 1993) and by others as a social and moral movement (Jasper and Nelkin 1992; Richards 1990). As a new social movement, it is sometimes linked to the environmental movement (Eckersley 1992) and eco-pax movements (Pakulski 1991).

'The eco-pax movements in the West', write Crook, Pakulski and Waters, 'attract civil rights campaigners, feminist supporters, animal-liberationists and a host of other groups' (1992 p. 153). Agnew (1998) , Nibert (2002; 2003) and Sztybel (2007) assert that the animal movement represents a rejection of oppressive structures of domination including the notorious trio of classism, racism, sexism, and especially speciesism; the latter, given its unfamiliarity to most people, has not attracted anything like the trio's vast network of scholarly commentators.

Sutherland and Nash (1994) describe animal rights as a new environmental cosmology while Eder (1990) includes vegetarianism and animal rights as movements against modernity; meanwhile, Tester (1991) dismisses these movements as puritanical cults and Wolfe (1993), a strong critic of animal rights, nominates ecological and animal rights issues as the fastest growing political movements in the West and the most threatening to humanist values.

These disparate views indicate the absence of any clear consensus on what makes the animal movement tick. Crook et al however suggest a possible clue when they assert that what is 'new' about NSMs, is 'their *specific orientations* combined with international *mass media exposure*' (1992 p.148). In the case of the animal movement these orientations include unique moral concerns , namely the rights of animals; self-organization such as do-it-yourself (DIY) activism; and importantly, the use of drama and spectacle often involving scandalizing images intended to achieve mass media exposure; hence Jasper's (1999) emphasis on the importance of morally challenging images, 'extreme rhetoric' and 'moral shocks' in recruiting supporters to the animal rights movement.

At a broader level of analysis the work of a number of sociologists and their theoretical ideas have been touted as among the most likely candidates for explaining one of the most misunderstood social movements of our era: Eliasian theory (Van Krieken 2001), Marxist realism (Benton 1993), feminism and ecofeminism (Vance 1993), and social constructionism (Hannigan 1995; Yearley 1992). An account of these perspectives follows.

Eliasian theory is most promising in explaining long-term processes such as changing attitudes to animals over the past several centuries. Elias emphasises the importance of shame and changing thresholds of repugnance towards violence due to the 'civilising process' (Elias 1978). He shows how cruelty and violence towards animals including the display of animal bodies in public has come to be seen as repugnant by most people in the West. His theory is supported by evidence of a long-term trend associated with 'the civilizing of appetite' (Mennell 1991) and the increasing popularity of vegetarian and vegan diets. Thus, meat is purchased in drastically disguised forms and vegetarian diets become more popular along with demands for the more humane treatment of farmed animals (Fiddes 1991). Eliasian theory, although disputed by Tester (1991) and Franklin (1999), is nonetheless a useful resource for the animal movement, especially for what it has to say about long-term trends in meat eating, vegetarianism and a predicted decrease in cruel practices towards animals.

According to Martell (1994) Marxist ideas are useful for understanding the political economy of capitalism but for little else in society-nature relations; if that is the case, then Marx's critique of capitalism may be applied to what Noske (1989) calls 'the animal-industrial complex'. Martell does however acknowledge Marx's usefulness in contributing to (1) green politics; (2) a capitalist market analysis; and (3) ecological theory. Importantly, Martell notes eco-socialism's potential for 'widening agency from the productivist industrial working class to social movements outside the labour movement' (1994 p. 153). The Marxist realist Benton (1993; 1995) takes a more positive view of Marx's relevance to animal rights when he shows how humans are bound to animals in a variety of social relationships such as in nature parks, zoos and circuses, pet-keeping, animal experimentation and intensive farming. In each of these contexts, Benton argues, animals are treated as property and not as sentient beings. He also draws parallels between factory farming and the conditions of workers in slaughterhouses and in intensive animal factories. His wish for the emergence of 'affective ties of trust, loyalty, compassion and responsibility' (1995 p.175) is, as he acknowledges, not likely to develop given that it is against the interests of workers to object to the exploitation of animals. The women's movement, especially the strand known as ecofeminism, is much more in sympathy with these sentiments.

There is now a large ecofeminist literature on animals and the environment (see Vance 1993 for an outline) which provides a comprehensive resource for animal and environmental activists. The ecofeminist critique is particularly important as a corrective to the movement's most prominent philosophers, who Ruddick (1980) asserts, are obsessively fixated on reason while dismissive of what she calls a 'maternal epistemology' based on an ethic of care and humility. This should not be construed as a soft-hearted alternative to rational debate, as women, many with strong feminist leanings, constitute the majority of animal protectionists; to them, the abuse of animals as a social problem is no less deserving of moral condemnation than other, more recognised abusive practices such as racism and its offshoots ethnic cleansing, slavery, lynchings, hate crimes against people of color and so on and sexism with its related violations of bodily integrity including clitoridectomy, rape and wife bashing.

The theory that is arguably most in accord with the animal movement's ideology and campaigns as well as with the testimonies of animal protectionists is social constructionism; when it draws on social movement and social problems theories, social constructionism offers one of the most sociologically promising ways to analyse the animal movement.

A Social Constructionist Framework

Social constructionist theory, argues Buechler, 'brings a symbolic interactionist approach to the study of collective action by emphasizing the role of framing activities and cultural processes in social activism' (1995 p.441). In other words, the idea of animal rights is not natural; it has to be argued and contested as an issue in interaction with sympathisers and critics, typically as a collective enterprise ; the issue of animal rights as a social and moral problem is thus constructed and framed by the movement's activists (in the streets) and advocates (in the suites). According to Mauss (1989) social movements and social problems are 'alternative features of the same reality' (cited in Bash 1995 p. 248), a proposition also supported by Jenness (1995) and McCright and Dunlap (2000). My own contribution (Munro 2005) to this conceptual framework is to show how both traditions are utilised by activists in what Holstein and Miller (1993) and Miller and Holstein (1989) designate as 'social problems work'. McDonald (2000), also writing in this tradition, has described how individuals become animal activists, vegans and vegetarians by engaging in social problems work—'reading, thinking, talking, and becoming involved in animal rights or vegetarian-related activities'. Similarly, Irvine (2003) has shown how animal shelter workers in the USA engage in social problems work that includes educating the public about animal health, training and behaviour. Improving the fate of unwanted pets is part of the animal welfare agenda to rescue individual animals; more important for animal rightists and liberationists is the quest to expose the abuse of millions of animals in what Noske (1989) and Kew (1999) respectively label 'the animal-industrial complex' and 'the animal-using consensus'.

The concept of social movement framing pioneered by Wilson (1973) has since been comprehensively developed by Snow and Benford (1988; 1992) and more recently by Snow and Byrd (2007). These theorists argue that all social movements have three core framing tasks, namely diagnostic, prognostic and motivational framing, or in Wilson's (1973) original terminology, a movement's diagnosis, prognosis and motivation. In the case of the animal movement, issue entrepreneurs identify animal exploitation as a social problem in much the same way that environmental threats are increasingly constructed as anthropogenic social problems (Hannigan 1995; Yearley 1992). The animal movement's diagnostic frame is to target animal abuse as a social problem on a par with harming children, women, the elderly, and most pertinently, fauna and flora. This means that the animal movement seeks to gain social problems status for its concerns about our (mis)treatment of animals particularly in the culturally-sanctioned contexts of animal experimentation, intensive farming and recreational hunting.

While much of the movement's diagnostic work is associated with the ideas of philosophers, it is the social problems work of animal activists and advocates that transforms ethics into social action. Movement insiders discover, name and frame putative abuses primarily vivisection, factory farming and blood sports as injustices to living creatures no decent society should tolerate. The practical work of animal activism and advocacy is the movement's prognostic frame, that is, the tactics it employs to prosecute its cause. Mobilising structures in the iconic form of social movement organisations (SMOs) have been developed to organise various grassroots campaigns and to mobilise emotions and moral capital on behalf of individual animals. (See Cudworth 2003, Chapter 6 on some of these campaigns).

For most people the concept of animal rights is an alien one so that the task of the animal movement is to normalize it: 'If there is a telos of social movement activity', writes Scott, 'then it is the normalization of previously exotic issues and groups' (1990 p.10). Normalizing the idea of animal rights in the seminal campaigns against vivisection, factory farming and blood sports is what constitutes the social problems work in the mainstream animal movement. Thus far, social movement activists rather than social scientists have diagnosed these practices as unconscionable; while there are some notable exceptions, most social science writing on 'the animal issue' has focused on animals as inconveniently 'out of place' (Fine and Christoforides 1991; Irvine 2003; Jerolmack 2008; Marvin 2000) and dangerous animal rights extremists as 'out of control' (Bryant 1991; Bryant and Snizek 1993; Dizard 1994; Kerasote 1993; Wolfe 1993). In short, social scientists' interest in animal issues has generally been characterized by anthropocentric motives or silence on what Agnew (1998) and Sunstein (2000) refer to as one of the most seriously neglected moral and legal problems of our time.

A Closer Look at the Animal Movement's Styles of Advocacy and Activism

Pain and suffering have featured prominently in the campaigns initiated by reformers in civil rights, women's and animal movements to promote 'the sacred rights of the weak' (Clark 1995). Animal protectionists in the movement's three main strands—welfare, liberation and rights—are united on the principle that animals are sentient beings rather than 'things' to be commodified as food, research tools or sporting trophies. Sociologists who have used a constructionist approach in relation to animal-related issues as social problems include Maurer (1995) on meat, Kunkel (1995) on factory farming and Munro (1997) on duck shooting; these studies reveal how vegetarians, health advocates and opponents of blood sports use various rhetorical strategies to frame their concerns as social problems.

In anthropocentric thinking, exemplified in Wolfe's (1993) *The Human Difference,* humans and animals are perceived as entirely different species. In this dominant paradigm, animals deserve kindness rather than rights and their interests are always subordinated to the demands of human well-being. This corresponds to the most moderate form of animal protection represented by animal welfarism. The moral orthodoxy of animal welfare is what Clark (1997) calls 'the norm of *moderate* concern for animals. By contrast, animal rights calls for the *abolition* of animal exploitation, while animal liberation as espoused by Peter Singer (1975; 1990) falls in between these two extremes. Animal welfare/liberation/rights constitute the main ideologies and strategies of the animal movement and are discussed in the remainder of this review.

Animal Welfare: Supporting Moral Orthodoxy

The Royal Society for the Prevention of Cruelty to Animals (RSPCA) in the UK and Australia) and the Society for the Prevention of Cruelty to Animals (SPCA in North America) are the quintessential animal welfare non-government organisations (NGOs) responsible for lobbying policy makers on the humane treatment of (mainly) companion animals. The (R)SPCA's strategy of working within institutional politics has ensured that the NGO maintains a moderate, reformist agenda designed to achieve only incremental changes in legislation affecting animals. From its inception in the early 19th century in England up until the 1960s, the RSPCA has epitomised middle-class respectability in its membership and moral orthodoxy in its aspirations for the humane treatment of animals; that is, animals matter but not as much as humans.

Robert Garner (2006) has criticised the animal welfare ethic because it fails to reject speciesism, the idea that humans are superior to nonhuman animals. However, while he sees the animal welfare position as philosophically flawed, he defends its political strategy. Garner argues that it makes sense politically 'to focus on reforms improving the treatment of animals which do not compromise significant human interests, and to engage in campaigns to try and shift perceptions on what is regarded as unnecessary suffering'(2006 p.161).

Elsewhere, Garner (1993) suggests that legislative reform in animal welfare is more effective than moralising efforts to win over public opinion; in a subsequent paper, while acknowledging the importance of the British public's support in animal rights campaigns for example, in the long-running campaign against fox hunting Garner (1998) attributes the movement's success to both militant grassroots direct action by the Hunt Saboteurs Association (HSA) and the advocacy work of the League Against Cruel Sports (LACS); he explains how the mass media were eager to broadcast the dramatic images of confrontations between hunters and the hunt saboteurs whose respective claims the protagonists hoped, would influence public opinion in their favor. However, Garner believes the legislative- advocacy work of the League has ultimately been more effective in winning the issue for the anti-hunting campaigners as large numbers of British members of parliament have acknowledged the League's long-term commitment by voting successfully for a ban on fox hunting.

The hunting controversy in England highlights the importance of the political opportunity structure when access to political elites was achieved by the League with the support of many Labour parliamentarians sympathetic to the anti-hunting cause. However, the political-process model—the key concept of which is the political opportunity structure—has been found wanting by prominent social movement scholars including Goodwin and Jasper (1999) and Goldstone (2004). According to the former, the model biases structure and neglects culture while Goldstone finds the model too broad to take into account all the elements in a complex field of competing players (2004 p.358). Goldstone's alternative to the political-process model resembles Giugne's (1998) identification of two crucial aspects in any analysis of the relationship of a movement and its political environment, namely 'the system of alliances and oppositions and the structure of the state' (p. 381).

It would therefore seem obvious that the political context is a crucial factor in a movement's success or failure since strategies and tactics that are effective in one political environment may not be effective in another. Timing is also crucial in that the political climate may be either favourable or unfavourable to an idea or a tactic. An idea whose time had come by the mid-1970s—animal liberation—is discussed next.

The Pragmatism of Singer's 'Animal Liberation'

Peter Singer's *Animal Liberation* (1975) which many observers believe launched the modern animal rights movement came on the scene during 'the protest cycle of the 1960s and 1970s' (Goldstone 2004 p. 340); it was a heightened period of social movement activism that saw the emergence of liberation movements on behalf of women, gays, people of color and the environment. Animal liberationists espouse Peter Singer's (1975; 1990) utilitarian philosophy in seeking a balance between the interests of humans and other animals by advocating a pragmatic approach to our treatment of animals. Thus factory farming is seen as morally repugnant, but not traditional farming; recreational hunting is condemned but not subsistence hunting by say, indigenous peoples; and in the vexed issue of animal research, animal liberationists seek a compromise with animal experimentalists based on the 3 Rs: reducing, refining and replacing the use of animals with alternatives.

Animal rights activists and more extreme animal liberationists in what Fluekiger (2008) categorizes as the Radical Animal Liberation Movement (RALM) see this kind of compromise as morally bankrupt. Critics of animal rights activists are inclined to label them—in ascending order of deviance—as 'radicals', 'extremists', and 'terrorists'. Kew (1999) has noted the prevalence of such labels in the mass media and no doubt ordinary people are influenced by negative portrayals of 'animal people'. Animal protectionists counter these designations with their own labels e.g. 'animal defenders', 'animal protectionists', 'animal rescuers', 'animal advocates' and the like. While Singer's 1975 manifesto may have spawned the various groups and individuals who constitute the RALM, Singer himself is neither an abolitionist nor indeed a rightist; and nor are the vast majority of animal protectionists. Like Singer, their aims are pragmatic as is their acceptance of the idea of 'animal rights' as useful only as a political slogan.

Most animal liberationists are not concerned with the broader philosophical debate between animal welfare reformists and animal rights abolitionists as represented respectively by Robert Garner (1993; 2010) and Gary Francione (1996; 2000) and recently in their extended arguments in Francione and Garner (2010). Mainstream activists are more inclined to believe in Garner's preference for improvements in animals' lives via regulation rather than Francione's stance that calls for the abolition of all practices involving our use of animals. Garner's view is that animal welfare's pursuit of incremental legislation delivers more improvements in our treatment of animals than moral purity: 'Getting something of what you want is better than nothing' (2006 p.161). This strategy also endorses 'the psychology of small wins' (Weick, 1984) whereby activists are inspired by the success of a political win, no matter how small.

The pragmatism of animal liberation as indicated in Figure 11.1 below offers animal protectionists a position *between* the proponents of regulation or abolition as well as the prospect of finding common ground with like-minded groups in other social movements. Animal liberationists frame speciesism as a social problem comparable to sexism and racism and other forms of intraspecies exploitation and so are amenable to coalition-building with progressive social movements such as social justice, consumer , public health and environmental groups (see for example Hargrove 1992; Luke 1995). Elizabeth Cherry's (2010) study of animal activists in France and the USA revealed how the concept of 'anti-speciesism'—a term which fails to resonate outside the movement—was popular among her French informants because of its potential for making common cause with movements against racism and sexism. Cherry reports a second activist strategy whereby animal cruelty is explicitly invoked in tactics which are physical (e.g. a woman wearing a circus elephant's shackles), discursive (e.g. does a hen have a right to a beak?) and iconographic (foie-gras evoked in a poster where ducks and geese force-feed humans). Such tactics, designed to recruit members of the general public via moral shocks (Jasper and Poulsen 1995), may also alienate potential supporters as Cherry acknowledges. According to Jasper (1997 p.180) for a moral shock to stir people to action, it must have explicit cognitive, emotional and moral dimensions. However, if the impact on the audience is too shocking, it may well backfire and render the tactic counterproductive (for an example of such a case see Mika 2006).

Animal Rights: Challenging the Status Quo

In contrast to the animal welfare strategy of working within the political process, animal rights activists press their claims within civil society. Bypassing institutional politics is seen by grassroots activists as the most effective way to mount militant, disruptive (albeit non-violent) protests in pursuit of their abolitionist agenda. In contrast to the animal welfare lobby's focus on incremental change via legislative means, animal rights activists seek fundamental changes in the way individuals and industries treat animals. Following Regan (1984; 1987), animal rightists reject the pragmatism of animal liberation and argue instead for the abolition of all practices in which humans use other animals, including pet-keeping. Regan calls for the 'total abolition of the use of animals in science; the total dissolution of commercial animal agriculture; the total elimination of commercial and sport hunting and trapping' (1985 p.13). Garner has recently suggested that animal rights would be taken more seriously if the argument for moral egalitarianism was jettisoned and replaced by 'a much more (morally and politically) acceptable version of animal rights based on the sentience of animals and not their personhood' (2010 p.128).

Similarly, the issue of vegetarianism raises an important question about what Perlo (2007) calls 'strategies for promoting animal rights'. Purists in the animal rights stream almost always insist on a commitment to vegetarianism (and ideally veganism) as a basic principle of membership in the movement. To judge the success of animal rights by a widespread conversion to ethical vegetarianism would surely doom animal rights to obscurity in most countries. A more pragmatic strategy is suggested by Frank (2004). He emphasises the role of radical animal activists in providing information to consumers and argues that illegal, non-violent, undercover actions have revealed serious defects in food regulations as well as providing 'moral shocks' to consumers. It is on this issue that animal welfarists, liberationists and rightists could unite in common cause, but only if the subversive potential of vegetarianism is fully exploited. This means that the framing of a vegetarian lifestyle would need to include not just animal welfare considerations but also environmental and health improvements for humans.

Thus, Franklin (1999) argues that the destruction of habitat and the use of animals in research and commercial agriculture—once justified as necessary for the greater good of humanity—are now seen as creating unacceptable risks and problems. Food scares such as Bovine Spongiform Encephalopathy or BSE ('mad cow disease') , salmonella, and genetically modified food have been identified as social problems in a number of fields: the costs of agribusiness to small farmers (Dolan 1986); health (Fraser et al. 1990); environmental risks to consumers (Rifkin 1992); the physical environment (Coppin 2003); the spectre of third world hunger (Coats 1989); and genetic engineering (Kimbrell 1994). Although the concerns over these developments are primarily motivated by fears for human survival and rarely by animal welfare considerations, all animals—human and nonhuman—would ultimately benefit by a revolution in dietary habits along the lines described by Elias (1978) who predicts that vegetarianism will become the long-term dietary future of our species.

Thus far the review has focused on some of the main theoretical approaches employed by social scientists in analysing the animal movement. The rest of the review addresses the practices of animal protectionists as well as the question of how the social problems work of these activists can be helped or hindered by collaborating with the intellectual work of academics.

The Animal Movement in Action

It is through actions that social movements *move,* a process involving different levels and dimensions of movement 'mobilising and affecting opinions, engaging emotions, changing laws, preventing some actions while encouraging others' (Eyerman 2006 p.194).

Figure 11.1: Modes of Animal Protection

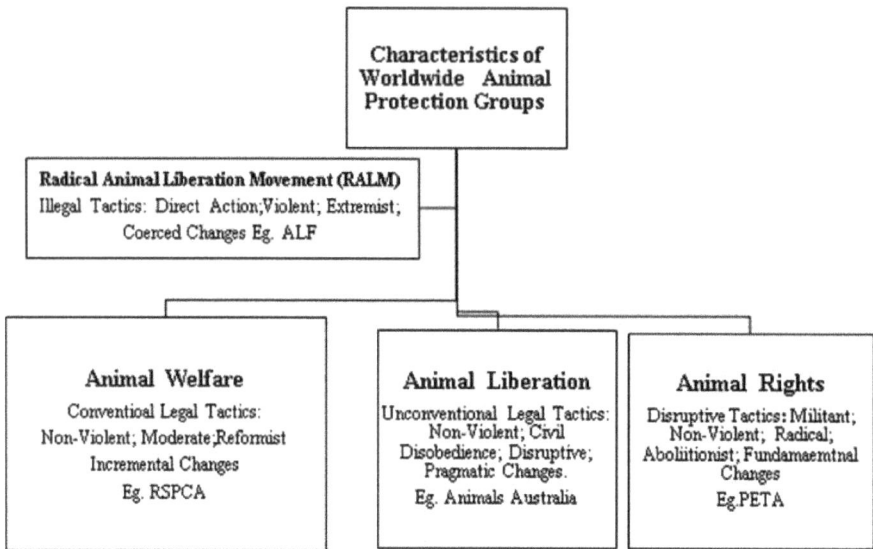

```
                    ┌─────────────────────┐
                    │  Characteristics of  │
                    │  Worldwide  Animal   │
                    │  Protection Groups   │
                    └─────────────────────┘

┌──────────────────────────────────────────────┐
│ Radical Animal Liberation Movement (RALM)     │
│ Illegal Tactics: Direct Action;Violent; Extremist; │
│         Coerced Changes Eg. ALF               │
└──────────────────────────────────────────────┘

┌──────────────────────┐  ┌──────────────────────┐  ┌──────────────────────┐
│    Animal Welfare    │  │   Animal Liberation  │  │    Animal Rights     │
│ Conventioal Legal Tactics: │ │ Unconventional Legal Tactics: │ │ Disruptive Tactics: Militant; │
│ Non-Violent; Moderate;Reformist │ │    Non-Violent; Civil │ │  Non-Violent; Radical; │
│  Incremental Changes │  │ Disobedience; Disruptive; │ │ Aboliitionist; Fundamaemtnal │
│     Eg. RSPCA        │  │   Pragmatic Changes.  │  │        Changes       │
│                      │  │  Eg. Animals Australia │ │       Eg.PETA        │
└──────────────────────┘  └──────────────────────┘  └──────────────────────┘
```

In Figure 11.1 strategies refer to the broad organising principles of the mainstream movement's three main strands: welfare, liberation and rights (and outside the mainstream in the case of the RALM); associated tactics are listed below these strategic categories. Singer's philosophical views in *Animal Liberation* (1975; 1990) are located between animal welfare and animal rights; politically, however, they are more in tune with animal rights practice. The latter is frequently and often deliberately confused with the violent, extremist actions of RALM groups. It should also be noted that Fluekiger's understanding of what is "radical" in the RALM covers direct actions, including sabotage and vandalism, the liberation of animals, arson, and home visits (2008 p.111), a list which misinterprets radicalism as extreme and violent; RALM groups do employ extreme and violent tactics but the activists are not radicals or terrorists in the conventional meanings of these terms as virtually all social activists who challenge the status quo can be viewed as radicals while the more sinister designation of 'terrorist' should only apply to those who plan and carry out deadly, random attacks in the public domain.

While some movement theorists and philosophers would question the accuracy of the above model, it broadly corresponds to the ideologies of the movement's three main strands and importantly, with the testimonies of animal protectionists; Figure 11.1 also closely resembles Orlans's (1993) 'preliminary classification chart' which in addition to animal welfare, rights and liberation organizations, includes details of legal and illegal animal industries. Orlans points out that the chart is an oversimplification since the categories resist strict demarcation; however, as intended, it is an approximation designed to highlight basic differences between the key terms: animal exploitation, animal use, and animal welfare/rights/liberation.

In reality, classification disputes are of little interest to animal protectionists; what really matters and what is most contentious for both supporters and opponents of the movement is its prognosis, that is, how activists seek to abolish cruel practices strategically and tactically. Marginally less problematic is the related issue of the movement's motivational framing or how it mobilises support. These tasks are about making strategic choices such as the use of violence or non-violence, direct or indirect action, collaboration or confrontation or in Tarrow's (1998) terms, choosing between conventional, disruptive and violent repertoires. Tarrow's terminology is an accurate categorisation of the strategies employed by animal welfarists (moderate and conventional); animal rightists (militant and disruptive); and liberationists (extremist and violent) in the RALM's case.

In the UK and North America, where animal rights activities are most in evidence, the media typically frame the campaigns as the actions of violent extremists or terrorists (Kew 1999), and in doing so support the backlash against animal rights by animal-user industries. Thus moderate reforms to improve anti-cruelty laws in Canada relating to individual acts of cruelty were strenuously opposed by animal-user industries when they exaggerated the effects of the reforms on their activities and cast the animal welfare reformers as 'terrorists', 'extremists' and 'radicals'(Sorenson 2003). The fact that the anti-cruelty amendments did not affect their interests was irrelevant as the animal-user lobby believes it has to be on constant guard lest the enhanced status of animals becomes 'a challenge to human uniqueness' (Sorenson 2003 p. 397). Meanwhile, the extremists in the RALM pose more of a threat to the financial and physical well- being of its targets, and academics engage in philosophical disputes of little interest to activists. However, the abolitionist Francione and reformist Garner claim that their comprehensive debate 'broad animal protectionism'—advocated by Garner and rejected by Francione as the 'new welfarism'—is not simply an academic exercise but rather something that is relevant and indispensable to practitioners: 'The practical strategy of animal advocates must necessarily be informed by theory, and their political, legal, and social campaigns will be determined by (it)' (Francione and Garner 2010 p. xi-xii). How this might be achieved is taken up in the next section.

Academic and Activist Collaboration: A Call to Action

In a rousing call to action, Reese (2001) has appealed to sociologists to confront troubling social problems affecting human beings; given the tone of her manifesto, the omission of any mention of nonhuman animals is no doubt inadvertent. In this mobilising tract, Reese appeals to sociologists to take to the streets and engage with social movement activists by documenting their causes and grievances. By critically evaluating the movement's issues, their strengths and deficiencies, she believes that sociologists will derive a sense of purpose and relevance. Similarly, Bevington and Dixon advocate 'dynamic engagement with movements' (2005 p.190). Social scientists, they believe, should have neither a detached association with social movements, nor an uncritical, unconditional stance towards a favourite movement. Sociologists, they suggest, need to develop 'movement-relevant theory' that can be utilized by activists in their various campaigns; for social movement scholars the relevance of their theories would be enhanced by what Maddison and Scalmer (2006) call 'activist wisdom'.

The idea of the social movement analyst as activist is controversial, with various commentators referring to both the risks and opportunities of scholar-activist collaboration. Space limitations preclude a detailed discussion of these ideas, many of which are described most recently by Eyal and Buchholz (2010) in what they refer to as 'a sociology of interventions'. Detailed accounts of scholar-activist collaborations can be found in Croteau et al. (2005), Maddison and Scalmer (2006) and Valocchi (2009). Although the present review will focus on the positives rather than the negatives of scholar-activist collaboration, Einwohner's (2002) study of the strategies animal rights activists use to maintain their motivation provides an example of the risks involved; one of the 'four fortifying strategies' refers to how the activists boost their morale by claiming credit for successful campaigns, a strategy that may be less viable if they were to accept substantial input from academic collaborators.

Many of the questions and dilemmas posed by activists in progressive social movements that might be resolved by social movement scholars are comprehensively described in Maddison and Scalmer (2006) and Valocchi (2009) who canvassed the ideas of grassroots activists in a range of progressive social movements in Australia and the USA respectively. Valocchi's (2009) *Social Movements and Activism in the USA* shares the aspirations of the Australian authors to discover what activists and scholars can learn from each other. If, as the Australian scholar activists claim, academic theories are enhanced by their informants' 'practical knowledge' and 'activist wisdom', can animal activists profit from an understanding of social movement theories and concepts?

'There is Nothing as Practical as a Good Theory'

As the best- known scholar activist in the animal movement, Peter Singer has been both praised and condemned for practicing what he preaches. Many animal activists attribute Singer's 'activist wisdom' to the pragmatism that characterises the style of animal liberation he described in his 1975 best-seller of the same name. Although social movement scholars would be hard pressed to achieve Singer's credibility in the animal movement, their academic 'tool kit' might prove to be more useful than the philosopher's more abstract concepts and reasoning; this would certainly be the case in the everyday practice of activism where strategy and tactics are of paramount importance. For example, Jasper (2004) has identified about two dozen 'strategic dilemmas' of concern to activists such as 'the organization dilemma' the choice between activism in the streets or advocacy in the suites. Maddison and Scalmer (2006) devote two chapters to this dilemma of 'expressive *or* instrumental action' and 'democracy *or* organization'. Saul Alinsky's (1971) advice 'If you want drama, get a movement; if you want results, get an organization' may be a satisfactory solution to this dilemma; on the other hand, social movement scholars would be obliged to point out the dangers of bureaucratization when organizations develop a CEO culture obsessed with fundraising or impression management.

The six additional activist dilemmas identified by Maddison and Scalmer (2006) deserve a brief comment on their relevance to the animal movement. The *Unity Difference* dilemma is one that confronts animal activists whenever strategic and tactical choices are debated. As argued in the present review, the mainstream animal movement consists of three main strands which differ in their tactical repertoires but are united in their ideological and strategic opposition to speciesism. Movement scholars, in their role as 'critical friends' of activists (Yearley 1992), would serve them well with this analysis as disunity is one of the main threats to a movement's viability. Similarly, the choice between *Revolution or Reform* and the issue of *Counter-publics and Mainstream* are causes of conflict inside and outside the animal movement which the discussion of strategies in the review highlights. The present review suggests activists would benefit by exposure to the debate between Francione and Garner (2010) on the merits of abolition *versus* regulation and fundamentalism *versus* pragmatism; the review also indicates that non-violence rather than violence is more likely to achieve the goals of mainstream animal protectionists (Elias 1978). Furthermore, Elias's disdain for the abstract theorizing of philosophers, which accords with Marx's famous dictum—'The philosophers have only interpreted the world in different ways; the point is to change it'—is worth serious reflection by both movement scholars and activists.

One of the issues identified by Jasper (2004) 'the extension dilemma' corresponds broadly to what Maddison and Scalmer (2006) refer to as the *Local-Global* issue. Jasper makes the point that a movement will have difficulty in maintaining its collective identity if it forms coalitions with other cause groups. However, in the case of the animal movement, this may be a risk worth taking as it seems unlikely that a relatively unique conscience movement could prosecute its campaigns globally without initiating common cause with like-minded activists (see Szasz 1994; Munro 1999). As a NSM the animal movement does not seek a wholesale transformation of society in the manner of earlier movements inspired by socialism and so Maddison and Scalmer's couplet *Redistribution and Recognition* is only relevant to the extent that animal activists seek to destabilize 'the animal-industrial complex' (Noske 1989); and while activist campaigns are not about the redistribution of wealth or capital, they are about promoting the value of animals as sentient beings as opposed to commodities for exploitation by animal-user industries. In this way animal activists hope that their moral capital will triumph over the financial resources of the animal-exploiting industries. Moral capital, therefore, is a concept worth employing when activists challenge 'the animal-using consensus' (Kew 1999).

Occupying the moral high ground is not however enough to achieve widespread public support for a movement's cause; Tilly's (2004) WUNC idea is relevant in this context and well worth the consideration of animal activists in their quest for respect and recognition. WUNC—worthiness, unity, numbers, commitment—according to Tilly, are prerequisites for the success of social movements. Valocchi's engagement with local activists suggests how scholar activist discussions of such ideas are likely to generate useful information for both parties: 'Our discussion of goals, strategies and political opportunities, resources and organizations, participation, commitment, conflicts, and identities enabled a dialogue between scholars' theories and concepts and activists' concerns and dilemmas' (2009 p.167).

The last dilemma in Maddison and Scalmer's list *Hope or Despair* is especially important for the success of the animal movement not least because of the opportunities and promise scholar-activist collaboration might provide. One hopes, for example, that this review of the theories and practices relevant to the animal movement and the concluding summary below provide an accurate portrayal of the animal movement's grievances, goals, strategies, strengths and dilemmas from which both animal activists and movement scholars can profit.

Conclusion

The main topics covered in this review are the theories and practices of the animal rights movement and their possible integration by scholar-activist collaboration. I will now summarize some of the key ideas relating to these three themes in the hope that they might stimulate further research. First, Eliasian, Marxist, feminist and social constructionist theories provide insightful analyses of the animal movement. Elias's (1978) notion of the civilising process is relevant to changing attitudes toward violence against human and nonhuman animals and along with Mennell's (1991) work on 'the civilising of the appetite' point to vegetarianism as the dietary future of human beings; more work is needed on the political economy of the 'animal-industrial complex' (Noske 1989) along Marxist lines begun by Benton (1993); the latter's plea for the emergence of 'affective ties of trust, loyalty, compassion and responsibility' (1995 p.175) resonates with Elias's view that increases in mutual identification within and between species should lead to decreasing levels of cruelty; (eco) feminists also support these sentiments both in theory and practice, in particular in their approach to animal protection as social problems work against speciesism and sexism; finally, social constructionist theory emphasises the role of framing and cultural processes in social movement activism (Buechler 1995) ; as we have seen in this review, the efficacy of diagnostic, prognostic and motivational frames are of crucial importance to the success of the animal movement.

The practice of animal protection as depicted in Figure 11.1 is the second theme covered in the review. Animal activists and advocates, it is argued, are engaged in three modes of animal protection: welfare, liberation and rights characterised by different strategies of activism and advocacy; these non-violent mainstream animal movements should not be confused with extremist groups in the RALM. I have argued that the pragmatism of Singer's animal liberation occupies the middle ground between animal welfare's preference for regulation via legislation and the strict abolitionist goals of animal rights; again, the latter's methods of persuasive communication via militant, non-violent actions should not be confused with the violent tactics of the RALM.

Finally, the review's third theme of scholar-activist collaboration attempts to show some of the promises and pitfalls of such an engagement. It is surely logical that social movement theories and concepts are enhanced by a scholar's engagement with activists whose 'practical knowledge' provide empirical credibility for what otherwise is often perceived as arcane, abstract theory. On the activist side of the collaboration, as Francione and Garner (2010) maintain, campaign strategies need to be informed by relevant theory; an admittedly exploratory account of how this might work is outlined under the axiom 'there is nothing as practical as a good theory'. The themes summarised above eminently qualify as topics for future research by social movement scholars; this is especially true for the animal rights movement which remains one of the most misunderstood and understudied social movements of our era.

REFERENCES

Agnew, Robert 1998. 'The Causes of Animal Abuse: A Social- Psychological Analysis,' *Theoretical Criminology* 2: 177-209.

Alinski, Saul 1971. *Rules for Radicals: A Pragmatic Primer for Realistic Radicals.* New York: Random House.

Arluke, Arnold and Clinton Sanders 2009. *Between the Species: Readings in Human-Animal Relations.* Boston: Pearson Education.

Barnes, Barry 1995. *The Elements of Social Theory.* London: University College London Press.

Bash, Harry 1995. *Social Problems and Social Movements: An Exploration into the Sociological Construction of Alternative Realities.* Atlantic Highlands, N. J: Humanities Press.

Beirne, Piers 1995. 'The Use and Abuse of Animals in Criminology: A Brief History and Current Review.' *Social Justice* 22: 5-31.

Beirne, Piers 1999. 'For a Non-Speciesist Criminology: Animal Abuse as an Object of Study.' *Criminology* 37: 117-147.

Beirne, Piers 2007. 'Animal Rights, Animal Abuse and Green Criminology' in Piers

Beirne and Nigel South (eds) *Issues in Green Criminology: Confronting Harms Against Environments, Humanity and Other Animals.* Devon: Willan Publishing.

Benton, Ted 1993. *Natural Relations: Ecology, Animal Rights and Social Justice.* London: Verso.

Benton, Ted 1995. 'Animal Rights and Social Relations' in Andrew Dobson and Paul Lucardie (eds) *The Politics of Nature: Explorations in Green Political Theory.* London: Routledge.

Bevington, Douglas and Chris Dixon 2005. 'Movement-Relevant Theory: Rethinking Social Movement Scholarship and Activism.' *Social Movement Studies* 4: 185-208.

Bryant, Clifton 1991. 'Deviant Leisure and Clandestine Lifestyle: Cockfighting as a Socially Devalued Sport.' *World Leisure and Recreation* 133: 17-21.

Bryant, Clifton and William Snizek 1993. 'On the Trial of the Centaur.' *Society* 3: 25-35.

Buechler, Steven 1995. 'New Social Movement Theories.' *The Sociological Quarterly* 36: 441-461.

Cazaux, Geertrui 1999. 'Beauty and the Beast: Animal Abuse from a Non-Speciesist Criminological Perspective.' *Crime, Law and Social Change* 31: 105-126.

Cherry, Elizabeth (2010). 'Shifting Symbolic Boundaries: Cultural Strategies of the Animal Rights Movement.' *Sociological Forum* 25: 450-475.

Clark, Elizabeth 1995. "The Sacred Rights of the Weak": Pain, Sympathy and the Culture of Individual Rights in Antebellum America.' *The Journal of American History* September: 463-93.

Clark, S. R. L. 1997. *Animals and Their Moral Standing.* Routledge: London.

Coats, C. D. 1989. *Old McDonald's Factory Farm.* New York: Continuum Publishing.

Coppin, Dawn 2003. 'Foucauldian Hog Futures: The Birth of Mega-Hog Farms.' *The Sociological Quarterly,* 44: 597-616.

Crook, Stephen, Jan Pakulski, and Malcolm Waters 1992. *Post modernization: Change in Advanced Society.* London: Sage Publications.

Croteau, David, William Hoynes and Charlotte Ryan 2005. *Rhyming Hope and History: Activists, Academics, and Social Movement Scholarship.* Minneapolis and London: University of Minnesota Press.

Cudworth, Erika 2003. *Environment and Society.* London and New York: Routledge.

Dizard, Jan 1994. *Going Wild: Hunting, Animal Rights, and the Contested Meaning of Nature.* Amherst: University of Massachusetts Press.

Dolan, E. F. 1986. *Animal Rights.* New York: Franklin Walts.

Eckersley, Robyn 1992. *Environmentalism and Political Theory: Toward an Ecocentric Approach.* London: UCL Press.

Eder, Klaus 1990. 'The Rise of Counterculture Movements Against Modernity: Nature as a New Field of Class Struggle.' *Theory, Culture and Society* 7: 21-48.

Einwohner, Rachael 2002. 'Motivational Framing and Efficacy Maintenance: Animal Rights Activists' Use of Four Fortifying Strategies.' *The Sociological Quarterly* 43: 509-526.

Elias, Norbert 1978. *The Civilising Process, Vol 1, The History of Manners.* Oxford: Basil Blackwell.

Eyal, Gil and Larissa Buchholz 2010. 'From the Sociology of Intellectuals to the Sociology of Interventions.' *Annual Review of Sociology* 36: 117-137.

Eyerman, Ron 2006. 'How Social Movements Move' in J. Alexander, B. Giesen, and J. Mast. *Social Performance: Symbolic Action, Cultural Pragmatics, and Ritual.* Cambridge: Cambridge University Press.

Fiddes, M 1991. *Meat: A Natural Symbol.* London: Routledge.

Fine, Gary and Lazaros Christoforides 1991. 'Dirty Birds, Filthy Immigrants, and the English Sparrow War: Metaphorical Linkages in Constructing Social Problems.' *Symbolic Interaction* 14:375-393.

Fluekiger, J-M. 2008. 'The Radical Animal Liberation Movement: Some Reflections on its Future.' *Journal for the Study of Radicalism* 2: 111-132.

Flynn, Clifton 2008. (ed.) *Social Creatures: A Human and Animal Studies Reader.* New York: Lantern Books.

Francione, Gary 1996. *Rain Without Thunder: The Ideology of the Animal Rights Movement.* Philadelphia, PA.: Temple University Press.

Francione, Gary 2000. *Introduction to Animal Rights: Your Child or the Dog?* Philadelphia: Temple University Press.

Francione, Gary and Robert Garner 2010. *The Animal Rights Debate: Abolition or Regulation?* New York: Columbia University Press.

Frank, Joshua 2004. 'The Role of Radial Animal Activists as Information Providers to Consumers.' *Animal Liberation Philosophy and Policy Journal* 2: 1-13.

Franklin, Adrian 1999. *Animals and Modern Cultures: A Sociology of Human-Animal Relations in Modernity.* London: Sage.

Fraser, L., S. Eawistowski, J. Horwitz, and S. Turkel 1990. *The Animal Rights Handbook.* Los Angeles: Living Planet Press.

Garner, Robert 1993. *Animals, Politics and Morality.* Manchester: Manchester University Press.

Garner, Robert 1998. 'Defending Animal Rights.' *Parliamentary Affairs* 51: 458-469.

Garner, Robert 2006. 'Animal Welfare: A Political Defence.' *Journal of Animal Liberation and Ethics* 1: 161-174.

Garner, Robert 2010. 'Animals, Ethics and Public Policy.' *The Political Quarterly* 811: 123-130.

Giugne, Marco 1998. 'Was it Worth the Effort? The Outcomes and Consequences of Social Movements.' *Annual Review of Sociology* 98: 371-393.

Goldstone, Jack 2004. 'More Social Movements or Fewer? Beyond Political Opportunity Structures to Relational Fields.' *Theory and Society* 33: 333-365.

Goodwin, Jeff, and James Jasper 1999. 'Caught in a Winding, Snarling Vine: The Structural Bias of Political Process Theory.' *Sociological Forum* 14: 27-54.

Hannigan, John 1995. *Environmental Sociology: A Social Constructionist Perspective.* London: Routledge.

Hargrove, EC (ed) 1992. *The Animal Rights/Environmental Ethics Debate: The Environmental Perspective.* New York: State University of New York Press.

Hobson-West, Pru 2007. 'Beasts and Boundaries: An Introduction to Animals in Sociology, Science and Society', *Qualitative Sociology Review* 3: 23-41.

Holstein, James, and Gale Miller 1993. 'Social Constructionism and Social Problems Work' in Gale Miller and James Holstein (eds) *Constructionist Controversies: Issues in Social Problems Theory.* New York: Aldine de Gruyter.

Irvine, Leslie 2003. 'The Problem of Unwanted Pets: A Case Study in How Institutions "Think" about Clients' Needs.' *Social Problems* 50: 550-566.

Irvine, Leslie 2008. 'Animals and Sociology.' *Sociology Compass* 2:1954-1971.

Jasper, James 1997. *The Art of Moral Protest: Culture, Biography and Creativity in Social Movements.* Chicago: University of Chicago Press.

Jasper, James 1999. 'Recruiting Intimates, Recruiting Strangers: Building the Contemporary Animal Rights Movement' in Jo Freeman and Victoria Johnson (eds) *Waves of Protest: Social Movements Since the Sixties.* Latham: Rowman and Littlefield Publishers, Inc.

Jasper, James 2004. 'A Strategic Approach to Collective Action: Looking for Agency in Social Movement Choices.' *Mobilization* 9: 1-16.

Jasper, James, and Dorothy Nelkin 1992. *The Animal Rights Crusade: The Growth of a Moral Protest*. New York: The Free Press.

Jasper, James, and Jane Poulsen 1995. 'Recruiting Strangers and Friends: Moral Shocks and Social Networks in Animal Rights and Anti-Nuclear Protests.' *Social Problems* 42: 493-512.

Jenness, Valerie 1995. 'Social Movement Growth, Domain Expansion, and Framing Processes: The Gay/Lesbian Movement and Violence Against Gays and Lesbians as a Social Problem.' *Social Problems* 42: 145-170.

Jerolmack, Colin 2008. 'How Pigeons Became Rats: The Cultural-Spatial Logic of Problem Animals.' *Social Problems* 55: 72-94.

Kerasote, Ted 1993. *Blood Ties: Nature, Culture, and the Hunt*. New York: Random House.

Kew, Barry 1999. *Fearsome Truths: The Challenge of Animal Liberation*. Unpublished PhD Thesis in Sociology, Durham: University of Durham.

Kimbrell, Andrew 1994. *The Human Body Shop: The Engineering and Marketing of Life*. San Francisco: Harper Collins.

Kunkel, Klaus 1995. 'Down on the Farm: Rationale Expansion in the Construction of Factory Farming as a Social Problem.' In Joel Best (ed.) *Images of Issues: Typifying Contemporary Social Problems*. New York: Aldine de Gruyter.

Luke, Brian 1995. 'Solidarity Across Diversity: A Pluralistic Rapprochement of Environmentalism and Animal Liberation.' *Social Theory and Practice* 21: 177-206.

McCright, Aaron and Riley Dunlap 2000. 'Challenging Global Warming as a Social Problem: An Analysis of the Conservation Movement's Counter-Claims.' *Social Problems* 47: 499-522.

McDonald, Barbara 2000. "Once You Know Something, You Can't Not Know It": An Empirical Look at Becoming Vegan', *Society & Animals* 8: 1-23.

Maddison, Sarah, and Sean Scalmer 2006. *Activist Wisdom: Practical Knowledge and Creative Tension in Social Movements*. Sydney: UNSW Press.

Martell, Luke 1994. *Ecology and Society: An Introduction*. Cambridge: Polity Press.

Marvin, Garry 2000. 'The Problem of Foxes: Legitimate and Illegitimate Killing in the English Countryside. 'in John Knight (ed.) *Natural Enemies: People Wildlife Conflicts in Anthropological Perspective*. London and New York: Routledge.

Maurer, Donna 1995. 'Meat as a Social Problem: Rhetorical Strategies in Contemporary Vegetarian Literature.' In Donna Maurer and Jeffrey Sobal (eds) *Eating Agendas: Food and Nutrition as Social Problems*. New York: Aldine de Gruyter.

Mauss, Arnaud 1989. 'Beyond the Illusion of Social Problems Theory' in James Holstein and Gale Miller (eds) *Perspectives on Social Problems: A Research Annual* 1: London: JAI Press Inc.

Mennell, Stephen 1991. 'On the Civilising of Appetite' in M. Featherstone, M. Hepworth, and B.S. Turner (eds) *The Body: Social Processes and Cultural Theory*. London: Sage Publications.

Mika, Marie 2006 'Framing the Issue: Religion, Secular Ethics and the Case of Animal Rights Mobilization', *Social Forces*. 85: 915-941.

Miller, Gale and James Holstein 1989. 'On the Sociology of Social Problems' in James Holstein and Gale Miller (eds) *Perspectives on Social Problems*. 1: 1-18, Greenwich, CT: JAI Press.

Miller, Gale and James Holstein 1997. *Social Problems in Everyday Life: Studies of Social Problems* Greenwich, CT: JAI Press.

Munro, Lyle 1997. 'Framing Cruelty: The Construction of Duck Shooting as a Social Problem.' *Society & Animals* 5: 137-154.

Munro, Lyle 1999. 'From Vilification to Accommodation: Making a Common Cause Movement', *Cambridge Quarterly of Healthcare Ethics*. 8: 46-57.

Munro, Lyle 2005. *Confronting Cruelty: The Challenge of the Animal Rights Movement* Leiden and Boston: Brill.

Nibert, David 2002. *Animal Rights/Human Rights: Entanglements of Oppression and Liberation*. Lanham, MD: Rowman and Littlefield.

Nibert, David 2003 'Humans and Other Animals: Sociology's Moral and Intellectual Challenge.' *The International Journal of Sociology and Social Policy* 23: 5-25.

Noske, Barbara 1989. *Humans and Other Animals: Beyond the Boundaries of Anthropology*. London: Pluto Press.

Orlans, F. Barbara 1993. *In the Name of Science: Issues in Responsible Animal Experimentation.* Oxford: Oxford University Press.

Pakulski, Jan 1991. *Social Movements: The Politics of Moral Protest* Melbourne: Longman Cheshire.

Perlo, Katherine 2007. 'Extrinsic and Intrinsic Arguments: Strategies for Promoting Animal Rights.' *Journal of Critical Animal Studies* V: 1-14.

Reese, Ellen 2001. 'Deepening Our Commitment, Hitting the Streets: A Call to Action.' *Social Problems* 48: 152-157.

Regan, Tom 1984. *The Case for Animal Rights.* London: Routledge.

Regan, Tom 1985. 'The Case for Animal Rights' in Peter Singer (ed.) *In Defence of Animals.* New York: Harper & Row Publishers.

Regan, Tom 1987. *The Struggle for Animal Rights.* Clarks Summit PA: International Society for Animal Rights Inc.

Richards, Rebecca 1990. *Consensus Mobilization Through Ideology, Networks, and Grievances: A Study of the Contemporary Animal Rights Movement*, PhD Dissertation, Printed by University Microfilms International, Ann Arbor.

Rifkin, Jeremy 1992. *Beyond Beef: The Rise and Fall of the Cattle Culture.* New York: Dutton Books.

Ruddick, Sara 1980. 'Maternal Thinking.' *Feminist Studies* 6: 350-351.

Scott, Alan 1990. *Ideology and New Social Movements.* Boston and London: Unwin Hyman,

Singer, Peter 1975. *Animal Liberation: A New Ethics for Our Treatment of Animals.* New York: New York Review and Random House.

Singer, Peter 1990. *Animal Liberation 2nd ed.* London: Jonathon Cape.

Snow, David, and Robert Benford 1988. 'Ideology, Frame Resonance and Participant Mobilization' in B. Klandermans, H. Kriesi and S. Tarrow (eds) *From Structure to Action: Comparing Social Movement Research Across Cultures.* International Social Movement Research, A Research Annual: 197-217 Greenwich, CT: JAI Press.

Snow, David, and Robert Benford 1992. 'Master Frames and Cycles of Protest' in Aldon Morris and Carol McClurg Mueller (eds) *Frontiers in Social Movement Theory.* New Haven and London: Yale University Press.

Snow, David, and S. Byrd 2007. 'Ideology, Framing Processes, and Islamic Terrorist Movements.' *Mobilization* 12: 119-136.

Sorenson, John 2003. 'Some Strange Things Happening in Our Country: Opposing Proposed Changes in Anti-Cruelty Laws in Canada.' *Social and Legal Studies* 12: 77-402.

Sunstein, Cass 2000. 'Standing for Animals', *UCLA Law Review* 47: 1333-1368.

Sutherland, Anne, and Jeffrey Nash 1994. 'Animal Rights as a New Environmental Cosmology.' *Qualitative Sociology* 17: 171-186.

Szasz, Andrew 1994. *Eco populism: Toxic Waste and the Movement for Environmental Justice.* Minneapolis: University of Minnesota Press.

Sztybel, David 2007. 'Animal Rights Law: Fundamentalism versus Pragmatism.' *Journal of Critical Animal Studies* **v**: 1-35.

Tarrow, Sidney 1998. *Power in Movement: Social Movements and Contentious Politics*, 2nd edition. Cambridge: Cambridge University Press.

Tester, Keith 1991. *Animals and Society: The Humanity of Animal Rights.* London: Routledge.

Tilly, Charles 2004 *Social Movements 1768-2004.* Boulder: Paradigm Publishers.

Tovey, Hilary 2003. 'Theorising Nature and Society in Sociology: The Invisibility of Animals.' *Sociologia Ruralis* 43: 196-214.

Valocchi, Stephen 2009. *Social Movements and Activism in the USA.* Hobboken: Routledge.

Vance, Linda 1993. 'Remapping the Terrain: Books on Ecofeminism.' Bibliographic Essay. *Choice* June: 1585-1593.

Van Krieken, Robert 2001. 'Elias and Process Sociology' in George Ritzer and Barry Smart (eds) *Handbook of Social Theory.* London: Sage Publications.

Weick, Karl 1984. 'Small Wins: Redefining the Scale of Social Problems.' *American Psychologist* January: 40-49.

Wilkie, Rhoda and David Inglis (eds) 2007. *Animals and Society: Critical Concepts in the Social Sciences Vols 1-5.* London: Routledge.

Wilson, John 1973. *Introduction to Social Movements*. New York: Basic Books Inc.
Wolfe, Alan 1993. *The Human Difference: Animals, Computers, and the Necessity of Social Science*. Berkeley CA: University of California Press.
Yearley, Steven 1992. *The Green Case: A Sociology of Environmental Issues, Arguments and Politics*. London: Routledge.

Chapter 12

Contesting Moral Capital in Campaigns Against Animal Liberation

According to Klandermans (1990, pp. 122-123), social movement scholars would provide better explanations of the way social movement organizations mobilize resources, use opportunities, and exert influence if they paid more attention to the multi-organizational field of movements. For Klandermans, the multi-organizational field consists of an alliance system (supporters) and a conflict system (opponents, as in countermovement organizations). Countermovement tactics listed by Klandermans (1990) include (a) criminalizing social movements and their activities; (b) undermining their organizational strength; and (c) using repression, threats, anti-propaganda, and litigation. Crucial to the backlash against animal liberation, the tactics are also effective in "undermining the moral and political bases of [a] social movement organization" (p. 128). Singer (1975) has argued that the animal movement stands or falls on its capacity to occupy "the moral high ground."

In mobilizing support for their respective causes both the animal liberation movement and its corresponding counter-movements are involved in moral entrepreneurial activities designed to build moral capital. In their quest for respectability, both sides engage in the "social construction of moral meanings" (Douglas, 1970). Animal movement activists seek to stigmatize and mark as deviant what many people perceive as normal, legitimate, mainstream activities such as raising animals for food, hunting wild animals for pleasure or profit, and conducting experiments in the interests of scientific research on animals kept in laboratory environments. In doing so, the campaigners confront not only the vested interests behind these enterprises—the scientific/medical fraternity, agribusiness, and the hunting and gun lobbies—but also the individual who sees nothing wrong with using nonhuman animals to provide for human needs and wants.

The animal movement seeks to transform the moral meanings associated with the worst of these practices, redefining them as socially irresponsible. When animal activists challenge any of the uses to which animals are put, however, vested interests—individuals who profit from animal exploitation or animal industries and lobbyists—attempt to protect their investments by mobilizing public sentiment. The appearance of adversaries represents both a sign of success and an important test of the original movement's effectiveness (Dowie, 1995). In short, a counter- movement signals that the social movement is doing its job. For example, Putting People First (PPF) was formed in 1991, when its founder objected to the claims made by People for the Ethical Treatment of Animals (PETA) at her daughter's s primary school in Washington, D.C. The founder, Marquardt, has attacked both animal rights and environmentalists as "cultists" and the Humane Society as "a radical animal rights cult and a front for a neo-pagan cult that is attacking science, health, and reason" (Deal, 1993, pp. 83-84). According to Deal, Marquardt is the rising star of the Wise Use movement, a lobbyist for businesses that use animals for food, research, recreation, clothing, and entertainment. She claims, however, to speak for "the average American who drinks milk and eats meat; benefits from medical research; wears leather, wool, and fur; hunts and fishes; owns a pet; goes to zoos, circuses, and rodeos; and who benefits from the wise and rational use of the earth's resources" (Deal, 1993, p. 83).

Mottl (1980) defines a countermovement as "a response to the social change advocated by an initial movement [that] mobilizes human, symbolic, and material resources to block institutional social change or to revert to a previous status quo." This article argues that in the controversy over animal rights, moral resources or moral capital are more pertinent. Contemporary initial movements, against which counter-movements have been mobilized, include gay rights, animal rights, gun control, and cigarette smoking (Meyer et al., 1996). In analysing movement-countermovement conflicts as well as cross-national studies of movements for social change and their counter-movements, this article also addresses organized opposition to animal liberation in the United States, the United Kingdom, and Australia.

Moral Capital in the Animal Liberation Movement

Goode (1992) has claimed that widely enjoyed practices such as those listed by PPF severely restrict the animal movement's capacity to accumulate "moral capital" or "moral resources." Animal activists sometimes speak of a reservoir of goodwill or people's level of compassion for animals. Activists believe they can draw on a considerable reserve of moral capital and goodwill in their anti-cruelty campaigns. A prominent critic of animal rights suggests that a remarkable result of the animal movement has been the extension of a "shadow citizenship" to animals in modern democracies, where they have become part of "the web of public concern" (Scruton, 1996, pp. 103-104). Animal welfare organizations like the Royal Society for the Prevention of Cruelty to Animals (RSPCA) epitomize the respectability of the widespread concern for animals that is manifested in anti-cruelty campaigns especially in the United Kingdom, the United States, and Australia.

Yet according to Goode (1992), the moral boundaries drawn by the movement are hopelessly out of kilter with those of the general public. Therefore, many of the animal movement's appeals for public support lack moral capital, in that their arguments do not resonate with what most people believe and with how most people behave. Thus, many individuals who dislike the vanity of fur will welcome the utility of leather. An abhorrence of the Draize test—observing the effects on the eyes of rabbits in order to test the safety of cosmetics—need not translate into a rejection of animal experiments that might lead to improved human health and happiness. Public disquiet over the worst excesses of factory farming is not likely to change the dietary habits of a lifetime, although it may lead to the elimination of such cruelties as debeaking, cattle branding, and tail-docking. As animal protection leaders are quick to point out, the movement can cite many real reforms that refute Goode's thesis: the worldwide decline in fur sales; the ban on animal testing by several international cosmetics firms; the ban in many jurisdictions on the use of wild animals by circuses; opposition to the confinement of dolphins and other sea creatures in aquaria; and the mass support for the protection of charismatic wildlife and endangered species (1992, pp. 461-463). Most of these issues were, at one time, considered beyond the reach of the animal movement or, arguably, constituted appeals that did not resonate with what many people consider reasonable. Some of our most pleasant pastimes—eating a ham sandwich, visiting the zoo or McDonald's; going fishing or duck shooting; displaying a leather sofa; and even keeping pets—have become less innocent than they used to be. Attitudes toward animals have changed profoundly. In liberal democracies, a strengthened public goodwill toward animals has compelled opponents of animal rights to adopt novel tactics in their campaigns to defend the use of animals in science, agriculture, and hunting. In a recent study of the protagonists involved in the controversy over laboratory animals, Groves argued that "whereas animal rights activists rationalize their emotions for animals, pro-researchers emotionalize their rationality" (1997, p. 14). The present study confirms this analysis with respect to the pro-hunting, pro-meat eating, and the pro-research lobbies. And for the ordinary citizen who is subjected to the tactics of both movement and countermovement, Wright's experience rings true in that both reason and emotion play a part in the way people think about animals (1990).

Although Wright (1990) finds the stridency in many animal rights campaigns obnoxious, he acknowledges the moral strength of the animal liberationist defence of animals as sentient beings (Singer, 1975). Wright expresses what many thinking individuals seem to be saying at the end of the 20th century: "I still eat meat, wear a leather belt, and support the use of animals in important scientific research. But not without a certain amount of cognitive dissonance" (1990, p. 20). These sensibilities, changing attitudes, and practices underpin a "web of public concern" for animals (Scruton, 1996). Together with the steadily increasing popularity of vegetarianism among young people in the West, this concern constitutes the growing reserve of moral capital from which the animal movement can draw.

Although Goode's thesis to the contrary is unconvincing, groups opposing animal liberation understand that no animal protection strategy will succeed if it is perceived by the public as detrimental to human interests and well-being. A movement, that is, will not attract moral capital if the majority of its supporters are thought to come from the ranks of misanthropic animal lovers. These are individuals who love their pets more than babies, to paraphrase a common charge against the antivivisectionists in the last century (French, 1975; Buettinger, 1993); such sentiments are recycled in contemporary countermovement rhetoric.

In its critique of instrumentalism and its challenge to anthropocentric thinking (Jasper & Nelkin, 1992), the animal movement has been condemned as inimical to human welfare, particularly when it campaigns against animal experimentation or the rights of indigenous peoples to hunt for food and fur. Even when animal protection social movement organizations extend their frames to include human welfare—such as the Australian Association for Humane Research's emphasis on human health and well-being in its anti-vivisection campaign in Australia—they attract criticism from those who want to put animals in their place (Leahy, 1991; Wolfe, 1993).

Apart from the critics of the philosophy of animal rights, formidable, organized groups and counter-movements seek to subvert animal liberation as a political movement. According to Meyer and Staggenborg (1996, p. 1635), counter-movements emerge under three conditions: (a) when the movement shows signs of success; (b) when the movement's goals threaten vested interests; and (c) when political allies are available to the countermovement. Each of these preconditions was found to exist in the recent movements against animal liberation.

Staging Counter Offensives

> *In an activist society like ours, the only way to defeat a social movement is with another social movement*

> –Ron Arnold, in *Tokar*, 1995, p. 151.

Just as the emancipation of blacks and women has led to a backlash, social movements in defence of nature and animals have spawned virulent countermovements that defend anthropocentrism and speciesism in the simple "common sense" language of the common man: "There is nothing greater on Earth than a human being. A turtle can't build a ship or read a blueprint, can he?" (Harding, 1993, p. 45-47). PPF is one of many counter-movements that have been mobilized to protect vested interests in government, the medical-scientific fraternity, and in the corporate-commercial sector. Staging counter-offensives in the United States are the National Cattlemen's Association; the Safari Club International; the Texas Wildlife Association; the National Rifle Association (NRA); the Cosmetic, Toiletry, and Fragrance Association; the American Medical Association (AMA); and universities such as Stanford and Berkeley. It is from this cluster that counter-movements are formed to challenge the claims of animal protectionists in their specific campaigns against factory farming, animal experimentation, and recreational hunting.

Although counter-movements take different forms in the United Kingdom, the United States, and Australia, they represent essentially the same interests. In the campaign against blood sports, the NRA in the United States, the British Field Sports Society (BFSS) in the United Kingdom, and the Sporting Shooters' Association in Australia represent the main countermovement organizations. The pro-hunting lobby, although well organized and resourced in all three countries, pales in insignificance compared to the wealth and power of the medical-scientific establishment and the commercial interests of agribusiness. All three counter-movements have adopted a strategy of survivalist anthropocentrism to appeal to the widest possible constituency.

Counter-movements launched by the medical and scientific fraternities represent a response to the animal movement's success in threatening the continued use of animals in scientific/medical experiments. The pro-research lobby frames its counterattack against animal rights as literally a matter of life and death. Counter-movements in defence of the ancient pastimes of hunting and meat eating are framed as a values war in which the "salt of the earth" is pitted against "animal rights-vegetarian activists from hell" (Vidal, 1975). These countermovements use a survivalist rhetoric similar to that of the scientists when they emphasize quality-of-life issues in hunting and standard-of-living arguments in eating meat. Unlike the more focussed, human welfare campaigns of the pro-research movement, the countermovements in defence of hunting and agribusiness are designed to contest broader social values such as freedom of choice, which allow their claimsmakers to appeal to a wider constituency.

Suffering for Science

Organized opposition to the animal movement is especially strong in the biomedical fraternity and is motivated by all three criteria identified by Meyer and Staggenborg (1996): a) The animal liberation movement has succeeded in building moral capital; b) the animal liberation movement threatens research interests; and c) the countermovement is appealing to elites. Not surprisingly, therefore, the backlash against animal rights has been well organized and widespread within the pro-research fraternity. Arluke and Groves (1998) have identified categories of oppositional groups as grassroots, patient-originated, advocacy, and professional. They include Putting People First, Americans for Medical Progress, the incurably ill for Animal Research (iiFAR), the National Association for Biomedical Research, the AMA, and the National Institute on Mental Health (NIMH).

In a detailed study of how medical scientists seek to build moral respectability in their profession, Arluke et al. argued that they primarily attempt to construct a "moral identity that is superior to their opponents" (1998, p. 145). This strategy is evident in some of the countermovement campaigns. Adams (1991) claims that during the 1980s, animal rights, more than any other grass roots movement in the United States, attracted the best financed, most concerted and consistent opposition to its objectives. Adams identified the AMA, the Department of Health and Human Services (DHHS), and the giant pharmaceutical company, Procter & Gamble, as the movement's main adversaries in the United States. According to the AMA's own action plan outlined in a brochure obtained by Adams, the AMA sought to deplete the animal movement's moral capital by demonizing it as anti-scientific, violent, and threatening to the public's right of free choice. The brochure went on to list a number of actions that could be taken against the animal rights movement, the objective of which Adams (1991) suggested, was to shift public opinion, which has tended to favour the animal movement.

In 1989, the medical fraternity resolved to go on the offensive by denouncing animal protectionists when NIMH claimed, "the movement's philosophy is based on a degradation of human nature" (Adams, 1991, p. 130). The NIMH went on to list a dozen tactics for members to use to replace the passive "bunker mentality" that had been the medical fraternity's response to attack by "the animal people." Procter & Gamble took a similar offensive stance when it sought the cooperation of other large corporations—Gillette, Eastman Kodak, Monsanto, Colgate Palmolive, Lever Brothers, IBM, and Johnson & Johnson to name a few. These would form an industry coalition on animal testing that would counter the animal rights movement by improved public relations and lobbying efforts in support of animal testing.

The threat to big business posed by the animal movement can be gauged in a proposal dated June 9, 1990, which set out a detailed 3-year plan that was estimated to cost the bigger companies somewhere between $35 and $250 million (Adams, 1991, p. 310). Adams pointed out that "the big three" adversaries had strikingly similar plans to attack the animal rights movement and, most importantly, sought to unite against the threat to their continued use of animal tests. The coalition was meant to work with existing pro-research organizations such as the Foundation for Biomedical Research (FBR) and the National Association for Biomedical Research (NABR), although its proposed budget underwrote a vastly more ambitious plan of attack. According to Animals' Agenda, the FBR compiled a 290-page resource kit that advertises video recordings, publications, and other materials that can be used to promote vivisection and attack the animal rights movement (Church, 1997, p.31).

Groves (1995) suggested that social movement theorists have generally neglected the role of emotions in the lives of activists, although elsewhere (1997), he noted that pro-research activists rely on mothers with sick children, patient groups, and so on to promote their causes. In their promotional literature, he suggests, animals and children are often represented as objects of compassion (Groves, 1997, p. 163). In borrowing some of the tactics of animal protection campaigns such as the image of suffering innocents, pro-research bodies like the NABR and the AMA have recently used the politics of emotion to convince the public that animal experimentation saves the lives of children and HIV/AIDS sufferers.

Images of innocent children make for good television and print copy as *Newsweek* demonstrated with its cover story (McCabe, 1988), "The Battle over Animal Rights: A Question of Suffering versus Science." This story featured a young mother, Jane McCabe, and her 9-year-old daughter, Clair, who was suffering from cystic fibrosis. McCabe's personal story makes a strong, emotional appeal for animal research. According to her mother, Clair would not be alive without pancreatic enzymes from pigs and antibiotics tested on rats. Clair's mother responded to the animal rights bumper sticker—"Lab animals never have a nice day—by asking "Why is a laboratory rat's fate more poignant than that of an incurably ill child?" (McCabe, 1988).

One of the United States' senior medical officers, Goodwin, a U.S. DHHS official claiming to speak for 100 percent of his scientist colleagues, insisted that "there is no middle ground as to whether or not animals should be used for biomedical research. Either it is ethical, or it is unethical" (1992, p. 10). For him, the issue is not whether, but how animals should be used in research. He encourages scientists to get out of the bunker and defend their work, for example, by insisting that the role of animals be explicitly mentioned in public relations communications. He goes on in his speech to recommend the involvement of patient groups: "[T]hey speak with an authenticity and passion that is hard to rival" (1992, p. 10). Living, speaking symbols of medical progress are powerful tools exploited by research bodies in the form of patient testimonials.

Jasper and Nelkin (1992, p. 133) noted that the FBR uses a similar style of propaganda to their animal rights opponents when it puts patients on display alongside Hollywood celebrities and famous transplant surgeons as testimony to the achievements of animal research. The most dramatic example of patient testimonials comes from iiFAR, which is funded by the AMA. Individuals in wheelchairs or on life-support systems make compelling proselytes for their medical saviours. Nonetheless, animal protectionists have retaliated with the claim that the funding for animal experimentation could be better spent on alternatives to animal research and on preventive measures. And it does seem that an organization whose several thousand members are "incurably ill" is hardly a good advertisement for either animal research or medical progress.

It is perhaps for this reason that some pro-research groups are changing their tactics, including the use of vilification, which was a feature of the vivisection controversy in the 19th century. According to Vanderford (1989), vilification in the abortion debate served a number of functions. It identified abortionists as "them" and anti-abortionists as "us"; it cast abortionists in an exclusively negative light, attributing diabolical motives to them and magnifying them as a powerful enemy capable of doing great evil. In the vivisection debate, both sides have attempted to delegitimize each other by one or more of these means. Not surprisingly, research on the controversy indicates a gap in communications between animal rights campaigners and scientists as well as a strongly "us versus them" mentality in the two fraternities (Munro, 1993; Paul, 1995). Americans for Medical Progress, the self-proclaimed key watchdog over the animal rights agenda, has sought to discredit America's leading moderate animal welfare organization—the Humane Society of the United States (HSUS)—by linking it with the more radical agenda of PETA. Sinister reports and images of "animal libbers" on the wrong side of the law make for good media stories, even in far-off Australia.

Raids and Devices

Terrorist-like raids on poultry farms incendiary devices in letter boxes.

–The Age, 1997, p. 19.

This is how the Police Commissioner in the Australian state of Victoria describes animal liberationists in defending covert police operations against community groups like the Coalition Against Duck Shooting (CADS) during the 1990s. In October of 1997, The Age newspaper in Melbourne revealed that a secret police surveillance unit had infiltrated a number of community groups they considered to be a threat to public order. Many of the people targeted were environmentalists and animal rights campaigners including Peter Singer and Laurie Levy, Director of CADS. One man on the police's list of suspected deviants was an anti-war campaigner who had been awarded the Order of Australia for services to peace! Another had been singled out 10 years earlier for having won the right as a school student, in 1987, to obtain documents on animal experimentation in Victoria.

In *The Age* article (1997, p. 19), the Police Commissioner chose to invoke the exploits of the notorious Animal Liberation Front (ALF) to support his case for spying on animal welfare groups. He pointed out that ALF is an anarchist-based organization in the United Kingdom and claimed that their Australian disciples had been active in 96 criminal incidents (from 1982 to 1996) in Melbourne, attacking butcher shops, furriers, and clothing outlets. The Commissioner noted that ALF members were subsequently charged, and the bomb-making equipment was seized. Although ALF engages in unlawful activity in Australia and elsewhere, it is a mistake to confuse Animal Liberation branches in Australia with the infamous ALF which does not share the non-violent philosophy of the mainstream animal liberation movement. Yet, police surveillance of animal protectionists in Australia and elsewhere and the surreptitious labelling of movement leaders as "terrorist extremists," blurs this distinction in the public mind. Counter-movements are thus provided with an additional weapon to devalue the mainstream animal movement's moral currency.

The Defense of Meat: McLibel and the "Veggie Libel Laws"

Two recent events on both sides of the Atlantic highlight the vulnerabilities of the meat industry to the slogan "Meat is Murder!" Needless to say, anyone who openly attempts to reveal the dark side of "Hamburger Heaven" runs up against the unpleasant prospect of having to deal with the ubiquitous Strategic Lawsuits Against Public Participation (SLAPP), which powerful interests are increasingly using against their critics. Beder argues that "companies and organizations taking this legal action are not doing so in order to win compensation, but rather their aim is to harass, intimidate, and distract their opponents" (1997, p. 64).

This seems to be the motivation in the case against Morris and Steel in the trial involving McDonald's versus the vegetarian activists known as the McLibel Two. As the activists were virtually penniless, McDonald's could not hope to gain monetary compensation for the alleged libel. In fact, some of the McLibel Two's colleagues had agreed to apologize to the company for distributing an offending leaflet in order to avoid litigation and possible financial ruin. Morris and Steel, the "animal rights vegetarian activists from Hell," were the exception in that they were prepared to go to court to defend their right to free speech. The McLibel trial turned out to be the longest trial of its kind in British history. Although McDonald's prevailed, some of the activists' most important charges were upheld (Vidal, 1997).

A similar U.S. case revealed the depth of the beef industry's sensitivity to unfavourable commentary. The Texas Cattlemen's Association instituted a multimillion-dollar lawsuit against television personality Oprah Winfrey who told an April 1996 worldwide television audience that stories of mad cow disease had turned her off hamburger. The Cattlemen invoked food disparagement laws. A Texas jury, however, found for the right to free speech, particularly on matters involving public health, and acquitted Winfrey.

The two cases demonstrate that vested interests in the animal food production industry do not take kindly to their critics. The cases also suggest that opponents of animal protectionism who are unable to gain the high moral ground will resort to legal processes to silence their critics. McDonald's and the Texas cattlemen were unlucky in that their respective targets had the backing or resources to fight back. In most cases, however, SLAPPs are the equivalent of a secular *fatwa*, allowing corporations to deter potential critics from speaking out in public.

SLAPPs put would-be activists on notice that they too could end up in court, Beder (1997) points out, transforming a public issue into a private, legal adjudication. The corporation has the advantage of wealth and power, and the defendant has the most to lose. Yet litigation can be counterproductive for the claimants as well. Writing in *The Ecologist*, Lilliston & Cummins (1997, p. 219) observed that the food industry in the United States plans to block food safety activists by introducing food slander laws in 50 states but is reluctant to do so. The action could give the activists their day in court and result in unfavourable publicity.

Beder notes that, in the United States, environmental and animal rights controversies are among the most common issues in which SLAPPs have been used (1997, p. 66). Interests that have the most to lose in animal rights campaigns against factory farming include the National Farmers Union (NFU) in the United Kingdom and its equivalents in Australia and the United States. Johnson pointed out that the NFU did not welcome the introduction of Welfare Codes designed to give farm animals a number of basic protections after Harrison exposed the worst excesses of factory farms in her 1994 book, *Animal Machines*. He noted that it took the British government 25 years to act on the recommendation to ban veal crates, in a country where the veal industry is a fairly soft target (Johnson, 1991, p. 206). More formidable adversaries for the animal protection lobby are the bacon and egg producers in the United Kingdom. As an illustration of their power, Johnson describes the failure of Compassion in World Farming and other animal protection organizations to place advertisements in the media on the plight of battery hens.

Agribusiness is much greater than the farming lobby and, indeed, most of the animal protectionists I have interviewed are not critical of individual, small-scale farmers at all. What concerns the animal liberation movement is the increasing intensification of farming in which the family farmer becomes a victim no less than the animals. Agribusiness incorporates a large number of interests and therefore potential adversaries of the animal movement who include feed suppliers, machinery and farm equipment manufacturers, agricultural chemical suppliers, fertilizer suppliers, and farm labourers, as well as the many scientists and research assistants employed in the agri-technology industry. To this incomplete list can be added the increasing number of researchers in biotechnology and genetic engineering industries who may be counted on to support any group that will make the world safe for science.

Finally, Lilliston et al. (1997, p. 220) highlighted the movement-countermovement dialectic. They point out that food safety advocacy and the natural/organic food movement are on the rise, and so too are agribusiness lobby groups that seek to weaken federal regulations to the advantage of food multinationals.

Hunting Rights: The Countryside Movement and Wise Use

Eat British lamb. 50,000 foxes can't be wrong

–Marcher's placard

Although there are many pro-hunting organizations in the United Kingdom, the United States, and, to a lesser extent, in Australia, two movements against animal liberation campaigns to ban blood sports typify the countermovement against animal rights: the Countryside Movement in the United Kingdom and the Wise Use movement in the United States. Wise Use has a longer history of opposition to animal rights and environmentalism.

In England, the defence of traditional values has led to the formation of the Countryside Alliance, an amalgamation of the BFSS, founded in 1930, and the recently formed Country Business Group and the Countryside Movement. Soon after the Labour Party was elected in 1997, a Countryside rally was held in Trafalgar Square to persuade the new government that its inclination to ban hunting with hounds was ill-conceived. One media report claimed the rally attracted 100,000 hunt supporters and was the largest mass meeting since Dunkirk. The keynote address at the rally by Baroness Anne Mallalieu captured what was at stake for the hunting fraternity. In her impassioned speech to the converted, the Baroness described hunting as "our music, it is our poetry, it is our art, it is our pleasure. It is our whole way of life." In short, the hunting issue in the United Kingdom has become a weapon in the values war over the ancient pastimes of the English countryside. What is striking about this call to arms is the frequent reference to lifestyle, livelihood, and life itself that, according to the BFSS, depends on the death of wild animals for its survival: "Our communities and way of life [are being] destroyed it is about the people who live in the countryside people who know, love, and live among animals and those who hunt have been their guardians and protectors over generations" (BFSS, 1997).

Anti-hunting and anti-factory farming campaigners tend to believe that these traditional guardians of farm animals have been responsible for the bovine spongiform encephalopathy (BSE) crisis, and as protectors of wild animals, their conservationist claims rest on the dubious notion of culling wildlife. On the other hand, their conservationist credentials have to be acknowledged in that they are primarily interested in conserving what they see as rural values and what remains of the traditional country pastimes like hunting.

Mocking the Turtle

While the Countryside Movement is a recent development, the Wise Use movement in the United States has followed a much more aggressive anti-environmental agenda since the 1980s. The term "wise use of resources," first used in 1907 by the first head of the U.S. Forestry Service, has come to represent the interests of a coalition of industrial, agricultural, and conservative political groups. They seek to protect private property and private enterprise from excessive interference by green groups. Wise Use is supported by a multitude of special interests—anglers, off-road vehicle enthusiasts, real estate developers, and hunters and trappers—as well as industry groups such as chemical and pesticide manufacturers and the timber industry. Arnold and Gottlieb founded Wise Use in 1988 and coordinate the movement's activities from their "educational foundation" at the Centre for the Defence of Free Enterprise. Populist in tone, the movement claims to occupy the middle ground between the extreme environmentalism of "eco-freaks" and the most rapacious forms of capitalism. According to Beder (1997, p. 56), however, the Wise Use agenda, as the name of its propaganda wing at the educational foundation implies, has a corporate agenda making the ostensibly grassroots movement a front for big business. It is a coalition of conservative interests with no formal structure. Its cohesion derives from its common enemy, the environmental and animal rights movements.

Arnold, who had previously worked at the Sierra Club before it became "environmental," has adapted the tactics of the greens and grassroots activists in promoting Wise Use's anti-environmentalist agenda by the use of direct mail. This medium provides an effective form of fundraising as well as a tool for managing emotions in controversial public issues. Arnold, however, tends to target individuals, anonymous and otherwise, rather than issues. The Australian Wise Users do this with stickers on their four-wheel vehicles that urge supporters to "Fertilize the forest and bury a Greenie!" In Australia and the United Kingdom, environmentalists and animal liberationists tend to be portrayed as "ferals," "dole bludgers," and "no-hopers" by their critics, whereas in the United States, Wise Users paint them as "elitist" and "overeducated" city people (Beder, 1997, p. 51). In both cases, the stereotyped group is one that is easy to vilify or hate. Arnold believes that "fear, hate, and revenge are the oldest tricks in the direct mail handbook" (Tokar, 1995) and has argued that there is no room for compromise with greenies and animal libbers, that they must be dismantled and replaced (Beder, 1997, p. 51). A Wise Use tactic is to highlight the most extreme elements of these groups to mobilize rural people, whose interests are threatened by animal rights, anti-hunting, and gun control campaigns (Beder, 1997, p. 51). Beder argues that the Wise Use movement uses an anti-city rhetoric to appeal to the anti-intellectual tradition of the American West where "common sense" is valued more than book learning and where farmers and hunters know how to manage the land better than any city-based critic or professional (1997, p. 52). The same rhetoric was used by the pro-hunting lobby during the emergence of the Countryside Movement in the United Kingdom when Edelstein, hunting correspondent for *The Times*, wrote:

> We get homilies via the media, not least from adulterous politicians telling us to be kinder to our fellow creatures, diktats from distant bureaucrats, whose secure employment and overheated offices it is our privilege to underwrite, of how we should organize our lives, care for our livestock and make our livelihoods. We get hoodlums, of both sexes, informed, it seems, by hatred and ignorance in equal parts, trying to destroy our ancient pastimes (1995, p. 17).

Here we see, in summary form, the main grievances of the movement as a counter to animal rights claims about factory farming and fox hunting. It is a classic framing of the city versus country divide, as a war over values in which the politics of emotion feature prominently in countermovement tactics.

Like the Countryside Movement, Wise Use is unashamedly anthropocentric and places great emphasis on property rights and issues of livelihood: "Which would you rather have, a family wage or a kangaroo rat?" (Wise Use campaign proposition). Like the Countrysiders, Wise Users claim to be better stewards of the land than their green critics. On the other hand, the Countryside Movement is more genuinely environmental in that it wants to preserve the "remaining glories of the English countryside" (Waldegrave, 1998, p. 36). The Wise Use movement is still fueled by the notion that it is America's "Manifest Destiny" to conquer what still remains of the nation's wilderness.

Putting the Case

In the age of downsizing and job loss however, the Wise Use movement in the United States, with its appeal to grassroots constituencies, has succeeded in scuttling environmentalism. Like the Countryside Movement in the United Kingdom, Wise Use puts its case in dramatic, survivalist rhetoric as in a recent campaign drive among various U.S. corporations: "Like it or not, we are involved in a war with the preservationists and animal rights radicals. To win this war we must gain control of the hearts and minds of the public" (Tokar, 1995). Tokar describes the increasing militancy of sections of the Wise Use movement and its success in using the mass media to publicize anti-environmental initiatives.

In the Countryside Movement, there are also signs that the ideological war is heating up. On March 1, 1998, the second Countryside March took place in London to warn the British government that they should "listen to the countryside." *Country Life's* March 5, 1998, cover story (Mitchell, 1998) on the march claimed that 300,000 took part in the good-natured event but suggested that the mood in the countryside could turn sour if rural people continued to be ignored. The accompanying editorial noted that the most memorable placard of the day conveyed this message with the words, "Civil Rights not Civil War," an ominous warning of the rural uprising to come.

Rural people in England perceive several threats to the countryside , such as farmers being forced off the land, ramblers, more houses on greenfield sites, the ban on beef on the bone, and, of course, hunting. Prime Minister Blair admitted that hunting was a major concern of the Countryside Movement, but added that he could not believe support for the private member's bill to ban hunting with hounds could be equated with the end of the countryside (*Country Life*, 26 February, 1998).

By framing its agenda in terms of freedom of choice, the Countryside Movement and Wise Use have effectively used survivalist rhetoric to contest the moral capital of movements that attempt to defend the rights of nature. Thus, no one should underestimate the power of elite groups involved in making the English countryside safe for hunters. Nor should anyone underestimate the appeal to ordinary people of anti-liberationists who—in vivisection, factory farming, and recreational hunting—put the interests of humans ahead of those of nonhuman animals.

Conclusion

This article draws attention to the neglect of counter movements by social movement scholars who focus on "initial" movements rather than on those emerging in response to or in opposition to the original social movement. In taking up Meyer & Staggenborg's (1996) call for more cross-national studies of movement-counter-movement conflicts, I have attempted to show that the backlash against animal liberation in the United States, the United Kingdom, and Australia is characterized by the common rhetorical strategy of survivalist anthropocentrism. I have argued that the moral capital accrued in animal liberation campaigns has been vigorously contested by various counter-movements in the case study countries.

Whereas the pro-research lobby argues its case as a life and death matter, the meat and agriculture industries and sport hunting fraternity use standard-of-living and quality-of-life arguments in defence of their activities. All three counter campaigns, in defending the use of animals for science, food, and sport, seek to undermine the animal movement's moral capital by a variety of tactics that include the use of emotion, condemnation, and vilification. These counter campaigns display images of suffering children and the incurably ill in the pro-research campaign. Mass rallies by hunting enthusiasts condemn the condemners by vilifying animal activists as "terrorists" and "extremists", while McWrits are increasingly used by agribusiness to silence the claims by opponents of the meat industry that "Meat is Murder".

The three counter movements discussed in this paper have assumed the characteristics of a moral crusade and have adopted some of the moralizing tactics borrowed from the animal activist toolkit. These tactics include the use of emotion, negative labelling, atrocity stories, protest rallies, and direct mail, which typically features images of suffering innocents ranging from sick children to long-suffering farmers and country folk. Such tactics are used by both sides in the animal rights controversy and, indeed, in all three case-study countries. Clearly, these tactics are not the exclusive monopoly of any single country or countermovement. The politics of emotion ranges from the rhetoric of vilification to the mass protest rally. Even so, the paper has identified cross-national differences. The United States and American companies use litigation. The United Kingdom, where grassroots activism is common, uses participation in mass protest rallies. The politics of emotion is evident in Australia, as demonstrated by the attacks of the elites and police authorities against animal rights "extremists" and "terrorists".

Emotion, as Groves (1995; 1997) has argued, is an important, but neglected, component of social movement activism. Mottl (1980) notes how counter movements seek to mobilize human, symbolic, and material resources against their opponents but fail to include moral resources such as feelings, emotions, and sensibilities. This article has shown that moral resources or moral capital—in the form of people's compassion for animals—is contested by opponents of animal liberation who appeal to the anthropocentric inclinations of ordinary people to put their interests before those of other animals. By "mocking the turtle," they hope to deplete the animal movement's moral capital in ways that are, in the main, predicated on emotional rather than rational, economic, or legal grounds. For in the final analysis, the competition for moral resources is not about winning minds, it's s about winning hearts.

Note: I thank Ken Shapiro and an anonymous reviewer for helpful comments on an early draft of this paper.

REFERENCES

Adams, T. (1991). *Grassroots: How ordinary people are changing America.* New York: A Citadel Press Book, Carol Publishing Group.

Arluke, A. & Groves, J. M. (1998). Pushing the boundaries: Scientists in the public arena. In L. Hart (Ed.), *Responsible Conduct in Research* (pp. 145-164). New York: Oxford University Press.

Beder, S. (1997). *Global spin: The corporate assault on environmentalism.* Melbourne: Scribe Publications Pty. Ltd.

BFSS, (1997, July). British Field Sports Society Home Page.

Buechler, S. M. & Cylke, F. K. (1997). *Social movements: Perspectives and issues.* Mountain View, CA: Mayfield Publishing Company.

Buettinger, C. (1993). Anti- vivisection and the charge of zoophilia-psychosis in the early twentieth century. *The Historian,* 55(2), 277-288.

Church, J. H. (1997). The politics of animal research. *The Animals' Agenda,* 17(1),

Country Life, (1998, February 26). 300,000 march for the countryside. pp. 56-59.

Deal, C. (1993). *The Greenpeace guide to anti-environmental organizations.* Berkeley: Odonian Press.

Douglas, J. (1970). *Deviance and respectability: The social construction of moral meanings.* New York: Basic Books, Inc.

Dowie, M. (1995). *Losing ground: American environmentalism at the close of the twentieth century.* Cambridge, MA: The MIT Press.

Edelstein, D. (1995, February 25). Hunting: A free country. *The Times Magazine,* pp. 16-20.

French, R. D. (1975). *Anti -vivisection and medical science in Victorian society.* Princeton: Princeton University Press.

Goode, E. (1992). *Collective behaviour.* Florida: Harcourt Brace Jovanovich, Inc.

Goodwin, F. K. (1992). Animal rights-medical research and product testing: Is this a "hang together or together we hang" issue? *Contemporary Topics in Laboratory Animal Science,* 31 (1), 6-11.

Groves, J. M. (1995). Learning to feel: The neglected sociology of social movements. *The Sociological Review,* 43(3), 435-461.

Groves, J. M. (1997). *Hearts and minds: The controversy over laboratory animals.* Philadelphia: Temple University Press.

Harding, T. (1993, September 24). Mocking the turtle. *New Statesman and Society,* 45-47.

Harrison, R. (1964). *Animal machines: The new factory farming industry.* London: Vincent Stuart Ltd.

Jasper, J. & Nelkin, D. (1992). *The animal rights crusade: The growth of a moral protest.* New York: The Free Press.

Johnson, A. (1991). *Factory farming.* Oxford: Blackwell

Klandermans, P. B. (1990). Linking the "old" and the "new": Movement networks in the Netherlands. In R. Dalton & M. Kuechler (Eds.), *Challenging the political order: New social and political movements in western democracies* (pp. 122-136). Cambridge: Polity Press.

Leahy, M. (1991). *Against liberation: Putting animals in perspective.* London: Routledge.

Lilliston, B. & Cummins, R. (1997). The food slander laws in the U.S.: The criminalization of dissent. *The Ecologist,* 27(6), 216-220.

McCabe, Jane (1988, December 26). Is a lab rat's fate more poignant than a child's? *Newsweek,* 50-57.

Meyer, D. & Staggenborg, S. (1996). Movements, counter-movements, and the structure of political opportunity. *American Journal of Sociology,* 101 (6), 1628-1660.

Mitchell, S. (March 5, 1998). Save the country way of life, say marchers. *Country Life.*

Mottl, T. L. (1980). The analysis of counter-movements. *Social Problems,* 2 7(5), 620-634.

Munro, L. (1999). From vilification to accommodation: Making a common cause movement. *Cambridge Quarterly of Healthcare Ethics* (special edition in honour of Henry Spira).

Munro, L. (1993). Hands up those who have pets! Bridging the gap between scientists and animal liberationists. In N. E. Johnston (Ed.), *Proceedings of the Animal Welfare Conference* (pp. 111-116). Melbourne: Animal Ethics Unit, Monash University.

Paul, E. S. (1995). Us and them: Scientists' and animal rights campaigners' views of the animal liberation debate. *Society & Animals,* 3(1), 1-21.

Scruton, R. (1996). *Animal rights and wrongs.* London: Demos.

Singer, P. (1975). Animal liberation: A new ethics for our treatment of animals. London: Jonathan Cape.

The Age, (October 10, 1997). Terrorist-like raids on poultry farms: Incendiary devices in letter boxes.

Tokar, B. (1995). The "wise use" backlash: Responding to militant anti-environmentalism. *The Ecologist*, 25(4), 150-157.

Vanderford, M. (1989). Vilification in social movements: A case study of pro-life and pro- choice rhetoric. *Quarterly Journal of Speech*, 75, 166-182.

Vidal, J. (1997). *McLibel: Burger culture on trial.* London: Pan Books.

Waldegrave, W. (1998, February 5). Right to roam: A new crossroads? *Country Life*, 32-38.

Wolfe, A. (1993). *The human difference: Animals, computers and the necessity of social science.* Berkeley: University of California Press.

Wright, R. (1990, March 12). Are animals people too? *The New Republic*, 20-27.

Chapter 13

Future Animal:

Environmental and Animal Welfare
Perspectives on Genetic Engineering

The gods are just, and of our pleasant vices
Make instruments to plague us

—Edgar in Shakespeare's *King Lear*

Introduction

Genetic engineering is a social invention as much as a biological one. Ordinary citizens interested in the well-being of life on the planet should therefore be involved in the ethical debates concerning the future of nonhuman animals. The creations of genetic engineers ought to be evaluated on a case-by-case basis by what the American philosopher R G Frey (1983) calls 'a jury of concerned individuals'. Frey is an advocate for putting animals in perspective, which means that animals matter, but not as much as humans. He therefore supports the prevailing moral orthodoxy which currently in the West means that animals can be eaten, dissected, hunted and exhibited provided these things are done humanely and the benefits to humans outweigh the harms to the animals. The 'concerned individual', he suggests, would have no objection to humans killing animals as long as the animals do not suffer. In the present paper, my aim is to raise some of the ethical, welfare and social issues from an animal protectionist perspective which ordinary citizens would need to consider if they were ever asked to vote on the benefits or otherwise of the impact of genetic engineering on animal welfare. With the assistance of the writings from a number of 'concerned individuals' with different professional interests in animals—animal protection and environmental advocates, sociologists, scientists, veterinarians, moral philosophers and theologians—the paper is an attempt to guide them in this task.

Genetic engineering is for many animal protectionists the latest example of what the environmentalist John Muir derisively called 'Lord Man's creativity', a creativity that is both promising and menacing. The capacity to alter the telos or intrinsic nature of an animal has profound implications for both human and nonhuman animals which I will explore in this paper.

The sociologist Barbara Katz Rothman (1995) has suggested that genetic engineering is a social problem rather than a biological or ecological problem. Sociologists use the term social problem to include a wide range of perceived ills from the largescale issues of war, poverty and disease (Simon 1982) to the more manageable ills associated with such things as child abuse, hate crimes and the trio of oppressions—racism, sexism and speciesism—which are the targets of new social movements that include the animal rights movement. Rothman points out that social problems lie in the social world and not in the quality and behaviour of individual human beings. She sees genetic engineering as 'more the problem than the solution. Diversity is being bred out; the square tomato bred in' (1995). Like many other critics of genetic engineering, Rothman fears that those who bring us more packageable, cost-effective tomatoes will eventually turn their attention to producing 'better' animals, both human and nonhuman.

Animal experimentation and the technology of intensive farming are the forerunners of what might turn out to be, in the form of genetic engineering, the proverbial straw that will inadvertently subvert the moral orthodoxy on how we treat other animals. In this latest and most dramatic example of 'Lord Man's creativity', the risks, and according to its disciples, the promises involved, are greater for humans and nonhumans than any other single event in the history of our relationship with other animals. The phrase 'the point of no return' is used by opponents of genetic engineering, not in an apocalyptic sense, but rather as a catalyst to collective mobilisation and action against environmental risks.[1] More important than anything we might do to control risk, however, is the idea that nature herself has reacted to unnatural and excessive meddling in the sensitive balance that must exist between society and nature. G P Marsh made this point more than a century ago when he wrote in *Man and Nature* (1864):

> 'The ravages committed by man subvert the relations and destroy the balance which nature had established between her organised and her inorganic creations; and she avenges herself upon the intruder by letting loose upon her defaced provinces destructive energies hitherto kept in check by organic forces destined to be his best auxiliaries, but which he has unwisely dispersed and driven from the field of action' (cited in Passmore 1980).

In less apocalyptic language, the sociologist Luke Martell (1994:24) describes the nature/society relation as 'constituted by natural limits on society, society's effects on nature and the effects of society's impact on nature as they rebound on society'. This reciprocal relationship can be thought of as a triangle, the sides of which represent the various impacts described by Martell; for example, environmentally unsound practices lead to pollution of the environment which leads to ozone depletion which

---

[1] See Woods (1998) who suggests that the creation of transgenic animals may awaken in people emotions which will produce an increase in individual and cultural resistance to animal exploitation. She implies that this might turn out to be even more tenacious than conventional animal rights and antivivisectionist campaigns.

leads to skin cancer. Tampering with nature, according to both Marsh and Martell, is a perilous venture, if not a suicidal folly.

Hello Folly: Is Genetic Engineering a New Species of Trouble?

Genetic engineering is concerned with the intentional alteration of an organism's genetic material made possible by the discovery in the 1950s of the structure of deoxyribonucleic acid or DNA. For science, the genetic engineering of microorganisms, plants, animals and humans suggests the prospect of scientific advancement that few researchers could resist. Its impact will be felt in commercial agriculture, in biomedical and behavioural research, product and toxicity testing, veterinary and biology education as well as in other contexts in which animals are presently used. In the animal kingdom, the experimental possibilities range from the sublime to the ridiculous. Scientists have already started work on producing sheep resistant to flies and more productive turkeys that have had their broody behaviour programmed out of their natures (Reiss and Straughan, 1996: 175,182). Genetically engineered farm animals that produce better meat and other consumer products will no doubt be offered to the consumer as attractive options. Genetic engineering might also come to the aid of the incompetent hunter in the form of animals bred to be less alert or less dangerous (McCarthy and Ellis (1994).

In recent years, the magazine *New Scientist* has featured reports of animal patents ranging from cows to fish as well as the oncomouse which carries a cancer-causing gene that makes the animal a highly marketable product to medical researchers. Apart from the moral, welfare and ethical implications, patenting life, as in the case of the "oncomouse", opens a new battleground between biotechnologists and religious groups, environmentalists, lawyers and even between countries. Every month, *New Scientist* and other serious technical magazines describe the latest developments in organ transplants, xenotransplantation, transgenic animals, and the genetic engineering of microorganisms, plants and even the prospect of human clones. The magazine *Mother Jones* (January-February,1997) ran a cover story on biotech crops as 'the food of the future' in which the aims of leading biotechnology companies were described as providing more affordable, available and nutritious food for the future of humankind (Benson, Arax & Burstein, 1997). Solving food shortages in this way would seem to be a worthy initiative and one that would be universally welcomed. Nonetheless, there are costs as well as benefits in this kind of project. According to Reiss and Straughan (1996: 156), socio-economic reasons associated with issues of fairness to small farmers and poorer countries must be taken into account. For most people, however, the genetic engineering of animals is of greater concern simply because viscerally, animals matter more to them than plants. The rest of the paper reviews the work of a number of authors associated with both the genetic engineering of animals and the animal welfare/rights movement. Space limitations will not permit a full discussion of the often complex and detailed arguments in these sources. I hope that the review does at least hint at the essential arguments and will encourage interested readers to consult the authors' works where necessary.

Michael Reiss (Biologist) and Roger Straughan (Philosopher)

Improving Nature? (1996) is the title of a comprehensive account of the science and ethics of genetic engineering by Michael Reiss and Roger Straughan in which animals feature mainly as organ donors, as food sources and as models for human diseases in the science of genetic engineering. The last is seen by some animal liberationists as old wine in new bottles in that genetic engineering is perceived as a more objectionable form of animal experimentation. In 1990 researchers in Edinburgh succeeded in transferring copies of a human gene into the embryos of sheep which has resulted in one of the sheep, Tracey, producing a much-needed protein in her milk. She has been labelled 'the most valuable sheep in the world' as the protein is used to combat emphysema. Genetically engineered rats and mice are currently used to model human diseases such as cancer and Alzheimer's; and although new therapies for cystic fibrosis have been developed in this way, some people remain sceptical of the value of such experiments compared to preventive measures.

Genetic engineering enthusiasts like Dr Roy Calne, a pioneer of kidney transplantation, look forward to the coming of the "self-pig", a custom-made transgenic animal that will provide its human twin with body parts in an emergency. Animal liberationists, notably Peter Singer, have publicly denounced the idea as unacceptable, claiming that it ignores the legitimate rights of animals (quoted in Ewing, 1995). Yet many ordinary people would argue that using pigs for their body parts is no worse than eating them. But this may not be enough to override the public's disquiet over xenotransplantation as yet another example of 'Lord Man's creativity'. The will to master nature or 'the vivisection of our planet' as one of Sperling's (1988) animal liberation informants called it, is what many people perceive as a metaphor for all that is wrong with our relationship with other life forms.

This brings us to the moral and ethical issues associated with genetic engineering which Reiss and Straughan (1996) examine for their intrinsic and extrinsic properties. Animal liberationists I have interviewed believe the genetic engineering of animals is wrong *in itself* (the intrinsic concern) because it interferes with the animal's telos. According to this view, animals are an end in themselves and should not be used as a means to an end either to prolong life or to satisfy human wants and needs. For many people, particularly those with environmental sensitivities, the genetic engineering of animals is extrinsically wrong *because of its consequences*; in short, it is risky. Yet not all genetic experiments are detrimental to the welfare of animals although the motives behind them may well be selfish. Reiss and Straughan (1996) give the example in Australia where the aim is to genetically engineer sheep resistant to blowflies and other insect parasites. This would save the sheep from the torment of mulesing—the process of cutting away skin and tissue folds from the sheep's tail area in order to prevent flystrike—and save the sheep industry of up to $300 million annually on pesticides which also contribute to human illness and environmental damage.

Reiss and Straughan believe that each case involving genetic manipulations of animals has to be decided on its merits. According to them, the genetic engineering of animals to produce life-saving pharmaceuticals—as in the case of Tracey the protein-producing sheep—is a moral necessity; but when animals suffer to satisfy trivial human wants or needs, or when the benefits are uncertain, they oppose it as morally dubious. One such case which would seem to be typical of the treatment of farm animals, genetically engineered or otherwise, concerns attempts to produce genetically engineered turkeys deficient in the hormone prolactin which triggers broody behaviour in the animal. Researchers claim that turkeys would lay 15-20% more eggs if the animal's natural "broodiness" could be curbed (Reiss and Straughan, 1996:182).

In considering the ethics of genetically engineered farm animals on a case-by-case basis, Reiss and Straughan (1996) note that Tracey, for example, as 'the most valuable sheep in the world', has an entirely different life—one that is free of undue suffering—to the oncomouse which is genetically programmed to succumb to cancer. For animal protectionists this is undoubtedly more objectionable than conventional experiments on animals since they would see any attempt to alter the animal's telos as morally more questionable than the infringement of the animal's bodily integrity by conventionally cruel methods such as inducing disease, debeaking, mulesing, face branding and so on. When Reiss and Straughan pose the question 'do animals have rights?', animal protectionists ask, 'does a hen have a right to a beak?' which for most people goes without saying. Similarly, altering the telos or essence of an animal as in the proposal to genetically engineer a turkey in which broody behaviour has been eliminated, is seen as 'a serious violation of the intrinsic value of the creature (and) is ethically unconscionable' (Jeremy Rifkin quoted in Reiss and Straughan, 1996). Other critics of the 'scientist as God' concept—and this would include millions of God-fearing carnivores and spiritually inclined individuals—view these developments as the secular equivalent of blasphemy.

Bernard Rollin (Scientist and Philosopher)

One of the few books to examine comprehensively the ethical issues associated with the genetic engineering of animals is Bernard Rollin's (1995) provocatively titled *The Frankenstein Syndrome*. Dr Frankenstein's hubris in seeking to create life produces in fictional form a rampaging monster that for many people is emblematic of the folly of modern-day genetic engineering. Rollin examines the genetic engineering of animals for its alleged intrinsic and extrinsic wrongness. He concludes that the technology is not intrinsically, or in itself wrong , and therefore should not be banned outright as some environmental philosophers have demanded; he is scathing of the environmentalists' 'new ethic' which fosters the erroneous idea that "nature is perfect as it is". Nonetheless, Rollin's remarks apply only to an extreme fringe of the ecology movement since mainstream environmentalists know only too well that nature is "red in tooth and claw" and that the dangers it poses for humans need to be controlled. But genetic engineering is a level of interference in natural processes that immediately invokes the environmentalists' precautionary principle that is, if there is reasonable suspicion that a particular substance or practice might pose an unacceptable risk to the environment, it is better to eliminate the risk even in the absence of scientific evidence that the risk is real.

Rollin argues that the risks associated with 'the rampaging monster' are many and include the folly of leaving their management to scientists and other experts. He suggests that most scientists he has encountered care little about taking risks when faced with 'the sheer joy of scientific inquiry'. A powerful and dangerous alliance is therefore forged when 'the excitement of the chase' joins forces with industry's rapacious quest to profit from biotechnology.[2] Rollin runs off a list of the dangers to human and nonhuman life posed by the new technology and notes that decisions are being made in the absence of any public debate as to its ethical and social consequences; the patenting of life forms for instance has gone ahead without the benefit of these considerations. Rollin proposes therefore, a moratorium on the genetic engineering of animals rather than an outright ban. He sees no virtue in a unilateral banning of a project which others will gladly exploit.

For Rollin, an animal welfare advocate, genetic engineering does offer some major benefits for animals and humans such as the creation of disease and insect resistant animals like the fly-resistant sheep that will be spared the agony of mulesing and save farmers time and money. The idea of hornless cattle is also a possibility thus sparing the animal the pain of dehorning. Rollin has no moral qualms about altering the telos of the animal if this does not endanger other animals, humans or the environment. In theory, he suggests, the telos of battery hens could be altered by genetically expunging their urge to nest so that their confined lives would be made more bearable. However, he acknowledges that animal protectionists and probably most other people would want to change the system of battery farming rather than the nature of the beast. And Rollin himself believes, any fair-minded jury of concerned individuals would reject the genetically-engineered solution in favour of better animal husbandry and more humane methods of rearing chickens.

For Rollin, the bottom line in genetic engineering is 'the principle of the conservation of welfare' which means that any genetically engineered animals should be no worse off in terms of suffering and ideally better off than the parent stock. According to Rollin, society demands less, not more animal suffering. Thus while genetic engineering is not intrinsically wrong in Rollin's view, 'it is likely to lead to

---

[2] See for example Biocapitalism: what price the genetic revolution in *Harper's Magazine*, December 37-45, 1997

(greater suffering) in the current exploitative business context' (1995).[3] In this sense, he believes the conservation of welfare principle that animal welfare standards should be better not worse is more relevant to commercial agriculture than to research although I would suggest both are closely enmeshed. For instance, one of Rollin's informants indicated as much when he claimed that scientists would eventually create animal protein in fermentation vats without the further use of agricultural animals whose welfare would no longer be an issue.

Genetic engineering has the potential to reshape the human-nonhuman animal relationship, the ethical and health consequences of which have not been seriously addressed. 'What will it mean to come across a rabbit in the woods after genetically engineered 'rabbits' are widespread?' asks Bill McKibben. 'Why would we have any more reverence, or even affection, for such a rabbit than we would for a Coke bottle?' (quoted in Dobson 1997). Such questions are also raised in the Christian and humane perspectives outlined in the next two sections.

Andrew Linzey (Christian Theologian) and Stephan Clark (Moral Philosopher)

The Christian theologian Andrew Linzey (1994) holds the view that genetic engineering is 'animal slavery' and against the will of God. Like many other animal protectors, he is concerned with 'Lord Man's' attempts to play God with an animal's telos. 'The genetic manipulation of animal nature is not just some small welfare problem of how we should treat some kinds of animal species; it is part of a much more disturbing theological question about 'who do we think we are' in creation, and whether we can acknowledge moral limits to our awesome power, not only over animals, but also over our own species'. While Linzey acknowledges there may be instances where the wellbeing of individual animals is enhanced by genetic engineering, he argues that in the final analysis it 'represents the concretization of the *absolute* claim that animals belong to us and exist for us' (Linzey 1994). To him, the idea of humans creating new life in the form of patented transgenic animals is idolatrous.

Stephen Clark (1997) also believes that to use animals in this way, to see them as 'animal preparations' or 'living test-tubes', exceeds the limits of moral orthodoxy which he calls 'the 'norm' of *moderate* concern for animals'. He condemns experimentalists, not for any lack of compassion, but for acting out 'assumptions deeply ingrained in contemporary culture which are actually false or wicked', adding that animal experimentation of which genetic engineering is the latest and most controversial example 'represents our single greatest sin: the intention always to

---

[3] See Meg Gordon (1997) in *New Scientist* in which Caren Broadhead of FRAME warns that genetic engineers have little understanding of how transgenic animals like sheep suffer. Consequently, FRAME has called for the establishment of an international committee to examine the welfare of transgenic animals.

control what's going on, to evade all penalties'. Clark's condemnation of animal experimentation of all kinds is a reminder of the rhetoric of vilification that characterised the conflict over vivisection in the nineteenth century. Even so, is it the case that transgenic animals suffer more or less than God's natural creatures? This question is addressed in the next section.

Michael W. Fox (Veterinarian)

Like Linzey, Reiss and Straughan, and Rollin, the veterinarian Michael Fox (1990) concedes that there could be many benefits arising from the *appropriate* use of genetic engineering. However, Fox is adamant that there is clear evidence of suffering in genetically engineered animals. These include developmental abnormalities which cannot be predicted and can develop later in the animal's life; deleterious pleiotropic effects multiple harmful effects by one or more genes on the animal's phenotype, for example, when pigs became arthritic, had defective vision due to abnormal skull growth and were prone to illnesses which impaired their immune systems; genetically engineered 'bio-boosters' designed to increase disease resistance and to produce more marketable animals likewise jeopardise the animal's immune systems (1990: 182). Fox claims that growth-hormone treated pigs and dairy cows must be kept under intensive conditions which add to the stress of these high product 'factory animals.'

As a veterinarian, Fox is more concerned with the practical consequences of genetic engineering on animal welfare than what he calls 'the moralist polemics of right and wrong' of the animal rights movement. He is in no doubt that genetic engineering is the latest manifestation of 'the industrialized commercial exploitation of life' and as such, is against the interests of animals, nature and ultimately humans. To be sure, the religious and spiritual sensitivities exhibited respectively by Linzey, Clark and Fox would not satisfy the majority of people who believe that human beings have the right to use animals humanely for food, clothing, product safety tests and the like. Yet it has to be acknowledged that ordinary people who use animal products for these purposes have little understanding of the effects of genetic engineering on an animal's well-being. The public's understanding of genetic engineering is slim and even professionals who work with animals are unlikely to be informed on the many ethical issues concerning transgenic animals. For example McCarthy and Ellis (1994) ask, how can researchers, laboratory technicians and animal caretakers know their animals and promote their welfare if a new strain or species of animal has been created with altered or even unprecedented behavioral habits? The practice's understanding is shaped either by the generally sensationalist claims in media reports of genetic engineering or in the dire warnings of animal rights and environmental advocates. Many people seek the elusive 'middle way' advocated by John Webster (1994) and others.

John Webster (Animal Husbandry)

According to Webster, a professor of animal husbandry, animals are affected not by how we feel, but by what we do. He has little time for the abolitionists of the animal rights movement, preferring the 'middle way' or 'the pragmatic common sense of the reasonable man'. Elsewhere (Munro, 1999) I have suggested that the middle way will not resolve the many conflicts over how we use other animals, particularly in product testing for scientific, medical and commercial reasons which offers the best prospect for finding common ground—as distinct from a middle way—between experimentalists and animal activists. Product testing can be framed not just as an animal welfare/rights issue, but as a common cause involving health and environmental problems in addition to the concerns of animal protectionists. Much the same case can be put concerning the impact of genetically engineered animals. Webster is not interested in the moral dilemmas associated with patenting life forms as commercial products for this has nothing to do, he claims, with animal welfare. What matters, he argues, is what we do to animals in the process of 'adding value to an animal or its products... (say) a cheaper piece of meat from a chicken (or) a new heart from a pig' (Webster, 1994).

Webster lists nine manipulations of animals which might be considered by the moral entrepreneur. For the alert concerned individual, warning bells are sounded in the first procedure on the list—manipulation of animal feedstuffs to increase nutrient yield and composition—which Webster evaluates as unlikely under normal conditions to have any direct effect on animal welfare. He seems unaware of the practices which led to reports of mad cow disease in the UK and notes that apart from branding and castrating, and the practice of the unnatural feeding of cereals and growth hormones to cattle in feedlots, 'the practice (of beef production) is seen to be reasonably natural and therefore acceptable'. Using Webster's criterion of common sense, I could find only one of the eight remaining procedures [4] involving genetic manipulations of animals as of possible benefit to animals, namely conferring genetic resistance to infectious disease. Yet Webster's own evaluation of the list leads him to conclude that on balance, the effects of genetic engineering on animal welfare are likely to be beneficial. However, he is prepared to let the jury of public opinion and the common sense of the reasonable man decide whether or not we really need the genetic engineer's animals of the future.

---

[4] (1) Manipulation of animal feedstuffs to increase nutrient yield and composition; (2) Manipulation of digestion to increase nutrient availability; (3) Manipulation of metabolism to increase the production or alter the composition of meat, milk or fibre; (4) Increasing the rate of reproduction in the breeding female; (5) Artificial manipulation of breeding (genetic progress) by embryo transfer or cloning; (6) Conferring genetic resistance to infectious disease; (7) Manipulation of cognition by gene deletion within the central nervous system; (8) Insertion of human genes into animals for the manufacture of pharmaceuticals; (9) Genetic manipulation of animals to become universal donors of organs such as hearts and kidneys. (In Webster, 1994:243)

An Imaginary Jury of 'Concerned Individuals' and Animal Protectionists

According to a recent review by Orlans *et al* (1998) of the ethics of genetically engineering animals, advocates of transgenic technology reject the claim that its impact is overwhelmingly negative. Not surprisingly, they argue that creatures can be engineered to take the place of unmodified animals in farms and in laboratories, an idea which does not appeal to most animal protectionists who see attempts to improve nature as both futile and arrogant. Orlans *et al* point out that the predominant response to transgenic animals has been to evaluate them within the same animal welfare regulatory framework used in deciding on the ethics of our conventional treatment of animals. The authors believe that decisions about transgenic animals should be made on a case-by-case basis using customary ethical principles and existing animal welfare provisions.

Yet there are novel problems associated with the creation of these future animals which Orlans and her colleagues seem to downplay such as the harmful results of induced diseases and unintended side effects. In addition, Smith and Boyd (1991), and more recently, McKibben (in Dobson,1997) as mentioned above, warn that the idea of a transgenic animal could contribute to the further exploitation of all animals by reducing sentient beings to the status of 'inanimate object', 'living factory', 'research tool', 'commercial bioreactors' and the like. It seems likely that the possibility of a rise in neo-Cartesianism[5] that the spectre of transgenic animals represents would be the proverbial straw to test the willingness of animal lovers to tolerate animal experimentation. There can be little doubt that antivivisectionists would not attempt to use the idea of the transgenic animal to mobilise support from religious constituencies and other groups that have until now remained outside the animal experimentation debate.

Genetic engineering threatens to distort the boundaries between society and nature, thereby straining the prevailing moral orthodoxy concerning our treatment of other animals. Ironically, genetic engineering promises to be a mobilising resource for the mainstream animal protection movement by alerting ordinary and otherwise uninterested citizens to the ethical and social dimensions of animal exploitation. There are few practices that can rival the genetic engineering of animals as both a symbol of nature besieged and as a catalyst for the mobilisation of animal rights protest. In my survey of animal welfare supporters in Australia (Munro, 1997)[6] , animal experimentation procedures (items 2, 4 and 6) ranked high in terms of moral

---

[5] By neo-Cartesianism I mean a new variation on an old theme fathered by Descartes, namely that animals are machines or beings with very limited sentience.

[6] The Animal and Social Issues Survey (ASIS) was completed by 87% (n=347) of the membership of the Australian and New Zealand Federation of Animal Societies (ANZFAS) which represents a wide range of animal protectionists including animal welfarists, animal liberationists and animal rights advocates.

reprehensibility as it did in an American study by Richards (1990)[7]. Although genetic engineering per se was not included in the survey, the purpose-breeding of animals was ranked high in the list of what respondents considered ethically objectionable procedures on animals. All of the activities associated with animal experimentation registered a 'very high level of concern' among the respondents. These results suggest that for animal lovers and no doubt for Frey's (1983) 'concerned individual' as well, some experiments involving genetic engineering will only be acceptable if there is a fair balance between the overall benefits and the harm done to individual animals.

Conclusion

Reiss and Straughan's *Improving Nature?* is much more skeptical about genetic engineering than Rollin's *Frankenstein Syndrome*. Rollin does not believe that an environmental ethic is needed to guide us in addressing the ethical and social issues raised by genetic engineering. In this he is surely wrong. Relying on the conservation of welfare principle is not likely to work when the potential profits from animal exploitation are so massive for the biocapitalist. As so often happens, human greed will conveniently be framed as 'human welfare' when animal protectionists advocate the interests of animals in any genetic revolution of the future. And in dismissing the environmentalists' creed that 'nature cannot be improved', Rollin seems to deny the undeniable, namely the ecological law that governs our relations with nature. Environmentalists advocate 'the precautionary principle' whenever there is a threat of ecological catastrophe and are denounced as 'catastrophists' by their opponents for doing so. In a cover story on xenotransplants, *The Economist* (October 21, 1995) was unequivocal in condemning xenotransplantation and advocating a precautionary approach towards the technology. In short, *The Economist* warns of the danger of transplanting not just organs, but epidemics too. For individuals who are attracted to the promise but are fearful of the threat posed by genetic engineering, dangers of this kind will be more important than the animal protectionist's insistence on the animal's right to bodily integrity or the allegedly intrinsic immorality of the technology. Ironically, genetic engineering may turn out to be the mobilising issue that generates most individual and cultural resistance to the continued exploitation of animals.

One does not have to adopt a spiritual or religious frame of reference such as those advocated by Andrew Linzey or Stephen Clark to understand that the risks involved in 'improving nature' are immense. While Linzey and Clark offer more philosophical reflections on the concept of the future animal, Fox and Webster are more concerned with what we actually do to animals once they exist.

And as I indicated at the outset of this review, the concept of the social should not be forgotten in the debate over the future animal for in the final analysis, genetic

---

[7] The survey by Rebecca Richards was completed by 854 subscribers to *The Animals' Agenda*, a leading animal rights magazine in the United States.

engineering, like other issues and campaigns of concern to the animal protection movement, involves social conflict and hence is a social problem to be resolved by ordinary citizens. More importantly, however, the promises and and pitfalls of genetic engineering need to be debated publicly so that Frey's "jury of concerned citizens" is able to reach some kind of reasonable verdict on the issues at stake. A good starting point for such a discussion might be Wheale and McNally's (1995) *Animal Genetic Engineering: Of Pigs, Oncomice and Men.*

REFERENCES

Archer J 1994 Miracles that Never Happen. *The Independent Monthly*. July 78-79

Benson S, Arax M and Burstein R 1997 A Growing Concern. *Mother Jones* February 36-43

Clark S R L 1997 *Animals and their Moral Standing*. Routledge: London

Dobson A 1997 Genetic Engineering and Environmental Ethics. *Cambridge Quarterly of Healthcare Ethics* 6: 205-221

Ewing T 1995 Body Parts. *The Age*: 27 October, 13

Fox M W 1990 *Inhumane Society: The American Way of Exploiting Animals*. St Martin's Press: New York

Frey R G 1983 *Rights, Killing and Suffering: Moral Vegetarianism and Applied Ethics*. Blackwell: Oxford

Gordon M 1997 Suffering of the Lambs. *New Scientist* 154: 16-17

Linzey A 1994 *Animal Theology*. SCM Press Ltd: London

Martell L 1994 *Ecology and Society: An Introduction*. Polity Press: Cambridge UK

McCarthy C and Ellis G 1994 Philosophic and Ethical Challenges of Animal Biotechnology. *The Hastings Center Report* 24: PS 14-30

Munro L 1997 Animal Rights/Welfare Downunder. Based on a paper presented at the International Society for Anthrozoology Conference at Downing College, Cambridge UK, 24-26 July 1996. *ISAZ The Newsletter 14*: 15-19

Munro L 1999 From Vilification to Accommodation: The Making of a Common Cause Movement. *Cambridge Quarterly of Healthcare Ethics 8*: 46-57

Orlans B F, Beauchamp T L, Dresser R, Morton D B and Gluck J P 1998 *The Human Use of Animals: Case Studies in Ethical Choice*. Oxford University Press: Oxford

Passmore J 1980 *Man's Responsibility for Nature: Ecological Problems and Western Traditions*. Duckworth: London

Reiss M J and Straughan R 1996 *Improving Nature: The Science and Ethics of Genetic Engineering*. Cambridge University Press: Cambridge, UK

Richards R 1990 *Consensus Mobilization through Ideology, Networks, and Grievances: A Study of the Contemporary Animal Rights Movement*, PhD Dissertation, Printed by University Microfilms International: Ann Arbor

Rollin B 1995 *The Frankenstein Syndrome: Ethical and Social Issues in the Genetic Engineering of Animals*. Cambridge University Press: Cambridge

Rothman B K 1995 Of Maps and Imagination: Sociology Confronts the Genome. *Social Problems* 42: 1-10.

Simon H A 1982 Are Social Problems Problems that Social Science can Solve? In Kruskal W H (ed) *The Social Sciences: Their Nature and Uses*. The University of Chicago Press: Chicago

Smith J A and Boyd K M 1991 *Lives in the Balance: The Ethics of Using Animals in Biomedical Research*. Oxford University Press: Oxford

Sperling S 1988 *Animal Liberators: Research and Morality*. University of California Press: Berkeley CA

Webster J 1994 *Animal Welfare: A Cool Eye Towards Eden*. Blackwell Science Ltd: London

Wheale P 1995 and R. McNally 1995 *Animal Genetic Engineering: Of Pigs, Oncomice and Men*. Pluto Press: London

Woods T 1998 Have a Heart: Xenotransplantation, Nonhuman Death and Human Distress. *Society & Animals 6*: 47-65.

Chapter 14

From Vilification to Accommodation:
Making a Common Cause Movement

It is the rarest thing in the world to hear a rational discussion on vivisection

—C.S. Lewis, 1944

The history of the vivisection debate is a case study in the use of vilification not unlike its rhetorical use by adversaries in the pro-life/pro-choice controversy. According to Vanderford, vilification in that debate serves a number of functions: to identify adversaries as "them and us"; to cast opponents in an exclusively negative light; to attribute diabolical motives to one's adversaries; and to magnify the opposition's power as an enemy capable of doing great evil.[1] In the vivisection debate, both sides have attempted to delegitimize each other by one or more of these means. On the anti- vivisection side, Samuel Johnson in 1758 produced the fiercest attack up to that time on "the inferior Professors of medical knowledge" and "race of wretches whose lives are only varied by varieties of cruelty."[2] When the antivivisectionist movement peaked in England in the 1870s, the animal experimentalists began to organise in earnest to fend off the charge that vivisection was both cruel and useless. By the turn of the century, an American neurologist, Charles Loomis Dana, identified a way to discredit the mainly female anti-science "cranks" in the anti- vivisection movement by inventing the disease "zoophil-psychosis" to describe one of the diseases affecting mainly women who, having no children or a useful occupation, joined animal protection societies and campaigned against vivisection. Zoophil-psychosis, it was claimed, was a form of mental illness, an incurable insanity that afflicted the hysterical opponents of vivisection.[3] A century later, these attacks on female animal protectionists as "crazed spinsters" and the like continue to be used by predominantly male supporters of animal exploitation.

---

[1] Vanderford ML. "Vilification and social movements: a case study of pro -life and pro- choice rhetoric. *Quarterly Journal of Speech* 1989; 75: 166-82
[2] Quoted in Maehle AH, Troehler U. Animal Experimentation from Antiquity to the End of the Eighteenth Century: Attitudes and Arguments in Nicholaas AR (ed) *Vivisection in Victorian Perspective.* London: Routledge, 1990:14-47
[3] Buettinger C. Anti- vivisection and the charge of zoophil-psychosis in the early twentieth century. *The Historian.* Winter 1993;55(2):277-288

During the first half of the twentieth century, the rhetoric of vilification continued between "the idle, muddle-headed women" and "sob sisters" and the "evil" vivisectionists who perpetrated unspeakable acts against cats and dogs.[4]

While vilification from both sides continues to alienate experimentalists and protectionists, the ideological gulf that separates the protagonists is currently more about the conflicting worldviews held by the members of the pro- and anti-research fraternities. The Australian animal researcher Paul Komesaroff believes these worldviews ensure that both sides talk at cross purposes since both conceptualise nature differently. Nonetheless, it appears that moral orthodoxy, as defined by what the public is prepared to accept, is on the side of the animal experimentalists. Yet as Komesaroff seems tacitly to acknowledge, science's links with survival anxieties about an impending ecological crisis cannot be denied.[5]

For many people, "the animal as victim has become a symbol of both humanity and nature besieged (in the) vivisection of our planet."[6] Thus despite science's hold on moral orthodoxy, there is a strong and widespread feeling as manifested in the popular media in feature films such as "Silkwood," "Under Siege" and "Outbreak," that it has gone too far and that the point of no return is imminent. Environmentalists and scientists in the existing movement are therefore asking can ecological disaster be averted? Animal activists are at the same time searching for ways to save animals from ecological calamity. This wider ecological crisis facing us all, human and non-human animals alike, will ultimately be the trigger that results in the mobilisation of a "common interest" social movement. In the remainder of the paper I discuss the crucial difference between finding a "middle way" and the quest for the common ground that underpins the common interest/cause movement I have in mind.

The Futile Quest for a Middle Way

Like most other critics of animal liberationists, Sperling sees controversy in terms of two opposing sides of researchers versus liberationists who need to be encouraged to find "a middle way" between the extremes on both sides. The middle way or the cultivation of "a sense of balance" as advocated by John Webster in relation to farm animals,[7] may well prevent the ascendancy of extremist views (e.g. that there are no alternatives to animal experimentation) but it will not act as a deterrent to anthropocentrism[8] or human self-interest.[9] Furthermore, whenever an issue is framed

---

[4] Lederer SE. Political Animals: The Shaping of Biomedical Research Literature in Twentieth Century America. *ISIS*. 1992; 83:61-79

[5] Komesaroff P. Bioethics and Nature: The Case of Animal Experimentation. *Thesis Eleven*. 1992; 32:55-75

[6] Sperling S. *Animal Liberators: Research and Morality*. Berkeley CA: University of California Press, 1988:39

[7] Webster J. *Animal Welfare: A Cool Eye Towards Eden*. Oxford: Blackwell Science Ltd: 1994

[8] Munro L. A Decade of Animal Liberation. *Current Affairs Bulletin*. WEA of NSW in association with the University of Sydney. 1993\4;70(7):12-19

as "two-sided," the temptation to find a middle way will be irresistible as in *Brute Science* by LaFollette and Shanks, a book which comprehensively examines the moral and practical issues on both sides of the animal research debate.[10]

Experimentalists claim that as there is no satisfactory alternative, the use of animals is essential to human health. The antivivisectionists maintain that the researcher's case is deeply flawed and that the availability of cruelty-free alternatives renders animal experimentation morally reprehensible. Neither side is willing to compromise since each perceives the other's position as evil. That it is no exaggeration to use the term "evil" is borne out by the language of vilification which continues to be used by some of the protagonists in the controversy.[11]

Antivivisectionists have been slow in recognising the common ground between their issues of cruelty and bad science and those of health and environmental advocacy groups when the broader issue of ecological calamity is drawn into the debate. This is not surprising given the way the vivisection debate has been framed as a classic "for and against" issue in which people are encouraged to choose between two sets of arguments or more challengingly, to find "a middle way."[12] One of the strongest defences of the middle way has been proposed by Dresser in her quest for a compromise in biomedical and behavioural research between the dogmatic abolitionists in the anti- vivisection movement and the equally intransigent anthropocentrism of the pro-research fraternity.[13] Dresser's intermediate standards (which appear to be a watered-down version of the 3 R's i.e. reduce and refine but not replace!) are designed, she claims, "to balance the competing morally significant interests at stake: the experience and lives of laboratory animals, and the freedom of inquiry and animal research benefits important to modern society."[14]

Dresser acknowledges the wide variation of opinion within these moderate reform positions and the difficulty of reaching any compromise. For instance, it may be agreed that animal welfare takes precedence over researcher convenience and financial considerations, but a harder question to resolve arises when the needs of science are pitted against the well-being of animals; it may be possible to avoid duplicative projects, but it would be difficult to agree on what constitutes minimum use of animals consistent with good experimental design; while it might be agreed

---

[9] See note 7, Webster 1994:247

[10] LaFollette H, Shanks N. Brute *Science: Dilemmas of Animal Experimentation*. London: Routledge, 1996.

[11] Mukerjee M. Trends in Animal Research, in Forum on the Benefits and Ethics of Animal Research. *Scientific American*. 1997; Feb:79-93

[12] *Ibid*

[13] Dresser R. Standards for Animal Research: Looking at the Middle. *The Journal of Medicine and Philosophy*. 1988; 13:123-143. In "looking at the middle," Dresser calls for an intermediate standard of ethical research in four areas: (1) Enriching the physical and social environments of laboratory animals and minimizing their pain, suffering and distress; (2) A reduction in the number of animals' lives sacrificed in animal research; (3) Assessing the merit of protocols that will harm laboratory animals; (4) The external review and enforcement of regulations governing the treatment of laboratory animals.

[14] *Ibid*, p.124

that some experiments are unnecessary, for example—fetal alcohol syndrome research (FAS)—(see below), and others are ethically flawed, say when animals are used in military research, for testing cosmetics, and in some behavioural psychology experiments, a middle way will be much more difficult to achieve whenever the cost of doing so exceeds what society is prepared to accept. Dresser suggests that standards aimed at improving the lives of laboratory animals currently enjoy the highest chance of acceptance, but even here pragmatists know the line will be drawn on how much people are prepared to pay, say, for bigger cages, non-animal alternatives or more rigorous animal welfare enforcement laws.

In "looking at the middle," Dresser seems only too well aware that finding an intermediate way will only be possible if important advances in research are not hindered by the increasing concern for animal welfare. Like Webster's "sense of balance," Dresser's proposals are too heavily weighted against the interests of laboratory animals to appeal to most animal liberationists. And for different reasons, it is unacceptable to leaders of the pro-research lobby. Dr. Frederick Goodwin, a senior official at the Department of Health and Human Services in the USA, rejects "the mythical middle" because, as he bluntly declared to an audience of animal researchers, "there is no middle ground as to whether or not animals should be used for biomedical research. Either it is ethical or it is unethical."[15] For strict advocates of animal experimentation like Goodwin's followers, the middle ground is only relevant in considering *how* animals are used, not whether to use them. Let us suppose that we accept this position and the only problem that remains is to determine how animals should be used in research. At the very least, in what many believe is "the most sensitive and polarizing issue in the animal rights controversy"[16] there would need to be goodwill between the experimentalists and the protectionists for any meaningful dialogue and communication to take place. As we have seen, the controversy thus far has been characterised by the rhetoric of hostility and vilification over the issue of whether animals should be used or not in research. The issue of how they should be used is unlikely to fare much better given the entrenched positions of the main protagonists.

In the same speech to animal researchers mentioned above, Goodwin criticised a *Newsweek* cover story, which featured a young mother, Jane McCabe and her nine-year-old daughter Clair who was suffering from cystic fibrosis.[17] McCabe's personal story makes a compelling case for animal research. According to her mother, Clair would not be alive without the enzymes from the pancreas of pigs and antibiotics tested on rats. In reacting to the animal rights bumper sticker—"Lab animals never

---

[15] Goodwin FK. Animal Rights-Medical Research and Product Testing: Is this a 'Hang Together or Together We Hang' Issue? *Contemporary Topics in Laboratory Animal Science.* 1992;31(1):6-11

[16] Jasper J, Nelkin D. *The Animal Rights Crusade: The Growth of a Moral Protest.* New York: The Free Press, 1992.

[17] The story was called "The Battle over Animal Rights: A Question of Suffering versus Science." *Newsweek.* 1988; Dec. 26.

have a nice day"—she responds with the question "Why is a laboratory rat's fate more poignant than that of an incurably ill child?"[18]

In responding to this generally pro-research article, Goodwin found it necessary to criticise *Newsweek's* captioning of the issue as "suffering versus science" and for "tacitly accepting one of the major lies of the animal rights movement namely, that research with animals is inherently cruel."[19] He went on to complain that the mass circulation magazine had failed to educate the public about the complex issues associated with animal research. As noted above, I read the article as generally pro rather than antivivisectionist, notwithstanding the fact that the views of animal movement leaders such as Peter Singer and Ingrid Newkirk were reported.

If I am right and Goodwin's objections to the article are exaggerated, then the medical-science community which he represents appears to be stubbornly resistant to any kind of public debate or democratic conversation in which their case is not presented as the sane alternative to what Goodwin labels the "anti-intellectual," "anti-humanistic philosophy" of the pro-animal lobby. This exercise in name-calling, like Goodwin's inaccurate reading of Singer's *Animal Liberation*[20] as an articulation of animal rights philosophy, is a throwback to the rhetoric of vilification described at the beginning of this paper.

The "positions" or stances taken by the protagonists like Goodwin and his opposite numbers such as Gary Francione in the animal rights movement make any hope for compromise unattainable.[21] Francione is critical of some of the most prominent animal protection organisations for adopting moderate, welfarist objectives rather than a radical, animal rights position that accepts nothing short of the abolition of vivisection , factory farming, blood sports and the like. These hard-line approaches on both sides of the animal rights debate allow for no middle way since both positions claim to occupy the high moral ground. In the last part of this paper I suggest that progress towards improving the lot of laboratory animals can best be made by substituting "interests" for "positions" and by focusing on particular areas of animal research in which there is "common ground" between the protagonists and other interested parties.

---

[18] McCabe J. Is a Lab Rat's Fate More Poignant than a Child's? Cover story *Newsweek*. Dec. 26:59 1988:50-57.

[19] See note 15, Goodwin 1992:6

[20] Singer P. *Animal Liberation: A New Ethics for Our Treatment of Animals.* London: Jonathan Cape, 1975

[21] Francione G. *Rain without Thunder: The Ideology of the Animal Rights Movement.* Philadelphia: Temple University Press. 1996

Banning Product and Toxicology Animal Tests and Unnecessary Animal Research

Of the main contexts for animal experimentation, product and toxicity testing for medical-scientific, industrial, agricultural and household uses offer the best prospect for finding common ground and common interests between animal activists and other interested groups such as consumer protection and women's groups, health and environmental advocates. And by narrowing the focus to a single campaign like product testing, it is possible to frame the issue as a common cause in which even the interests of experimentalists—as consumers and people interested in quality of life issues—are part of the common cause in which a citizen's interests might conceivably override one's position as a professional scientist.

According to Galvin and Herzog,[22] American animal protectionists believe that consumer product testing is the most important issue in the animal rights movement and the one they are most likely to win. The task for the animal movement is to convince other social movement organisations such as consumer protection groups of the dangers of using products tested on animals. In their study of the animal rights crusade, the sociologists Jasper and Nelkin claim that by attacking *all* animal research, the fundamentalist *position* on science has gone against *common moral intuitions* "which ultimately perceive *links between vivisection, scientific progress, and improved public health.*"[23] I have italicised these words to draw attention to how animal protectionists might redefine the "common moral intuitions" that appear to support animal research.

The fundamentalists who want to ban all animal research do so from the non-negotiable position of the abolitionist. It is an extreme position which offends individuals like Jane McCabe who believes that her nine-year old daughter Clair owes her life to animal experimentation. Faced with a choice between "suffering versus the life of a child," rather than *Newsweek's* caption "suffering versus science," the intuitive response of most people would be to save the child, for this is a relatively simple choice. "Suffering versus science" is a much more complex proposition, or at least it ought to be, since the *links between vivisection, scientific progress and public health* by no means always yield desirable results. Nowhere is this more apparent than in animal experimentation for product and toxicity testing. Yet as Coles argues "commercial need and pragmatic concerns ensure that funding for animal tests overwhelmingly overshadows that put into the development of a fundamental, predictive science."[24]

---

[22] Galvin SL, Herzog HA. Attitudes and Dispositional Optimism of Animal Rights Demonstrators. *Society and Animals.* 1998;6(1):1-11

[23] See note16, Jasper and Nelkin. 1992

[24] Coles A-M. Protecting the consumer: The development of animal tests for evaluating toxic hazards. *Impact of Science on Society.* 1989; 155:241-252.

A recent book by Alix Fano makes a convincing case for banning animal tests that have legitimised the production and use of dangerous toxic chemicals. The subtitle of *Lethal Laws* sums up Fano's argument that the links between "animal testing, human health and environmental policy" are causal and malignant. She points out that there are more than 75 000 chemicals currently being used in the USA and that animal tests have failed to protect humans and their environment from both known and unknown health risks. Globally, the chemical industry is a $1.3 trillion business and the third largest manufacturing business in the USA with a profit margin in 1992 of $24 billion. [25] Apart from the manufacturers of chemicals and pharmaceuticals, toxicologists, pathologists, animal breeders and animal experimentalists are some of the vested interests in this lucrative business. Fano lists about a dozen non-animal methods for toxicological testing but notes that many activists and some scientists see the search for alternatives as a cynical bid to buy time. As one activist told me, many scientists are "addicted to animals" and are not prepared to even consider their replacement by alternatives.

A Case Study in Bad Science, Bad Ethics and Bad Policy

Nowhere is this more apparent than in what must be one of the most pointless animal experiments yet devised by research career scientists, namely the use of animals for studying fetal alcohol syndrome (FAS). In a paper by Becker and his four colleagues, the authors point out how animals of different species can be given alcohol at different stages of their pregnancy to determine how, when and which birth defects occur in the animals' offspring. [26] They describe FAS as "a thriving area of research" in which non-human primates as well as rodents can be used for understanding "this formidable (human) disorder," which others have described as a form of child abuse. [27]

Fetal alcohol syndrome is evidently the only cause of birth defects that can be completely prevented by mothers avoiding alcohol consumption during pregnancy. The career scientists say nothing about prevention and instead are fixated on the idea of inflicting the damage on animals that some mothers inflict on their unborn children so that they can study birth weight, body size, craniofacial, skeletal and cardiovascular defects as well as sensory and behavioural effects amongst other things.

---

[25] Fano A. *Lethal Laws: Animal Testing, Human Health and Environmental Policy.* New York: Zed Books Ltd: 1997

[26] Becker CR, Randall CL, Allen SL, Saulnier JL, Weathersby RT. Animal Research: charting the course for Fetal Alcohol Syndrome (FAS). *Alcohol and Research World.* Winter 1994;18(1):10-16

[27] Manson R, Marlot J. A New Crime: Fetal Neglect. *Californian Western Law Review.* 1988; 24:161-182; Parness J. The Abuse and Neglect of the Human Unborn. *Family Law Quarterly.* Summer 1986; 20:197-212

The use of animals for studying FAS is unnecessary given what we already know about the problem from human studies. [28] Since 1983, the American Medical Association has recommended that its members advise women of the dangers of alcohol consumption during pregnancy; education and special targeting of "at risk" groups remain the best means of preventing further instances of this incurable condition. It would seem obvious that career scientists who insist on using animals to study FAS do so because they are addicted to animal research. Since the data already exist, experiments of this kind are redundant and, in such cases, to do them again, according to the American toxicologist Ellen Silbergeld "is bad science, bad policy and bad ethics." [29]

Spira's Strategy of Reintegrative Shaming

Henry Spira has consistently demonstrated the effectiveness of exposing dubious products and experiments like FAS. His success, in ending experiments on cats at the American Museum of Natural History in 1977, is at first glance puzzling given the long and largely unsuccessful campaigns against similar experiments by antivivisectionists a century earlier. Spira's campaign succeeded where his predecessors failed for a number of reasons. In the 1970s the public was receptive to the various liberation movements of the time such as black liberation and women's liberation. At the same time, the mass media were attracted to the spectacle of activists protesting against bizarre "cat sex studies" carried out behind the closed doors of a publicly funded museum. In short, it was good television. But more importantly, Spira used the approach now known as "reintegrative shaming" [30] which proved more effective than the stigmatising or disintegrative shaming of the earlier antivivisectionists. The rhetoric of vilification was replaced by a more subtle form of accommodation whereby he offered to work with animal experimenters to find more acceptable alternatives to the Draize test and LD50.[31] Spira's strategy in dealing with companies like Revlon and Procter & Gamble was to use reintegrative shaming by which the company's deviant practices were publicised, or the threat was made to do so, if it was not prepared to mend its ways. Reintegration occurred when the targeted

---

[28] Dufour MC, Williams GD, Cambell KE, Aitken SS. Knowledge of FAS and the risks of heavy drinking during pregnancy, 1985 and 1990. *Alcohol and Research World.* Winter 1994;18(1):86-92
[29] Silbergeld is quoted in Pardue L. Testing for toxins: Environmental and Humane groups seek alternatives to animal tests. *E.* February 1994;5(1):14-5
[30] Braithwaite J. *Crime, Shame and Reintegration.* Cambridge: Cambridge University Press, 1989
[31] Spira targeted the LD50 test by approaching Procter & Gamble and suggesting the company itself could develop alternatives that could become the benchmark for other companies. In the aftermath of the campaign, according to Spira, Procter & Gamble has spent more than $14 million since 1986 on developing alternatives and has become the leader in promoting alternatives to animal tests. Details of the Revlon and Procter Gamble campaigns are reported in Spira H. Animal Rights. *Fellowship.* 1991; Sept;57(9):13-15.

companies agreed to change their practices and were then publicly commended for doing so.

Spira, who is content if the company is willing to *reduce* the number of animal tests, has been attacked by abolitionists in the animal movement for accommodating the enemy. The abolitionist's rhetoric of vilification has usually proven counterproductive as is their negative, disintegrative approach to shaming "animal abusers." According to Braithwaite's theory, stigmatising white collar offenders as "criminals" is not as effective as moralising with them and encouraging them to change their deviant ways.[32] Spira's work with major commercial companies has indicated that they are first and foremost interested in protecting their reputations as good corporate citizens. It is therefore in their interest to avoid any hint of cruelty towards animals or public disputes with animal protection organisations.[33]

Common Interest Strategies: Forming Collaborative Coalitions

Alix Fano believes there are two strategies available to activists who oppose animal experimentation: the first is to work within the current system to achieve incremental change and the second, which she advocates, is to work outside the system for radical change.[34] Henry Spira's approach is clearly to work at least initially with, rather than against, companies like Procter & Gamble, Gillette as well as with the National Institutes of Health (NIH), the organizational centre of US biological research. Fano suggests that while this approach might be expected to work in banning cosmetics testing, more radical, "grassroots" activism will be needed to apply social, political and economic pressure if toxicology tests are ever to be phased out. I believe it is unwise to jettison either strategy in favour of the other, as each can be used for different campaigns. Indeed Fano cites approvingly the repertoire of tactics used by one Virginian animal advocacy group which uses methods of exerting pressure on companies that could have been taken straight from a "Guide to Activists," drawn up by Henry Spira himself. Most of the grassroots tactics listed by Fano were used by Spira in the abovementioned campaigns and included the key concepts of pressure group politics, the promotion of alternatives, the use of international coalitions, advertising, public information, education and accommodating the interests of compassionate companies. Although reintegrative shaming was not included in the list, its effectiveness as a campaign strategy is clear from Spira's campaigns and from John Braithwaite's own applications of the theory.

---

[32] See note 30, Braithwaite 198
[33] Singer P. *Henry: One Man's Way.* A film written and co-produced by Peter Singer. 1997
[34] See note 25, Fano 1997

Reintegrative shaming has direct relevance to a number of interest groups implicated in toxic pollution including animal experimentalists and even environmentalists [35]

While these tactics are important resources for pressuring the animal movement's opponents, a different strategy is needed if the movement is to mobilise kindred spirits in other lobby groups. Alix Fano's campaign for "fewer pesticides, fewer food additives, and fewer toxic ingredients in industrial, household, and personal care products," [36] entails building coalitions with potential allies in the environmental movement, and individuals with common interests in health and consumer advocacy groups to oppose the commercial interests that support these products, that harm the environment, humans and other animals. At first glance, coalitions of this kind would appear logical; however, the willingness of such groups to extend their mobilisation frame is often severely restricted. Like their opponents in the chemicals industry, they too are captive to organisational objectives and positions. Nonetheless, the common interests of environmentalists and animal rights activists are more important than their ideological differences concerning the value of species versus individual animals. At least this is the view of a select sample of leaders of both movements interviewed recently for *E* magazine. [37]

The most likely allies of animal activists in their anti-toxics campaign are supporters of the environmental justice movement, which frames the problem of toxic products and waste primarily as a race issue, arguing that people of colour in poor neighbourhoods are the most seriously affected by the environmental impact of the chemicals industry. Yet people of colour are underrepresented in the animal protection movement and are unlikely to see speciesism, as animal liberationists do, as a societal evil on a par with racism. How then is any alliance possible? One strategy for animal activists is to show that what happens to animals in toxicology experiments is the beginning of a process of degradation that endangers the environment and human health. [38] That this sometimes impacts more profoundly on racial and ethnic minorities is self-evident to environmental justice activists; the animal connection and specific cases of toxics or product testing are usually not. For example, in an American sample of females aged 18 to 44 years, the level of understanding of fetal alcohol syndrome was lower among black women, Hispanic women and low income women than all the remaining women combined. [39] It should

---

[35] Rosenberger J. EPA: Environmental Poisoning Agency? *The Animals' Agenda.* 1998;18(1):10-11.

[36] See note 25, Fano 1997

[37] The January\February 1996 edition included several interview excerpts with prominent animal rights and environmental activists and advocates.

[38] In a review of John Wargo's *Our Children's Toxic Legacy: How Science and Law Fail to Protect Us from Pesticides,* Daniel Kevles suggests that the risks associated with pesticides are often disputed not least because of the unreliability of tests done on animals, typically mice. (See Kevles DJ. Endangered Environmentalists). *The New York Review of Books.* 1997; Feb 20:30-35

[39] See note 28, Dufour et al 1994

not be difficult to convince supporters of the environmental justice movement that money wasted on pointless animal experiments like FAS, could be more effectively put to use in FAS education and prevention campaigns. The women's movement also provides the greatest recruitment potential in anti-toxics campaigns since women, more than men are closer to, and more sensitive to the daily risks that many of these products pose for themselves and their families. Carolyn Merchant points out how ecofeminists confront the contradictions between production and reproduction by calling a halt to the assault on their bodies and those of their children by toxic household products and industrial pollutants [40]; animal liberationists campaigning against animal tests used to certify these products as "safe" are the natural allies of ecofeminists.

Thus, common ground between women and ecofeminists, health and consumer advocates, environmental justice and animal protectionists could be identified for a host of products that have been let loose on the market after dubious safety tests on animals. Dioxins, the by-products of a range of industrial processes, are a case in point. According to Sharon Beder, dioxins have been studied more than any other chemical and have been found to be toxic to all the animals used to test the chemical. These studies indicated that dioxin was a complete carcinogen and in 1985 the Environmental Protection Authority (EPA) in the USA classified it as such. The EPA adopted the precautionary principle in assuming there was no safe level of dioxin exposure for humans. These dangers were comprehensively downplayed by the chlorine industry and its allies who mobilised their resources to counter the claims of Greenpeace and other environmentalists. [41]

The Art of Accommodation: "Solidarity Across Diversity"

Animal protectionists have much to learn from industry's assault on environmentalism in the dioxin controversy as told by Sharon Beder. In the face of threats to the chlorine industry, the Chlorine Chemistry Council was advised by its paid public relations consultants to adopt a number of measures which boiled down to making friends and influencing people on editorial boards, among home builders, realtors, product manufacturers, hospital personnel, scientists and the medical fraternity including paediatric groups (to counter the claims of chlorine-related dangers to children) and even moderate environmental groups. Alliances were made between representatives of the paper and pulp and chlorine industries, chemical companies, conservative think tanks, the Wise Use Movement and the National Cattlemen's Association amongst others. In short, any industries or organisations whose interests could be seen as being potentially threatened by environmentalism

[40] Merchant C. *Radical Ecology: The Search for a Livable World.* New York: Routledge, 1992
[41] Beder S. *Global Spin: The Corporate Assault on Environmentalism.* Melbourne: Scribe Publications Pty. Ltd. 1997

were mobilised to press the claims of the industrial polluters. While these diverse groups have different positions on a wide range of social issues, it is economic and financial interests that ultimately provide the common ground for their alliance against green activism. In much the same way, the interests of animal protectionists, ecofeminists, consumers, environmental and health advocates as opposed to their positional stances on various issues across and within these movements are what unites their campaigns against industrial polluters and the scientists who underwrite them. The common interests of these eco-oriented movements concern postmaterialist, quality of life issues (e.g. clean air, healthy living) in contrast to the standard of living or materialist interests of the growth-oriented industry lobby (e.g. two cars in every garage). Put differently, advocates of materialist values maintain that there is no money in poetry while post materialists say there is no poetry in money.

Even so, in the world of *Realpolitik* where money rules over poetry, Beder notes that environmentalists have not been successful in competing with the corporate world in gaining influence over decision-makers. Instead of lobbying government, she argues, environmentalists would do better by focusing on the ideological sphere which means "exposing corporate myths and methods of manipulation"[42] and opening up new issues for public debate including, I suggest, the idea of shaming industrial polluters and their allies. As noted in the previous paragraph, social movement activists will also need to promote their own ideologies as a coherent and unified alternative to corporate greed. In the past it has been all too easy for their opponents to exploit the schisms and philosophical differences within and between progressive social movement organisations.[43]

In his collection of articles on the difficulty of any rapprochement between animal liberationists and environmentalists, Hargrove acknowledges that the ethical differences between the movements may ultimately prove academic as environmentalists and concerned citizens will resolve the controversy "at the practical level". Hargrove's own study of the history of environmental/animal liberation ideas suggests that the key frames of these movements were respectively, *wanton destruction* and *unnecessary cruelty*. He argues that the ethics of these positions are distinct, "involving completely different concerns and completely different animals."[44] This fails to see the wood for the trees, so to speak, since the *wanton destruction* of nature (the environmentalists' grievance) usually results in *unnecessary cruelty* to animals who lose their habitat (the animal liberationists' grievance). Brian Luke reinforces the idea that the interests of both movements coincide when the environment is degraded. He points out how the widespread sense of ecological calamity has united animal liberationists and deep ecologists in "solidarity across

---

[42] See note 41, Beder 1997

[43] Hargrove EC. (ed) *The Animal Rights/Environmental Ethics Debate: The Environmental Perspective.* New York: State University of New York Press. 1992; Varner GE. The prospects for consensus and convergence in the animal rights debate. *The Hastings Centre Report.* 1994; Jan\Feb;24(1):24-29

[44] See note 43, Hargrove 1992

diversity" against anthropocentrism, the primary culprit in the crisis.[45] As I have noted earlier in relation to the anti-toxics movement, the despoiling of nature should also encourage the mobilisation of consumer and health advocates, ecofeminists, environmental justice movement activists, and anyone whose quality of life is threatened by a toxic environment.

What are the prospects for a common cause or interest movement that includes these and other social movement activists? Can a cacophony of voices in defence of nature become a symphony? Unless environmentalists with whom animal protectionists are usually linked in the public mind as kindred spirits were prepared to participate, the movement would have little prospect of success. Greanville believes that environmentalists have much to gain from a tactical alliance with animal liberationists "since animal liberation insists on respecting and protecting *all* sentient life, a position that must include the protection of all life-sustaining mechanisms."[46] If the logic of this argument is accepted, it becomes possible to frame the issue of product and toxicology tests on animals as one that affects all sentient life, human and non-human alike. For as Alix Fano's book demonstrates, there is an undeniable link between animal testing, human health and environmental problems. And the way to expose the vested interests that profit from animal experimentation can best be achieved by the promotion of a "common interest" movement along the lines of the common cause lobby which was mobilised in 1970 in the USA.[47]

The social movement I am proposing takes its cue from Common Cause which sought to represent "public interests" against the more narrow objectives of "special interests." Mancur Olson has pointed out in his classic study of collective action that the state is usually expected to further the common interests of its citizens but instead, it often promotes its own interests and ambitions.[48] A "common interest" movement, originating in civil society, is therefore needed to promote the interests of like-minded individuals in the various progressive social movements discussed in this paper. As Olson argues, common or collective interest needs to be *organised*. Social movement organisations perform that function under the umbrella of the social movement itself. A common interest movement along the lines of an expanded *EcoPopulism*[49] would operate in ways that would maximise its issues at the national level. This could take different forms depending on the political culture of the country or region concerned.

---

[45] Luke B. Solidarity Across Diversity: A Pluralistic Rapprochement of Environmentalism and Animal Liberation. *Social Theory and Practice.* Summer 1995;21(2):177-206

[46] Greanville PD. Environmentalists and Animal Rightists-The New Odd Couple? *The Animals' Agenda.* 1989; Oct: 22-24

[47] McFarland AS. *Common Cause: Lobbying in the Public Interest.* Chatham New Jersey: Chatham House Publishers, Inc. 1984

[48] Olson M. *The Logic of Collective Action: Public Goods and the Theory of Groups.* Cambridge, Mass: Harvard University Press, 1971

[49] Szasz A. *Ecopopulism: Toxic Waste and the Movement for Environmental Justice.* Minneapolis: University of Minnesota Press, 1994

What is more important than these organisational features, is the idea that a coalition of existing social movement organisations—environmental, animal liberation, ecofeminist, consumer, health, social justice organisations to name the main ones—is needed to promote effectively the common interests of these groups. In making this point, I agree with Andrew's Szasz's conclusion to *EcoPopulism,* when he urges social movement activists to widen their particular issues to include the more universal ones of global social change. Social movements, he suggests, "take on greater historical significance when they not only mobilize participants to fight for their own interests but also provide a broader radicalizing experience (and) to be the brains, heart, and muscle of a more global challenge to the status quo."[50]

I have suggested throughout this paper that accommodating the interests of diverse and even opposing groups will be easier for some issues (e.g. fetal alcohol syndrome research, product and toxics testing with animals) than for others (e.g. biomedical and veterinary animal research). Nonetheless, by focusing on vulnerable targets where the strategy of reintegrative shaming can be employed, activists and advocates for social change not only win the issue, but credibility for their cause as well. Henry Spira's activism is testimony to that.

---

50 Ibid

Chapter 15

Conclusion and
Recommended Reading on Four Themes

There are two parts to the conclusion: Part 1 covers the topical and troubling subject of global pandemics and Part 2 is an annotated list of recommended books on the four main themes of this book: History, Cruelty, Activism and Perspectives. The section on pandemics is taken from my book *Life Chances, Education and Social Movements* (2019) in which I discuss two of the most troubling existential threats to our collective wellbeing: 1. Climate change and 2. Pandemics originating in zoonotic diseases. I argue that both these threats are linked to our treatment of nonhuman animals. In the case of pandemics, most of the authors cited below warned of the likely threat of a pandemic well before the current coronavirus crisis in late 2019 and now appearing to be something we will need to live with at least until a vaccine is found to halt the disease's spread.

Part 1: Pandemics and Life Chances

Robert Wuthnow dreads four main species of trouble confronting humanity: terrorism, nuclear annihilation and weapons of mass destruction, pandemics and environmental devastation.[1] He is however, optimistic about the ability of government organisations , think tanks and experts to make a substantial difference in confronting the nightmare scenarios he describes. As a sociologist, his omission of any discussion of more pessimistic writers in the risk fraternity, especially the many disciples of Ulrich Beck, is surprising.

Although Wuthnow has virtually nothing to say about 'the power of movement'[2], his argument implicitly acknowledges the fundamental tasks of SMs, namely diagnosis, prognosis and mobilisation as the *modus operandi* of social movement: 'The prevailing narratives concern themselves with defining the problem (diagnosis), discussing possible solutions (prognosis) and then calling on citizens (call to action) to live up to their moral obligations to help protect the common well-being and to be good stewards of the earth' (parentheses added).[3] His view is that social movements ebb and flow, whereas organisations are more stable [4], a view in accord with Saul Alinsky's dictum 'If you want drama, get a movement, if you want results, get an

---

[1] Wuthnow, 2010.
[2] Tarrow, 1998.
[3] Ibid., 5.
[4] Ibid., 216.

organisation.'[5] However, both activists in the streets and advocates in the suites—the iconic example being Greenpeace—are needed if campaigns hope to succeed.

It seems obvious that both social institutions such as education and collective action via SMOs are necessary for understanding and effectively dealing with safeguarding our collective wellbeing. Wuthnow rightly believes in the power of ideas, if not in 'the power of movement' and pays homage to Rachel Carson's (1962) ground-breaking book *The Silent Spring* which alerted authorities to the damaging effects of DDT, an insecticide that was a lethal concoction for birds and a health hazard more broadly. Most significantly, as Wuthnow and other commentators have declared, *Silent Spring* launched the modern environmental movement. Wuthnow lists other seminal books (listed below as recommended reading) that changed the public's attitudes on a number of social and environmental problems. He believes that books and expert reports are among the most effective agents of social change as they typically attract wide media coverage and a growing band of activists. There can be little doubt that certain books, some including the recommended reading, have been instrumental in influencing the emergence and mobilisation of important social movements. It remains to be seen whether or not well-argued books on the existential threats we are confronting will make an impression on the public.

Fred Guterl, the executive editor of *Scientific American,* lists six major threats to life on the planet: superviruses, species extinction, synthetic biology, machines (AI and computers), ecosystem damage and climate change with the latter, according to him, the most vexing problem of all and viruses the most immediate threat to our wellbeing.[6] The subtitle of Guterl's book *Why the Human Race May Cause Its Own Extinction and How We Can Stop It* does not live up to its promise. While his descriptions of the threats are convincing, the solutions he proposes are piecemeal and depend too much on the science and technology responsible for so many of our problems; the behavioural changes he claims that would reset our practices in tune with nature—eating synthetic meat and cutting back on the use of energy-intensive modern conveniences—would be unlikely to be adopted in affluent countries.

As the focus of this chapter is on risk movements attempting to mitigate the impact of these national and existential threats, there is space only for two of the most serious and challenging risks to both human and nonhuman beings, namely risks associated with the animal-human link and its connection with climate change.

The Long Shadow of Intensive Animal Agriculture

Guterl's issue of immediate concern, the spread of viruses, has been comprehensively explained by the veterinarian Mark Walters, who identifies seven modern plagues and their causes mostly associated with our manipulation of the environment. The diseases

---

[5] Alinsky 1971.
[6] Guterl 2012: 182.

or 'ecodemics' and their causes are described in convincing detail in each of the seven chapters: 1.Mad Cow Disease; 2.HIV/AIDS; 3. Salmonella DT104; 4. Lyme Disease; 5.Hantavirus; 6.the West Nile Virus; and 7. New Strains of Flu Viruses.[7] Walters does not say much about how these diseases might be prevented as his intention is to call for action and a plea to respect nature's integrity.

Walters describes some old and new diseases, many originating in both domestic and wild animals, and how we are causing them. His key argument is that global environmental disruption (especially intensive agriculture and its use of antibiotics in livestock), urbanisation and climate change are largely responsible for the emergence of new infectious diseases such as pandemic flu. Walters offers little in the way of solutions, content only to vividly explain what our abuse of nature has meant for the planet and its species. In the epilogue, he refers to intensive agriculture as a giant genetic engineering laboratory responsible for much of the damage to the health of human and nonhuman species alike.[8]

This theme is taken up by Karesh and Cook on the dark side of the human-animal link.[9] They point out how modern advances in transportation of live animals, animal products, goods and people, along with an increasing dependence on intensive farming for food, have led to the spread of harmful viruses and bacteria. This has resulted in outbreaks of avian flu, severe acute respiratory syndrome (SARS), the Ebola virus and mad cow disease among others. The authors are deeply pessimistic about controlling these threats because there are no government agencies or multilateral organisations set up for the sole purpose of preventing the spread of zoonotic and anthropozoonotic diseases. They advocate the need for building stronger knowledge-sharing networks among different disciplines, achieving a dramatic reduction in the wildlife trade, and more effective regulation of the livestock industry. Unless these strategies succeed, they warn, global pandemics are likely.

Michael Greger M.D. in his focus on zoonotic diseases warns of the consequences of rearing animals in factory farms. [10]According to the World Health Organisation's (WHO) flu expert in Asia and virologist Earl Brown, intensive chicken rearing is 'a perfect environment for generating (the) virulent avian flu virus'. [11] Greger goes on to assert that the only virus deadly enough to kill billions of people worldwide is the bird flu virus that in 1918 killed an estimated 50 to 100 million individuals.[12] Intensive animal agriculture and the consumption of animal products in 2018 have increased to the extent that even a moderate impact of a flu pandemic

---

[7] Walters 2014.
[8] Ibid., 2014: 178.
[9] Karesh & Cook 2005.
[10] Greger 2010.
[11] Cited by Greger 2010: 110-11.
[12] Ibid., 109-10. For a full discussion of the topic see Greger's Bird Flu: A Virus of Our Own Hatching. 2006.

would be catastrophic according to Michael Osterholm, director of the Center for Infectious Disease Research and Policy. [13]

Akhtar links the deadly consequences of intensive agriculture and our consumption of animal products with the increase in infectious disease epidemics, environmental destruction and global warming . [14] The risks in consuming animal products include deadly zoonotic pathogens, heart disease, cancer, obesity and diabetes. She argues that a plant based diet is the only option 'which will single-handedly thwart food shortage crises in parts of the world, increase longevity and dramatically decrease rates of chronic diseases, keep us slimmer, prevent epidemics and pandemics, decrease tremendous suffering in animals, and maybe even keep the planet from overheating'. [15]

In Michael Pollan's considered view it will be difficult if not impossible to tackle climate change without a complete overhaul of the industrial food system that is responsible for so many environmental, social and public health 'bads'. [16]Animal welfare concerns feature in all three of these contexts , as documented by Gunderson and Stuart, who provide a list of a dozen or so papers on these 'bads'. [17] The authors refer to the well-known risks of food-borne illness outbreaks associated with industrial food processing in concentrated animal feeding operations (CAFOs), and note how the imperatives of economic efficiency and profit motivate the meat industry to ignore farm animal and consumer welfare. [18] The *Livestock's Long Shadow* report by the UN's Food and Agricultural Organization (FAO) has had little impact on the meat industry, whose stakeholders made no attempt to dispute the evidence in the report but simply carried on business as usual, a business the FAO has estimated is responsible for 18 percent of global anthropogenic greenhouse emissions, more than the gases emitted by the global transport system. [19]

Although Gunderson's prognosis of universal vegetarianism and community based agriculture may seem an impossible goal, it is surely the most rational path for the long term; his two-pronged solution[20] is notably supported by Norbert Elias and Wendell Berry respectively.[21] What is perhaps easier to digest is the recommendation proposed by Nierenberg and Niles to cut back on meat, dairy and egg consumption and to avoid factory farmed- animal products all together. [22]

Pollan also supports a smaller-scale, more humane animal agriculture alongside the proliferation of farmers' markets for the 'goods' that they provide. With initiatives

---

[13] Cited by Greger 2010: 111.
[14] Akhtar 2012: 129.
[15] Ibid., 131.
[16] Pollan 2010.
[17] Gunderson & Stuart 2014. In Endnote 2: 69-70.
[18] Ibid., 68.
[19] Bristow & Fitzgerald 2010: 219.
[20] Gunderson 2011.
[21] Elias 1979; Berry 1977.
[22] Nierenberg & Niles2010.

such as farmers' markets, vegetable gardens in primary schools, organic food products and 'go veg' campaigns, food movements are offering an alternative way of eating in opposition to the fast-food corporations and their profit-making motivations. Pollan points out how the food movement is becoming impossible to ignore by the political class given some of the high-profile meat horror stories described at the beginning of the 20th century by Upton Sinclair and at the end by Eric Schlosser.[23]

Michael A Fox makes a strong case for linking vegetarianism to the health of our species and more broadly to planetary health. He claims vegetarianism is 'the best way to reduce the environmental harm and degradation caused by humans' quest for nourishment.'[24] He cites many like-minded writers from activists to academic philosophers who support the claim; a noticeable omission is the high-profile case of the 'Mclibel 2' (Helen Steele and Dave Morris), the UK supreme court trial of 'the vegetarian- animal activists from hell' which shone a light on the dark side of the 'burger culture', notably the McDonald's corporation.[25]

In researching the history of the animal diseases-human health link, Swabe warns that risks to the health of human and nonhuman animals, have dramatically increased as a consequence of industrialised animal processing; furthermore, the conveyor-belt slaughtering process increases the prospect of cross-infection and the contamination of human food.[26] Although Swabe does not belong to the animal rights movement, she acknowledges that the movement's increasingly vocal activists, most of whom are vegetarians or vegans, have secured improvements in the treatment of farm animals. The aforementioned trial of Steele and Morris is one such case. The Mclibel 2 trial was a high-profile case—the longest civil trial in British history—which made the public aware of a host of problems associated with the humble hamburger including deforestation, intensive agriculture, animal exploitation and human health, issues which have now re-emerged in the debates over climate change.

There is likely to be much greater legal, social and political action in relation to the current global crisis of the Covid-19 pandemic. At the time of writing, vaccines are being developed and tested to deal with this particularly infectious plague that has impacted catastrophically on most countries in the developing and developed world. Karesh and Cook warned in 2005 (three years after the SARS outbreak in China) there will be more pandemics unless the problems associated with wildlife trafficking and the intensive livestock industry are dealt wirh by governments. The world is now confronting Covid 19 some 15 years on from their warning. In the final section , I provide a list of book reviews that I hope will be useful in remedying the continuing crises resulting from the dark side of the human-animal link.

---

[23] Sinclair 1905; Schlosser 2001.
[24] Fox M A; 2000. 167.
[25] See Vidal 1997.
[26] Swabe 1999: 140.

REFERENCES

Akhtar, A. 2012. *Animals and Public Health: Why Treating Animals Better is Crucial to Human Welfare.*

Alinski, S. 1971. *Rules for Radicals: A Pragmatic Primer for Realistic Radicals.* New York: Random House.

Berry, W. 1977. *The Unsettling of America: Culture & Agriculture.* San Francisco: Sierra Club Books.

Bristow, E. & A. Fitzgerald. 2011. 'Global Climate Change and the Industrial Animal Agriculture Links: The Construction of Risk.' *Society & Animals* 19: 205224.

Carson, R. 1962/2002 *Silent Spring.* London: Penguin.

Elias, N. 1978. *The Civilising Process, Vol 1 The History of Manners.* Oxford: Basil Blackwell.

Fox, M. A. 2000. 'Vegetarianism and Planetary Health'. *Ethics & Environment* 5, no.2: 163-74.

Greger, M. 2010. 'Zoonotic Diseases', Chapter 9 in Moby with M. Park eds., *Gristle: From Factory Farms to Food Safety (Thinking Twice About the Food We Eat).* New York & London: The New Press.

Gunderson, R. 2011. 'The Metabolic Rifts of Livestock Agribusiness'. *Organization & Environment* 24, no. 4: 404-22.

Gunderson, R. & D. Stuart. 2014. 'Industrial Animal Agribusiness and Environmental Sociological Theory'. *International Journal of Sociology* 44, no. 1: 54-74.

Guterl, F. 2012. *The Fate of the Species: Why the Human Race May Cause Its Own Extinction and How We Can Stop It.* New York: Bloomsbury.

Karesh, W. & R. Cook. 2005. 'The Human-Animal Link'. *Foreign Affairs* July-August, 84, no. 4: 38-50

Nierenberg, D. & M. Niles. 2010. 'Climate Change' Chapter 5 in Moby with M. Park (eds) *Gristle: From Factory Farms to Food Safety: Thinking Twice About the Food We Eat.* New York and London: The New Press.

Pollan, M. 2010. 'The Food Movement, Rising', *The New York Review of Books* May, pp.1-6. http://michaelpollan.com/articles-archive/the-food-movement-rising/

Schlosser, E. 2001.*Fast Food Nation: The Dark Side of All-American Meal.* UK: Penguin.

Sinclair, U. 1905. *The Jungle.* New York: Doubleday.

Swabe, J. 1999. *Animals, Disease and Human Society.* London and New York: Routledge.

Tarrow, S. 1998. *Power in Movement: Social Movements and Contentious Politics,* 2nd edition. Cambridge: Cambridge University Press.

Vidal, J. 1997. *McLibel: Burger Culture on Trial.* London: Macmillan.

Walters, M. J. 2014. *Seven Modern Plagues: and How We Are Causing Them.* Washington: Island Press.

Wuthnow, R. 2010. *Be Very Afraid: The Cultural Response to Terror, Pandemics, Environmental Devastation, Nuclear Annihilation and Other Threats.* Oxford and New York: Oxford University Press.

Recommended Reading on Four Themes

(An annotated guide was a supplement to my article, "The Animal Rights Movement in Theory and Practice: A Review of the Sociological Literature", *Sociology Compass* 6/2 (2012): pp. 166–181, 10.1111/j.1751-9020.2011.00440.x).

Books marked # appeared in the supplement of 2012.

On History

Evans. E.P. (1906/1998) *The Criminal Prosecution and Capital Punishment of Animals: The Lost History of Europe's* **Animal Trials. London: William Heinemann.**

This book is a most interesting account of one of the strangest practices involving animal-human interactions. Up until the early 20th century animals in some European countries were put on trial and sometimes executed for various crimes attributed to them. Pigs were the most prosecuted. In one famous case in 1836 France, a sow accused of infanticide was dressed in human clothes and brought before the judge and sentenced to death, possibly as a warning to her owner. Unlike today, animals were considered to have agency and were treated like humans by the law. Another pig and her piglets came before a court accused of killing a child; the sow was sentenced to death while the piglets were spared due to their youth. Between the 9th and 19th century all kinds of creatures from termites, horses, snakes to bees featured in animal trials. In some cases, for example when locusts were charged with destroying crops, they were tried *in absentia*. Animal trials peaked between 1600 and 1700 and may have continued after 1906 when Evans's book went to press.

(I acknowledge Piers Beirne's article in writing this short review. His article is titled "The law is an ass: Reading E.P. Evans' *The Medieval Prosecution and Capital Punishment of Animals,* in the journal *Society and Animals,* 1994, 2;1:27-46).

 # Garner, Robert. 1998. *Political Animals: Animal Protection Policies in Britain and the United States***. London: Macmillan Press Ltd.**

The book describes the progress made by the animal protection movement in the two countries where animal rights protests have been most prominent. The author presents a comprehensive examination of animal welfare policies in Britain and the US thus providing an informative comparative study of the movement's relationship with the state in these two countries. Garner's focus on policy networks corresponds to the sociologist's concept of social movement organizations. More than fifty such organizations—balanced evenly between animal protectionists and animal-user industries—are discussed in the book. *Political Animals* provides an excellent introduction to the politics of animal rights; missing in the accounts, however, are the voices of the animal activists and their opponents. In the final analysis, it is the meaning activists attribute to their cause that drives the movement, a fact which Garner tacitly acknowledges.

Gibson, Graeme (2009) *The Bedside Book of Beasts: A Wildlife Miscellany.* **London: Bloomsbury Publishing Plc.**

This book is well named and well suited for the bedside table. The illustrations are striking and feature all kinds of animals; a random sample from each of the eight lengthy chapters: the bear; the owl; the wolf; the elephant; the shark; the rabbit; the tiger; the falcon and the stag. The animals are the main characters due to the power and beauty of their extraordinary bodies alongside the stories that accompany their representation. Writers of fiction and nonfiction, poems, literature and myths (the Minotaur and the Leviathan) are featured. The excerpts range from the obscure (an American writing on the balance of nature in Africa) to the familiar fairy tale of Little Red Riding Hood. Gibson remarks on how the natural world can restore and even heal our minds and bodies; while no substitute for time spent in the wild, the Bedside Book inspires a greater respect for the natural world and its many species.

 # Kean, Hilda. 1998. *Animal Rights: Political and Social Change in Britain since 1800.* **London: Reaktion Books Ltd.**

In this informative book, the historian Hilda Kean provides one of the most comprehensive and interesting surveys of the early animal protection movement in England, the birthplace of animal rights. Kean tells an engaging story of how and why people's attitudes and practices involving animals changed over the past two centuries. She attributes these changes largely to the seemingly simple idea of "sight", or how people were influenced by seeing for themselves how animals such as horses and dogs were ill-treated in public spaces primarily in streets and markets. Animals "out of sight" in vivisection laboratories and in abattoirs also came to the attention of the early animal protectionists, most of whom were women. The sight and spectacle of animal abuse turned hearts and stomachs once a light on these everyday cruelties was shone by the pioneers of animal rights in England. Kean's book is nicely illustrated in keeping with the theme of *seeing* animals in their various relationships with humans.

Lansbury, Coral (1985) *The Old Brown Dog: Women, Workers and Vivisection in Edwardian England.* **Madison, Wisconsin: The University of Wisconsin Press.**

This is a lively account of riots that took place in England the "home of the animal lover" in 1907 when anti-vivisectionists (mainly women) and working class men found common cause against middle class medical students who practised and defended animal experimentation.. The riots were a rare example in the history of the animal movement of workers and women finding common cause in the defence of dogs, in this case, a little brown dog whose suffering in the hands of vivisectors they memorialised in a statue in Battersea. The inscription described in some detail the cruelty involved in animal experimentation and was designed to be provocative.

Medical students demanded that the "offensive" inscription be removed and when this failed, they escalated their protests by removing the statue itself.

Riots broke out with mounted police brought in to disperse the crowds of anti-vivisectionists, workers and students. Working class men resented the temperance society's idea that they should quench their thirst by drinking at fountains erected for horses and dogs rather than enjoying a pint of bitter in the local pub. These same men were also opposed to women getting the vote and so it is curious that they were prepared to join forces with women in "the old brown dog affair". Suffragettes were not known to be members of the anti-vivisection movement and their demands for the right to vote threatened the jobs of working-class men who believed female cheap labour would lead to their unemployment. Workers were not threatened by the female membership in the anti-vivisectionist movement. On the other hand, they had little in common with the middle-class medical students and no doubt resented their privileged background, a town versus gown story perhaps, with the little brown dog at its centre. Incidentally, Coral Lansbury is the mother of Australia's 29th prime minister, MalcolmTurnbull.

Ritvo, Harriet (1987) *The Animal Estate: The English and Other Creatures in the Victorian Age.* **Cambridge, MA: Harvard University Press.**

Ritvo's history of human-animal relations focuses on 19th century England. She uses the tools of the historian such as the primary sources of cattle breeders' manuals, records kept by the Zoological Society of London, veterinary reports and humane society documents on animal protection to explore these relations on a range of topics: cattle breeding; exotic animal collection and collectors; pioneering activist campaigns against animal cruelty; the role of household pets in Victorian England; big game hunting and zoos.

The attitudes of the Victorians toward animals reveal strong class biases such as the dog breeders who sought to improve the "quality" of their dogs over the mongrel dogs kept by the working class. Cattle breeders were motivated by producing bulky animals that would attract prize money and status for the owners; according to Ritvo, the weight of cattle and sheep virtually doubled by century's end. Academics mainly wrote about animals as business products for profit and not as sentient beings. Collectors of exotic animals for private and public zoos and big-game hunters were also condemned, but not field sports such as fox hunting, favoured by the upper classes.

Pet-keeping slowly led to the view that animals deserved kindness and respect. In 1840, the Royal Society for the Prevention of Cruelty to Animals (RSPCA) was established to advocate these values and even employed a private police force to expose animal cruelty.

Zoos, where exotic, wild animals were contained, represented the Victorians' idea of man's superiority over nature and also as a symbol of England's imperial prowess. Ritvo ventured outside England in her discussion of zoological gardens using the pioneering zoo owner Carl Hagenbeck and Hagenbecks Tierpark in

Hamburg, Germany as her unit of analysis. She reports that Hagenbeck was an international animal trader as well as a pioneer of building larger enclosures for megafauna from the wild that influenced other zoos to follow suit. She suggests that zookeepers in the 19th century acknowledged a zoo was really no place for large animals such as elephants. *The Animal Estate* is a welcome follow up book to Keith Thomas's informative study to be discussed next.

Thomas, Keith (1983) *Man and the Natural World: Changing Attitudes in England 1500-1800.* **England: Penguin Books.**
The British historian Sir Keith Thomas has written a most engaging and detailed book on the early history of our changing relations with the natural world. The focus of my comments is on the changing attitudes as reported by Thomas toward nonhuman animals in the early modern period 1500-1800. In 1500, anthropocentric attitudes towards nature reigned supreme; by 1800, different attitudes, especially toward animals, prevailed, but not without contradictions. These views are still prevalent in the 21st century: We love our pets but are happy to exploit those that are not regarded as companion animals. Thomas explains how pet-keeping was popular and widespread in middle class families and along with Harriet Ritvo in *The Animal Estate,* the emotional attachment to pets like cats, caged birds and dogs, would eventually induce people to campaign against cruelty to animals.

Thomas writes: "Economic independence of animal power and urban isolation from animal farming had nourished emotional attitudes which were hard, if not impossible, to reconcile with the exploitation of animals by which most people lived". The contradictions are many and some are still evident in our present-day relations with animals. The chapter headings provide the themes of the book; of the six chapters, the following dwell on these relations and contradictions:

Men and Animals (including domestic companions and privileged species).

Compassion and the Brute Creation (including cruelty and the dethronement of man).

The Human Dilemma (including town or country; meat or mercy).

Turner, E.S. (1992) *All Heaven in a Rage.* **Fontwell Sussex: Centaur Press.**
Another much praised book on animals takes its title from William Blake's couplet "A Robin red breast in a cage/ Puts all heaven in a rage". Turner describes cruelty to animals over a period of 2000 years in his thought-provoking and action-inspiring book. The reader is told of the animal atrocities committed in Roman times when the emperors hosted brutal contests between gladiators and animals as well as animals pitted against animals. In the latter, bears, elephants, bulls, lions, rhinos and other megafauna were pitted against each other with only the elephant able to survive

the rampaging attack of a rhino. He documents the cruelty of hunters involved in big-game hunting as well as duck shooting and the like.

Turner, like Keith Thomas, sees the contradictions in our attitudes and practices concerning animals: "fox hunters who are revolted at the idea of performing animals. Old ladies assault men who try to kill pigeons, but keep cats which destroy birds."

All Heaven in A Rage documents evidence of progress in animal welfare and its author asserts that the British can claim to be more compassionate than most other peoples. Britain's achievements, he notes, include the banning of the leg-hold trap (1963) and regulation of vivisection (1876). Turner was also pleased with the emergence of the modern animal rights movement and its compassionate supporters:

> "It is astonishing how many creatures, from whales to hedgehogs, now have their own pressure groups. Vegetarianism has made extraordinary advances. The cause of animals has disturbed the calm of company boardrooms, sown self-doubt in universities, driven airlines and airports to show respect for their animal freight (and) rattled the defenders of animal slaughter."

On Cruelty

D' Silva, Joyce and John Webster (eds.2017) *The Meat Crisis: Developing More Sustainable Production and Consumption.* **London and Washington: Earthscan.**

This updated edition (from 2010) consists of 21 chapters that includes additional topics on the dietary effects of meat and dairy products, the use of antibiotics in animal production and the impact of meat consumption on the well-being of humans, animals and the environment. The book is divided into four sections:

1. The impact of animal farming on the planet

2. Farming practices and animal welfare

3. The implications of meat production for human health

4. Politics, philosophy and economics.

The editors point out how 70 billion farm animals are slaughtered annually for food and that number is expected to double by 2050. The biggest increases are likely to be in developing countries which are expected to demand access to a richer diet based on meat and dairy. The message of the book is that the world needs to eat less meat if the negative impact on our collective health is to be avoided. The goal of this very comprehensive book is to contribute to the building of a more sustainable and equitable world. As Gandhi once remarked: "We must live more simply, if others are to simply live". That implies the reduction and eventual replacement of a meat-based diet with a vegan or vegetarian diet.

 # Imhoff, Daniel (ed) 2010. *The CAFO Reader: The Tragedy of Industrial Animal Factories*. Published by the Foundation for Deep Ecology with Watershed Media, Berkeley, LA: University of California Press.

The *Reader's* subject concentrated animal feeding operations (CAFOs) covers most of the topics relevant to factory farmed animals and is divided into seven parts: (1) The pathological mindset of the CAFO; (2) Myths of the CAFO; (3) Inside the CAFO; (4) The loss of diversity; (5) Hidden costs of the CAFO; (6) Technological takeover; (7) Putting the CAFO out to pasture. The acronym CAFO suggests a bland, mundane practice and is therefore a name which the editor believes should be replaced by the more accurate label "animal concentration camps". The chapter titles indicate what is in store for the reader, but the content is perhaps less confronting than the book's companion photo-format volume of the same name. The *Reader* is a comprehensive survey of how living creatures are subjected to inhumane practices for their body parts by "corporate food purveyors" and is essential reading for anyone wanting to understand the global scale and impact of industrialised animal factories.

Munro, Lyle (2005) *Confronting Cruelty: Moral Orthodoxy and the Challenge of Animal Rights*. Leiden, The Netherlands: Brill NV.

This is the first book in the *Human and Animal Studies* (HAS) Series which currently lists more than two dozen monographs published by Brill under the editorship of Kenneth Shapiro of the Society & Animals Institute in the US. As the author of the book, I am reluctant to "review" it and will leave it to two independent reviewers (one positive and one negative) who provide some helpful comments to the reader in the excerpts which follow. The full reviews can be found in the relevant journals.

Review by Pru Hobson-West (University of Nottingham) "Joint Review", *Society and Animals,* 2007, 41, 2:375-7.

Munro's research on animal activists in the USA, England and Australia and, using empirical work, aims to address the question: 'Why and how do people campaign on behalf of a species that is not their own. (After reviewing the contents of Chapters 1-3, the review continues):

> Chapter 4 then discusses the reasons given by participants for joining the movement, as well as various definitions of cruelty, and the historical origins of the concept of speciesism. Whilst enjoyable to read and impressively referenced, the author does not make sufficiently clear what the function of these chapters is, in relation to the text as a whole, and exactly how the book improves on the numerous typologies that already exist in the academic literature.(Hobson-West then remarks on Chapters 5,6 and 7 and finally on Chapter 8):

Munro concludes that the animal protection movement should be credited with 'transforming a previously exotic philosophical issue into a social problem that is taken seriously'. As a whole, *Confronting Cruelty* can also be credited with successfully promoting the value of a social problems approach, in combination with elements of social movement theory. Having just grappled with the abstract ethical arguments and sub-arguments in Garner's *Animal Ethics,* however, this reader would have appreciated more weight being given to the new empirical data and also some sense of what it was actually like to study the animal movement.

Review by Nik Taylor (now at the University of Canterbury, New Zealand). *Journal for Critical Animal Studies*, 2008, Volume VI, Issue 1, 2008 68-70. (In her review of Chapters 1-4 Taylor suggests that.the book is "eurocentric (sic) and anthropocentric"—an opinion that doesn't stand up) Chapter 5 moves to address vivisection, blood sports and factory farming as three main campaign areas of organizational activism. Accordingly, the data this chapter is based on is taken from interviews with those working amongst prominent animal protection agencies. Here organizational strategy, as opposed to individual motivation, is discussed. The chapter presents an interesting overview but docs not, in my opinion, offer enough detailed analysis (or even presentation) of what the participants had to say. This holds true for chapter 6 as well. This is a shame as these two chapters represent the most interesting heart of the book. Had the author presented participants' views more often and analysed them in more depth these chapters would have been much more interesting and would have offered much more insight into the animal protection movement from the perspective of those within it.

Pachirat, Timothy (2011) *Every Twelve Seconds: Industrialized Slaughter and the Politics of Sight.* **New Haven and London: Yale University Press.**

Hilda Kean (1998) argued the importance of "sight" in the rise of animal protection groups in England, when people saw for themselves how animals were ill-treated in public spaces such as in streets, markets and abattoirs. As part of the "civilizing process" Norbert Elias (1979) explained how butchers and slaughterhouses were gradually removed "out of sight" in order to prevent the public and especially animal sympathisers and defenders from protesting against the enterprises. The title of Timothy Pachirat's book succinctly sums up the enormity of animal suffering and death when living animals are killed for their meat. He claims some 8.5 billion animals are slaughtered for their meat annually. It is not an argument about animal rights but rather a first-hand account of "the killing work" in a slaughterhouse with chapter headings such as "Kill Floor", "Killing at Close Range" and "The Politics of Sight'. He notes what Kean and Elias have also described as "the power of distance and concealment to make the unacceptable acceptable and the extraordinary ordinary".(see Chapter 6 in the present book for an Australian case study on "the bloody business" of live animal exports).

On Activism

Munro, Lyle. 2001. *Compassionate Beasts: The Quest for Animal Rights.* Westport, CT and London: Praeger.

As the author of this book, my first on the animal movement, I will leave the verdict to the independent reviewers. The excerpts which follow can be read in full in the relevant journal.

A review by Suzanne R. Goodney, Indiana University, srg@indiana.edu In *Contemporary Sociology* 2002, 31,6: 762-764

To date, hardly any of the literature examining the animal rights movement has provided significant insight into the motivations, lifestyles, and sensibilities of the actual activists and participants who animate this effort. In *Compassionate Beasts*, Lyle Munro, aspires to remedy this lack. And while he does succeed at amassing the information necessary for constructing this particular wing of the social movement literature, he leaves readers with but a vague sketch of a design plan for organizing what is an intriguing compilation of activists' accounts of their motivations and strategies. The first chapter of Part One is perhaps the strongest of the entire volume. Here, Munro skilfully compiles a social history of animal rights activism within the United Kingdom, the United States, and Australia, the spatial bounds of his study.

In Part Two, he returns to his strong suit with additional social-historical insight. He offers a sound set of chapters examining the issues and politics that have animated the Australian animal rights movement over the last several decades. These are less analysis than summary, but the summation is intriguing. Munro incorporates in Part Two the voices of the activists and participants he interviewed. Their words provide the reader with an understanding of what motivates and sustains participants in this movement, and of their amateur and professional distinctions, as well as an excellent clarification of the commitment to ethical vegetarianism. Munro returns at the end of Part Two and throughout Part Three to a more robust social movement analysis of the animal rights crusade. Comparative responses to intensive and factory farming are examined first. Here, Munro summarizes the ways in which animal rights social movement organizations have combined efforts within each particular country to address specific issues more effectively. Militancy, size, and novelty, he concludes, distinguish the British campaign on behalf of farm animals, in that this effort ultimately raised a threat to the state. Munro displays quite a talent for analysis and synthesis, along with a great comparative framework. Too often, though, he merely summarizes the data he has collected.

The final part of *Compassionate Beasts* outlines some of the strategies that animal rights organizations have effectively used to counter such "offenses" against animals such as experimentation or vivisection, hunting, meat eating, and now, genetic experimentation.

In sum, Munro provides readers several worthwhile insights. First, he offers a better sense of the recent social history of the Anglo-American animal rights movement, reflecting nicely some of the political disparities among the three locales examined and the variant strategies that derive from such differences. Additionally, one finds an interesting, if unsystematic, sense of these activists' world views, particularly with regard to the use and consumption of animal products.

Singer, Peter (1975) *Animal Liberation: A New Ethics for Our Treatment of Animals*. **New York: Random House.**

This is the book by the Australian philosopher Peter Singer that launched the modern animal protection movement first in Australia in the mid-1970s and soon after in several other countries. The book was a best seller and a leading British newspaper described the concept of animal liberation as one of the 10 best ideas of the 1970s. Singer has also been described by Michael Spector in *The New Yorker* (1999) as "The Dangerous Philosopher" for in part, his philosophy of animal liberation: "The anguish of a pig that lives only to be confined and then butchered counts as suffering to Singer in just the same way that human anxiety does. Singer's laudable desire to reduce suffering in the present can be seen as a recipe for the ruin of the world economy". This may seem like an overreaction to Singer's two main targets of factory farming and animal experimentation but not according to his critics in the animal-user industries. As an academic advocate for animals, activist and vegetarian, Singer practises what he preaches; his *Animal Liberation* even includes vegetarian recipes.

Waldau, Paul (2011) *Animal Rights: What Everyone Needs to Know.* **Oxford: Oxford University Press.**

This is a basic introduction to many of the issues pertaining to the animal protection movement including a glossary of terms, a chronology of key events in animal rights and the author's suggestions for further reading. I think the best way to illustrate the promise of the book's title is to set out the main themes as presented in the 11 chapter headings with one example from each to whet the interest of potential readers.

1. General information (e.g. definitions of animal rights)
2. The animals themselves (e.g. how science categorizes animals)
3. Philosophical arguments (e.g. moral versus legal rights)
4. History and culture (e.g. the origins of animal protection)
5. Laws (e.g. "animal law" today)
6. Political realities (e.g. successes and failures of animal politics)
7. Social realities (e.g. how are attitudes changing today?)
8. Education, the professions and the arts (e.g. what are "animal studies")
9. Contemporary sciences (e.g. natural and social)
10. Major figures and organizations in the animal rights movement (e.g. pioneers, theologians, women, philosophers, feminists, lawyers, leaders in New Zealand, India and China)
11. The future of animal rights (e.g. the role of the individual citizen).

Designed for the reader interested in a straightforward account of animal rights issues, Waldau's book is just that.

On Perspectives

The animal rights movement has been described as one of the most neglected and misunderstood social movements of our era. However, social movement scholars are beginning to realise the political and moral significance of the world wide animal protection movement at a time when nature itself has been included in the specialist field of environmental sociology. Just as people are beginning to see that nature matters and is not separate from society, nonhuman animals (hereafter animals) too are increasingly perceived as worthy of our respect and consideration. The long-running animal protection movement which began in England in the 18th century is today better known as the animal rights movement. It is the men and women of this movement who, atypically for a social movement, are campaigning for a species that is not their own. The movement's theories and practices are important for what they do for animals and also because of what the animal rights controversy reveals about human beings.

Adams, Carol (1990) *The Sexual Politics of Meat: A Feminist-Vegetarian Critical Theory*. **Cambridge: Polity Press.**

For readers unfamiliar with animal rights, feminism and vegetarianism, the very title *The Sexual Politics of Meat* would be likely to raise eyebrows. Were they to read the book, most would be challenged by the writing, if not the ideas, while others would be enlightened. Adams writes of four chronological stages in the development of meat: vegetarian; hunting; subsistence farming and intensive agricultural farming. The latter is what animal rights activists are most concerned about. But why "sexual politics"? As a feminist, Adams and many of her feminist colleagues believe women and animals are victims of male oppression; meat as "animal flesh" is therefore associated with masculinity as in the advertising slogan "Give the man meat" and indeed with toxic masculinity as in the abuse of animals (eating them) and women (beating them). "Real men eat meat" contrasts with the male vegetarian or vegan labelled negatively as a "fruit". Adams believes that words and language matter. There is often hostility towards vegetarians and especially vegans who are viewed as being on a quest to undermine patriarchy as well as the animal-industrial complex.

Francione, Gary and Garner, Robert (2010) *The Animal Rights Debate: Abolition or Regulation.* **New York: Columbia University Press.**

In this book, the legal philosopher Francione and the political scientist Garner debate the virtues of strict animal rights versus moderate animal welfarism. Francione is an influential advocate for the abolition of all human uses of animals who he argues are treated in the law as property and this is morally wrong. He takes to the moral high ground by insisting there are only two approaches to animal protection issues, namely animal rights and what he criticises as "new welfarism" represented by the likes of Garner. Francione is a vegan and believes that ethical veganism is the only sure way to end animal exploitation, a position Garner contends is "dogmatic", "inflexible" and "fundamentalist".

For Garner, the abolitionist's demands are unrealistic, noting that it's an "all or nothing" demand that is much less effective than animal welfare's strategy of incremental improvements via regulation. One could also add that there is such a thing as the "psychology of small wins" which supports regulation. Also, Garner argues that regulation is more effective politically than abolition which is likely to be rejected by most people (who like their animals as pets, food and entertainment) and politicians (who like to please their electors).

Both contestants in this debate fail to acknowledge "animal liberation" as the pragmatic alternative to welfare and rights. Singer is not an advocate for animal rights, nor does he support the animal welfare lobby, the members of which tend to be averse to activist campaigns that Singer himself has participated in. My own position is that there are three main branches of animal protection: welfare, liberation and rights that animal protectionists I have surveyed and interviewed belong to. To be committed to animal rights like Francione, one has to be a vegan; most of Singer's supporters in animal liberation groups, like Singer himself, are vegetarians; animal welfare supporters, for example in the RSPCA, tend to be ordinary folk who are happy to eat meat as long as they think the animals do not suffer during their conversion to meat.

Noske, Barbara. 1989. *Humans and Other Animals: Beyond the Boundaries of Anthropology*. London: Pluto Press.

As an anthropologist, Noske brings a different perspective to our relationship with nature, especially in the long process of animal domestication. Her chapter on "the animal industrial complex" shows how both human and nonhuman animals suffer within this structure of domination; for example, slaughterhouse work takes a heavy toll on the meat workers while the animals experience atrocious pain and misery on the assembly line of mass execution. Noske's book is valuable for its broad treatment of animal-human relations in which she describes cultural, historical, structural and sociological aspects of these relations particularly in America and Australia.

Wilkie, Rhoda and Inglis David (eds.) 2007. *The Social Scientific Study of Nonhuman Animals: A Five-volume Collection–Animals and Society: Critical Concepts in the Social Sciences*. (Vols 1–5), London: Routledge.
(The following is a shorter version of the original)

This is a collection of 90 previously published articles and book chapters in approximately 2,000 pages on the social-scientific study of animals. The papers range from the earliest in 1928 on "the culture of canines" to the latest in 2006 on "religion and animals." Three quarters of the papers were published in the last two decades and are derived from anthropology, sociology, psychology, geography, philosophy and feminist studies.

In their introduction, the editors suggest that social scientists have in some ways been forced to take animals seriously:

"It is increasingly the case today that neither the citizen in the street, nor the consumer in the supermarket, nor the social scientist in the academy can afford to ignore the often highly charged ideas and feelings that surround animals and their relation with humans".

A summary of the topics covered in the anthology:

Vol I. Representing the animal (Introduction and critical concepts in the social sciences): Ethical issues; Animal welfare; The characteristics of animal protectionists; "Wilderness"; The role of animals in the lives of children; and The animal rights movement.

The main topics included in the collection provide a hint of its value to researchers:

Vol II. Social science perspectives on human-animal interactions: (I) Anthropology; Geography; Feminist studies.

Vol III. Social science perspectives on human-animal interactions (II): Sociology; Psychology.

Vol IV. Forms of human-animal relations and animal death; The dynamics of domestication: Human-pet relationships; Human-livestock relations; Animal abuse and animal death.

Vol V. Boundaries and quandaries in human-animal relations: Border troubles: are humans unique and what is an animal? The legal, ethical and moral status of animals; "The Frankenstein syndrome": animals, genetic engineering, and ethical dilemmas.

This anthology is an excellent resource for students of HAS.

Wolfe, Alan (1993) ***The Human Difference: Animals, Computers and the Necessity of Social Science.*** **Berkeley CA: University of California Press.**
    Wolfe is a strong critic of the animal rights movement which he considers to be one of the fastest-growing political movements in the West and like its bigger cousin, the environmental movement, an unwanted threat to humanism. In short, he argues that animal rights, computers and artificial intelligence (AI) in their different ways undermine human cognitive capacities (e.g. computers are smarter than us) and pleasures (animal rights seek to deprive us of fantasy, excitement and creativity). He suggests these pleasures add meaning to the lives of everyday folk. *Fantasy* might be a visit to a zoo, circus or animal theme park; *excitement* could come in the form of hunting and shooting big game, foxes or ducks; and *creativity* involves such things as using animals for experimentation, food or entertainment. Wolfe has a narrow view of

the social sciences when he fails to see animals and nature are part of our social world, a fact that sociologists have only in recent decades accepted. We now have many humanities and social science disciplines studying the human-animal-environment link as detailed in the five volumes by Wilkie and Inglis (2007) in the previous review. *The Human Difference* is an eloquent defence of humanism which nonetheless from Wolfe's perspective is undermined by animal rights and ecological issues as "one more nail in the coffin of anthropocentrism."

Acknowledgements

My first acknowledgement is, of course, to Common Ground Publishing for accepting and supporting the publication of this book. In particular, I want to thank Kerry Dixon the Managing Editor (Books) for her prompt and detailed replies to my queries and her professionalism during the publishing process. I was especially pleased to find an academic publisher prepared to publish previously published and peer reviewed work by a sole author on a topic that has become increasingly relevant during the worldwide calamity caused by the Covid-19 pandemic. It is obvious that there is something seriously wrong with our relationships with non-human animals, a fact that has been argued for decades by animal defenders and environmentalists. Unfortunately, many journals are inaccessible to the public and there are relatively few books on the animal-human link compared to books on other social problems. I hope this book will be accessible to a much wider audience .

I want to acknowledge Friedrich Nietzsche for providing the succinct title for the book. *Man is the Cruelest Animal* comes from his *Thus Spoke Zarathustra* written between 1883 and 1886. At the age of 45, Nietzsche died after suffering a severe mental breakdown. The story goes that while he was visiting Turin in Italy, he caused a civil disturbance by attempting to stop a horse from being beaten. The police intervened and seeing Nietzsche clinging to the horse protectively, they had him admitted to a mental asylum where he died soon after. Whether or not the story is true, it would seem that the philosopher was outraged by the cruel treatment of the horse and so his adage is a relevant one for a book that is about the quest for animal rights. Incidentally, in Dostoyevsky's *The Brothers Karamazov,* Ivan Karamazov states: "An animal can never be as cruel as a human being, as artfully, artistically cruel". It will be noted that the word "cruelty" appears in only two of the 15 chapter titles, a figure that represents the absence of explicit descriptions of animal cruelty in most of the chapters. Writers and activists tend to use striking phrases to evoke, rather than describe animal deaths in gruesome detail: "the hog-squeal of the universe"; "the suffering of innocents"; "meat is murder"; "photographs of agony"; "spectacles of suffering" and the like. I mention these image-phrases by way of acknowledging the activists and many authors I have drawn on for this book. While there are too many to mention by name , I am keen to acknowledge the following individuals for their support in my study of the animal protection movement over several years: Sue Burney, Jan Clark, Joan Court, Adele Douglass, Les Hardy, Laurie Levy, Glenys Oogjes, Barry Richardson, Ken Shapiro and Di Wuillemin.

Finally, I am very grateful to my partner Jennifer Barlow who has been my best reader and critic patiently reading and commenting on all of the book's chapters.

Permissions

My thanks to the publishers of my sole-authored publications. I have made every effort to contact the original publisher for permission to publish the papers I have used in the book, except for material for which I hold the copyright. The following lists the sources on which the chapters of the book are based:

Chapter 1: *Compassionate Beasts: The Quest for Animal Rights. Westport, CT and London: Praeger. Chapter 1, pp. 9- 24 , 2001.*

Chapter 2: *Current Affairs Bulletin. 70, 7: pp. 12-19, December/January, 1993/1994.*

Chapter 3: *Confronting Cruelty: Moral Orthodoxy and the Challenge of the Animal Rights Movement. Leiden and Boston: Brill. Chapter 4, pp. 64-96, 2005.*

Chapter 4: *Compassionate Beasts: The Quest for Animal Rights. Westport, CT and London: Praeger. Chapter 3, pp. 39-53, 2001.*

Chapter 5: *Society and Animals: Journal of Human – Animal Studies. 5, 2: pp.137-154, 1997.*

Chapter 6: *Social Movement Studies: A Journal of Social, Cultural and Political Protest. 18, 8: pp.1-16, 2014.*

Chapter 7: *Social Movement Studies: A Journal of Social, Cultural and Political Protest. 4,1: pp. 75-94, 2005.*

Chapter 8: *Regional Journal of Social Issues. 28: pp.37-49, 1994.*

Chapter 9: *Society and Animals: Journal of Human – Animal Studies. 10, 2: pp.173-191, 2002.*

Chapter 10: *Society and Animals: Journal of Human – Animal Studies . 9, 1: pp. 43-61, 2001.*

Chapter 11: *Sociology Compass. 6,2: pp.166-181,2012.*

Chapter 12: *Society and Animals: Journal of Human – Animal Studies. 7,1: pp.35-50, 1999.*

Chapter 13: *Cambridge Quarterly of Healthcare Ethics. 10,3: 314-324, 2001.*

Chapter 14: *Cambridge Quarterly of Healthcare Ethics. 8,1: pp. 46-57, 1999.*

Chapter 15: *Life Chances, Education and Social Movements. London and New York: Anthem. An excerpt from Chapter 8, pp. 175- 178: 2019.*

www.ingramcontent.com/pod-product-compliance
Lightning Source LLC
Chambersburg PA
CBHW052010030426
42334CB00029BA/3157